PASCAL FOR THE APPLE

To Jennifer

Disclaimer of all Warranties and Liability

Acknowledgements

The Apple Pascal™ system incorporates UCSD Pascal™ and Apple extensions for graphics and other functions. UCSD Pascal was developed largely by the Institute for Information Science at the University of California at San Diego, under the direction of Kenneth L. Bowles.

"UCSD PASCAL" is a trademark of the Regents of The University of California. Use thereof in conjunction with any goods or services is authorized by specific license only and is an indication that the associated product or service has met quality assurance standards prescribed by the University. Any unauthorized use thereof is contrary to the laws of the State of California.

PASCAL FOR THE APPLE

Iain MacCallum
University of Essex, England

Prentice/Hall International

ENGLEWOOD CLIFFS, N.J.   LONDON   NEW DELHI   SINGAPORE
SYDNEY   TOKYO   TORONTO   RIO DE JANIERO   WELLINGTON

Library of Congress Cataloging in Publication Data

MacCallum, Iain.
    Pascal for the Apple

    Bibliography: p.
    Includes index.
      1. Apple II (Computer) — Programming.
  2. Pascal (Computer program language) I. Title.
  QA76.8.A662M3 1983 001.64'24 82-16483
  ISBN 0-13-652891 0 (pbk)
  ISBN 0-13-652909 7 (with floppy disk)

British Library Cataloging in Publication Data

MacCallum, Iain
    Pascal for the Apple.
    1. Pascal (Computer program language)
    2. Apple computer — Programming
    I. Title
    001.64'24 QA76.73.P2
  ISBN 0-13-652891 0

For permission within the United States contact Prentice-Hall Inc., Englewood Cliffs, NJ 07632.

ISBN 0-13-652891 0
ISBN 0-13-652917 8 {DISK}
ISBN 0-13-652909 7 {TEXT & DISK PACKAGE}

Prentice-Hall International, London
Prentice-Hall of Australia Pty Ltd, Sydney
Prentice-Hall of Canada Inc., Toronto
Prentice-Hall of India Private Ltd, New Delhi
Prentice-Hall of Japan Inc., Tokyo
Prentice-Hall of Southeast Asia Pte Ltd, Singapore
Prentice-Hall Inc., Englewood Cliffs, New Jersey
Prentice-Hall do Brasil Ltda, Rio de Janiero
Whitehall Books Ltd, Wellington, New Zealand

10 9 8 7 6 5 4 3 2

Printed in the United States of America

Contents

Contents

Contents

Contents

Part 1

In part 1 the reader will gain confidence in the use of the Apple Pascal Operating System, and in the writing and executing of programs that display interesting patterns on the screen. The hopefully entertaining nature of these chapters should not be allowed to obscure the serious matter of program construction by the method of "structured programming". To this end procedures, iteration, decision making and recursion are all introduced early in the book, with appropriately selected examples and exercises.

Part 2

Now the party is over, and we must face up to the fact that computers are required to do tasks other than drawing pictures. It is the need to process numerical and textual information that leads to an awareness of data and restrictions on the kind of values that variables may take. Communication with the world outside (output and input) is introduced and hierarchical structures (arrays, records and sets) are developed from more elementary components.

Part 3

The final part of this book explores some applications of the two remaining types that Pascal offers. Pointers lead to a new kind of data object (one with value, but no name) whose creation is under the direct control of the program, thus permitting the modelling of dynamic structures in the world outside. Lists, queues, trees and graphs are discussed in some detail, culminating in a solution to one of the fundamental problems of computer science, the shortest path problem. In the midst of this, the other remaining type is introduced, namely the file. This exemplifies yet another property of data, for here we find a type of data whose values both precede and survive the duration of the program's execution.

Preface

"I cannot do't without compters."
(W. Shakespeare. Winter's Tale, iv, 3)

Beware! This book is different. It differs from most books on programming by treating the learning of programming as an essentially practical matter. In fact, in contrast to the more traditional textbook which presents programming as a means for the reader to communicate instructions to a computer, the dedication of this book to the Apple also enables the computer to be used as a means of communicating the essence of programming to the reader. Together with the disk, it perhaps resembles certain courses in foreign language tuition which are accompanied by a record or cassette. If you follow this book closely, you will find that you are spoken to in a language called Pascal, and that you will soon be speaking back in that same language.

The book is in three Parts.

Part 1 introduces the essential features of the Apple Pascal Operating System (which is based on the UCSD p-System) and through the use of a simple graphics, called TURTLEGRAPHICS, some basic features of the Pascal programming language, namely procedures, iteration, decision making and recursion. If the reader finds this section to be fun, this is no accident. Nevertheless, the principles of program construction used in these opening chapters are quite serious, and their application to perhaps less entertaining problems will be maintained throughout the book.

In Part 2 the reader is led back to the more realistic computer world of characters, numbers and simple structures, first by enhancing programs written in Part 1 to make use of data supplied conversationally, and then by the introduction of derived types and records. Only at this stage does it become necessary to consider the assignment statement. Arrays and sets are then introduced after which it is possible to treat strings of text as records in standard Pascal. Much of this part will draw its programming examples from the realm of text handling. Functions and sets are introduced and procedures are tidied up. Finally, reals are introduced, being deferred to this relatively late stage since they play no significant role in learning to program, and they can be deceptively simple to the beginner.

In Part 3, two types in Pascal remain to be discussed: pointers and files. Pointers open the way to a new realm of programming wherein the dynamic structures of the outside world may be realistically modelled within the computer. Pointers are used to create circular lists (which can model queues and lists) trees and graphs. Files give programs the ability to deal with arbitrarily large volumes of data; to relate more meaningfully to the real world and to other programs; and to leave behind tangible evidence of their having been run. The experimental/formal sequence of the chapters is broken in the last 4 chapters, where the balance is in favor of practical programming problems.

I wish to put on record my thanks to those who have assisted me in the preparation of this book. Few staff in the Department of Computer Science at the University of Essex have escaped having their valuable opinions sought, and all their names ought to be mentioned. But in particular, I must thank Adrian Wheal for implementing the system software, Jim Doran for useful criticism of earlier forms of the course, Debbie Goody for programming assistance, Mary Barnett for word-processing assistance and Fiona MacCallum and members of the Lower Sixth Form at Colchester Royal Grammar School for allowing me to use them as guinea-pigs. The running of the courses on which the book has been based would not have been possible without the considerable efforts of John Tierney, Mike Millman and John Ford. I am deeply indebted to Dan Simpson of Sheffield Polytechnic, who first suggested that a course at the University of Essex become this book and then, with John Cookson of Edinburgh Regional Computing Centre and Alan Whittle, made valuable comments on the final draft. The production of this combined book and disk was a new venture for both author and publisher, and I therefore wish to acknowledge the particular assistance in this area afforded by Giles Wright of Prentice-Hall International. Finally I must record my thanks to Professor C.A.R. Hoare of Oxford University for his encouragement at the outset.

The book was prepared for publication using an implementation of the UCSD Pascal on a Vector Graphic System 3 microcomputer and was printed on a Qume Sprint 9 printer fitted with a Prestige Elite ASC11 96 wheel.

I.R. MacCallum
Colchester
October 1982

Preliminaries

What You Should Have

The course in programming which this book describes assumes that the reader has access to an Apple II or Apple II Plus computer with Apple Pascal. This in turn requires a minimum of 48K bytes of memory (but preferably 64K), one disk drive (but preferably two) and the Apple Language Card. (The color card is not necessary.) If you have added an 80-column display, you will also need high-resolution graphics which may be selected by some kind of "software switch" or which may be sent to the original 40-column display. (If you are in any doubt about this, consult your dealer.) The standard system for a 40-column display on a domestic TV needs no modification. It is also assumed that you have the following disks:

APPLE0:
APPLE1:
APPLE2:
APPLE3:

supplied with Apple Pascal,

MACC: (the disk which accompanies this book)

and at least 2 other blank disks. The MACC: disk is *write-protected*. This means that you cannot use the Apple to add to or change the information on that disk. It therefore greatly reduces the likelihood of the MACC: disk becoming accidentally corrupted. You are strongly advised to make a working copy of the MACC: disk on a disk which is not write-protected, that is, one which has a square notch on the right-hand edge. See the appropriate section entitled "How To Prepare The Disks".

It will also be useful to have occasional access to the Apple Pascal Reference Manual and the Apple Pascal Operating System Reference Manual.

How To Use This Book

Throughout Parts 1 and 2 and most of Part 3, the chapters are intended to be studied alternately at the computer and away from the computer. Material is generally presented first in an experimental or laboratory situation in the odd numbered chapters, and then more formally in succeeding even numbered chapters. For this reason, the juxtaposition of unrelated material in a chapter may seem rather unconventional. The exercises, being placed in the text at the most apposite points, are an integral part of the book, and unless otherwise stated, should be attempted if continuity is to be maintained.

The practical chapters (mainly odd numbered) will not all take the same time to work through. As a rough guide, the reader should alllow about 80 hours of Apple time and a similar amount of private reading and study time to complete the course.

If the book is used in a group teaching situation (with two-drive Apples), then it is recommended that each student is supplied with the appropriate system disk(s) plus the MACC: and USER: disks prepared in accordance with the instructions in the appropriate section entitled "How To Prepare The Disks." That is, the MACC: disk and a blank disk should have the Compiler copied to them. Students thus equipped may then start at chapter 1.

If the book is used by an Apple owner, then the appropriate section "How To Prepare The Disks" must be read and followed through, in conjunction with the relevant sections of the Apple Pascal documentation. In particular, users of one-drive Apples are strongly advised to familiarize themselves with the facilities of the Filer before starting chapter 1. Read appendix 2, sections 1 and 2 of this book, or better still, chapter 3 of the Apple Pascal Operating System Reference Manual.

How To Prepare The Disks (on a two-drive Apple)

Before embarking upon the course, certain preparations must be made. Following appendix E of the Apple Pascal Language Reference Manual (sections entitled "Pascal in Seconds" and "Making Backup Diskette Copies") make backup copies of the APPLE1:, APPLE2:, and APPLE3: disks. Keep the originals in a safe place and use only the copies you have made.

Still referring to appendix E, format another two new disks. Make a backup copy of the disk MACC: onto one of these disks. (If during the copying of the MACC: disk an error of the form "I/O ERROR#64" is displayed, then the copy has failed. Refer to the section below entitled "What To Do If The MACC: Disk Cannot Be Read".) Change the name of the other disk from BLANK:, the name the formatter program gave it, to your initials. To do this,

— check that the Apple is displaying the COMMAND prompt line,
— type F to enter the Filer,
— load the formatted disk in drive 2,
— type C to Change the name of the disk, and in response to the message "CHANGE ?"
— type

        BLANK:,ABC:

    except that in place of ABC, put your initials (not more than 7 characters). If your initials happen to be MACC, use something else, such as MAC, to avoid confusion with the disk which accompanies this book. Follow the second colon (:) with RETURN and wait until disk activity stops. Remove the blank disk and apply a sticky label with its new name.
— Type Q to Quit the Filter.

Throughout this book, the disk which now bears your intials (and similar disks) will be referred to as your USER: disk.

On a two-drive Apple you will find it more convenient to have a copy of the Compiler on your working copy of MACC: and also on each USER: disk. To do this, follow these instructions.

(a) Load the system disk APPLE1: in drive 1.
(b) Type F to enter the Filer.
(c) Remove APPLE1: from drive 1 and load APPLE2: in its place.
(d) Type T to prepare to transfer a File.
(e) Load your working copy of MACC: in drive 2.
(f) Type (very carefully)

APPLE2:SYSTEM.COMPILER,MACC:$

followed by the RETURN key. Note that $ is obtained by holding down SHIFT and pressing the key marked

```
$
4
```

(g)   Wait about 16 seconds.
(h)   Remove MACC: from drive 2.
(j)   Repeat these instructions from (d) above replacing MACC: by your USER: disk.
(k)   Replace APPLE1: in drive 1.
(l)   Type Q to Quit the Filer.

Note that all Apple software and the MACC: disk are copyright and that the copies you have made must be treated as a backup of the software on APPLE2: and MACC:.

How To Prepare The Disks (on a one-drive Apple)

Before embarking on the course, certain preparations must be made. Following appendix D of the Apple Pascal Language Reference Manual (sections entitled "The Two-Step Startup" and "Making Backup Diskette Copies") make backup copies of the APPLE0:, APPLE1:, APPLE2: and APPLE3: disks. (Some later Apple Pascal systems require that APPLE3: (not APPLE1:) be loaded first in the startup, followed by APPLE0:.) Copying a disk on a one-drive Apple requires much patience. Keep the original disks in a safe place and use only the copies you have made.

Still refering to appendix D, format another two new disks. Make a backup copy of the disk MACC: onto one of these disks. (If during the copying of the MACC: disk an error of the form "I/O ERROR#64" is displayed, then the copy has failed. Refer to the section entitled "What To Do If The MACC: Disk Cannot Be Read".) Change the name of the other disk from BLANK:, the name the formatter program gave it, to your initials. To do this,

— check that APPLE0: is loaded and that the Apple is displaying the COMMAND prompt line,
— type F to enter the Filer,
— unload APPLE0: and load the formatted disk
— type C to Change the name of the disk, and in response to the message "CHANGE ?"
— type

BLANK:,ABC:

except that in place of ABC, put your initials (not more than 7 characters). If your initials happen to be MACC, use something else, such as MAC, to avoid confusion with the disk which accompanies this book. Follow the second colon (:) with RETURN and wait until disk activity stops. Remove the blank disk and apply a sticky label with its new name.
— Type Q to Quit the Filter.

Throughout this book, the disk which now bears your initials (and similar disks) will be referred to as your USER: disk.

Note that all Apple software and the MACC: disk are copyright and that the copy you have just made must be treated only as a backup of the software on MACC:.

What To Do If The MACC: Disk Cannot Be Read

First check that your Apple will still load Apple Pascal and run the demonstration programs on APPLE3:. Then check that your Apple will still make a satisfactory copy of one of the Apple system disks. If it will not, suspect your disk drive and contact your Apple dealer.

If your Apple copies a system disk but not the MACC: disk, try copying *both* these disks from the other drive (if you have two) or on another Apple (preferably your dealer's). If the MACC: disk can be read on another drive, it sounds like trouble with your drive (see your dealer), but if the MACC: disk consistently refuses to be read on two or more drives which successfully read the Apple system disks, then post the suspect disk, suitably packaged, *within one month of the date of purchase,* to

Prentice-Hall Inc.	or	Prentice-Hall International
Attn: Ben C. Colt		Department 207
College Marketing		66 Wood Lane End,
Englewood Cliffs,		Hemel Hempstead,
New Jersey 07632		Herts HP2 4RG
U.S.A.		England

together with
- your name and address
- date of purchase
- name and address of bookshop or source of disk.

Prentice-Hall will replace a defective disk free of charge.

Versions of Pascal

The reader will notice that three different versions of Pascal are mentioned in this book.

— *Standard Pascal* refers to the second draft proposal of the ISO standard | ISO, 1981 |. The main differences between this proposal and the Revised Report, | Jensen and Wirth, 1978 | are noted in the text.

— *UCSD Pascal* is an evolving system, widely available on microcomputers and originally written at the University of California at San Diego, under the direction of Professor K.L. Bowles. Where UCSD Pascal is mentioned in the text, it is to highlight some important difference between it and Standard Pascal, such as UCSD Pascal's type STRING or its lack of function and procedure parameters. See the UCSD Pascal User Manual | SofTech, 1981 |, | Clark and Kohler, 1982 | and a brief history of UCSD Pascal in chapter 1. UCSD Pascal is a product of SofTech Microsystems, San Diego.

Apple Pascal is an implementation of UCSD Pascal (somewhere between version I.5 and IV.0) for the Apple II. Where it is specifically mentioned in the text, it is generally to highlight some aspect of Apple Pascal, not specific to versions I.5 and IV.0 of UCSD Pascal. Apple Pascal is described in detail in | Apple, 1980a |.

PART 1
The Basic Principles of Programming

In part 1 the reader will gain confidence in the use of the Apple Pascal Operating System, and in the writing and executing of programs that display interesting patterns on the screen. The hopefully entertaining nature of these chapters should not be allowed to obscure the serious matter of program construction by the method of "structured programming". To this end procedures, iteration, decision making and recursion are all introduced early in the book, with appropriately selected examples and exercises.

CHAPTER 1
Introduction to Programming

The art of programming is complex. It requires the exercising of several different skills. It is at the same time both analytical and synthetic; a problem must be analyzed before its solution may be synthesized. Programming demands both precision and imagination. The written form of a program must be sufficiently precise for consumption by a computer and yet must be sufficiently readable to be understood by humans. Programs which work for a living must reflect today's requirements and yet be readily adaptable, by someone other than the original author, for tomorrow's.

Program writing is similar in many ways to the composition of music commissioned for a specific purpose. And just as a sheet of music is a means of communicating a set of commands to a musician for interpretation, so the text of a program is a means of communicating a set of commands to a computer for it to interpret. Musical notation is a kind of language which happens to combine the precise with the vague. Pitch and the relative duration of notes are quite precisely represented and typical of the kind of commands given to a computer, but advice such as "with a swing but not too fast" is not. Communication with a computer has to be precise. This in turn means that the language (or notation) used will be formal and the interpretation fairly unforgiving, whilst the additional need to communicate with other programmers means that our use of that (formal) language should be as expressive as possible.

The language adopted for the book is Pascal, the work of Professor Niklaus Wirth of Zurich. It was devised to be a language for both teaching the principles of programming, and to a lesser extent for systems programming. A further objective was that the language should be "small" and simple, which, in 1971, nicely anticipated today's generation of personal computers.

The principal architect of Pascal on small computers is Professor Kenneth Bowles of the University of California at San Diego (UCSD). In 1975 under his leadership, a team at UCSD produced the first Pascal system to run on a microcomputer (an LSI version of the ubiquitous PDP-11). It was noted for being highly portable and for being a complete single-user program development system with its own editor, file handler and other utility programs. Within a few years UCSD Pascal was available on most commonly available microprocessor families. More recently other languages have been implemented under the same programming development system, and the language independent program development part (notably the Editor and the Filer) has become known as the UCSD p-System. The disks APPLE1: and APPLE2: (APPLE0: and APPLE1: for one-drive Apples) contain the p-System and the means by which the Apple can interpret the Pascal language.

There are many places where we might begin. Following the musical
analogy, we could begin where the experienced composer begins, by considering
a problem, analyzing it, abstracting the essential details and discarding the
inessential, and creating an outline structure of a solution in some more or
less formal notation. But we are not yet experienced composers of programs
and neither are we yet familiar with the notation, so let us begin by looking
at a program which has already been composed in the language (or notation)
called Pascal. We shall, first of all, "play through" the program (or, to use
computing jargon, execute or run it) to see what it does; then we shall
look in a little more detail at some of the principles of programming which it
demonstrates.

1.1 INTRODUCING THE UCSD p-SYSTEM

Before we can examine a program on the Apple itself, we must be introduced
to some of the program development features of the UCSD p-System. First the
UCSD p-System must be loaded, and how you do that depends on how many disk
drives are connected to the Apple.

1.1.1 Loading the p-System (two-drive Apples)

Switch the Apple off. If it is not already loaded, load APPLE1: in drive
1 and switch the power on. In about 16 seconds the screen will display the
prompt line

        COMMAND: E(DIT, R(UN, F(ILE, C(OMP, L(IN

The Apple is now loaded with the UCSD Pascal system. Throughout the rest of
this book, we will refer to the APPLE1: disk of a two-drive Apple as the
system disk.

If the prompt line fails to appear, you have a problem either with the
Apple itself or with the working copy of the APPLE1: disk. Repeat this section
with the APPLE1: disk supplied with Apple Pascal, and if that succeeds, make
another working copy of the system disk. If the Apple is at fault, consult
your dealer.

1.1.2 Loading the p-System (one-drive Apples)

Switch the Apple off. Load the disk APPLE3: in the drive and switch the
power on. (Early Apple Pascal systems require that APPLE1: be loaded here, not
APPLE3:.) When the top of the screen shows the prompt line asking you to

        INSERT BOOT DISK WITH SYSTEM.PASCAL ON IT, THEN PRESS RESET

remove APPLE3: from the drive and load APPLE0:. Hold down the CTRL key and
press RESET. (On early Apples, just press RESET alone.) In about 16 seconds
the screen will display the prompt line

        COMMAND: E(DIT, R(UN, F(ILE, C(OMP, L(IN

The Apple is now loaded with the UCSD Pascal system. Throughout the rest of
this book, we will refer to the APPLE0: disk of a one-drive Apple as the
system disk.

        If the prompt line fails to appear, you have a problem either with the
Apple itself or with the working copy of the APPLE0: disk. Repeat this section
with the APPLE0: disk supplied with Apple Pascal, and if that succeeds, make
another working copy of the system disk. If the Apple is at fault, consult
your dealer.

1.1.3 Levels of Command

    The top line of the display currently on the screen, namely

        COMMAND: E(DIT, R(UN, F(ILE, C(OMP, L(IN

is essentially a menu of things to do. The computer is now said to be at
the outermost level of command. Each letter represents a level of the
system which can be invoked to allow us to do some particular job. In this
section we shall mainly be concerned with

        E - Editor
        R - Run the program you have just been looking at
        F - File handler (or Filer).

1.1.4 The Apple Screen

    If your Apple has a TV type display of width 40 characters, then lines of
more than 40 characters will be truncated at the 40th character. To see
the rest of the line type CTRL-A; that is, hold down the key marked CTRL and
type A. To flip back to the original display, type CTRL-A again. This may be
done at almost any time that the Apple is waiting for you to type something,
but it is not recommended during the display of pictorial information or when
it is busy doing something such as compiling a program.

1.1.5 Checking your Disks

    The UCSD p-System contains a means for checking that a disk is at least
readable, known as a bad block scan. No guarantee is thereby implied
that what it reads is sensible, of course, but it does mean that there is a
high probability that the disk is not physically damaged. To check your MACC:
disk,

- ensure that the system disk is loaded in drive 1,
- check that the Apple is at the outermost level of command,
- type F to obtain the Filer and wait about 2 secs,
- type B to execute the Bad block scan module,
- one-drive Apples only: unload the APPLE0: disk,
- load the working copy of the MACC: disk, and in response to "BAD BLOCK SCAN OF ?", type MACC: followed by RETURN (not forgetting to type the colon (:)),
- in reply to the question, "SCAN FOR 280 BLOCKS ? (Y/N)", type Y,
- wait for about 10 seconds.

During this time the red light on the drive under test should remain on, accompanied by a gentle purring sound. The message "0 BAD BLOCKS" means all is well. If a bad block exists, you should, at this stage, repeat the instructions in the preliminaries on making a working copy of the MACC: disk, possibly with a physically different disk. Type Q to Quit the Filer and return to the outermost level of command. (One-drive Apples will then ask you to reload the APPLE0: disk. Do so, and the Apple will shortly be back at the outermost level of command.)

To check the system disk, repeat the instructions above using APPLE1: for a two-drive Apple, or APPLE0: for a one-drive Apple in place of MACC:.

If you take care of your disks, bad blocks will be very rare, but if at any time the Apple behaves abnormally, it is worth attempting a bad block scan of the disks in use. Problems arising in this chapter should be dealt with by attempting to remake working copies of the disks in question. Later, reference should be made to appendix 4 which describes the selective recovery of information from corrupt disks.

1.2 AN INTRODUCTION TO PROGRAMMING

First we will look at the text of a program, and then get the computer to obey it, usually known as running or executing the program.

1.2.1 Examining a Program

Check that the system disk is in drive 1 and that the Apple is at the outermost level of command. We are going to look at the program text in the file called FIVESTAR on the disk MACC:. Follow the instructions appropriate to your Apple.

(two-drive Apples)

- Ensure that the MACC: disk is loaded in drive 2.

- Type F to obtain the Filer.

- Type G to Get a file. (If the display replies with "THROW AWAY CURRENT WORKFILE ?", type Y. This will be explained later.)

- In response to the somewhat brief question "GET ? ", type MACC:FIVESTAR followed by RETURN.

(one-drive Apples)

- Type F to obtain the Filer.
- Next copy the file FIVESTAR from the MACC: disk to APPLE0: disk.
  To do this,
    - type T
    - remove APPLE0: and load MACC:
    - type MACC:FIVESTAR.TEXT,APPLE0:$ followed by RETURN. Note
      that the system disk is called A-P-P-L-E-zero, not A-P-P-L
      E-letter O.
    - When requested, remove MACC:, load APPLE0: and tap the
      spacebar.
- Type G to Get a file. (If the display replies with "THROW AWAY
  CURRENT WORKFILE ?", type Y. This will be explained later.)
- In response to the somewhat brief question, "GET ? ", type FIVESTAR
  followed by RETURN.

The response should be "TEXT FILE LOADED". If the response is "NO FILE
LOADED", you have made an error; type G and try a bit harder to get the name
right. If you spot a mistake before you press RETURN, you can correct it with
the ← key. When you have the "TEXT FILE LOADED" message,

- type Q to Quit the Filer, and then
- type E to obtain the Editor.

The Editor is a subsystem specially designed for creating and modifying
program text. It is also useful for displaying text, and that is why we use
it here. After a few seconds the following program will be in the Apple's
internal memory and will also be displayed on the screen.

```
PROGRAM FIVESTAR;

USES TURTLEGRAPHICS;

VAR SIDENUMBER : INTEGER;

BEGIN
     INITTURTLE;
     MOVETO(80, 80);
     PENCOLOR(WHITE);
     FOR SIDENUMBER := 1 TO 5 DO
         BEGIN
              MOVE(120);
              TURN(144)
         END;
     READLN
END.
```

Check that the screen corresponds with this program.

1.2.2 Running the Program

To find out what happens when the computer obeys this program ask the computer to Run it. To do this,

- type Q to Quit the Editor,
- type U (to be explained later) and
- type R to Run the program.

Watch the screen carefully during this process. It all happens in 3 phases.

- WRITING...   the program text is transferred from memory to the system disk.

- COMPILING... the program is translated from Pascal into P-code a language closer to that which the Apple itself understands. The translation is placed in a codefile.

- RUNNING...   the codefile is loaded back into the memory where it is interpreted and obeyed.

EXERCISE 1A: Draw the shape which is now displayed on the screen.

The program above has not quite finished. It is waiting at the line

        READLN

for you to type in anything ending with the RETURN key. This enables you to see the picture it has drawn, before returning to the outermost level of command in which state the screen reverts to display only text. Press the RETURN key now. For an action replay you can run the program again by pressing R.

1.2.3 Understanding the Program

It is essential at this stage to understand the relationship between the text of the program (see section 1.2.1) and the outcome of the program, namely a pentagram, which you should have drawn for the exercise above. Type E to have the program text displayed again.

The action of the program is described by a set of commands placed between the first **BEGIN** and the last **END**. We call this part the main program.

The three lines before the first **BEGIN** give information about what is to follow, both to the reader and the computer. More precisely, in the first line the word **PROGRAM** marks the beginning of the program text whilst the word FIVESTAR is the program name given principally for the benefit of the human reader. Here the program name and the name of the file are the same, namely FIVESTAR. There is no need for these names to be the same, but in the interests of simplicity they will generally be the same in this book. The semicolon marks the end of the program name and is essential. The second line indicates that the program needs material which is not part of Pascal, but is in the library of useful things. The part of the library called TURTLEGRAPHICS contains all the drawing equipment needed for the graphical examples used in this course. Any program which uses these facilities must have this line immediately after the program heading. The turtlegraphics package is

explained in more detail in appendix 1. For the time being, it should be
sufficient to regard the package as providing the means for commanding the
movement of a pen-carrying turtle on the x-y plane, the origin of which
is at the bottom left-hand corner of the screen. The third line states that
the program needs a variable; that the name of the variable is
SIDENUMBER; and that the variable must be able to accommodate an integer (or
whole number) value. A variable is like a box which can hold one and only one
value at any instant in time, but from time to time the value may change.
There will be more about variables in the next chapter (section 2.2), but it is
sufficient here to note that this variable takes the values 1, 2, 3, 4 and 5
during the execution of this program.

Rerun the program (type Q E R) and attempt to match the outcome of the
program with the program text.

If you are not satisfied that you understand this, execute the program in
the file XPLAIN1.1 on the MACC: disk, and follow the instructions and
information given on the screen. To execute that program on a two-drive
Apple,

- make sure you are at the outermost level of command,
- type X to eXecute a program,
- in response to the prompt "EXECUTE WHAT FILE?", type
  MACC:XPLAIN1.1 followed by RETURN, and
- follow the instructions on the screen.

To execute this program again, repeat the sequence above. (The difference
between eXecute and Run will be explained in section 3.6.4.)

On a one-drive Apple, you must first copy the file MACC:XPLAIN1.1.CODE
from MACC: to APPLE0: (see section 1.2.1) and then follow the instructions
above, replacing MACC:XPLAIN1.1 by XPLAIN1.1.

EXERCISE 1B: What do you think would have been drawn if,

(a) instead of   FOR SIDENUMBER := 1 TO 5 DO
     there had been   FOR SIDENUMBER := 1 TO 4 DO

(b) instead of   MOVE(120)
     there had been   MOVE(60)

(c) instead of   MOVE(120);
                       TURN(144)
     there had been   MOVE(60);
                       TURN(72)

EXERCISE 1C: Explain the meaning of

(a) MOVE(120)
(b) TURN(144)
(c) MOVETO(80, 80)
(d) PENCOLOR(WHITE)

If you wish to repeat the whole of section 1.2, you may do so by going
back to paragraph 1.2.1. One-drive Apple users need not repeat the copying of
files from the MACC: disk if they were successful first time through.

1.2.4 Note for One-drive Apples

Free space on APPLE0: is severely limited. It was only 32 blocks when you started, and by now it is only 14 blocks. When a disk has insufficient space for a file being written to it, the message "OUTPUT FILE FULL" is displayed. As soon as any file that has been temporarily copied to APPLE0: is no longer required, it should be either removed or transferred to another disk. (See appendix 2.)

One-drive users will find themselves Transferring files frequently. If a message of the form "DESTROY ABC: ? " appears, it means you have probably made a typing error and the disk called ABC: is about to lose all its files unless you type N. Retype the Transfer command correctly.

1.3. CORRECTING A PROGRAM

The program whose name was FIVESTAR, and which lives in the file called FIVESTAR, was a correct program. Usually when we write a program there are mistakes (known in the trade as bugs) of various kinds: typing errors, grammatical errors, logical errors. Typing and grammatical errors (called syntax errors) are generally found during the compiling process. Other errors found whilst the program is being obeyed are execution errors. The next program you are going to try to run has errors of each kind.

Before we look at the next program, the system date should be set to the correct date, a job you should always do whenever starting to use the Apple for the first time on a given day. It is the Filer that maintains the system date on the system disk. You should be at the outermost level of command, in which case type F to enter the Filer. Type D to prepare to change the Date. The date displayed will probably not be correct. Type in the correct day number (1 or 2 digits) followed by a dash (top row of the keyboard, to the left of the RESET key) followed by the first 3 letters of the month, followed by another dash, followed by the last two digits of the year, followed by RETURN. For example, if the date is 26 March 1982, type

        26-MAR-82   followed by RETURN.

If the leading one or two components of the date happen to be correct, you can just type the components that are incorrect followed by a RETURN. If the date is completely correct, just press RETURN. For example, if the date is given as 26-MAR-82, then type

        RETURN   for 26 March 82.

        30   followed by RETURN   for 30 March 82.

        2-APR   followed by RETURN   for 2 April 82.

        26-MAR-83   followed by RETURN   for 26 March 83.

The Apple responds by confirming the newly entered date and returns you to the Filer.

We are now ready to get the file called TWOBUGS from the diskette MACC:. (On a one-drive Apple, the file MACC:TWOBUGS.TEXT must first be transferred to the system disk as in section 1.2.1.) To display it on the screen,

- type G to Get a new file,
- type Y to say "Yes, throw away the workfile", (to be explained later)
- type MACC:TWOBUGS (just TWOBUGS on a one-drive Apple) followed by the RETURN key, and in response to "TEXT FILE LOADED",
- type Q to Quit the Filer and
- type E to enter the Editor).

The program now displayed has two mistakes which we will not look for just yet; we will let the Compiler do that. But before the program disappears notice the line

                (* PROGRAM SHOULD DRAW A SQUARE *)

This is a comment. Comments are always enclosed in the special brackets, (* and *). They may be placed anywhere in a program, are disregarded by the Compiler, and should be used in moderation to assist the human reader to understand what it's all about.

Now, to find the bugs, type Q, U and R (see section 1.2.2). Relax for 15 secs and you'll see that one of them has been spotted by the Compiler.

The information on the screen is not too helpful but if you now type E to return to the Editor, the precise location of the error in this program will be marked by a character in reversed video. This is known as the cursor. The top line says what the error is, and the cursor shows where it is. (Unfortunately, not all errors are reported as accurately as this one, but with a little practice you'll soon learn to recognize quickly what has gone wrong.) If you have not yet discovered what is wrong, compare the screen with a similar program in section 1.2.1. You should now have identified the error, and realized that one character of the program is incorrect. Do what the top line says, noting that on the screen, <SP> stands for the spacebar, and you will find yourself in the Editor, the program designed specifically to enable you to make changes to programs. Before we make the correction let us first learn how to move the cursor around the screen.

1.3.1 Moving the Cursor

On the right-hand side of the keyboard there are 2 keys marked with arrows. Press one of these keys and note what happens to the cursor. Try the other key marked with an arrow. Now type CTRL-O. (Remember to hold down the key marked CTRL whilst the letter O key is typed.) Then type CTRL-L. These are the four basic cursor moving keys. Move the cursor to the following positions.

- the A of DRAW
- the S of SQUARE
- the 4 of the FOR ... TO ... DO command
- the + of the FOR ... TO ... DO command
- the (of line 3 of the program (the comment line)

With the cursor on the (of the comment, type CTRL-I (TAB). Press ← twice and TAB again and notice that the response of the cursor is like that of the tab key on a typewriter, moving to character positions 8, 16, 24, etc. (The leftmost column is column 0.) Now press the spacebar, and notice that it has the same effect as →. Press ← until the cursor is at the start of the line; hold down the key marked REPT and then hold down the spacebar (or →) for a second or two. Note that this has a repeating effect. Any key can be repeated in this mannner. Next press RETURN 12 times.

EXERCISE 1D: How does the effect of the RETURN key differ from that of CTRL-L
               in the Editor?

    Finally, type CTRL-O until the cursor is at the top of the screen. Press
the spacebar (or →) several times and observe what happens to the cursor at
the end of a line. Move the cursor down to the second **BEGIN**; press ←
and observe what happens at the start of a line. This shows that trailing
spaces and leading spaces are represented on the screen but not in the file.
Special care must be taken when extending a line at either end. Get the cursor
back to the + sign.

    Although the cursor is shown on the screen located at a character, it is
more correctly thought of as being between the indicated character and the
character to its left. The significance of this will become more apparent when
we come to insert text into a file.

1.3.2 Editor Modes and Commands

1.3.2.1 X - eXchange

    The Editor's modes and commands are summarized on the top line of the
screen (known as the prompt line). Use the CTRL-A feature (section 1.1.4)
to see more modes and commands available in the Editor. To correct this
program, only the exchange mode is needed. From the prompt line you will
notice that X stands for eXchange. Type X and then, just for fun, type

         QWERTY

Obviously this makes matters worse, not better; so we had better reject these
changes. Press the key marked ESC, and the original is restored. Type X and
then type QWERTY again. Press ← a few times, noting how typing errors may
be corrected in eXchange mode. Press ESC and the original is again restored.
Whenever you press ESC in the exchange mode, the text is restored to its
previous state. With the cursor on the erroneous + sign, type X again. This
time, make the proper correction (just one character is wrong) and if you are
happy that you've now got it right, type CTRL-C. Think of CTRL-C as meaning
accept and ESC as meaning reject. You cannot use →, or CTRL-L or
CTRL-O in the eXchange mode in Apple Pascal.

    Execute this program (Q, U, R) and see what happens. Make a note of
what it drew on the screen. Press RETURN to terminate this program and Type E
to return to the Editor. You have a program which is syntactically correct,
but does not do what it is supposed to do. It will probably be the first of
many.

EXERCISE 1E: Use the Editor to display the program text again. Study it, make
               the necessary corrections, and execute it.

EXERCISE 1F: Where does the pen appear to start from? Make a guess at a
               MOVETO command to move the pen to

                    (a)   the center of the screen
                    (b)   the top right-hand corner of the screen

EXERCISE 1G: Using only the exchange mode, modify the program to draw a
               regular pentagon (5 sides) which fits nicely onto the screen.
               Leave the picture on the screen.

Before we explore further features of the Editor, you might care to have
a permanent copy of the pentagon drawing program on your user disk.

On a two-drive Apple,

- Press RETURN to terminate the program.
- Load one of your user disks (see the preface) in drive 2, in place
  MACC:
- type F to obtain the Filer, and
- type S to Save the program you have just run.

The screen will reply "SAVE AS MACC:TWOBUGS ?" for this was the original name
of the file that held the faulty program. Now you want to save the program
on a different disk with a different name so,

- type N (for No) and in response to "SAVE AS WHAT FILE ?"
- type USER:PENTAGON followed by RETURN, where USER stands for
  your initials, or whatever volume name you initially gave to this
  disk.

(If you are repeating this you may, at this and later stages get messages of
the form: "REMOVE OLD USER:PENTAGON.TEXT ?". Answer by typing Y.)
Confirmatory messages then state that the program text has been transferred to
USER:PENTAGON.TEXT and that the code file has been transferred to
USER:PENTAGON.CODE.

On a one-drive Apple, leave APPLE0: in the drive, and save the program
first as APPLE0:PENTAGON using the method above. Then use the Filer to
transfer APPLE0:PENTAGON.TEXT to USER:PENTAGON.TEXT and APPLE0:PENTAGON.CODE
to USER:PENTAGON.CODE.

Note that the two files named

        SYSTEM.WRK.TEXT
        SYSTEM.WRK.CODE

on the system disk, were collectively known as the workfile. There will
be more about the workfile in section 3.6.4. Type Q to return to the outermost
level of command.

1.3.2.2   I - Insert and D - Delete

We are going to make some more changes to the pentagon drawing program
saved above.

- Type F to obtain the Filer,
- type G Y (you may throw away the workfile),
- type USER:PENTAGON (APPLE0:PENTAGON on a one-drive Apple)
  followed by RETURN,
- type Q to Quit the Filer, and
- type E to get the Editor to display the pentagon drawing program.

Depending on how you responded to exercise 1G, the program name and the comment
may no longer be appropriate.

- Move the cursor to the first letter of the program name.
- Type D (for Delete) and
- press → (or the spacebar) four times.
- Press ←; smart, isn't it?
- Continue to press → until the cursor is on the semicolon.
- Type CTRL-C.

To insert PENTAGON at this position,

- type I (for Insert). Has the semi-colon disappeared completely? ‾Type CTRL-A to find out. Type CTRL-A again.
- Type PENTAGON
- type CTRL-C.

If you make a mistake whilst inserting, correct it with ← but note that you cannot go back beyond the start of the insertion. Whilst inserting you may type CTRL-I (TAB) but not →. In both I and D modes you can abandon what you are doing at any stage by pressing ESC, but if you want the insertion or deletion to take place you must finish with CTRL-C. Using the insert and delete modes, make the comment line appropriate to what the program does.

Quit the Editor, Update the workfile, enter the Filer and Save this file again as USER:PENTAGON in exactly the same manner as in section 1.3.2.1. Note that this time the Filer suggests that the program be saved with the same file name as it was Got with. Type Y at this suggestion. When the message "REMOVE OLD USER:PENTAGON.TEXT ?" appears (and if you think about it, quite correctly this time) type Y and the newer version supersedes the older one.

Return to the Editor (type Q E) and

- change **PROGRAM** PENTAGON to **PROGRAM** REVERSAGON
- change PENCOLOR(WHITE) to PENCOLOR(REVERSE)
- change **FOR** SIDENUMBER := 1 **TO** 5 **DO** to
  FOR SIDENUMBER := 1 **TO** 95 **DO**

Check that the comment line reads (* PROGRAM SHOULD DRAW A PENTAGON *) and run the program. Save this program as USER:REVERSAGON. Get back to the Editor displaying the latest version of the program. (Only two keys need to be pressed.)

1.3.2.3   Inserting and Deleting Lines

When inserting, you can add several lines simply by pressing RETURN at the end of each line. Do not use CTRL-O or CTRL-L when inserting. When deleting, you can use either of the arrows, RETURN and CTRL-I (TAB). As an example,

- put the cursor on the P of PENCOLOR(BLACK)
- type D
- press RETURN
- and CTRL-C.

A line has been removed. (Don't worry, it was not necessary, for at the start of a program the pen is effectively BLACK anyway.) If you delete too many lines, use CTRL-O to recover those you don't want to lose. You can also delete lines above the cursor. To see how forgiving the Editor can be,

- type D
- type CTRL-O 5 times
- type CTRL-L 8 times
- and then ESC.

We will now modify the program to draw a five-sided spiral.

- Put the cursor on the P of PENTAGON in the comment,
- type I
- press RETURN and then type SPIRAL and then the spacebar,
- and CTRL-C to accept.

Using the Insert and Delete modes,

- Change PENCOLOR(REVERSE) to PENCOLOR(WHITE).
- Change MOVE(...) to MOVE(100 - SIDENUMBER).

Note that the modified MOVE command requires a calculation to be performed, in order to determine how far each move should be made. In the parentheses, you have an example of an <u>expression</u>, a rule or formula for calculating a value. Run the program and save it on your user disk as USER:SPIRAL in the same manner as you saved the pentagon drawing program. Quit the Filer.

1.3.2.4   Adjusting Lines

Get back to the Editor which should display the program you have just saved. Move the cursor to the S of SPIRAL. Type A, press the > key a few times and notice what happens. Try the < key. Now get the S of SPIRAL directly under the P of **PROGRAM** and press CTRL-C to accept. (Whilst in the Adjust mode, ESC has no effect.) Type A again, and then type C, L and R noticing what happens. (You will have to type CTRL-A to see the effect of R.) Get the S of SPIRAL back under the P of **PROGRAM** and accept (CTRL-C).

The Adjust mode can be used to improve the layout of several lines of program. Note that this program uses 4 spaces per level of indentation. Suppose we wish to make this 6 spaces per level. Move the cursor down to the line containing INITTURTLE. Then make Adjustments as follows.

- Type A, >, >, CTRL-L
- CTRL-L
- CTRL-L
- CTRL-L
- >, >, CTRL-L
- >, >, CTRL-L
- CTRL-L
- <, < CTRL-L
- <, < CTRL-C (to terminate the Adjust mode)

(If during the above sequence you get lost, type CTRL-C, Q, E, Y, E and the original version is restored.) When you are happy with the layout change the program name to SPIRAL, leave the Editor (Q, U) and use the Filer to save the program again as USER:SPIRAL. Type Q to quit the Filer.

You must become very familiar with the use of Adjust. You should always keep your programs properly set out so that whenever you have to look at a program text, it is in its most readily understandable form.

1.4. PROCEDURES

Get the file STARTIME from the MACC: disk (you can safely throw away the workfile) and check that the program corresponds to the following.

```
PROGRAM STARTIME;

USES TURTLEGRAPHICS;

VAR STARNUMBER : INTEGER;

PROCEDURE DRAWSTAR(S : INTEGER);

    VAR SIDENUMBER : INTEGER;

    BEGIN
        FOR SIDENUMBER := 1 TO 5 DO
            BEGIN
                MOVE(S);
                TURN(144)
            END
    END; (* DRAWSTAR *)

BEGIN
    INITTURTLE;
    MOVETO(80, 80);   PENCOLOR(WHITE);
    DRAWSTAR(120);
    READLN
END.
```

The program does not quite fit onto the screen. Press RETURN 23 times, and on the final RETURN you will see the program scroll up and reveal the last line. The screen is effectively a window through which the file may be viewed. Run the program. Then return to the Editor.

This program has quite a different appearance and structure to the one called FIVESTAR, yet the outcome is the same. The action is described in the main program (between the last END and its corresponding BEGIN). The name DRAWSTAR has been introduced as the name of a new command known as a procedure. Comparison of the programs FIVESTAR and STARTIME shows that the new command

```
    DRAWSTAR(120)
```

in the program STARTIME, must be equivalent to

```
    FOR SIDENUMBER := 1 TO 5 DO
        BEGIN
            MOVE(120);
            TURN(144)
        END
```

in the program FIVESTAR. Inspection of the program STARTIME reveals that it contains the section

```
PROCEDURE DRAWSTAR(S : INTEGER);

    VAR SIDENUMBER : INTEGER;

    BEGIN
        FOR SIDENUMBER := 1 TO 5 DO
            BEGIN
                MOVE(S);
                TURN(144)
            END
    END; (* DRAWSTAR *)
```

immediately after the line saying that the program needs a variable. This section says that the program needs a new command (procedure) whose name is

DRAWSTAR

and which means

```
FOR SIDENUMBER := 1 TO 5 DO
    BEGIN
        MOVE(S);
        TURN(144)
    END
```

Note the use of the comment (* DRAWSTAR *) to mark the end of the section introducing the new command. If you are still unsure of the operation of this program, eXecute the program in the file XPLAIN1.2 on the MACC: disk.

EXERCISE 1H: (a) Modify the program above to draw four pentagrams of side 25, 65, 120 and 160 with a common starting point as in figure 1.1. Do not attempt to use a **FOR ... TO ... DO** command in this program. Save it as USER:FOURSTARS. Note that the procedure is written only once, but the new command which it defines can appear many times in the program.

(b) Modify USER:FOURSTARS to draw 5 pentagrams of side 20, 40, 60, 80 and 100. This time use a **FOR ... TO ... DO** command, noting that the equivalent of

starnumber times twenty

in Pascal is

STARNUMBER*20

EXERCISE 1J: The identifier S appears twice in the procedure DRAWSTAR. If it were replaced by say SIDELENGTH in both places, would the procedure do the same thing, or something different?

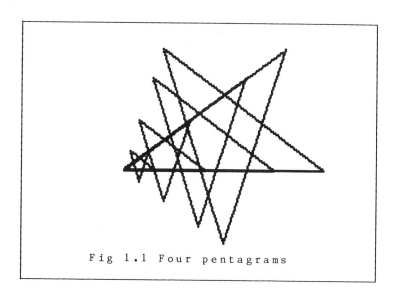

Fig 1.1 Four pentagrams

EXERCISE 1K: Explain in your own words the difference between

PROCEDURE DRAWSTAR(S : INTEGER);

    VAR SIDENUMBER : INTEGER;

    BEGIN
      FOR SIDENUMBER := 1 **TO** 5 **DO**
          BEGIN
             MOVE(S);
             TURN(144)
          END
      END; (* DRAWSTAR *)
   and

DRAWSTAR(120).

EXERCISE 1L: Using the program in the file STARTIME as a starting point, write
a program to draw the picture in figure 1.2. To see it drawn
slowly on the screen, eXecute the program in the file STARTURN on
the MACC: disk. Save your program as USER:MYSTARTURN.

Change the pencolor from WHITE to REVERSE and observe what
happens. Save this as USER:STARFISH.

SOLUTIONS TO THE EXERCISES

1A: See figure 1.3. The first line drawn is the horizontal one across the
lower part of the screen. It is drawn left to right. The remaining
four lines are drawn with their starting points coinciding with their
predecessor's end point.

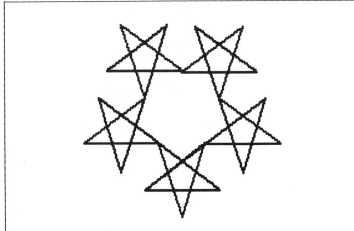

Fig 1.2   Picture drawn by STARTURN

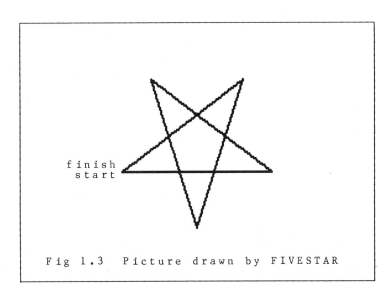

Fig 1.3   Picture drawn by FIVESTAR

1B: (a)   The final line is not drawn. The start and the finish are not
               connected. See figure 1.4.

         (b)   The picture is half of the size (linearly). See figure 1.5.

         (c)   A regular pentagon of side 60 units. The external angle of a
               regular pentagon is 72 degrees. See figure 1.6

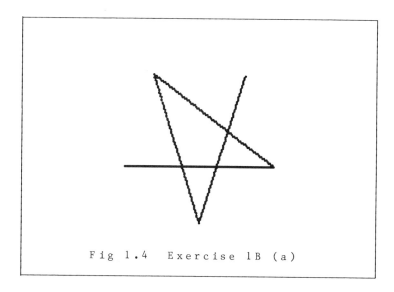

Fig 1.4   Exercise 1B (a)

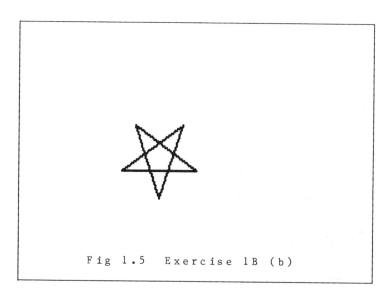

Fig 1.5   Exercise 1B (b)

1C:	(a)	MOVE(120)	Move forward 120 units in the direction the turtle is pointing. Draw line with the current pencolor.
	(b)	TURN(144)	Turn anticlockwise through 144 degrees. Do not move from current position.
	(c)	MOVETO(80, 80)	Move to a point 80 units right of the origin and 80 units above. Draw line with current pencolor.
	(d)	PENCOLOR(WHITE)	Change the pencolor to WHITE. On subsequent moves pen leaves white trace.

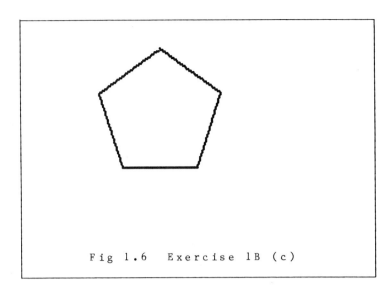

Fig 1.6   Exercise 1B (c)

1D: RETURN moves the cursor to the first non-blank character of the next
        line; downward arrow moves the cursor to the next line, keeping the
        same column position.

1E: **PROGRAM** FOURSQUARE;

        (* PROGRAM SHOULD DRAW A SQUARE *)

        USES TURTLEGRAPHICS;

        VAR SIDENUMBER : INTEGER;

        BEGIN
             INITTURTLE;
             PENCOLOR(BLACK);
             MOVETO(70, 20);
             PENCOLOR(WHITE);
             FOR SIDENUMBER := 1 **TO** 4 **DO**
                 BEGIN
                     MOVE(100);
                     TURN(90)
                 END;
             READLN
        END.

1F: Pen starts at the center of the screen.
        (a) MOVETO(139, 95) puts the pen at the center of the screen (or
             thereabouts).
        (b) MOVETO(279, 191) puts the pen at the top right-hand corner.

1G: **PROGRAM** PENTAGON ;

(* PROGRAM SHOULD DRAW PENTAGON *)

USES TURTLEGRAPHICS;

VAR SIDENUMBER : INTEGER;

```
BEGIN
    INITTURTLE;
    PENCOLOR(BLACK);
    MOVETO(70, 20);
    PENCOLOR(WHITE);
    FOR SIDENUMBER := 1 TO 5 DO
        BEGIN
            MOVE(100);
            TURN(72)
        END;
    READLN
END.
```

1H: (a) **PROGRAM** FOURSTARS;

USES TURTLEGRAPHICS;

VAR STARNUMBER : INTEGER;

PROCEDURE DRAWSTAR(S : INTEGER);

VAR SIDENUMBER : INTEGER;

```
    BEGIN
        FOR SIDENUMBER := 1 TO 5 DO
            BEGIN
                MOVE(S);
                TURN(144)
            END
    END; (* DRAWSTAR *)

BEGIN
    INITTURTLE;
    MOVETO(80, 80);  PENCOLOR(WHITE);
    DRAWSTAR(25);
    DRAWSTAR(65);
    DRAWSTAR(120);
    DRAWSTAR(160);
    READLN
END.
```

(b) **PROGRAM** FIVESTARS;

USES TURTLEGRAPHICS;

VAR STARNUMBER : INTEGER;

PROCEDURE DRAWSTAR(S : INTEGER); ... **END**; (* DRAWSTAR *)

```
BEGIN
    INITTURTLE;
    MOVETO(80, 80);  PENCOLOR(WHITE);
    FOR STARNUMBER := 1 TO 5 DO DRAWSTAR(STARNUMBER*20);
    READLN
END.
```

We shall see, in section 2.8 that either a single command, such as
DRAWSTAR(STARNUMBER*20) above, or a group of one or more commands
bracketed by **BEGIN ... END** may be repeated by means of the
FOR ... TO ... DO command. Thus, in the program above,
FOR STARNUMBER := 1 **TO** 5 **DO** DRAWSTAR(STARNUMBER*20) could have
been written in the more verbose form

```
FOR STARNUMBER := 1 TO 5 DO
    BEGIN
          DRAWSTAR(STARNUMBER*20)
    END
```

1J: There is no difference. Only the name of a variable has been
        changed, not its use.

1K: The section of program

```
PROCEDURE DRAWSTAR(S : INTEGER); ... END; (* DRAWSTAR *)
```

        is an explanation of how to interpret the command DRAWSTAR whenever
        it is encountered and for any value of S. In other words, it is how
        to do it.

```
DRAWSTAR(120)
```

        is a command to execute the commands in the procedure DRAWSTAR. In
        other words, it means do it now, giving S the value 120.

1L: Observe that redrawing an extra three lines of a pentagram gets you
        to the start of the next pentagram to be drawn. However as a turn
        always follows a line, 8 lines and turns put you facing in the wrong
        direction. You have turned once too often. To undo the last turn
        you need to TURN(-144). Hence the program below. It is not unique.
        Can you think of another equivalent program?

```
PROGRAM MYSTARTURN;

USES TURTLEGRAPHICS;

VAR STARNUMBER : INTEGER;

PROCEDURE DRAW8SIDES(S : INTEGER);

    VAR SIDENUMBER : INTEGER;

    BEGIN
        FOR SIDENUMBER := 1 TO 8 DO
            BEGIN
                MOVE(S);
                TURN(144)
            END;
        TURN(-144)
    END; (* DRAW8SIDES *)

BEGIN
    INITTURTLE;
    MOVETO(140, 140);  PENCOLOR(WHITE);
    FOR STARNUMBER := 1 TO 5 DO DRAW8SIDES(60);
    READLN
END.
```

Other interesting patterns may be drawn if the constant 8 is replaced
by 2, 3, 4, 5, 6, 7 or 9, and the pencolor changed to REVERSE.

CHAPTER 2
The Basic Elements of a Program

From the previous chapter, you should have obtained a feel for the relationship between a program text and what happens when the program is executed. We sometimes use the term <u>trace</u> (of a program) to refer to the sequence of all effects of the execution of a program. You can also think of the trace of a program as the history of its execution. Much of the trace of the program text in the file FIVESTAR could be seen on the screen of the display. However, parts of the trace which could not be seen on the screen were the changes that took place in the values in the variable called SIDENUMBER. (These were, in fact, visualized by the XPLAIN programs on the MACC: disk.) Whilst we concentrate on graphical programs, most of the trace will be visible, and many mistakes will manifest themselves in the form of distorted (and often amusing) pictures. Under such conditions mistakes are relatively easy to find; hence the suitability of graphics for the early stages of learning to program.

In this chapter we look again in a little more detail at the program text, and the basic elements of which it is comprised.

2.1 NAMES OF THINGS

In our everyday life we take little care grammatically to distinguish objects from their names, for in most cases, the context enables any ambiguity to be resolved. For example

> "Amanda is making good progress."
> "Amanda is a girl's name."

are two sentences in which the word "Amanda" is used in 2 different contexts. In the first we use it to denote a person; in the second it denotes a name. However in the sentence

> "Amanda has 3 A's."

a wider context (possibly one or more preceding sentences) has to be considered in order to decide whether the reference is to her name or examination grades.

Programs consists of both things that are referred to by name and things that are referred to explicitly. Consider again the first program you looked at in section 1.2.1.

```
PROGRAM FIVESTAR;

USES TURTLEGRAPHICS;

VAR SIDENUMBER : INTEGER;

BEGIN
    INITTURTLE;
    MOVETO(80, 80);
    PENCOLOR(WHITE);
    FOR SIDENUMBER := 1 TO 5 DO
        BEGIN
            MOVE(120);
            TURN(144)
        END;
    READLN
END.
```

Things that are named, or referred to by their names are

FIVESTAR	– the name of the program.
TURTLEGRAPHICS	– the name of a <u>unit</u> or <u>package</u>, (part of the library) which contains the drawing equipment.
SIDENUMBER	– the name of a variable used to count from 1 to 5.
INTEGER	– the name used to describe the set of negative, zero and positive whole numbers able to be used in a program.
INITTURTLE) MOVETO) PENCOLOR) MOVE) TURN)	– the names of some of the commands in the turtlegraphics repertoire.
WHITE	– the name of one of the pencolors.
READLN	– the name of a command in Pascal itself which is used to absorb anything typed on the keyboard up to and including the next RETURN.

and things referred to explicitly are

    80   1   5   120   144

Words which are printed in bold face,

    PROGRAM, USES, VAR, BEGIN, FOR, TO, DO, END

are not names of things. They are called <u>reserved words</u> and are used to give concrete shape to a program in much the same way as, in a mathematical proof, you might use words such as "Theorem", "let", "therefore", etc. Reserved words should be thought of as indivisible words or extensions to the basic character set. An ideal Pascal computer would, perhaps, have a special key for each reserved word which, when pressed, caused the whole word to be displayed in bold face. A full list of reserved words in Apple Pascal is given in appendix 3. Reserved words must not be used as names.

Returning to the list of named things in the program FIVESTAR, we can see that there is a rich variety of things that can be named, ranging from the program itself to a humble variable used to count from 1 to 5. Two of the names

        FIVESTAR, SIDENUMBER

were chosen by the author of that program, whilst

        TURTLEGRAPHICS, INITTURTLE, MOVETO, PENCOLOR, MOVE, TURN, WHITE

were chosen by the author of the turtlegraphics package and

        INTEGER, READLN

were chosen by the author of Pascal itself. If you look at the program in section 1.4 you will see the name DRAWSTAR used to name a procedure or command which was introduced by the author of that program.

Names are sufficiently important to be given a special name of their own. We call them <u>identifiers</u>. We have much freedom in inventing identifiers provided they

        — start with a letter
        — contain only letters and digits
        — contain no spaces
        — do not straddle two or more lines, and
        — are not reserved words.

In Apple Pascal, there is one further restriction.

        — Only the first 8 letters are significant.

Thus the following pairs of identifiers are not distinguished.

        TURTLEGRAPHICS   TURTLEGRAVY
        FIVESTAR   FIVESTARS

Within these restrictions identifiers must be chosen to make programs as readable as possible. A variable should generally be named by a noun suggesting the entity it represents, whilst a procedure should be named by a verb in the imperative mood, suggesting its action. Examples of identifiers are

        LENGTH   EXTANGLE   PITCH   DURATION
        K9   R2D2   DOTHIS   DRAWTHAT
        PLAYTUNE   RATHERLONGTAKECARE

EXERCISE 2A: Which of the following are valid identifiers?

        CUBE   COLUMBIA   U.S.A.
        A$ 50P   U235
        ALPHA+   EXERCISE 2A   IDENTIFIER
        PROGRAM   TWO-THIRDS   TEN%

EXERCISE 2B: Are the following pairs of identifiers equivalent in Apple Pascal?

        (a)   POSITION1   POSITION2
        (b)   PENTAGON   PENTAGRAM
        (c)   DIAMETER   DIAMETERSQ
        (d)   SUBMARINE   SUBMARINER

2.2   VARIABLES

    The program called FIVESTAR refers to SIDENUMBER. This is a variable.
More precisely, SIDENUMBER is the name of a variable or, to use the proper
term, an identifier. Think of SIDENUMBER as the name of a box which can hold
only one number (value) at a time. At its creation, the variable holds no
number. It is like an empty box, and its value is said to be underlined.
During the course of the execution of this program, the box called SIDENUMBER
holds several different numbers, but only one at a time. For example, 1 is
the first number it holds, and 5 is the last. Thus

        a variable   is likened to a box
        an identifier   is likened to the name of the box
        a value   is likened to one and only one number in
                                       the box at a given time.

On the Apple computer, integer values are restricted to the range

        -32768 to +32767 $(-2^{15}$ to $2^{15} - 1)$

    Variables are created as the result of executing what is in the **VAR**
section of a program. In the third line of our program

        VAR SIDENUMBER : INTEGER;

VAR says this is the start of the section in which variables are introduced
and SIDENUMBER : INTEGER says that a variable, suitable for holding an integer
(whole number, natural number) is required, and that it is to be named
SIDENUMBER. The variable, as yet, has no value. This is known as a
declaration. Several variables may be declared in the **VAR** section,
for example, by writing

        VAR J, K, M, P, Q, R, Y : INTEGER;

EXERCISE 2C: If, in the program FIVESTAR, the identifier SIDENUMBER
               had been systematically replaced by

        (a)   EDGENUMBER
        (b)   SIDENUMB
        (c)   MOVE

    what would the outcome have been?

EXERCISE 2D: If, during the execution of the program FIVESTAR, it were
               possible to look into the variable SIDENUMBER immediately before
               the execution of MOVETO(80, 80), what would its value be?

                    (a)   0
                    (b)   1
                    (c)   5
                    (d)   undefined

     The declaration of a variable (or any other object) makes the variable
available throughout that part of the program text in which it is declared.
Referring back to the program STARTIME in section 1.4, this means that
STARNUMBER could be referred to throughout the program (although, in fact it
was not referred to at all) but SIDENUMBER could only be referred to within
the procedure DRAWSTAR. The proper word to use for that part of the text in
which a variable may be referred to, is the scope of a variable. We
shall return to this topic in chapters 4 and 15.

2.3 PROCEDURES

     In the program in section 1.4 we encountered a procedure whose name was
DRAWSTAR. The procedure consisted of the procedure declaration

```
          PROCEDURE DRAWSTAR(S : INTEGER);

               VAR SIDENUMBER : INTEGER;

               BEGIN
                    FOR SIDENUMBER := 1 TO 5 DO
                         BEGIN
                              MOVE(S);
                              TURN(144)
                         END
               END; (* DRAWSTAR *)
```

and the procedure was activated or called by executing the command or
procedure statement

```
          DRAWSTAR(120)
```

in the main program. In exercise 1K it was noted that the procedure
declaration plays the role of "how to do it", whereas the procedure statement
says "do it, now!". That part of the procedure declaration between the first
BEGIN and the last END, which contains the commands indicating "how to
do it", is known as the body of a procedure. In exercise 1H, it was
observed that, once the procedure declaration was written, several calls could
be written with little effort, and that the value put in the parentheses of
the procedure statement (known as the actual parameter) caused the effect
of the call to be varied. The procedure itself recognized the need for
variation by referring to the length of the side of the pentagram by the
identifier S. In this context S is known as a formal parameter.

     Thus, armed with this particular procedure, the business of drawing
pentagrams of different sizes was eased. It was as though the repertoire of
available commands had been extended for the purpose of that program.

There is another important benefit arising out of the use of procedures. If we focus attention on the main program

```
INITTURTLE;
MOVETO(80, 80);
PENCOLOR(WHITE);
DRAWSTAR(120);
READLN
```

it clearly gives an overview of what is going on, leaving the detail to the bodies of the procedures. In the case of the first three commands, the bodies are provided within the turtlegraphics package and are of no concern to us, but in the case of DRAWSTAR(120), the body is manifest in the text of the procedure. The casual reader will learn more from the 5 lines of program above, than from the equivalent program in section 1.2.1, yet the detailed enquirer can discover the full story by referring back to the procedure body. This ability to separate the detail from the overall structure is of great importance in creating readable programs. In the remaining chapters we shall adopt this approach to the solving of problems and the design of programs.

EXERCISE 2E: Another benefit of procedures, not apparent in the example above, is that of saving space. Explain.

EXERCISE 2F: If, during the execution of the program STARTIME in section 1.4, we had been able to look into the formal parameter S immediately before the execution of the **FOR ... TO ... DO** command, what do you suppose its value would have been?

> (a)   0
> (b)   80
> (c)   120
> (d)   undefined

Compare your answer with that to exercise 2D.

2.4   CONSTANTS

The program FIVESTAR contains several items that have values but no names. These are constants (strictly speaking, unsigned constants). The constants in that program are

> 80   1   5   120   144

all integers (whole numbers). (Other kinds of constants will be described in later chapters.) In UCSD Pascal, an integer constant has to be in the range

> 0 to 32767   (0 to $2^{15} - 1$)

Integer constants are always written without spaces or commas.

2.5 SIMPLE EXPRESSIONS

An expression is a rule (or formula) for calculating a value. At this stage we restrict ourselves to expressions which produce integer values. They are examples of <u>simple expressions</u>. Other kinds of expression will be introduced later. There were a few expressions in the previous chapter. One of the more obvious ones was in the program in the file #5:SPIRAL where

        100 - SIDENUMBER

was written as the actual parameter of the MOVE command. You will recall that, as SIDENUMBER increased, the length of the sides decreased. In fact, there were several less obvious expressions in chapter 1. In the program FIVESTAR,

        1   5   80   120   144

and in the program STARTIME, in the MOVE(S) command,

        S

are all expressions. They are rules for producing values, but in these instances the calculation is non-existent.

Expressions are <u>evaluated</u> each time they are encountered in the execution of a program. For example, in the program in USER:SPIRAL the expression 100 - SIDENUMBER was evaluated once for each line drawn. Its value on each occasion was 99, 98, ... , 6, 5.

Two aspects of expressions have to be examined in some detail, namely how they are written and where they may be written.

2.5.1 How to Write Simple Expressions

The structure of expressions in Pascal is intended to follow closely the formulas of mathematics, and at the same time be unambiguous and be able to be written as a typographically linear sequence of characters (no superscripts and no subscripts).

Expressions are made up from

- operators   (such as +, -)
- operands   (variables, constants)
- parentheses

The principal differences between the formulas of mathematics and simple expressions of Pascal are summarized below.

- Multiplication must be explicitly written. It is denoted by * and not x.

- There is no exponentiation operator in Pascal. There is however a function

      SQR(x)

   which computes the square of any expression x. Thus, SQR(x) yields the same value as x*x. You can even write SQR(A + B) instead of (A + B)*(A + B).

- For some time we shall restrict ourselves to integer division. The integer division of two integers yields an integer result which is truncated towards zero. The symbol for this operator is the the reserved word **DIV**. Thus the mathematical formula,

$$\left[\frac{i}{j}\right]$$

   which stands for the whole number part of $\frac{i}{j}$, is represented in Pascal by

      I **DIV** J.

   With a negative operand, (-I) **DIV** J and I **DIV** (-J) are both interpreted as -(I **DIV** J). Care must be taken to ensure that I **DIV** 0 is never attempted. It will cause a program to fail at execution time.

On the other hand, the formulas of mathematics and simple expressions of Pascal are similar in the following respects.

- Multiplication and division bind more strongly than addition and subtraction. That is, the operator precedence of multiplication and division is the same, but greater than that of addition and subtraction. For example, in neither of the equivalent expressions

      Mathematics: 2x - 1
      Pascal: 2*X - 1

   are parentheses needed. However, note the way the expression has been written in Pascal. You should have realized from chapter 1 that spaces are generally ignored in a Pascal program. We could have written the Pascal expression as

      2 * X-1

   and the meaning would have been the same. However, in the first form, spaces have been used to remind the human reader of the operator precedence, namely that * binds more strongly than -. The second version suggests precisely the opposite sense.

- Parentheses may be used in matching pairs to override the natural order of operator precedence above. For example,

      Mathematics: 2(x - 1)
      Pascal: 2*(X - 1).

- Where operators of the same precedence occur at the same level, they are evaluated from left to right. For example, in both mathematics and Pascal,

      M - N - 1   means   (M - N) - 1.

- A leading minus before an expression is interpreted as in mathematics. For example,

Mathematics: $-2x^2 + 1$
Pascal: $-2*SQR(X) + 1.$

In the examples of expressions that follow, we assume that the following variables already have the values shown.

I	3	P	19
J	7	Q	4
K	-2	R	11
M	5	Y	1982

Math formula	Pascal expression	Value
$j - i$	J - I	4
$2j - 1$	2*J - 1	13
$2(q + 3)$	2*(Q + 3)	14
$p - q - r$	P - Q - R	4
$[\frac{r}{q}]$	R **DIV** Q	2
$[\frac{r}{-2}]$	R **DIV** (-2)	-5
$[\frac{4m + 23}{10}]$	(4*M + 23) **DIV** 10	4

The integer division operator **DIV** turns out to be useful in many situations. To determine whether, for positive p and q, q divides into p exactly or leaves a remainder, the value of the expression

P - ((P **DIV** Q) * Q)

can be inspected. If it is zero, the division is exact, otherwise the expression gives the value of the remainder. Observe that none of the parentheses above is necessary, and the expression is equivalent to the slightly enigmatic

P - P **DIV** Q * Q

In mathematics, the remainder on dividing p by q is usually written

p(mod q)

The usefulness of this operation is reflected in Pascal by the provision of a special operator **MOD**. In Pascal, the expression above is written

P **MOD** Q

The operator **MOD** has the same precedence as **DIV** and *. Since **MOD** is defined in terms of **DIV**, it follows that P **MOD** 0 will also cause a program to fail at execution time.

In the examples of the use of **MOD** which follow, we assume the same variables and values as before.

Math formula	Pascal expression	Value
7(mod 3)	7 - ((7 **DIV** 3) * 3) or 7 - 7 **DIV** 3 * 3 or 7 **MOD** 3	7 - ((2) * 3) = 1
p(mod q)	P - P **DIV** Q * Q or P **MOD** Q	19 - 4 * 4 = 3
i(mod j)	I - I **DIV** J * J or I **MOD** J	3 - 0 * 7 = 3

EXERCISE 2G: Write down a Pascal expression whose value is 0 if n divides into 360 leaving no remainder.

EXERCISE 2H: For each of the following mathematical formulas, write down an equivalent Pascal expression and the corresponding value, assuming the variables and values given above.

$$-2(i + j) \qquad p^2 + q^2 + r^2 \qquad -k$$

$$pq - r^2 \qquad j(mod\ 2) \qquad y(mod\ q)$$

$$i - j - k \qquad [\frac{i + j}{2k}] \qquad [\frac{p + r}{q}]$$

$$\frac{[\frac{m}{q}]}{[\frac{j}{i}]} \qquad [\frac{y}{mq}] \qquad i^4$$

EXERCISE 2J: Prove that the following two expressions are equivalent.

P - ((P **DIV** Q) * Q)
P - P **DIV** Q * Q

EXERCISE 2K: If a and b are integers with positive values, write down an expression (using only the arithmetic operators mentioned in this chapter) whose value is the integer nearest to

$$\frac{b}{a}$$

EXERCISE 2L: You will meet the following expression in a later chapter. Write it as a Pascal expression.

$$y + 31(m - 1) + d + [\frac{y - 1}{4}] - \left[\frac{3[\frac{y + 99}{100}]}{4}\right]$$

2.5.2 Where to Write Expressions

An almost infallible guide to where expressions may be written is

"wherever it appears to be reasonable to write an expression,
    it is legal to write one."

Applying this rule to those statements which have been discussed so far, we
conclude that expressions are legal in the following contexts.

- FOR v := expression TO expression DO ...
- as an actual parameter of a procedure statement.

Examples of each of these situations are,

FOR V := I - 1 TO J + 1 DO ...

DRAWSTAR(STARNUMBER*20)

2.6 PROGRAM LAYOUT

Good programs should not only be acceptable to the computer and correct
in their actions, but should also be comprehensible by a programmer other than
the author. Programs which have to pay for themselves must be readily
modifiable when the external world to which they relate changes because, for
example, of financial, legal, commercial and technical developments. As
exercise 2M at the end of this section shows, the layout of a program can
significantly alter its readability.

2.6.1 Spaces

Spaces in Pascal programs are generally ignored except that they must not
be placed

- within an identifier
- within a constant, or
- within a reserved word

On the other hand, spaces are necessary to separate items from each
other, where otherwise an ambiguity would arise. A useful guide (if somewhat
strong) is always to put spaces immediately before and after a reserved word
unless it is at the beginning or end of a line.

2.6.2 Blank Lines

Blank lines make good visual separators for breaking up a long program into syntactic or logical sections. In long programs it is essential to be able to locate procedures easily.

The freedom to add spaces and blank lines almost anywhere in the text of a program presents a good opportunity to make the appearance of a program reflect its structure.

2.6.3 Indentation

The use of indentation in the programs discussed so far may not seem necessary, but the longer a program is, and the more complex it becomes, then the more necessary it is that the logical structure of the program be as apparent as possible. Indentation makes a significant contribution to the readability of programs. The style adopted in this course is but one possibility. Develop your own style and then stick to it.

2.6.4 Semicolons

Commands are separated from each other by semicolons (;). Note that this is not the same as saying that commands are terminated by semicolons. There was no semicolon after TURN(144) or READLN in the program FIVESTAR. (Pascal is designed to accept unnecessary semicolons, in particular those appearing immediately in front of an **END**, but it will not tolerate the omission of necessary ones.)

The end of a line has no special significance. Commands can be carried over onto more than one line. It would be acceptable to the computer, but misleading to a human reader, to write

```
FOR SIDENUMBER
:= 1 TO 5 DO BEGIN
MOVE(120); TURN(144) END
```

EXERCISE 2M: Rewrite the following program (which happens to be acceptable to Apple Pascal) so that it is intelligible to a human reader.

```
PROGRAM POLYS;USES TURTLEGRAPHICS;
VAR ORDER:INTEGER;PROCEDURE
DRAWPOLYGON(NUMSIDES,LENGTH:INTEGER);
VAR I:INTEGER;BEGIN FOR I:=1 TO
NUMSIDES DO BEGIN MOVE(LENGTH);TURN(360
DIV NUMSIDES)END END;(* DRAWPOLYGON *)
BEGIN INITTURTLE;MOVETO(110,10);PENCOLOR
(WHITE);FOR ORDER:=3 TO 6 DO DRAWPOLYGON
(ORDER,60);READLN END.
```

2.7 TERMINOLOGY

We have used the word "command" to describe a component of a program which causes some sort of action to happen. It is perhaps unfortunate that the generally used word for this in computing is statement. It is unfortunate because these two words have quite different meanings in the world outside computing. However, from now on we shall conform to the usual terminology and describe action-causing components of programs as statements.

2.8 THE FOR STATEMENT AND COMPOUND STATEMENT

Each program considered so far has had a construction of the form

      FOR identifier := expression1 **TO** expression2 **DO**

which has been followed either by a procedure statement such as

      DRAWSTAR(STARNUMBER*20)

(in exercise 1H(b)), or by **BEGIN** statement; ... statement **END**, such as

```
BEGIN
    MOVE(120);
    TURN(144)
END
```

in the program FIVESTAR. This construction causes either a single statement or a group of statements to be executed repeatedly in what is known as a loop.

In the first example above, it is the procedure statement that is to be repeated according to the values of the expressions in the **FOR** ... **DO** clause; and in the second case it is the group of statements between the **BEGIN** and **END** that is to be repeated. The pair, **BEGIN** ... **END**, serves as a pair of big brackets, having the effect of treating a number of statements as though they were one. The construction

      BEGIN statement-1; statement-2; ... statement-n **END**

is known as a compound statement.

We can now define a for statement provisionally as one of

    - **FOR** identifier := expression1 **TO** expression2 **DO**
        procedure statement

    - **FOR** identifier := expression1 **TO** expression2 **DO**
        compound statement

The identifier must be the name of an integer variable and the expressions must evaluate to integer values. The pair of characters ":=" is to be regarded as an indivisible unit. It is pronounced "becomes". Do not separate the colon and the equals sign.

The effect of the for statement is that the procedure statement or compound statement is executed repeatedly with the identifier taking successively the values

expression1, expression1 + 1, ..., expression2

If expression1 is equal to expression2, the procedure statement or compound statement is executed once. If expression1 is greater than expression2 the procedure statement or compound statement is not executed at all.

EXERCISE 2N: Write down how many times the statement P is executed in each of the following:

        (a) FOR I := 0 TO 7 DO P;
        (b) FOR J := -7 TO 0 DO P;
        (c) FOR K := -3 TO +3 DO P;
        (d) FOR M := -SQR(2) TO SQR(SQR(2)) DO P;
        (e) FOR N := 1 TO 360 DIV 7 DO P;
        (f) FOR Q := 3 TO 1 DO P;
        (g) FOR R := 100 DIV 4 TO SQR(5) DO P;

2.9 STATEMENTS

This is a good time to review the various kinds of statement encountered so far. There are, in fact, only the three described below.

Kind of Statement	Example(s)
procedure statement	MOVETO(80, 80) INITTURTLE

compound statement	BEGIN
	    MOVE(120);
	    TURN(144)
	END

for statement	FOR SIDENUMBER := 1 TO 5 DO
	    BEGIN
	        MOVE(120);
	        TURN(144)
	    END

The statement is such an important syntactic unit that the following rule applies: "wherever a statement can be written, any kind of statement can be written". Applying this to the for statement, we can redefine its form as

FOR identifier := expression1 TO expression2 DO statement

thus admitting the possibility of nested for statements. For example,

```
FOR RANK := 1 TO 8 DO
    FOR FIL := 1 TO 13 DO
        BEGIN
            PENCOLOR(NONE);
            MOVETO(FIL*20, RANK*20);
            PENCOLOR(WHITE);
            DRAWSTAR(10);
            PENCOLOR(NONE)
        END
```

Note that the effect of defining the for statement in terms of statement, and statement in terms of for statement (known as a pair of <u>mutually recursive</u> definitions), permits the nesting to an arbitrary <u>depth of</u> one for statement within another.

EXERCISE 2P: Assume you have available to you two procedures

                   PROCEDURE FLOGGLE(X, Y : INTEGER);

        and

                   PROCEDURE TOGGLE(X, Y : INTEGER);

        which draw a floggle or a toggle on the screen at coordinate
        position (x, y). Assume also that you have the variables
        RANK and FIL available, as above. Write a program
        fragment that draws 6 floggles at x-coordinates 30, 60, 90, 120,
        150 and 180 followed by a toggle at 210, on each of the lines
        whose y-coordinates are 40, 80 and 120.

2.10   THE TURTLEGRAPHICS PACKAGE

By now you should be fairly familiar with the turtlegraphics package. It is described in some detail in appendix 1, and you should read this appendix to the end of section 1 now.

SOLUTIONS TO THE EXERCISES

2A: Valid identifiers are

                CUBE   COLUMBIA   U235   IDENTIFIER

        Invalid identifiers are

                U.S.A.   (full stops)
                TWO-THIRDS   (minus sign/hyphen)
                A$ ($)
                50P   (begins with a non-letter)
                TEN%   (%)
                ALPHA+   (+)
                EXERCISE 2A   (contains a space)
                PROGRAM   (reserved word)

2B: (a) (c) (d)   equivalent pairs
        (b)   not equivalent pairs

2C: (a) (b)   outcome of program is the same.
        (c)   the identifier move cannot stand for two different
                           things at the same time. Program will fail in
                           compilation.

2D: (d) undefined

2E: Using a procedure to represent a section of program that is to be
        executed in several different parts of a program means the section is
        written only once (in the procedure declaration) and the very much
        shorter call (the procedure statement) is written several times.
        Without a procedure, the section of program is written several times.

2F: (c) 120
        A variable such as SIDENUMBER is created but its value is not
        defined. A formal parameter such as S is like a variable, but
        immediately after its creation it receives a value (120 in this case)
        given by the value of the actual parameter.

2G: 360 **MOD** N

2H: Values are in curly brackets following the expressions.

        $-2*(I + J)$ {-20} $SQR(P) + SQR(Q) + SQR(R)$ {498} $-K$ {2}

        $P*Q - SQR(R)$ {-45}   J **MOD** 2 {1}   Y **MOD** Q {2}

        $I - J - K$ {-2} $(I + J)$ **DIV** $(2*K)$ {-2} $(P + R)$ **DIV** Q {7}

        $(M$ **DIV** $Q)$ **DIV** $(J$ **DIV** $I)$ {0}
                                Y **DIV** $(M*Q)$ {99} $SQR(SQR(I))$ {81}

2J: $(P$ **DIV** $Q) * Q$ is equivalent to P **DIV** $Q * Q$ because
        DIV and * have equal precedence and are therefore applied left to
        right.
        $P - (P$ **DIV** $Q * Q)$ is equivalent to $P - P$ **DIV** $Q * Q$
        because - (minus) is of lesser precedence than **DIV** or *.

2K: The integer closest to $\dfrac{b}{a}$ is

$$[\frac{b}{a} + \frac{1}{2}] = [\frac{2b + a}{2a}]$$

        Therefore the expression is $(2*B + A)$ **DIV** $(2*A)$

2L: $Y + 31*(M - 1) + D + (Y - 1)$ **DIV** $4 - 3*((Y + 99)$ **DIV** $100)$ **DIV** 4

```
2M:     PROGRAM POLYS;

        USES TURTLEGRAPHICS;

        VAR ORDER : INTEGER;

        PROCEDURE DRAWPOLYGON(NUMSIDES, LENGTH : INTEGER);

            VAR I : INTEGER;

            BEGIN
                FOR I := 1 TO NUMSIDES DO
                    BEGIN
                        MOVE(LENGTH);
                        TURN(360 DIV NUMSIDES)
                    END
            END; (* DRAWPOLYGON *)

        BEGIN
            INITTURTLE;
            MOVETO(110, 10);
            PENCOLOR(WHITE);
            FOR ORDER := 3 TO 6 DO DRAWPOLYGON(ORDER, 60);
            READLN
        END.
```

```
2N:     (a)  8         (b)  8         (c)  7
        (d) 21         (e) 51         (f)  0
        (g)  1
```

```
2P:     FOR RANK := 1 TO 3 DO
            BEGIN
                FOR FIL := 1 TO 6 DO FLOGGLE(30*FIL, 40*RANK);
                TOGGLE(210, 40*RANK)
            END
```

CHAPTER 3
Divide and Conquer

The principal objective of this chapter is to explore the method of problem solving which leads to a programming methodology variously described as "Structured", "Top-down" and "Successive Refinement". Its essence is the replacement of individual tasks by a number of simpler tasks, the process of replacement being applied successively until all remaining tasks are sufficiently obvious to be written directly in the programming language itself. In contrast to the approach of chapter 1, where we studied completed programs, we will now start with a problem, albeit a simple one, and proceed towards a solution in terms of a program. Taking up the musical analogy at the beginning of chapter 1, it is as though we will compose a piece of music to meet some well-defined requirement.

A secondary objective of this chapter is to gain further experience with the Editor and Filer.

3.1   TO DRAW A WINDMILL

Our task is to write a program which, when executed, draws a windmill on the screen in the manner of figure 3.1. The first thing to notice is that the task itself is one which has been abstracted (from the Latin, meaning "taken out") from the real world. The windmill of figure 3.1 is but a simple two-dimensional representation of windmills in the real world. It lacks an entrance, windows, loading and unloading facilities (maybe they are all round the back); the direction of view is orthogonal to the plane of the sails; and "hidden lines" behind the sails are not removed. In other words, the windmill of figure 3.1 is an abstraction of a general view of a real world windmill, showing only limited features. From now on, we concentrate on the windmill of figure 3.1.

The first stage in the solution is reached by using powers of observation and classification which lead to the conclusion that to draw a windmill is equivalent to

```
        draw the body        (the rectangular part)
        draw the roof        (the triangular part)
        draw the sails
```

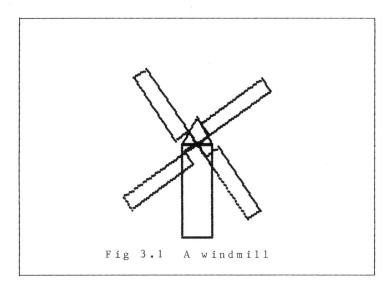

Fig 3.1   A windmill

In this example, it happens not to matter in which order the three parts are drawn, and an alternative equivalent decomposition is

        draw the roof
        draw the body
        draw the sails

The irrelevance of order shown here is not generally true of problem solving. Consider the culinary absurdities that might be generated if the original problem had been that of making a cup of coffee.

    At this stage it is worth starting to type in the solution to this problem. Check that the disk(s) are loaded, switch the computer on and load the system. You are about to create a brand new program in a new file, something you have not done before.

        - Type F to obtain the Filer,
        - type N to indicate you wish to create a New file,
        - type Y to say "Yes, throw away the workfile",
        - type Q to Quit the Filer, and
        - type E to obtain the Editor.

The Editor discovers that there is no workfile present and asks you to press RETURN so that you can start with a clean sheet, so to speak. The program you are about to enter has to be Inserted into that clean sheet, so type I. Then enter the following outline program.

```
PROGRAM MILL1;

USES TURTLEGRAPHICS;

BEGIN
      DRAWBODY;
      DRAWROOF;
      DRAWSAILS
END.
```

This represents the first stage in the production of the program.
Obviously we are far from finished, for it would be quite unreasonable to
expect a general-purpose programming language, even one equipped for graphics,
to know about the bodies, roofs and sails of windmills. Nevertheless, it is
instructive to attempt to run this program, if only to see the nature of the
problems the Compiler has with it. To do this type Q, U and R. Wait for
about 15 seconds and then as each syntax error is reported, press the spacebar
and note them. They all relate to the as yet undeclared identifiers DRAWBODY,
DRAWROOF and DRAWSAILS. Not surprising, if you think about it.

There are three ways to proceed. We could do something about DRAWBODY; we
could do something about DRAWROOF; or we could do something about DRAWSAILS.
It will be most instructive to look at DRAWSAILS first, since it is somewhat
different from the other two. As we examine DRAWSAILS we will put well to the
back of our minds the matters of DRAWBODY and DRAWROOF. At this stage the
title of this chapter should begin to become apparent.

From the picture we are aiming to draw, and maybe a background knowledge
of windmill sails, we see that each sail has the same shape but is in a
different orientation. Taking the axis of rotation of the sails as the origin
of the drawing, we can express

```
      DRAWSAILS
```

as

```
FOR SAILNUMBER := 1 TO 4 DO
    BEGIN
          DRAWSAIL;
          TURN(90)
    END
```

where SAILNUMBER is the name of a variable which can count from 1 to 4. The
statement DRAWSAILS is removed from the program and is replaced by the for
statement which includes the simpler, but still unexplained, DRAWSAIL. The
next level in the development of the program is therefore

```
PROGRAM MILL2;

USES TURTLEGRAPHICS;

VAR SAILNUMBER : INTEGER;

BEGIN
      DRAWBODY;
      DRAWROOF;
      FOR SAILNUMBER := 1 TO 4 DO
          BEGIN
                DRAWSAIL;
                TURN(90)
          END
END.
```

Get back to the Editor (if you are not already there) and make the changes necessary to bring the program up to this level. Do not run it yet.

3.2 THE WINDMILL REALIZED

We now focus our attention successively on the statements DRAWBODY, DRAWROOF and DRAWSAIL. First consider DRAWBODY. Our treatment of DRAWBODY will differ from that of DRAWSAILS. Rather than substitute simpler statements in the text for DRAWBODY, we will leave this statement in the program, and provide a definition of it in a procedure. The drawing of the windmill can be expressed directly in terms of the kinds of straight line traces made by the turtle. Starting at the axis of rotation of the sails and facing due east, suitable statements to draw the body of the windmill are

```
MOVE(12);
TURN(-90);
MOVE(72);
TURN(-90);
MOVE(24);
TURN(-90);
MOVE(72);
TURN(-90);
MOVE(12)
```

To embody this sequence of statements into a procedure (or a "here's how to do it when you need to" structure) we write

```
PROCEDURE DRAWBODY;

    BEGIN
        MOVE(12);
        TURN(-90);
        MOVE(72);
        TURN(-90);
        MOVE(24);
        TURN(-90);
        MOVE(72);
        TURN(-90);
        MOVE(12)
    END; (* DRAWBODY *)
```

Two things are worth noting. In chapter 1 we used positive degrees to denote anticlockwise rotation of the direction of the turtle; here we use negative degrees to represent clockwise rotations. Secondly, observe that by simple geometry it can be verified that the turtle finishes up at its initial position again facing due east. This is an example of an invariance, an important idea in the production of reliable programs. The procedure DRAWBODY does something to the screen but leaves the turtle precisely as it found it.

Applying similar principles to the roof of the windmill we get

```
PROCEDURE DRAWROOF;

    BEGIN
        MOVE(12);
        TURN(120);
        MOVE(24);
        TURN(120);
        MOVE(24);
        TURN(120);
        MOVE(12)
    END; (* DRAWROOF *)
```

and to a single sail we get

```
PROCEDURE DRAWSAIL;

    BEGIN
        MOVE(72);
        TURN(90);
        MOVE(12);
        TURN(90);
        MOVE(60);
        TURN(90);
        MOVE(12);
        TURN(90);
        MOVE(-12)
    END; (* DRAWSAIL *)
```

In both DRAWROOF and DRAWSAIL, the principle of invariance is again apparent. Furthermore, the invariance of DRAWSAIL ensures that the for statement in the main program

```
FOR SAILNUMBER := 1 TO 4 DO
    BEGIN
        DRAWSAIL;
        TURN(90)
    END
```

also preserves the invariance of the turtle.

Before we put all this together, recall from chapter 1 that the turtle has to be initialized and the pencolor set to WHITE before anything can be drawn. Remember also that if you are to be able to admire your artistic creation for more than a fraction of a second you need to include READLN as the last statement of the program. Thus the program is

```
PROGRAM MILL3;

USES TURTLEGRAPHICS;

VAR SAILNUMBER : INTEGER;

PROCEDURE DRAWBODY;

    BEGIN
        MOVE(12);
        TURN(-90);
        MOVE(72);
        TURN(-90);
        MOVE(24);
        TURN(-90);
        MOVE(72);
        TURN(-90);
        MOVE(12)
    END; (* DRAWBODY *)

PROCEDURE DRAWROOF;

    BEGIN
        MOVE(12);
        TURN(120);
        MOVE(24);
        TURN(120);
        MOVE(24);
        TURN(120);
        MOVE(12)
    END; (* DRAWROOF *)

PROCEDURE DRAWSAIL;

    BEGIN
        MOVE(72);
        TURN(90);
        MOVE(12);
        TURN(90);
        MOVE(60);
        TURN(90);
        MOVE(12);
        TURN(90);
        MOVE(-12)
    END; (* DRAWSAIL *)

BEGIN
    INITTURTLE;
    PENCOLOR(WHITE);

    DRAWBODY;
    DRAWROOF;
    FOR SAILNUMBER := 1 TO 4 DO
        BEGIN
            DRAWSAIL;
            TURN(90)
        END;

    READLN
END.
```

Get back to the Editor and the program MILL2 should be displayed. Note that the program MILL3 contains the whole of MILL2. Add the three procedures and the initializing and terminating statements, and save it as USER:MILL3 before attempting to execute it.

The program draws a different windmill from that in figure 3.1. The sails in figure 3.1 are at an angle of 35 degrees to the horizontal. Our replacement of DRAWSAILS by the for statement was not quite complete. Clearly, it should have been replaced by

```
TURN(35);
FOR SAILNUMBER := 1 TO 4 DO
    BEGIN
        DRAWSAIL;
        TURN(90)
    END;
TURN(-35)
```

Note that yet again invariance is preserved by these additional statements. Make these changes to the file USER:MILL3 and obtain the same picture as in figure 3.1.

What we have just done is to divide the problem into three independent sub-problems and conquer each sub-problem separately. If you are not convinced, take the program MILL3 and permute the three parts

- DRAWBODY

- DRAWROOF

- TURN(35);
  ```
  FOR SAILNUMBER := 1 TO 4 DO
      BEGIN
          DRAWSAIL;
          TURN(90)
      END;
  TURN(-35)
  ```

in any order and execute the program again. Invariance is not always so obvious or so abundant as seen here, but where it can be identified it is usually worth preserving.

EXERCISE 3A: (a)   Change the angle of the sails to 15 degrees.

(b)   Change the number of sails from 4 to 3, and ensure that the windmill is still balanced!

EXERCISE 3B: Enlarge the roof to become an equilateral triangle of side 36 units.

3.3   TOWARDS A BETTER WINDMILL

Our windmill appears to be what was asked for, but can our program respond to possible future market requirements? For example, if larger roofs and smaller sails become fashionable, how quickly can we respond to such demands? The program is not particularly good in this respect. To enlarge the roof in the exercise above, you had to change four closely related statements. We can make the procedure DRAWROOF (and the others) more flexible by the use of a parameter. DRAWROOF thus becomes

```
PROCEDURE DRAWROOF(S : INTEGER);

    BEGIN
        MOVE(S);
        TURN(120);
        MOVE(2*S);
        TURN(120);
        MOVE(2*S);
        TURN(120);
        MOVE(S)
    END; (* DRAWROOF *)
```

and the main program becomes

```
    BEGIN
        INITTURTLE;
        PENCOLOR(WHITE);

        DRAWBODY;
        DRAWROOF(12);
        TURN(35);
        FOR SAILNUMBER := 1 TO 4 DO
            BEGIN
                DRAWSAIL;
                TURN(90)
            END;
        TURN(-35);

        READLN
    END.
```

in order to draw the original picture. Do not make these changes to the program in USER:MILL3 yet.

EXERCISE 3C: What change to the main program immediately above would produce the larger-roofed windmill of exercise 3B?

EXERCISE 3D: Rewrite DRAWBODY and DRAWSAIL with a similar parameter. (You may safely use the same identifier S for the parameter in DRAWBODY and DRAWSAIL, since a parameter is only of relevance in the procedure in which it is defined.) Do not attempt to make these modifications yet.

   Modification of the program in USER:MILL3 is not quite so lengthy a job as might at first be expected. Follow these instructions carefully.

   1. Get the file USER:MILL3 ready for for editing.

   2. Replace all occurrences of "12" by "S". To do this the Replace mode of the Editor is used. (See appendix 2, section 3.6.6.) Type

                    /R/12//S/

   The first oblique (/) means repeat the Replacement until the end of the file is reached. It does not echo on the screen until R has been typed. The remaining 4 obliques are delimiters marking the bounds of what is to be replaced by what. Miskeying between delimiters can be corrected by pressing ←.

Replacements should have been limited to occurrences of "12" as an item (or <u>Token</u>) in its own right, and not as digits within another number (such as the "12" in "120") or within an identifier.

3. Next type J (for Jump) and then B to put the cursor back to the Beginning of the file.

4. Repeat steps 2 and 3 three more times to change all occurrences of

72	into	6*S
24	into	2*S
60	into	5*S

5. Change the first line of each procedure and make the three procedure calls in the main program

DRAWBODY(15)   DRAWROOF(18)   DRAWSAIL(12)

6. Change the name of the program to MILL4.

The modified program should be

```
PROGRAM MILL4;

USES TURTLEGRAPHICS;

VAR SAILNUMBER : INTEGER;

PROCEDURE DRAWBODY(S : INTEGER);

    BEGIN
        MOVE(S);
        TURN(-90);
        MOVE(6*S);
        TURN(-90);
        MOVE(2*S);
        TURN(-90);
        MOVE(6*S);
        TURN(-90);
        MOVE(S)
    END; (* DRAWBODY *)

PROCEDURE DRAWROOF(S : INTEGER);

    BEGIN
        MOVE(S);
        TURN(120);
        MOVE(2*S);
        TURN(120);
        MOVE(2*S);
        TURN(120);
        MOVE(S)
    END; (* DRAWROOF *)
```

```
PROCEDURE DRAWSAIL(S : INTEGER);

    BEGIN
        MOVE(6*S);
        TURN(90);
        MOVE(S);
        TURN(90);
        MOVE(5*S);
        TURN(90);
        MOVE(S);
        TURN(90);
        MOVE(-S)
    END; (* DRAWSAIL *)

BEGIN
    INITTURTLE;
    PENCOLOR(WHITE);

    DRAWBODY(15);
    DRAWROOF(18);
    TURN(35);
    FOR SAILNUMBER := 1 TO 4 DO
        BEGIN
            DRAWSAIL(12);
            TURN(90)
        END;
    TURN(-35);

    READLN
END.
```

When you have succeeded in making these modifications, and the program is correct, save it as USER:MILL4. You should now convince yourself that you have indeed a better windmill. Vary the actual parameters, and see what you can produce.

EXERCISE 3E: Suppose a file contains the text of a story about Jack and Jill, and a new file is to be produced with Jack replaced by Jill and Jill replaced by John. Write down two suitable Replacements to do this.

EXERCISE 3F: Do the same as in exercise 3E but this time replace all occurrences of Jack by Jill and all occurrences of Jill by Jack. (This needs more than two Replacements.)

3.4   WINDMILLS MADE TO MEASURE

You should now have a program which draws a windmill of given proportions, with its center of rotation at the center of the screen and its sails at an angle of 35 degrees to the axes. It is not difficult to change either its location or the angle of the sails by suitable modifications to the main program, but in this section we shall develop a more flexible means of drawing a windmill, and indeed of dignifying it by making it an entity in itself. Given this improved status for the windmill, we can easily draw several arbitrarily oriented windmills on the screen together. To keep things fairly simple, we shall fix the proportions of the body, roof and sail as they were in the program MILL3. We shall think of that windmill, whose sail was of width 12, as a "size 12" windmill.

For a moment let us forget what we have done so far, and rethink our requirements afresh. It would be very convenient if, for example, we could write

        DRAWMILL(6, 120, 100, 45)

in order to draw a windmill of size 6, whose center of rotation is at the point (120, 100) and whose sails are at an angle of 45° to the axes. We can enjoy this convenience, simply by providing an appropriate procedure which draws the entire windmill. It should not come as too great a surprise to see this written as

        PROCEDURE DRAWMILL(SIZE, X0, Y0, THETA : INTEGER);

            VAR SAILNUMBER : INTEGER;

            BEGIN
                MOVETO(X0, Y0);
                PENCOLOR(WHITE);

                DRAWBODY(SIZE);
                DRAWROOF(SIZE);
                TURN(THETA);
                FOR SAILNUMBER := 1 **TO** 4 **DO**
                    BEGIN
                        DRAWSAIL(SIZE);
                        TURN(90)
                    END;
                TURN(-THETA);

                PENCOLOR(NONE)
            END; (* DRAWMILL *)

Two points are worth noting.

- Where there is more than one parameter, the actual parameters (6, 120, 100, 45) must correspond in order with the formal parameters (SIZE, X0, Y0, THETA). Parameters are separated by commas.

- Further examples of invariance occur in the procedure DRAWMILL. The color of the pen is assumed to be NONE at entry, and is left as NONE on exit. Likewise the direction of the turtle and its position are unaffected by a call of the procedure DRAWMILL. Thus the main program is quite free to move the turtle between windmills without interconnecting lines being drawn on the screen.

The procedure, however, is incomplete, just as the program MILL2 was incomplete. It needs to know about DRAWBODY, DRAWROOF and DRAWSAIL. The most natural way to introduce these, which happen to be used only by the procedure DRAWMILL, is to declare them within the procedure DRAWMILL itself. In the program MILL5 which follows, notice how the structure of the procedure DRAWMILL begins to look remarkably similar to the structure of the program MILL4. The body of DRAWMILL has become textually separated from the procedure heading, and in order to improve the readability of the program, we have placed a comment on the first **BEGIN** of the body of DRAWMILL. Thus the complete program becomes

```
PROGRAM MILL5;

USES TURTLEGRAPHICS;

PROCEDURE DRAWMILL(SIZE, XO, YO, THETA : INTEGER);

    VAR SAILNUMBER : INTEGER;

    PROCEDURE DRAWBODY(S : INTEGER);

        BEGIN
            MOVE(S);
            TURN(-90);
            MOVE(6*S);
            TURN(-90);
            MOVE(2*S);
            TURN(-90);
            MOVE(6*S);
            TURN(-90);
            MOVE(S)
        END; (* DRAWBODY *)

    PROCEDURE DRAWROOF(S : INTEGER);

        BEGIN
            MOVE(S);
            TURN(120);
            MOVE(2*S);
            TURN(120);
            MOVE(2*S);
            TURN(120);
            MOVE(S)
        END; (* DRAWROOF *)

    PROCEDURE DRAWSAIL(S : INTEGER);

        BEGIN
            MOVE(6*S);
            TURN(90);
            MOVE(S);
            TURN(90);
            MOVE(5*S);
            TURN(90);
            MOVE(S);
            TURN(90);
            MOVE(-S)
        END; (* DRAWSAIL *)

    BEGIN (* DRAWMILL *)
        MOVETO(XO, YO);
        PENCOLOR(WHITE);

        DRAWBODY(SIZE);
        DRAWROOF(SIZE);
        TURN(THETA);
        FOR SAILNUMBER := 1 TO 4 DO
            BEGIN
                DRAWSAIL(SIZE);
                TURN(90)
            END;
        TURN(-THETA);

        PENCOLOR(NONE)
    END; (* DRAWMILL *)
```

```
BEGIN
    INITTURTLE;
    DRAWMILL(12, 70, 100, 45);
    READLN
END.
```

Note also that initialization and termination have been removed from the procedure DRAWMILL and placed in the main program, in anticipation of the need to draw several windmills in one picture.

Several of the lines in the program MILL5 stretch beyond character position 40. If you type CTRL-Z, the screen is put in a mode which automatically keeps the cursor in view. To cancel this mode type CTRL-A twice. It is easy to change the program MILL4 into MILL5. Do so now, check that it produces the correct picture and save it as USER:MILL5. To realize the full power of this new procedure, in the main program replace

```
DRAWMILL(12, 70, 100, 45)
```

by

```
FOR MILLNUMBER := 1 TO 4 DO
DRAWMILL(MILLNUMBER*2, 10 + 12*SQR(MILLNUMBER), 100, MILLNUMBER*10)
```

and add an appropriate declaration for MILLNUMBER after the line

```
USES TURTLEGRAPHICS;
```

EXERCISE 3G: Execute the modified program above and explain the effect of each parameter on the picture drawn. Save this as USER:MILL6.

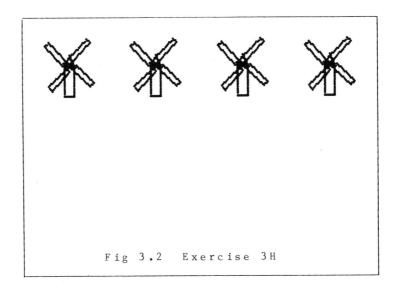

Fig 3.2   Exercise 3H

EXERCISE 3H: Modify the program to draw 4 small identical windmills of size 4
               across the top of the screen. See figure 3.2.

EXERCISE 3J: Modify the program again to draw 4 small windmills across the
               top and 4 across the middle of the screen. (Hint: read
               section 2.9 again.)

EXERCISE 3K: What about 4 across the top, 4 across the middle and 4 across
               the bottom?

3.5 COUNTING DOWN

Get the program in USER:MILL6 and replace

        FOR MILLNUMBER := 1 **TO** 4 **DO**

by

        FOR MILLNUMBER := 4 **DOWNTO** 1 **DO**

observing what happens when it is run. Whilst the for statement allows both
increments and decrements, it does not provide a mechanism for increments or
decrements by other than one. That is why, in exercise 3G, windmills of size
2, 4, 6 and 8 could not be obtained directly from the variable controlling the
for statement.

EXERCISE 3L: Express the syntax of this form of for statement in the manner
               of the definition in section 2.9.

3.6 MORE ABOUT FILES

3.6.1 Volumes

"Volume" is a word used to describe any UCSD p-System I/O device. A
volume may be referred to by number or by name. Load the p-System with the

Volume number	Volume name	Description
#1:	CONSOLE:	the video terminal
#4:	APPLE0: or APPLE1:	disk drive 1
#5:	USER:	disk drive 2

system disk in drive 1, and, on a two-drive Apple with your user disk in
drive 2. Enter the Filer, type V and a table roughly corresponding to the
first two columns above will be displayed. USER stands for the name you gave
your user disk. Volumes other than those above may be ignored.

It is important to appreciate the difference between referring to a
volume by name and by number, especially when referring to the disks. If you
refer to #4: for example, you refer to drive 1 regardless of what disk is
mounted. If you refer to ABC: then the Filer will proceed to search all drives
until it finds a disk whose volume name is ABC:. If the volume name or number
is omitted from any file reference, #4: (the system disk) is assumed.

3.6.2 File Directory

On each of your disks, a few blocks are set aside to hold a list of the
files currently on the disk. This is known as the file directory or
just directory. A directory listing may be obtained by typing L when
in the Filer. In response to the message "DIR LISTING OF ?" type the name of
your user disk followed by a colon (or #5: or just #5 without the colon)
followed by RETURN. If you have worked through all the exercises so far, your
user disk should contain

```
        SYSTEM.COMPILER
        PENTAGON.TEXT           PENTAGON.CODE
        REVERSAGON.TEXT         REVERSAGON.CODE
        SPIRAL.TEXT             SPIRAL.CODE
        FOURSTARS.TEXT          FOURSTARS.CODE
        MYSTARTURN.TEXT         MYSTARTURN.CODE
        STARFISH.TEXT           STARFISH.CODE
        MILL3.TEXT              MILL3.CODE
        MILL4.TEXT              MILL4.CODE
        MILL5.TEXT              MILL5.CODE
        MILL6.TEXT              MILL6.CODE
```

though not necessarily in this order. To obtain a directory listing of the
system disk, type L followed by APPLE1: or APPLE0: (or #4: or just #4) and
RETURN.

3.6.3 Kinds of Files

In this course you will mainly be dealing with files of 2 kinds, namely

- textfiles (whose names end in .TEXT) the files you create,
  edit and submit to the Compiler, and
- codefiles (whose names end in .CODE) the files the Compiler
  produces for eXecution.

The Get command assumes that the file is a textfile and .TEXT need not
be typed. The Save command appends the appropriate ending to the textfile
and codefile and so neither .TEXT nor .CODE must be typed. The eXecute
command (at the outermost level of command) assumes the file is a codefile and
.CODE need not be typed.

3.6.4 The Workfile

You have made use of the workfile in chapter 1 perhaps without realizing
it. The workfile is based on the pair of files #4:SYSTEM.WRK.TEXT and
#4:SYSTEM.WRK.CODE. Their special status makes the edit-compile-debug-edit
cycle easy to use. It is relevant to both one- and two-drive Apples. It
works as follows.

(a) Assuming you are in the Filer, typing G for Get, followed by
the name of a textfile (omitting .TEXT), does not copy anything.
It nominates the given file as the workfile in readiness for the
next use of the Editor. Type Q to Quit the Filer.

(b) Back at the outermost level of command, E for Edit enters the
Editor which reads the nominated file into the internal memory
of the computer where most editing commands operate.

(c) When you Quit the Editor and then type U (for Update the
workfile), the file is copied from internal memory to the system
disk where it is given the special name SYSTEM.WRK.TEXT

(d) The R (for Run) command then uses #4:SYSTEM.WRK.TEXT as input
to the Compiler, which produces the code to be executed in the
file #4:SYSTEM.WRK.CODE which it then loads into memory and Runs.

(e) If the Compiler detects an error you have to return to the
Editor to correct it. The actual workfile #4:SYSTEM.WRK.TEXT
takes precedence over the nominated file and so the Editor
loads #4:SYSTEM.WRK.TEXT into memory with the location and
description of the error highlighted.

The cycle continues at (c) above until you have something worth saving on
your user disk. At that stage the Filer is entered and S (for Save) will
cause #4:SYSTEM.WRK.TEXT to be copied to the textfile named in the most recent
Get. (With a one-drive Apple, the workfile should be saved on #4, and then
Transferred to the user disk.) Beware, if a file is saved on #4: the workfile
is merely renamed, and is not copied.

Once it has been saved, you can get rid of the workfile. Whilst in the
Filer type N (for New workfile) and in response to "THROW AWAY CURRENT
WORKFILE ?", type Y.

At the outermost level of command, the commands Run and eXecute are
subtly different. The eXecute command is the more basic. You supply the
name of a codefile (omitting .CODE) and it runs the program in that codefile.
The Run command does not need a file name. It looks specifically to the
workfile for a program to run. See appendix 2, section 1 for further details.

3.7 MORE ABOUT THE EDITOR

Only a few features of the Editor have been referred to so far, namely
eXchange, Insert, Delete, Adjust, Replace and Jump. These, together with the
cursor-moving keys, are sufficient for the development of short programs, but
work on longer files is eased by other facilities. The Editor is described in
more detail in appendix 2, and in full in the Apple Pascal Operating System
Reference Manual. You are advised to refer to one of these documents now, to
familiarize yourself with the following facilities which will make your use of
the Apple more efficient.

- V for Verify. The screen is displayed afresh with the cursor centrally placed.

- P for Page. This moves the cursor by a complete screenful (24 lines) at a time.

- F for Find. Searches the file for the specified string. (Find bears a close resemblance to Replace.)

- Direction. The Editor can search, and move the cursor in either the forwards (the default) or the backwards direction.

- Repeat-factor. Most cursor-moving commands, if preceded by an integer repeat-factor, can be repeated a specified number of times.

- The copy buffer. All text inserted or deleted is placed in the copy buffer (unless you are otherwise informed). The contents of the copy buffer may be copied back into the text at any place the cursor is moved to. This is useful for moving chunks of program, such as a procedure, from place to place or for inserting multiple copies of the same (or nearly the same) piece of program.

- C for Copy. You can also copy the contents of another file into the file being edited. This is useful when making use of procedures in other programs.

Other features of the Editor, of less importance to the development of programs, are provided for the processing of files of text.

3.8   FURTHER PROGRAMMING PROBLEMS

3.8.1   Regular Convex Polygons

A regular convex polygon of order n is defined to be an n-sided figure whose sides are of equal length and whose external angles are each 360/n degrees. This definition ensures that the polygon is closed.

EXERCISE 3M: Which regular convex polygon(s) of order between 3 and 10 have integral (whole number) external angles?

EXERCISE 3N: Write a program, similar to STARTIME in section 1.4, to draw the eight regular convex polygons (as best you can) as shown in figure 3.3, for n = 3 to 10 on a common base line of length 30. In place of the procedure DRAWSTAR, you should have a procedure whose first line is

PROCEDURE DRAWPOLYGON(N, S : INTEGER);

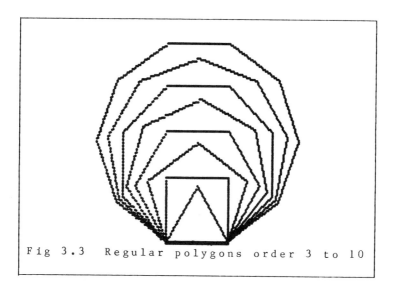

Fig 3.3   Regular polygons order 3 to 10

3.8.2 Non-convex Polygons

A regular non-convex polygon of order n is defined to be an n-sided figure whose sides are of equal length and whose external angles are each 360*k/n degrees for any integer k > 1. This definition also ensures that the non-convex polygon is closed.

EXERCISE 3P: Write a more general procedure, this time with 3 parameters (the order of the polygon, the external angle, and the length of the side) and try it out with the actual parameters

(24, 105, 80)

Under what circumstances does your program draw closed figures?

3.8.3 Roly-polygons

The roly-polygon is thought to have been discovered by a youngster in primary school. Some roly-polygons are shown in figures 3.4 and 3.5.

To draw a roly-polygon first, define an extended polygon of order n to be a regular convex polygon of order n in which the final turn is replaced by a move. For example, an extended polygon of order 3 and side s, is drawn by

```
MOVE(S);
TURN(120);
MOVE(S);
TURN(120);
MOVE(S);
MOVE(S)
```

A roly-polygon of order n is made by drawing n extended polygons of order n.

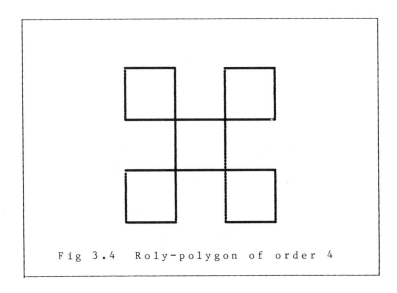

Fig 3.4   Roly-polygon of order 4

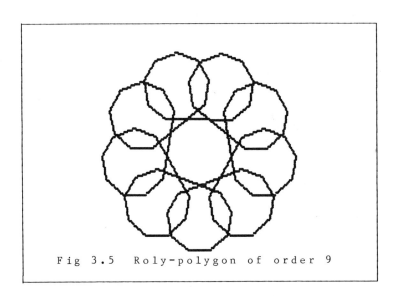

Fig 3.5   Roly-polygon of order 9

EXERCISE 3Q: Write a procedure whose first line is

PROCEDURE DRAWROLYPOLY(N, S : INTEGER);

and with it draw a roly-polygon of order 6. Why are roly-polygons closed? Can roly-polygons be defined in terms of non-convex polygons?

SOLUTIONS TO THE EXERCISES

3A: (a) In the program fragment above the exercise, change

                        35 into 15
                        -35 into -15

        (b) Change the for statement above the exercise into

                    FOR SAILNUMBER := 1 TO 3 DO
                        BEGIN
                            DRAWSAIL;
                            TURN(120)
                        END;

3B: In the procedure DRAWROOF

                12 becomes 18 (in 2 places)
                24 becomes 36 (in 2 places)

3C: Replace DRAWROOF(12); by DRAWROOF(18);

3D: **PROCEDURE** DRAWBODY(S : INTEGER);

            BEGIN
                MOVE(S);
                TURN(-90);
                MOVE(6*S);
                TURN(-90);
                MOVE(2*S);
                TURN(-90);
                MOVE(6*S);
                TURN(-90);
                MOVE(S)
            END; (* DRAWBODY *)

        PROCEDURE DRAWSAIL(S : INTEGER);

            BEGIN
                MOVE(6*S);
                TURN(90);
                MOVE(S);
                TURN(90);
                MOVE(5*S);
                TURN(90);
                MOVE(S);
                TURN(90);
                MOVE(-S)
            END; (* DRAWSAIL *)

3E: Before each of the Replacements, type JB to reset the cursor to the
        start of the file.

                /R/Jill//John/
                /R/Jack//Jill/

        in that order. What happens if the commands are given the other way
        round?

3F: Assuming that the string ZZZZ does not occur in the file

```
/R/Jack//ZZZZ/
/R/Jill//Jack/
/R/ZZZZ//Jill/
```

3G: MILLNUMBER*2   : windmills of size 2, 4, 6 and 8 are
                                   drawn

        10 + 12*SQR(MILLNUMBER) : windmills are drawn with increasing
                                    separation to allow more room for the
                                    sails. Their x-coordinates are 22, 58,
                                    118, 202

                        100   : axes of rotation of sails are all at
                                 height y = 100 (a little above the center).

             MILLNUMBER*10   : sail angles are 10, 20, 30, 40 degrees.

3H: One way to do this is

```
FOR MILLNUMBER := 1 TO 4 DO
   DRAWMILL(4, -35 + MILLNUMBER*70, 160, 45)
```

3J: **VAR** ROWNUMBER, MILLNUMBER : INTEGER;
            .
            .
            .
```
FOR ROWNUMBER := 2 TO 3 DO
   FOR MILLNUMBER := 1 TO 4 DO
      DRAWMILL(4, -35 + MILLNUMBER*70, -32 + ROWNUMBER*64, 45)
```

        If you are in any doubt about the use of nested for statements, then
        execute the program in the file XPLAIN3.1 on the MACC: disk. It
        describes

```
FOR ROWNUMBER := 1 TO 2 DO
   FOR MILLNUMBER := 1 TO 4 DO
      DRAWMILL(4, -35 + MILLNUMBER*70, -32 + ROWNUMBER*64, 45)
```

3K: As for exercise 3J, but

```
FOR ROWNUMBER := 1 TO 3 DO ...
```

3L: **FOR** identifier := expression1 **DOWNTO** expression2 **DO** statement

3M: All except the polygon of order 7

```
3N:       PROGRAM REGULARPOLYGONS;

          USES TURTLEGRAPHICS;

          VAR ORDER : INTEGER;

          PROCEDURE DRAWPOLYGON(N, S : INTEGER);

          (* THIS PROCEDURE FAILS TO MAINTAIN THE ANGULAR AND COORDINATE
             INVARIANCE OF THE TURTLE, BECAUSE N * (360 DIV N) IS NOT ALWAYS
             EQUAL TO 360 *)

              VAR SIDENUMBER : INTEGER;

              BEGIN
                  PENCOLOR(WHITE);
                  FOR SIDENUMBER := 1 TO N DO
                      BEGIN
                          MOVE(S);
                          TURN(360 DIV N)
                      END;
                  PENCOLOR(NONE)
              END; (* DRAWPOLYGON *)

          BEGIN
              INITTURTLE;
              FOR ORDER := 3 TO 10 DO
                  BEGIN
                      MOVETO(115, 20);    (* THESE TWO STATEMENTS ARE HERE *)
                      TURNTO(0);          (* BECAUSE OF THE DEFICIENCY NOTED
                                             ABOVE *)
                      DRAWPOLYGON(ORDER, 50)
                  END;
              READLN
          END.


3P:       PROGRAM NONCONVEXPOLYGONS;

          USES TURTLEGRAPHICS;

          PROCEDURE DRAWNCPOLYGON(N, A, S : INTEGER);

              VAR SIDENUMBER : INTEGER;

              BEGIN
                  PENCOLOR(WHITE);
                  FOR SIDENUMBER := 1 TO N DO
                      BEGIN
                          MOVE(S);
                          TURN(A)
                      END;
                  PENCOLOR(NONE)
              END; (* DRAWNCPOLYGON *)

          BEGIN
              INITTURTLE;
              MOVETO(100, 60);
              DRAWNCPOLYGON(24, 105, 80);
              READLN
          END.
```

The polygon is closed if (N*A) MOD 360 = 0.

3Q: The statement of the problem suggests the writing of a procedure to
         draw extended polygons first. This produces the following program.

```
PROGRAM ROLY;

USES TURTLEGRAPHICS;

PROCEDURE DRAWEXTPOLYGON(N, S : INTEGER);

    VAR SIDENUMBER : INTEGER;

    BEGIN
        FOR SIDENUMBER := 1 TO N-1 DO
            BEGIN
                MOVE(S);
                TURN(360 DIV N)
            END;
        MOVE(S);
        MOVE(S)
    END; (* DRAWEXTPOLYGON *)

PROCEDURE DRAWROLYPOLYGON(N, S : INTEGER);

    VAR EXPOLYNUMBER : INTEGER;

    BEGIN
        PENCOLOR(WHITE);
        FOR EXPOLYNUMBER := 1 TO N DO DRAWEXTPOLYGON(N, S);
        PENCOLOR(NONE)
    END; (* DRAWROLYPOLYGON *)

BEGIN
    INITTURTLE;
    MOVETO(152, 120);
    DRAWROLYPOLYGON(6, 24);
    READLN
END.
```

A similar program, with DRAWEXTPOLYGON nested within DRAWPOLYGON is
also correct, and would be the result of a more strictly "top-down"
approach.

If θ is the external angle of the basic polygon, then the definition
of an extended polygon is equivalent to "a regular convex polygon of
order n, plus a turn of $-\theta$, plus a move of s". A regular convex
polygon preserves the invariance of the turtle. Therefore the net
effect on the turtle of n extended polygons is n of { turn(θ);
move(s) }, which is a clockwise polygon. This is, in fact, the polygon
seen at the center of each roly-polygon.

Yes, and there is a polygon at the center. Try one based on the
pentagram of section 1.2.1.

CHAPTER 4
Structured Programming and Syntax Diagrams

In this chapter, we will work through another example of a problem solved in the top-down or structured manner. The solution will also serve to focus attention on the places where procedures and variables may be declared, and the effect that this has on the structure of a program. Then we introduce the somewhat unrelated topic, namely that of describing the allowable grammatical forms in a programming language in a pictorial manner.

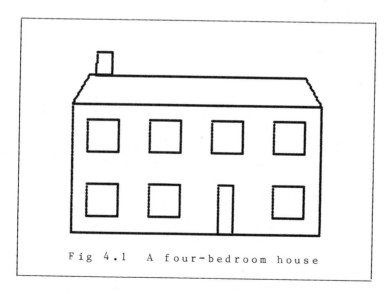

Fig 4.1   A four-bedroom house

4.1   THE DRAWING OF A HOUSE

Figure 4.1 depicits a "four-bedroom" house. Our task is to write a procedure to draw n-bedroom houses. That is, houses with n windows on the upper storey and n-1 windows and a door at or near to the center of the lower storey.

The size of the house is based on s, the size of its square windows (just as the size of the windmills of chapter 3 were based on the width of their sails). The house is 4s high, plus a roof whose sides slope at 60° and are of length s. The windows are a distance s apart. The door is s/2 wide and 3s/2 high. The chimney is s/2 wide, 3s/4 high, and at a distance s/4 from the left-hand end of the ridge of the roof.

We would like to have control over where the house is to be on the screen, the number of bedrooms, and the size of the house. The program to draw such a house would therefore appear to be something like

```
PROGRAM HOUSE1;

USES TURTLEGRAPHICS;

PROCEDURE DRAWHOUSE(XO, YO, BEDS, S : INTEGER);

    BEGIN
        FRAME;
        LOWERSTOREY;
        UPPERSTOREY;
        ROOF;
        CHIMNEY
    END; (* DRAWHOUSE *)

BEGIN
    INITTURTLE;
    DRAWHOUSE(40, 30, 4, 25);
    READLN
END.
```

where (XO, YO) are the coordinates of the lower left-hand corner of the frame of the house.

We are left with 5 procedures to be written, to give meaning to the commands we have invented, such as FRAME, LOWERSTOREY, etc. Before we do this, we should consider whether these procedures should have parameters.

- The procedures are unlikely to have any use except in connection with DRAWHOUSE. They should therefore be nested within DRAWHOUSE.

- If they are nested within DRAWHOUSE, then they already have access to all the parameters of DRAWHOUSE.

- The procedures are each referred to only once.

- If we gave them parameters, we would simply give them the same parameters as DRAWHOUSE, namely (XO, YO, BEDS, S).

We conclude that parameters are neither essential nor desirable in this context.

Next, consider the frame of the house, which is a rectangle of length

$$s/2 + beds*s + (beds - 1)*s + s/2 = beds*s*2$$

and height

$$s/2 + 2*s + s + s/2 = 4*s$$

The procedure FRAME could be written as

```
PROCEDURE FRAME;

    BEGIN
        MOVETO(X0, Y0);
        RECTANGLE(BEDS*S*2, 4*S)
    END; (* FRAME *)
```

We have used a little intuition and foresight here. The picture is made up largely of rectangular shapes, and the use of a procedure to draw rectangles will result in a clearer and shorter program.

Next consider the lower storey. It consists of, from left to right,

- $[\frac{beds}{2}]$ windows,
- one door
- enough windows to make beds items in all, namely
  $(beds - 1 - [\frac{beds}{2}])$ windows.

If we assume procedures for drawing windows and doors, which preserve the invariance of the turtle, then the procedure LOWERSTOREY is as follows.

```
PROCEDURE LOWERSTOREY;

    VAR WINDOWNUMBER : INTEGER;

    BEGIN
        MOVETO(X0, Y0);
        FOR WINDOWNUMBER := 1 TO BEDS DIV 2 DO
            BEGIN
                WINDOW;  MOVE(2*S)
            END;
        DOOR;  MOVE(2*S);
        FOR WINDOWNUMBER := 1 TO BEDS - 1 - BEDS DIV 2 DO
            BEGIN
                WINDOW;  MOVE(2*S)
            END;
    END; (* LOWERSTOREY *)
```

Similarly, the procedure UPPERSTOREY is

```
PROCEDURE UPPERSTOREY;

    VAR WINDOWNUMBER : INTEGER;

    BEGIN
        MOVETO(X0, Y0 + 2*S);
        FOR WINDOWNUMBER := 1 TO BEDS DO
            BEGIN
                WINDOW;  MOVE(2*S)
            END;
    END; (* UPPERSTOREY *)
```

The procedure ROOF is kept simple by the choice of 60° for the angle of the sloping ends. The ridge of the roof is thus exactly

```
beds*s*2 - s
```

in length. Ignoring the chimney, this procedure is

```
PROCEDURE ROOF;

    BEGIN
        MOVETO(X0, Y0 + 4*S);  TURN(60);
        PENCOLOR(WHITE);
        MOVE(S);  TURN(-60);
        MOVE(BEDS*S*2  - S);  TURN(-60);
        MOVE(S);  TURN(60);
        PENCOLOR(NONE)
    END; (* ROOF *)
```

Now the chimney presents a problem if we attempt to draw it as a separate entity. The x-coordinate of its bottom left-hand corner is 3s/4 but its y-coordinate is (4s + squareroot(3)) and we have yet to deal with the representation of numbers such as this. It would, therefore, be better to draw the chimney as part of the roof as and when we pass the point at which it is to be drawn. Thus, we remove the reference to CHIMNEY from the body of DRAWHOUSE, and rewrite the procedure ROOF as follows.

```
PROCEDURE ROOF;

    BEGIN
        MOVETO(X0, Y0 + 4*S);  TURN(60);
        PENCOLOR(WHITE);
        MOVE(S);  TURN(-60);
        MOVE(S DIV 4);
        CHIMNEY;
        PENCOLOR(WHITE);
        MOVE(BEDS*S*2  - 5*S DIV 4);  TURN(-60);
        MOVE(S);  TURN(60);
        PENCOLOR(NONE)
    END; (* ROOF *)
```

At this point, it is worth making a list of those procedures still to be written, and the procedures which refer to them.

Procedures required	Referred to by
WINDOW	LOWERSTOREY, UPPERSTOREY
DOOR	LOWERSTOREY
CHIMNEY	ROOF
RECTANGLE	FRAME, WINDOW, DOOR, CHIMNEY

The procedure CHIMNEY is required only by ROOF, and it may be nested within ROOF.

```
PROCEDURE ROOF;

    PROCEDURE CHIMNEY;

        BEGIN
            RECTANGLE(S DIV 2, 3*S DIV 4)
        END; (* CHIMNEY *)

    BEGIN (* ROOF *)
        MOVETO(XO, YO + 4*S);   TURN(60);
        PENCOLOR(WHITE);
        MOVE(S);   TURN(-60);
        MOVE(S DIV 4);
        CHIMNEY;
        PENCOLOR(WHITE);
        MOVE(BEDS*S*2  - 5*S DIV 4);   TURN(-60);
        MOVE(S);   TURN(60);
        PENCOLOR(NONE)
    END; (* ROOF *)
```

Similarly, the procedure DOOR is required only by LOWERSTOREY, and it may be nested within DOOR.

```
    PROCEDURE LOWERSTOREY;

        VAR WINDOWNUMBER : INTEGER;

        PROCEDURE DOOR;

            BEGIN
                MOVE(3*S DIV 4);
                RECTANGLE(S DIV 2, 3*S DIV 2);
                MOVE(-3*S DIV 4)
            END; (* DOOR *)

        BEGIN (* LOWERSTOREY *)
            MOVETO(XO, YO);
            FOR WINDOWNUMBER := 1 TO BEDS DIV 2 DO
                BEGIN
                    WINDOW;   MOVE(2*S)
                END;
            DOOR;   MOVE(2*S);
            FOR WINDOWNUMBER := 1 TO BEDS - 1 - BEDS DIV 2 DO
                BEGIN
                    WINDOW; MOVE(2*S)
                END;
        END; (* LOWERSTOREY *)
```

These instances of nesting are effectively saying that chimneys are only found on roofs, and doors are only found in lower storeys. If subsequently it is found necessary to depart from these conventions, the nesting of the procedures DOOR and CHIMNEY will have to be reconsidered.

Next, what about windows? They are drawn by both LOWERSTOREY and UPPERSTOREY. We could put a window-drawing procedure in each of LOWERSTOREY and UPPERSTOREY but that would be extravagant on space, taxing on our patience, and troublesome to maintain when windows of some different design become the order of the day. If we place the procedure WINDOW before the procedures that refer to it, that makes it available to them. The procedure itself has to preserve the invariance of the turtle and draw an s by s square centrally in an area 2s by 2s. Thus the procedure WINDOW may be written

```
PROCEDURE WINDOW;

    BEGIN
        MOVE(S DIV 2);  TURN(90);  MOVE(S DIV 2);  TURN(-90);
        RECTANGLE(S, S);
        MOVE(-S DIV 2);  TURN(90);  MOVE(-S DIV 2);  TURN(-90)
    END; (* WINDOW *)
```

At this stage it should be noticed that throughout the discussion, consideration of the pencolor has been limited to the procedure ROOF. This procedure assumed the pencolor to be NONE at the outset, and ensures that it is NONE at the end. All other drawing is done by the procedure RECTANGLE, and as you can see from the program below, it has the same policy regarding the pencolor. The procedure RECTANGLE, which requires parameters in order to draw rectangles of different size, is placed before all those procedures that refer to it.

The complete program is therefore

```
PROGRAM HOUSE2;

USES TURTLEGRAPHICS;

PROCEDURE DRAWHOUSE(X0, Y0, BEDS, S : INTEGER);

    PROCEDURE RECTANGLE(X, Y : INTEGER);

        BEGIN
            PENCOLOR(WHITE);
            MOVE(X);  TURN(90);
            MOVE(Y);  TURN(90);
            MOVE(X);  TURN(90);
            MOVE(Y);  TURN(90);
            PENCOLOR(NONE)
        END; (* RECTANGLE *)

    PROCEDURE FRAME;

        BEGIN
            MOVETO(X0, Y0);
            RECTANGLE(BEDS*S*2, 4*S)
        END; (* FRAME *)

    PROCEDURE WINDOW;

        BEGIN
            MOVE(S DIV 2);  TURN(90);  MOVE(S DIV 2);  TURN(-90);
            RECTANGLE(S, S);
            MOVE(-S DIV 2);  TURN(90);  MOVE(-S DIV 2);  TURN(-90)
        END; (* WINDOW *)

    PROCEDURE LOWERSTOREY;

        VAR WINDOWNUMBER : INTEGER;

        PROCEDURE DOOR;

            BEGIN
                MOVE(3*S DIV 4);
                RECTANGLE(S DIV 2, 3*S DIV 2);
                MOVE(-3*S DIV 4)
            END; (* DOOR *)
```

```
            BEGIN (* LOWERSTOREY *)
                MOVETO(XO, YO);
                FOR WINDOWNUMBER := 1 TO BEDS DIV 2 DO
                    BEGIN
                        WINDOW;  MOVE(2*S)
                    END;
                DOOR;  MOVE(2*S);
                FOR WINDOWNUMBER := 1 TO BEDS - 1 - BEDS DIV 2 DO
                    BEGIN
                        WINDOW;  MOVE(2*S)
                    END;
            END; (* LOWERSTOREY *)

        PROCEDURE UPPERSTOREY;

            VAR WINDOWNUMBER : INTEGER;

            BEGIN
                MOVETO(XO, YO + 2*S);
                FOR WINDOWNUMBER := 1 TO BEDS DO
                    BEGIN
                        WINDOW;  MOVE(2*S)
                    END;
            END; (* UPPERSTOREY *)

        PROCEDURE ROOF;

            PROCEDURE CHIMNEY;

                BEGIN
                    RECTANGLE(S DIV 2, 3*S DIV 4)
                END; (* CHIMNEY *)

            BEGIN (* ROOF *)
                MOVETO(XO, YO + 4*S);  TURN(60);
                PENCOLOR(WHITE);
                MOVE(S);  TURN(-60);
                MOVE(S DIV 4);
                CHIMNEY;
                PENCOLOR(WHITE);
                MOVE(BEDS*S*2  - 5*S DIV 4);  TURN(-60);
                MOVE(S);  TURN(60);
                PENCOLOR(NONE)
            END; (* ROOF *)

        BEGIN (* DRAWHOUSE *)
            FRAME;
            LOWERSTOREY;
            UPPERSTOREY;
            ROOF
        END; (* DRAWHOUSE *)

    BEGIN
        INITTURTLE;
        DRAWHOUSE(40, 30, 4, 25);
        READLN
    END.
```

EXERCISE 4A: Modify the program to draw a 3-storey house.

EXERCISE 4B: Add a garage to the right-hand side of the house.

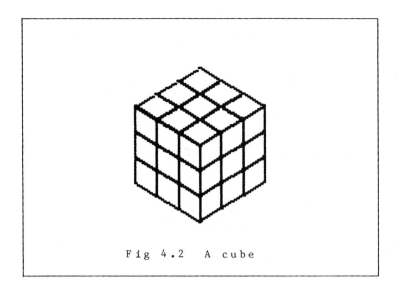

Fig 4.2   A cube

EXERCISE 4C: Figure 4.2 shows a cube viewed along a line through diagonally
               opposite corners. Construct a well-structured program to draw
               this view on the screen.

4.2   PROGRAM AND PROCEDURE STRUCTURE

     In this section we introduce diagrams which may be used to describe the
grammar (or syntax) of a Pascal program. They are called syntax diagrams.

     The general structure of each program we have looked at so far has been

          - program heading;

          - uses section; (optional. This is a UCSD Pascal feature, and
                            not in standard Pascal)

          - VAR section; (optional)

          - procedure section; (optional. Zero, one or more.)

          - BEGIN ... END.

which, expressed as a syntax diagram, is

program: [incomplete]

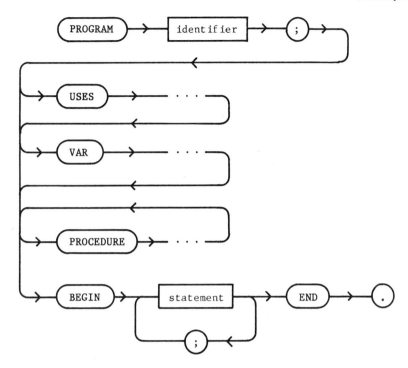

It should be noted that the syntax diagram above is incomplete, as only those features of Pascal already introduced have been included. An almost complete set of syntax diagrams for Apple Pascal may be found in appendix 6.

To interpret this diagram, first suppose that it represents a rail-road network, the lines being strictly one-way. Then, any possible route for a train defines a possible form of program. Dots are used to omit details which will be filled in later. A box with semicircular ends, such as

simply represents the symbol within it. A rectangular box, such as

represents any particular instance of the class of things named in the box. Rectangular boxes are usually described by further syntax diagrams. For example, the syntax diagram for program can be broken down into two diagrams.

program: [incomplete]

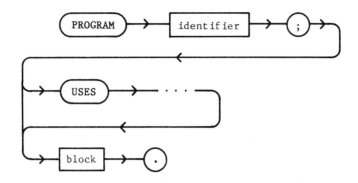

block: [incomplete]

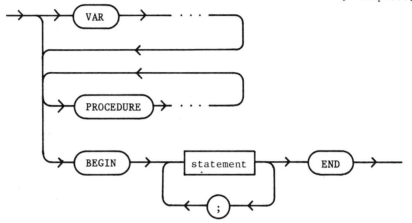

The usefulness of this form will become apparent shortly, when we express the syntax of a procedure declaration as a syntax diagram.

It can be seen from the syntax diagram above that a block can contain zero or one VAR sections; it may contain any number of procedure declarations; and it must contain one BEGIN ... END structure (compound statement).

EXERCISE 4D: Draw the syntax diagram for program heading. (See the beginning of this section.)

EXERCISE 4E: Draw the syntax diagram which defines a compound statement.

The syntax diagram of a procedure declaration is

procedure declaration:

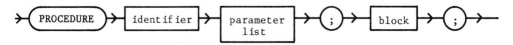

Ignoring the details of the box "parameter list" we notice something curious. If we incorporate the syntax diagram for "procedure declaration" in that of block, we have

block: [incomplete]

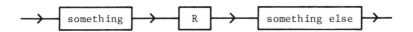

and we appear to have defined a block in terms of a block; but provided there is a path through the syntax diagram that does not include the thing being described, this is quite in order. Definitions of this kind are said to be recursive. However, the diagram

R:

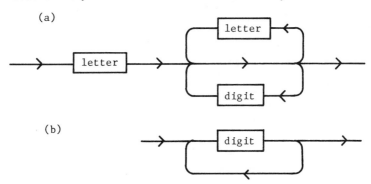

does not satisfy this condition, and is not permitted.

EXERCISE 4F: In the diagrams for program and block, given above, trace the path corresponding to the programs

        (a) FIVESTAR (section 1.2.1)
        (b) STARTIME (section 1.4)

EXERCISE 4G: Describe in your own words what is defined by

        (a)

        (b)

EXERCISE 4H: Here is a set of syntax diagrams defining members of the class
               sentence.

sentence:

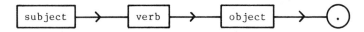

subject:

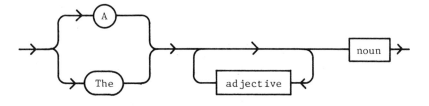

object:

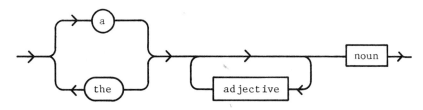

adjective: noun:

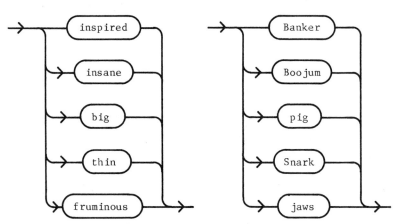

verb:

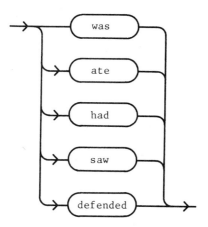

Which of the following are valid sentences according to these
diagrams?

    (a)   The Banker ate the pig.
    (b)   A pig ate the Banker.
    (c)   The Banker was insane.
    (d)   The Snark was a Boojum.
    (e)   The Snark had big fruminous jaws.
    (f)   A big pig saw the Shark.
    (g)   For the Snark was a Boojum you see.
    (h)   The inspired thin Banker defended the big pig.

EXERCISE 4J: Refer back to section 2.2 and draw a syntax diagram for the
               VAR section of a program.

EXERCISE 4K: Refer back to section 2.9 and complete the following syntax
               diagram of the for statement.

for statement:

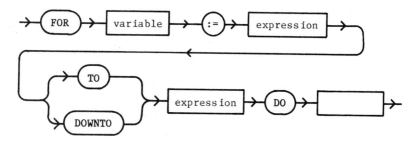

EXERCISE 4L: Draw a syntax diagram describing a statement.

EXERCISE 4M: Draw a syntax diagram describing the parameter list we have
               used so far in procedure declarations.

4.3   SIMPLE EXPRESSIONS REVISITED

It is possible to express the syntax of a simple expression in the form
of syntax diagrams which convey the various operator precedences. The least
strongly binding operators are + and -. Therefore we can define

simple expression: [incomplete]

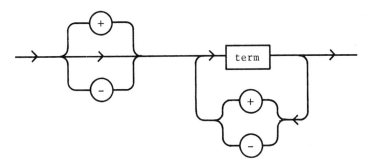

term: [incomplete]

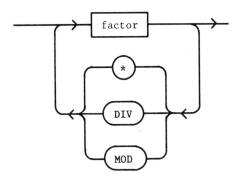

A factor is clearly what we called an operand in section 2.5.1. That is,
a constant, a variable (represented by its name or identifier), or SQR(x)
where x is a simple expression. We can also express the meaning of parentheses
and their effect on operator precedence by including a simple expression in
parentheses as a factor.

factor: [incomplete]

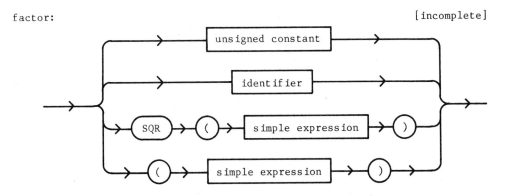

Note again the recursive nature of these three definitions. It is this that allows the nesting of parentheses in an expression. The earlier example, in the definition of a block, allows the nesting of procedures, and the mutual recursion of exercises 4K and 4L allows the nesting of for statements. Recursion seems to be an important idea in computing, and as we shall see in the next chapter it extends far beyond the sphere of language definition.

SOLUTIONS TO THE EXERCISES

4A: In the program at the end of section 4.1 four procedures should be modified, and a consequential change made to the main program. The procedure FRAME becomes

```
PROCEDURE FRAME;

    BEGIN
        MOVETO(X0, Y0);
        RECTANGLE(BEDS*S*2, 6*S)
    END; (* FRAME *)
```

The procedure UPPERSTOREY becomes STOREY, and takes a parameter.

```
PROCEDURE STOREY(N : INTEGER);

    VAR WINDOWNUMBER : INTEGER;

    BEGIN
        MOVETO(X0, Y0 + 2*N*S);
        FOR WINDOWNUMBER := 1 TO BEDS DO
            BEGIN
                WINDOW;   MOVE(2*S)
            END;
    END; (* STOREY *)
```

In the procedure ROOF

```
MOVETO(X0, Y0 + 4*S)      becomes      MOVETO(X0, Y0 + 6*S)
```

and the body of the procedure DRAWHOUSE becomes

```
    BEGIN
        FRAME;
        LOWERSTOREY;
        STOREY(1);   STOREY(2);
        ROOF
    END;  (* DRAWHOUSE *)
```

4B: Add the procedure

```
PROCEDURE GARAGE;

    BEGIN
        MOVETO(X0 + BEDS*S*2, Y0);
        RECTANGLE(5*S DIV 2, 2*S)
    END; (* GARAGE *)
```

so that it may be called from the body of DRAWHOUSE.

```
4C:     PROGRAM CUBEVIEW;

        USES TURTLEGRAPHICS;

        PROCEDURE DRAWFACE;

            PROCEDURE DRAWROW;

                PROCEDURE DRAWRHOMB;

                    BEGIN
                        PENCOLOR(WHITE);
                        MOVE(20); TURN(120); MOVE(20); TURN(60);
                        MOVE(20); TURN(120); MOVE(20); TURN(60);
                        PENCOLOR(NONE)
                    END (* DRAWRHOMB *);

                BEGIN (* DRAWROW *)
                    DRAWRHOMB;   TURN(120);  MOVE(20);   TURN(-120);
                    DRAWRHOMB;   TURN(120);  MOVE(20);   TURN(-120);
                    DRAWRHOMB;   TURN(120);  MOVE(-40);  TURN(-120)
                END (* DRAWROW *);

            BEGIN (* DRAWFACE *)
                DRAWROW; MOVE(20);
                DRAWROW; MOVE(20);
                DRAWROW; MOVE(-40)
            END (* DRAWFACE *);

        BEGIN
            INITTURTLE;
            TURN(30);
            DRAWFACE;   TURN(120);
            DRAWFACE;   TURN(120);
            DRAWFACE;
            TURN(90);
            READLN
        END.
```

An alternative solution based on non-nested procedures produces the
same result.

4D: program heading: [incomplete]

4E: compound statement:

4F: The path through the syntax diagrams can be traced as follows.

(a)   diagram   box in diagram   text in program
      ───

      program: PROGRAM   PROGRAM
                           identifier   FIVESTAR
                           ;   ;
                           USES ...   USES TURTLEGRAPHICS;
      block: VAR ...   VAR SIDENUMBER : INTEGER;
                           BEGIN   BEGIN
                           statement   INITTURTLE
                           ;   ;
                           statement   MOVETO(80, 80)
                           ;   ;
                           statement   PENCOLOR(WHITE)
                           ;   ;
                           statement   FOR SIDENUMBER := 1 TO 5 DO
                                                    BEGIN
                                                        MOVE(120);
                                                        TURN(144)
                                                    END
                           ;   ;
                           statement   READLN
                           END   END
      program: .   .

(b)   diagram   box in diagram   text in program
      ───

      program: PROGRAM   PROGRAM
                           identifier   STARTIME
                           ;   ;
                           USES ...   USES TURTLEGRAPHICS;
      block:(1)   VAR ...   VAR STARNUMBER : INTEGER;
                           PROCEDURE   PROCEDURE
                           identifier   DRAWSTAR
                           parameter list   (S : INTEGER)
                           ;   ;
      block:(2)   VAR ...   VAR SIDENUMBER : INTEGER;
                           BEGIN   BEGIN
                           statement   FOR SIDENUMBER := 1 TO 5 DO
                                                    BEGIN
                                                        MOVE(S);
                                                        TURN(144)
                                                    END
                           END   END
      block:(1)   ;   ;
                           BEGIN   BEGIN
                           statement   INITTURTLE
                           ;   ;
                           statement   MOVETO(80, 80)
                           ;   ;
                           statement   PENCOLOR(WHITE)
                           ;   ;
                           statement   DRAWSTAR(120)
                           ;   ;
                           statement   READLN
                           END   END
      program: .   .

4G: (a)   A letter followed by any sequence of letters and digits (an
             identifier).
       (b)   An unsigned constant (see section 2.4).

4H: (a) Valid
        (b) Valid
        (c) Invalid (object must have "a" or "the" and a noun)
        (d) Valid
        (e) Invalid (object must have "a" or "the")
        (f) Invalid (it's all about Snarks, not Sharks)
        (g) Invalid (it's what Lewis Carroll wrote, but "For" and
                       "you see" are spurious)
        (h) Valid

4J: **VAR** section: [incomplete]

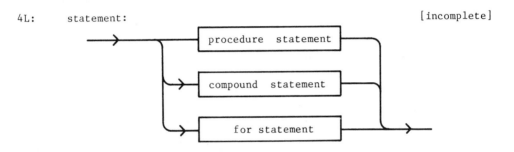

4K: Statement. Any of the answers: compound statement, procedure statement
        or for statement are only partly correct. All three together are
        equivalent to statement.

4L: statement: [incomplete]

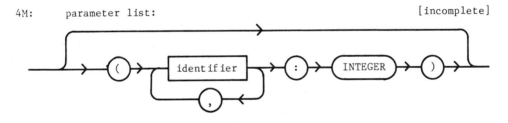

4M: parameter list: [incomplete]

CHAPTER 5
Decisions, Decisions

There are three important features of programs which exploit the power of
the computer. One is iteration (or the loop) which allows statements written
only once to be executed several times in succession; and this we have met in
the context of the for statement. Another is the procedure which enables
statements written only once to be executed at arbitrary points in the program.
The third, which we meet here, is the ability to make a program select between
two or more courses of action depending on the state of things discovered
during the execution of a program.

5.1 HOBSON'S CHOICE

For an example of a situation in which this kind of decision making is
desirable, get the program which you saved as USER:MILL5, and at the end,
replace the call of DRAWMILL by

        DRAWMILL(12, 70, 90, 45);
        DRAWMILL(-12, 210, 90, 45)

In other words, an additional windmill of size -12 is to be drawn. Before
you run the modified program, can you anticipate what it will draw? Run the
program and save it as USER:MILL5A.

We will assume that there is no demand for inverted windmills, and
therefore take steps to prevent their being drawn. Three questions arise.

- Where does the responsibility lie for checking? Is it in the main
  program, in DRAWMILL, in DRAWSAIL etc.?
- How do you stop windmills of size ≤ 0 being drawn?
- How do you express it in Pascal?

Consideration of the main program of MILL5 (see section 3.4) shows that
this is no place to apprehend the inappropriate request. Looking at DRAWSAIL,
we see that this is possible, but not drawing the sails is not enough; we also

have to not draw the roof and not draw the body. Clearly, the best place to
check is at at the start of DRAWMILL, either before or after the MOVETO(X0, Y0)
statement. If we allow the MOVETO(X0, Y0) to take place, then a statement
requesting a zero or negative-sized windmill would cause the turtle to move to
the place at which the windmill is to be not drawn. If we check before the
MOVETO(X0, Y0), no movement takes place. At this stage we cannot say that one
way is correct and the other wrong. Either has some merit. In the example
that follows we shall not allow movement to take place. The other arrangement
is left as an exercise for the reader.

To allow the turtle to draw only in the case of a strictly positive value
of SIZE, we use one of the forms of the Pascal if statement. The body
of the procedure DRAWMILL becomes

```
        BEGIN (* DRAWMILL *)
          IF SIZE > 0 THEN
              BEGIN
                  MOVETO(X0, Y0);
                  PENCOLOR(WHITE);

                  DRAWBODY(SIZE);
                  DRAWROOF(SIZE);
                  TURN(THETA);
                  FOR SAILNUMBER := 1 TO 4 DO
                      BEGIN
                          DRAWSAIL(SIZE);
                          TURN(90)
                      END;
                  TURN(-THETA);

                  PENCOLOR(NONE)
              END
        END (* DRAWMILL *)
```

Make this modification to the program in USER:MILL5A, noting that the 14
lines above from the second BEGIN to the corresponding END inclusive
are identical to the body of the procedure DRAWMILL in USER:MILL5A. Check that
all pairs of BEGIN and END are aligned, and that the program is
properly indented. Execute the program and check that only the first windmill
is drawn on the left-hand side of the screen. Save this as USER:MILL7.

If you are still uncertain of the use of the if statement in the context
of the program above, execute the program XPLAIN5.1 on the MACC: disk.

An alternative approach is to allow the windmill to be drawn with the
pencolor NONE. This takes time, but leaves no trace on the screen. It is
useful only as an illustration of another use of the if statement. To the
program in USER:MILL5A, add immediately after the line

```
        PENCOLOR(WHITE);
```

the line

```
        IF SIZE <= 0 THEN PENCOLOR(NONE);
```

and check again that only the left-hand windmill is drawn.

In Pascal, we have to write <= (with no intervening space) for $\leq$, >=
for $\geq$ and <> for $\neq$.

EXERCISE 5A: How should the procedure DRAWMILL in USER:MILL5 be modified if,
              for requests for windmills of size $\leq$ 0, the turtle is to be
              moved to the origin of the undrawn windmill?

The general form of the if statement we have used in these two examples is

if statement: [incomplete]

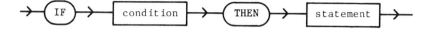

condition:

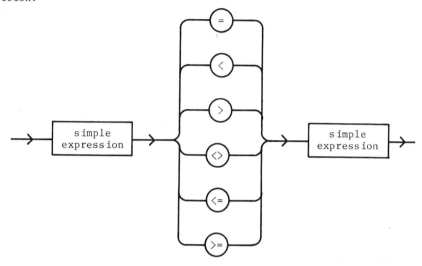

statement: [incomplete]

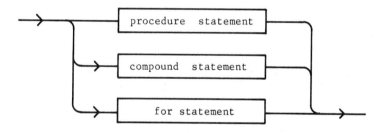

This form of if statement offers a "take it or leave it" choice. A seventeenth century Cambridge carrier, Tobias Hobson, who rented horses is said to have compelled his customer to take the horse nearest to the stable door, or go without; hence the phrase "Hobson's choice".

In both programming examples, when the condition is not satisfied, the statement is equivalent to "do nothing". What about a real choice between alternatives?

5.2 THIS OR THAT

Suppose the demand for windmills is such that it is decided that requests
for negative and zero-sized windmills should be met by drawing a windmill of
size 1, as a token response. Using a somewhat different form of if statement,
we turn the body of DRAWMILL in USER:MILL5A into

```
       BEGIN (* DRAWMILL *)
           IF SIZE <= 0 THEN DRAWMILL(1, X0, Y0, THETA)
           ELSE
               BEGIN
                   MOVETO(X0, Y0);
                   PENCOLOR(WHITE);

                   DRAWBODY(SIZE);
                   DRAWROOF(SIZE);
                   TURN(THETA);
                   FOR SAILNUMBER := 1 TO 4 DO
                       BEGIN
                           DRAWSAIL(SIZE);
                           TURN(90)
                       END;
                   TURN(-THETA);

                   PENCOLOR(NONE)
               END
       END (* DRAWMILL *)
```

Make this amendment to the program in USER:MILL5A, check that it works, and
save it as USER:MILL8. You can now safely remove MILL5A from your user disk.

    If you are uncertain of the use of this kind of if statement, execute the
program XPLAIN5.2 on the MACC: disk.

    This kind of if statement has the form

if statement: [incomplete]

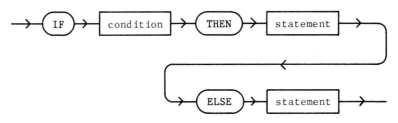

    Recall that the definition of statement in section 5.1 gives us the
freedom to put a procedure statement, a compound statement or a for
statement either between THEN and ELSE or after the ELSE.

EXERCISE 5B: Rewrite the version of DRAWMILL above so that it starts

```
             BEGIN
                 IF SIZE > 0 THEN ...
```

EXERCISE 5C: Draw the combined syntax diagram which describes both forms of
              if statement.

5.3 THE FLAGS OF COMPUTOPIA

In Computopia, where programs always work first time, they have not one but many national flags. On state occasions they always fly the flag appropriate to the order of the highest ranking official in attendance.

The flag of order 0 (which may be flown at any time by any non-official) is a plain white square, except when depicted on a video terminal when it is represented by a blank screen.

The flag of order 1 (used by the humblest official) is a white square with a black cross (white on a video terminal) dividing the flag into four equal white squares.

The flag of order 2 is a white square with a black cross, and a quarter size flag (by area) of order 1 in the upper right-hand quadrant.

The flag of order n (≥ 1) is a white square with a black cross, and a quarter size flag (by area) of order n-1 in the upper right-hand quadrant.

EXERCISE 5D: Draw, in the space below, the flag of order 3.

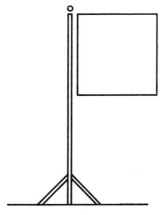

A procedure to draw the flag of order n is remarkably simple. It is virtually a direct translation of the essential information in the paragraphs above into Pascal. Suppose the procedure is called FLAG. It needs at least 2 parameters, one to give the order of the flag, the other to denote its (linear) dimension. The heading might be

   PROCEDURE FLAG(N, SIZE : INTEGER);

If we are to be able to specify where the flag is to be drawn, we need two more parameters, the coordinates of the center of the flag.

   PROCEDURE FLAG(N, SIZE, X0, Y0 : INTEGER);

Now the flag of order 0 needs no drawing at all, so we can write

```
PROCEDURE FLAG(N, SIZE, XO, YO : INTEGER);

    BEGIN
      IF N > 0 THEN
        BEGIN
             .
             .
             .
        END
    END; (* FLAG *)
```

All we need between the inner **BEGIN** and **END** is how to draw the flag of
order n, where n > 0. Following the essential information in the paragraphs
above, this is simply

```
PROCEDURE FLAG(N, SIZE, XO, YO : INTEGER);

    BEGIN
      IF N > 0 THEN                 (* NOTHING TO DRAW IF N <= 0 *)
        BEGIN
          MOVETO(XO, YO);  PENCOLOR(WHITE);

          (* FIRST DRAW THE CROSS THROUGH (XO, YO) *)

          MOVE(-SIZE);  MOVE(2*SIZE);  MOVE(-SIZE);  TURN(90);
          MOVE(-SIZE);  MOVE(2*SIZE);  MOVE(-SIZE);  TURN(-90);
          PENCOLOR(NONE);

          (* AND THEN THE STUFF IN THE UPPER RIGHT-HAND QUADRANT *)

          FLAG(N-1, SIZE DIV 2, XO + SIZE DIV 2, YO + SIZE DIV 2)
        END
    END; (* FLAG *)
```

Note again the invariances preserved by this procedure. Provided that
the call FLAG(N-1, ...) leaves the pencolor NONE and leaves the direction
unchanged, the procedure will do likewise. (This kind of reasoning is called
"induction" in mathematics.)

EXERCISE 5E: Type in the complete procedure, and incorporate it into a program
               whose main part consists only of

                         FLAG(5, 64, 139, 95)

               Execute the program and compare its result with the flag of order
               5 in figure 5.1. Save your program as USER:COMPFLAG.

               If you would like a step by step explanation of how this program
               works, execute the program XPLAIN5.3 on the MACC: disk.

EXERCISE 5F: Modify your program to draw the mirror image of the flag, that
               is, the design as seen from the back.

EXERCISE 5G: A separatist group in the heavily forested northern region known
               as Dendrotopia, has the same flag of order 0. (This frequently
               confuses the officials of Computopia.) The Dendrotopian flag of
               order n (> 0) is the flag of order 0 with a black cross (white
               on a video terminal) and a quarter size (Dendrotopian) flag of
               order n-1 in both the upper left and upper right quadrants.

               Modify the program in USER:COMPFLAG to draw the Dendrotopian flag
               of order 3 and save it as USER:DENDFLAG.

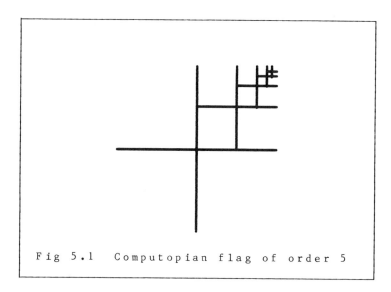

Fig 5.1   Computopian flag of order 5

You may be surprised at the result of this program. If so, note
that the Dendrotopian flag of order n-1 is drawn in both upper
quadrants of the cross of order n for all n > 0.

Draw the flag, and mark on it the sequence in which the crosses
were drawn.

If you would like a step by step explanation of how this program
works, execute the program XPLAIN5.4 on the MACC: disk.

EXERCISE 5H: Another rebel group known as Abacus is continually hatching
                plots to take over the entire country. Its flag of order 0 is
                again the same as that of Computopia. However its flag of order
                n (> 0) has a quarter size flag of order n-1 in each of the
                four quadrants. Modify the program in USER:DENDFLAG to draw the
                flag of Abacus of order 4 and save it as USER:ABAFLAG.

5.4 PICTURE FRAMES

     This section may be omitted at the first reading. Its main purpose is to
demonstrate the relative ease with which carefully written procedures may be
combined to produce enhanced effects. We shall begin by writing a procedure
for drawing square frames, and then apply it to the framing of some of the
pictures we have produced so far.

EXERCISE 5J: Write a procedure DRAWFRAME(S, X0, Y0 : INTEGER); which draws
                a square of side S whose center is at (X0, Y0). Make sure the
                turtle first goes to the south-west corner (with its pencolor
                NONE) and then draws the southerly border in an easterly
                direction. Also make sure that the turtle finishes up pointing
                due east when it has finished, and to preserve the invariance,
                return the turtle to (X0, Y0) at the end.

Check that it works by executing a program with the call

DRAWFRAME(64, 139, 95)

Save your program as USER:PICTURE1.

EXERCISE 5K: Modify the procedure so that after drawing the first side of the
frame, it draws a windmill of size (S **DIV** 16) at the point
(X0, Y0), and then completes the frame. Check your procedure
against the the solution, save it as USER:PICTURE2, but do not
attempt to execute it.

The program in USER:PICTURE2 is incomplete because the procedure DRAWMILL
is missing. You need not type this in again; you can have it copied from one
of the earlier programs you saved.

- Get back to the Editor displaying the file USER:PICTURE2.
- Move the cursor to the blank line before the line

PROCEDURE DRAWFRAME(S, X0, Y0 : INTEGER);

- Type C for Copy and then F for File.
- In response to the prompt "FROM WHAT FILE[MARKER,MARKER]?", type
USER:MILL5 followed by RETURN. Don't type the .TEXT.

This copies the whole of the file USER:MILL5.TEXT into the program you are
editing. It is clearly too much, but the excess is easy to delete. Do this
now, so that all that remains of the copy is the procedure DRAWMILL and the
procedures nested within it. If necessary, use the Adjust mode in the Editor
to ensure that the program is properly indented. Check that the program is
complete, and execute it. When correct, save it again as USER:PICTURE2.

The next step is to put multiple frames around the windmill. Inner frames
are to be of size 8 less than the next outer frame. For this, the procedure
DRAWFRAME needs to know M, how many frames to draw, as well as S, the size of
the largest one. The procedure heading becomes

PROCEDURE DRAWFRAME(M, S, X0, Y0 : INTEGER);

and in place of the call DRAWMILL(S **DIV** 16, X0, Y0, 35) we write

IF M > 1 **THEN** DRAWFRAME(M-1, S-8, X0, Y0)
            ELSE DRAWMILL(S **DIV** 16, X0, Y0, 35);

Try this with the main program call

DRAWFRAME(3, 64, 139, 95)

and save it as USER:PICTURE3. Remove **ELSE** DRAWMILL(S **DIV** 16, X0, Y0, 35)
from the if statement and try it with the main program call

DRAWFRAME(8, 80, 139, 95)

EXERCISE 5L: Modify one of the Computopia Flag programs to put

(a) a single frame round the flag of order 4.
(b) three frames round the flag of order 4.

Two principles of program design should have emerged from the exercises of this section. First, invariance within a procedure which is to be incorporated into another program eases the task of transportation from one environment to another. This is especially true of procedures that act upon external objects such as the turtle. The ease or difficulty with which a procedure may be used in some other environment is a measure of its portability. The second principle is that of modularity, which is reflected in the use of procedures to perform recognizably complete subtasks. If a close association exists between a procedure and a well-defined subtask in the real world, then that procedure is likely to have greater applicability in other programs. There is rather more to portability and modularity than this, but even at this comparatively early stage in programming, they are design characteristics which cannot be over emphasized.

5.5 THE ARGYLL SOCK

The final set of programs in this chapter is presented in the form of a series of exercises. The pattern produced is characteristic of that part of Scotland which used to be called Argyll (now Strathclyde) and is featured on thick woollen socks originating from that area.

Before embarking on this, note that if a program appears to be running for ever, you may only be able to stop it by pressing RESET (that is, CTRL and RESET on later Apples). You cannot re-enter the program at the place where it was stopped by RESET. However, the workfile is not lost when RESET is pressed, so the offending program text can be recovered and studied to find the error. (Programs which write text to the screen (see chapter 9) can be interrupted by pressing CTRL-S.)

EXERCISE 5M: Write a procedure CLOCK(S : INTEGER) which draws the diamond
              shape in figure 5.2 in a clockwise direction. The procedure

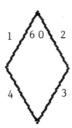

Fig 5.2   Clockwise diamond

should assume that in the main program the turtle has been turned to face the correct direction (60°). The numbers show the sequence in which the sides are to be drawn. Each side should be of length S. Start off with a move, then a turn, etc. Use only moves and turns, and do not attempt to use MOVETO or TURNTO statements, or a for statement. Make sure the procedure preserves the invariance of the coordinates and direction of the turtle. Test the procedure and leave it in the workfile.

EXERCISE 5N: Add to the program in the workfile a similar procedure called
ANTICLOCK which draws the same diamond, but in the opposite
orientation as shown in figure 5.3. Check this and leave it in
the workfile.

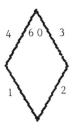

Fig 5.3   Anticlockwise diamond

EXERCISE 5P: The next objective is to draw the pattern shown in figure 5.4.
making use of procedures based on CLOCK and ANTICLOCK. The sides
of the smaller diamonds are to be exactly half the length of the
sides of the larger diamonds whose sides are assumed to be of an
even number of units in length.

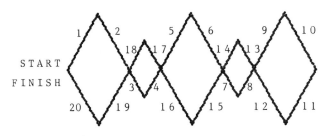

Fig 5.4   The Argyll sock pattern

First note where the turtle is, and its direction, immediately
after drawing the second side of the first large (clockwise)
diamond. Is not this just the place to call for the smaller
(anticlockwise) diamond, and draw the sides numbered 3 and 4 in
the diagram immediately above? Modify CLOCK accordingly.

Next consider the drawing of the smaller diamond. Where should
ANTICLOCK call CLOCK? The symmetry that CLOCK and ANTICLOCK
originally possessed should not be lost. Modify ANTICLOCK.

By this stage, you should have 2 procedures, each of which calls
the other. These are mutually recursive procedures.
However, as they stand, they will probably go on calling each
other for ever. To place a limit on the number of mutually
recursive calls made, add another parameter to each procedure
which says how many more diamonds (of either sort) are still to
be drawn. Make the execution of each procedure body subject to
the condition that there is at least one diamond still to be
drawn.

Since the first of your 2 procedures calls the second one, and the second one has not yet been declared, it is necessary to include a <u>forward declaration</u> of the second procedure before the declaration of the first procedure. (Pascal insists on almost everything being declared in the text in advance of its use.) For example,

      PROCEDURE SECOND(...); **FORWARD**;
        (* all parameters are declared here *)

      PROCEDURE FIRST(...);

        BEGIN ... **END**; (* FIRST *)

      PROCEDURE SECOND;
        (* note no parameters this time *)

        BEGIN ... **END**; (* SECOND *)

Your Argyll sock pattern should be capable of being drawn at any angle. In the main program, add immediately before the call of CLOCK,

      TURNTO(20);

and check that the pattern is as before, but at a different angle. Save the program as USER:SOCK.

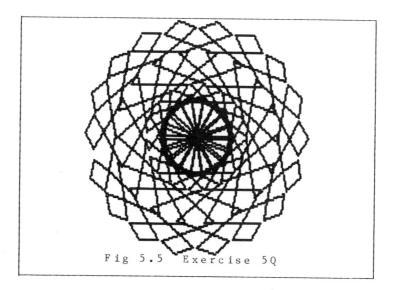

Fig 5.5   Exercise 5Q

EXERCISE 5Q: Add a variable SOCKNUMBER to the program, and obtain the design in figure 5.5.

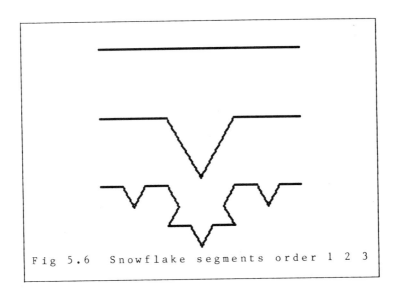

Fig 5.6   Snowflake segments order 1 2 3

EXERCISE 5R: The family of snowflakes, three of which are shown in figure
5.7 are made up from the segments shown in figure 5.6. Write a
recursive procedure DRAWSEGMENT(N, S : INTEGER) which draws a
segment of order n, of length s; and hence write a program to
draw one of the family of snowflakes. To test your program,
draw the snowflake of order 4 made from three segments of length
162.

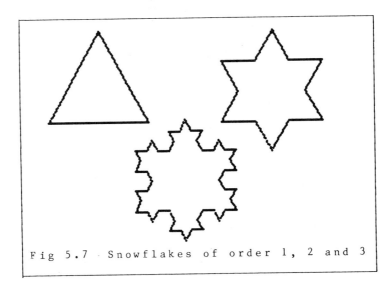

Fig 5.7 Snowflakes of order 1, 2 and 3

SOLUTIONS TO THE EXERCISES

```
5A:     PROCEDURE DRAWMILL(SIZE, X0, Y0, THETA : INTEGER);

            VAR SAILNUMBER : INTEGER;

            PROCEDURE DRAWBODY(S : INTEGER); ...;
            PROCEDURE DRAWROOF(S : INTEGER); ...;
            PROCEDURE DRAWSAIL(S : INTEGER); ...;

            BEGIN (* DRAWMILL *)
                MOVETO(X0, Y0);
                IF SIZE > 0 THEN
                    BEGIN
                        PENCOLOR(WHITE);

                        DRAWBODY(SIZE);
                        DRAWROOF(SIZE);
                        TURN(THETA);
                        FOR SAILNUMBER := 1 TO 4 DO
                            BEGIN
                                DRAWSAIL(SIZE);
                                TURN(90)
                            END;
                        TURN(-THETA);

                        PENCOLOR(NONE)
                    END
            END; (* DRAWMILL *)


5B:     BEGIN (* DRAWMILL *)
            IF SIZE > 0 THEN
                BEGIN
                    MOVETO(X0, Y0);
                    PENCOLOR(WHITE);

                    DRAWBODY(SIZE);
                    DRAWROOF(SIZE);
                    TURN(THETA);
                    FOR SAILNUMBER := 1 TO 4 DO
                        BEGIN
                            DRAWSAIL(SIZE);
                            TURN(90)
                        END;
                    TURN(-THETA);

                    PENCOLOR(NONE)
                END
            ELSE DRAWMILL(1, X0, Y0, THETA)
        END (* DRAWMILL *)
```

5C: if statement: [incomplete]

5D:

5E: **PROGRAM** COMPFLAG;

USES TURTLEGRAPHICS;

PROCEDURE FLAG(N, SIZE, XO, YO : INTEGER);

```
    BEGIN
        IF N > 0 THEN
            BEGIN
                MOVETO(XO, YO);   PENCOLOR(WHITE);

                MOVE(-SIZE);  MOVE(2*SIZE);  MOVE(-SIZE);  TURN(90);
                MOVE(-SIZE);  MOVE(2*SIZE);  MOVE(-SIZE);  TURN(-90);
                PENCOLOR(NONE);

                FLAG(N-1, SIZE DIV 2, XO + SIZE DIV 2, YO + SIZE DIV 2)
            END
    END; (* FLAG *)

BEGIN
    INITTURTLE;
    FLAG(5, 64, 139, 95);
    READLN
END.
```

5F: In the solution to exercise 5E, change

           FLAG(N-1, SIZE **DIV** 2, XO + SIZE **DIV** 2, YO + SIZE **DIV** 2)

       to

           FLAG(N-1, SIZE **DIV** 2, XO - SIZE **DIV** 2, YO + SIZE **DIV** 2)

5G: In the solution to exercise 5E, change the name of the procedure
       FLAG to FLAG2, and change

           FLAG(N-1, SIZE **DIV** 2, XO + SIZE **DIV** 2, YO + SIZE **DIV** 2)

       to

           FLAG2(N-1, SIZE **DIV** 2, XO - SIZE **DIV** 2, YO + SIZE **DIV** 2);
           FLAG2(N-1, SIZE **DIV** 2, XO + SIZE **DIV** 2, YO + SIZE **DIV** 2)

       The sequence in which the crosses are drawn is shown in figure 5.8.

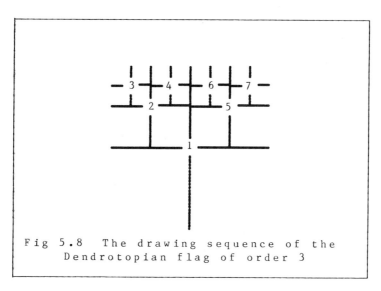

Fig 5.8   The drawing sequence of the
Dendrotopian flag of order 3

5H: In the solution to exercise 5E, change the name of the procedure to
        FLAG4 and change

            FLAG(N-1, SIZE **DIV** 2, X0 + SIZE **DIV** 2, Y0 + SIZE **DIV** 2)

        to

            FLAG4(N-1, SIZE **DIV** 2, X0 - SIZE **DIV** 2, Y0 + SIZE **DIV** 2);
            FLAG4(N-1, SIZE **DIV** 2, X0 + SIZE **DIV** 2, Y0 + SIZE **DIV** 2);
            FLAG4(N-1, SIZE **DIV** 2, X0 - SIZE **DIV** 2, Y0 - SIZE **DIV** 2);
            FLAG4(N-1, SIZE **DIV** 2, X0 + SIZE **DIV** 2, Y0 - SIZE **DIV** 2)

5J: The complete program is

```
PROGRAM PICTURE1;

USES TURTLEGRAPHICS;

PROCEDURE DRAWFRAME(S, X0, Y0 : INTEGER);

    VAR SIDENUMBER : INTEGER;

    BEGIN
        PENCOLOR(NONE);
        MOVETO(X0 - S DIV 2, Y0 - S DIV 2);
        PENCOLOR(WHITE);
        FOR SIDENUMBER := 1 TO 4 DO
            BEGIN
                MOVE(S);
                TURN(90)
            END;
        PENCOLOR(NONE);
        MOVETO(X0, Y0)
    END; (* DRAWFRAME *)
```

```
            BEGIN
                INITTURTLE;
                DRAWFRAME(64, 139, 95);
                READLN
            END.
```

5K: PROGRAM PICTURE2;

        USES TURTLEGRAPHICS;

        PROCEDURE DRAWFRAME(S, X0, Y0 : INTEGER);

```
                VAR SIDENUMBER : INTEGER;

            BEGIN
                PENCOLOR(NONE);
                MOVETO(X0 - S DIV 2, Y0 - S DIV 2);
                PENCOLOR(WHITE);
                MOVE(S);
                PENCOLOR(NONE);
                DRAWMILL(S DIV 16, X0, Y0, 35);
                MOVETO(X0 + S DIV 2, Y0 - S DIV 2);
                PENCOLOR(WHITE);
                TURN(90);
                FOR SIDENUMBER := 2 TO 4 DO
                    BEGIN
                        MOVE(S);
                        TURN(90)
                    END;
                PENCOLOR(NONE);
                MOVETO(X0, Y0)
            END; (* DRAWFRAME *)

        BEGIN
            INITTURTLE;
            DRAWFRAME(64, 139, 95);
            READLN
        END.
```

5L: The solutions are based on the Dendrotopian flag of exercise 5G.

        (a)

        PROGRAM FRAMEDFLAG1;

        USES TURTLEGRAPHICS;

        PROCEDURE FLAG2(N, SIZE, X0, Y0 : INTEGER);

```
            BEGIN
              IF N > 0 THEN
                BEGIN
                  MOVETO(X0, Y0);  PENCOLOR(WHITE);

                  MOVE(-SIZE);  MOVE(2*SIZE);  MOVE(-SIZE);  TURN(90);
                  MOVE(-SIZE);  MOVE(2*SIZE);  MOVE(-SIZE);  TURN(-90);
                  PENCOLOR(NONE);

                  FLAG2(N-1, SIZE DIV 2, X0 - SIZE DIV 2, Y0 + SIZE DIV 2);
                  FLAG2(N-1, SIZE DIV 2, X0 + SIZE DIV 2, Y0 + SIZE DIV 2)
                END
            END; (* FLAG2 *)
```

```
PROCEDURE DRAWFRAME(S, XO, YO : INTEGER);

    VAR SIDENUMBER : INTEGER;

    BEGIN
      PENCOLOR(NONE);
      MOVETO(XO - S DIV 2, YO - S DIV 2);
      PENCOLOR(WHITE);
      MOVE(S);
      PENCOLOR(NONE);
      FLAG2(4, S DIV 2, XO, YO);
      MOVETO(XO + S DIV 2, YO - S DIV 2);
      PENCOLOR(WHITE);
      TURN(90);
      FOR SIDENUMBER := 2 TO 4 DO
          BEGIN
              MOVE(S);
              TURN(90)
          END;
      PENCOLOR(NONE);
      MOVETO(XO, YO)
    END; (* DRAWFRAME *)

BEGIN
    INITTURTLE;
    DRAWFRAME(64, 139, 95);
    READLN
END.
```

(b)

```
PROGRAM FRAMEDFLAG2;

USES TURTLEGRAPHICS;

PROCEDURE FLAG2(N, SIZE, XO, YO : INTEGER);

    BEGIN
      IF N > 0 THEN
        BEGIN
          MOVETO(XO, YO);  PENCOLOR(WHITE);

          MOVE(-SIZE);  MOVE(2*SIZE);  MOVE(-SIZE);  TURN(90);
          MOVE(-SIZE);  MOVE(2*SIZE);  MOVE(-SIZE);  TURN(-90);
          PENCOLOR(NONE);

          FLAG2(N-1, SIZE DIV 2, XO - SIZE DIV 2, YO + SIZE DIV 2);
          FLAG2(N-1, SIZE DIV 2, XO + SIZE DIV 2, YO + SIZE DIV 2)
        END
    END; (* FLAG2 *)
```

```
PROCEDURE DRAWFRAME(M, S, XO, YO : INTEGER);

    VAR SIDENUMBER : INTEGER;

    BEGIN
      PENCOLOR(NONE);
      MOVETO(XO - S DIV 2, YO - S DIV 2);
      PENCOLOR(WHITE);
      MOVE(S);
      PENCOLOR(NONE);
      IF M > 1 THEN DRAWFRAME(M-1, S-8, XO, YO)
              ELSE FLAG2(4, S DIV 2, XO, YO);
      MOVETO(XO + S DIV 2, YO - S DIV 2);
      PENCOLOR(WHITE);
      TURN(90);
      FOR SIDENUMBER := 2 TO 4 DO
          BEGIN
              MOVE(S);
              TURN(90)
          END;
      PENCOLOR(NONE);
      MOVETO(XO, YO)
    END; (* DRAWFRAME *)

BEGIN
    INITTURTLE;
    DRAWFRAME(3, 64, 139, 95);
    READLN
END.
```

5M: ```
       PROCEDURE CLOCK(S : INTEGER);

           BEGIN
               MOVE(S);
               TURN(-120);
               MOVE(S);
               TURN(-60);
               MOVE(S);
               TURN(-120);
               MOVE(S);
               TURN(-60)
           END; (* CLOCK *)
       ```

5N:    ```
       PROCEDURE ANTICLOCK(S : INTEGER);

           BEGIN
               MOVE(S);
               TURN(120);
               MOVE(S);
               TURN(60);
               MOVE(S);
               TURN(120);
               MOVE(S);
               TURN(60)
           END; (* ANTICLOCK *)
       ```

5P: ```
       PROGRAM SOCK;

       USES TURTLEGRAPHICS;

       PROCEDURE ANTICLOCK(S, N : INTEGER); FORWARD;
       ```
       ```

```
          PROCEDURE CLOCK(S, N : INTEGER);

              BEGIN
                IF N > 0 THEN
                  BEGIN
                      MOVE(S);
                      TURN(-120);
                      MOVE(S);
                      ANTICLOCK(S DIV 2, N - 1);
                      TURN(-60);
                      MOVE(S);
                      TURN(-120);
                      MOVE(S);
                      TURN(-60)
                  END
              END; (* CLOCK *)

          PROCEDURE ANTICLOCK;

              BEGIN
                IF N > 0 THEN
                  BEGIN
                      MOVE(S);
                      TURN(120);
                      MOVE(S);
                      CLOCK(S*2, N - 1);
                      TURN(60);
                      MOVE(S);
                      TURN(120);
                      MOVE(S);
                      TURN(60)
                  END
              END; (* ANTICLOCK *)

          BEGIN
            INITTURTLE;
            MOVETO(80, 95);   TURN(60);
            PENCOLOR(WHITE);
            CLOCK(30, 5);
            READLN
          END.


5Q:       PROGRAM DESIGN;

          USES TURTLEGRAPHICS;

          VAR  SOCKNUMBER : INTEGER;

          PROCEDURE ANTICLOCK(S, N : INTEGER); FORWARD;

          PROCEDURE CLOCK(S, N : INTEGER); ... END; (* CLOCK *)
          PROCEDURE ANTICLOCK; ... END; (* ANTICLOCK *)

          BEGIN
              INITTURTLE;
              MOVETO(139, 95);
              PENCOLOR(WHITE);
              FOR SOCKNUMBER := -8 TO 9 DO
                  BEGIN
                      TURNTO(60 + SOCKNUMBER*20);   CLOCK(30, 4)
                  END;
              READLN
          END.
```

```
5R:     PROGRAM SNOWFLAKE;

        USES TURTLEGRAPHICS;

        PROCEDURE DRAWFLAKE(ORDER, SEGLENGTH : INTEGER);

            VAR SEGNUMBER : INTEGER;

            PROCEDURE DRAWSEGMENT(N, S : INTEGER);

                BEGIN
                    IF N = 1 THEN MOVE(S)
                      ELSE
                        BEGIN
                          DRAWSEGMENT(N - 1, S DIV 3); TURN(-60);
                          DRAWSEGMENT(N - 1, S DIV 3); TURN(120);
                          DRAWSEGMENT(N - 1, S DIV 3); TURN(-60);
                          DRAWSEGMENT(N - 1, S DIV 3)
                        END
                END; (* DRAWSEGMENT *)

            BEGIN (* DRAWFLAKE *)
                IF ORDER > 0 THEN
                    FOR SEGNUMBER := 1 TO 3 DO
                      BEGIN
                        DRAWSEGMENT(ORDER, SEGLENGTH); TURN(120)
                      END
            END; (* DRAWFLAKE *)

        BEGIN
            INITTURTLE;
            MOVETO(59, 48);
            PENCOLOR(WHITE);
            DRAWFLAKE(4, 162);
            READLN
        END.
```

The snowflake is but one of many recursively defined figures which are
readily drawn by turtlegraphics programs. In [Wirth, 1976] a few of
the better known examples are discussed and programs given in Pascal,
although these use calls to conventional graph-plotting software.
Rather more space is devoted to these figures in [Abelson & diSessa,
1980] where they are described in terms of turtlegraphics commands, in
the LOGO language.

CHAPTER 6
Conditional Statements and Recursion

The if statement, introduced in the previous chapter, is one of two kinds of conditional statement provided in Pascal. The other is the case statement which is introduced in this chapter.

The if statement was used in chapter 5 to enable decisions to be made during execution of a program, resulting in the selection of one course of action or another (or maybe no action at all). For example, it was used to suppress inverted windmills (section 5.1); replace inverted windmills by very small ones (section 5.2); to decide whether the flag of order 0 or the flag of order n-1 should be drawn (section 5.3); to decide whether more picture frames were required (section 5.4) and to decide whether more diamonds were needed for the Argyll sock pattern (section 5.5). In each case the decision was based on a numerical comparison of two expressions in what was called a condition. (In chapter 12, we shall see that a condition is in fact a particular instance of an expression.) The if statement is rather more powerful than the examples of chapter 5 might suggest as reference to its syntax diagram will reveal.

6.1 THE SYNTAX OF THE IF STATEMENT

In exercise 5C, using the syntax diagrams developed in chapter 4, we described the if statement thus.

if statement: [incomplete]

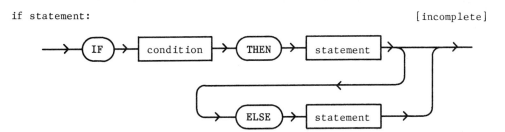

We can extend the definition of statement (see exercise 4K) to include the
if statement.

statement: [incomplete]

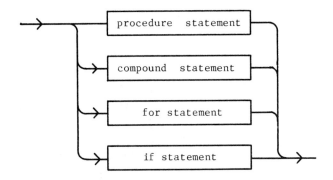

        Since the if statement itself is a member of the class statement, we have
another situation similar to the one met in section 2.9 and exercises 4K and
4L, where we defined

            for statement in terms of statement, and
            statement in terms of for statement.

Here we have defined

            if statement in terms of statement, and
            statement in terms of if statement.

This means that if statements may be nested within other if statements, or
within for statements.

        For example, suppose we want to put three frames round the picture of the
four windmills of exercise 3G, then, in the solution to exercise 5L(b) we
could replace the procedure FLAG2 by the procedure DRAWMILL, and write, in
place of the if statement in the procedure DRAWFRAME,

            IF M > 1 THEN DRAWFRAME(M-1, S-8, X0, Y0)
            ELSE
              FOR MILLNUMBER := 1 TO 4 DO
                DRAWMILL(MILLNUMBER*2, 10 + 12*SQR(MILLNUMBER), 100,
                                                           MILLNUMBER*10)

(A few other minor modifications are necessary in order to draw rectangular
frames of appropriate size.) As an example of nested if statements, consider
an extension to the version of the procedure DRAWMILL given in section 5.2, in
which the maximum size of windmill is also controlled. Suppose any size > 8 is
to be replaced with a windmill of size 8. The procedure would then, quite
naturally, and quite correctly, be written

```
PROCEDURE DRAWMILL(SIZE, XO, YO, THETA : INTEGER);

    VAR SAILNUMBER : INTEGER;

    PROCEDURE DRAWBODY(S : INTEGER); ...;
    PROCEDURE DRAWROOF(S : INTEGER); ...;
    PROCEDURE DRAWSAIL(S : INTEGER); ...;

    BEGIN (* DRAWMILL *)
      IF SIZE <= 0 THEN DRAWMILL(1, XO, YO, THETA)
        ELSE
          IF SIZE > 8 THEN DRAWMILL(8, XO, YO, THETA)
            ELSE
              BEGIN
                MOVETO(XO, YO);
                PENCOLOR(WHITE);
                DRAWBODY(SIZE);
                DRAWROOF(SIZE);
                TURN(THETA);
                FOR SAILNUMBER := 1 TO 4 DO
                    BEGIN
                        DRAWSAIL(SIZE);
                        TURN(90)
                    END;
                TURN(-THETA);
                PENCOLOR(NONE)
              END
    END; (* DRAWMILL *)
```

In this example, two if statements of the same kind (both are
IF ... THEN ... ELSE) are nested, but the syntax diagrams showed that
either kind of if statement may be nested within either kind. This is an
example of the regularity of the language. However, in the particular
case of nested if statements of different kinds, a question of interpretation
arises, and this is dealt with in section 6.3.

The other kind of conditional statement was not encountered in the
previous chapter. It is covered in the next section completing the discussion
of conditional statements.

6.2 THE CASE STATEMENT

In the late eighteenth century, times became hard in the windmill
manufacturing business. In a final bid to maintain competitiveness a
manufacturer decided to offer a range of 8 windmills made from a small
number of standard components. His range can be summarized as follows.

Size of windmill	Size of body	Size of roof	Size of sails
1	4	4	4
2	4	6	4
3	6	6	4
4	6	6	6
5	6	8	6
6	8	8	6
7	8	8	8
8	8	10	8

We have to provide the marketing manager with the ability to draw any one of
these windmills, and for this, the <u>case statement</u> is useful in that it
shortens the text and helps preserve the tabular nature of the specification
of the problem. In the version of the procedure DRAWMILL above, the three
calls

```
DRAWBODY(SIZE)
DRAWROOF(SIZE)
DRAWSAIL(SIZE)
```

are each replaced by a case statement.

```
PROCEDURE DRAWMILL(SIZE, X0, Y0, THETA : INTEGER);

    VAR SAILNUMBER : INTEGER;

    PROCEDURE DRAWBODY(S : INTEGER); ...;
    PROCEDURE DRAWROOF(S : INTEGER); ...;
    PROCEDURE DRAWSAIL(S : INTEGER); ...;

    BEGIN (* DRAWMILL *)
      IF SIZE <= 0 THEN DRAWMILL(1, X0, Y0, THETA)
        ELSE
          IF SIZE > 8 THEN DRAWMILL(8, X0, Y0, THETA)
            ELSE
              BEGIN
                MOVETO(X0, Y0);
                PENCOLOR(WHITE);

                CASE SIZE OF
                    1, 2 : DRAWBODY(4);
                    3, 4, 5 : DRAWBODY(6);
                    6, 7, 8 : DRAWBODY(8)
                END;

                CASE SIZE OF
                    1 : DRAWROOF(4);
                    2, 3, 4 : DRAWROOF(6);
                    5, 6, 7 : DRAWROOF(8);
                        8 : DRAWROOF(10)
                END;

                TURN(THETA);
                FOR SAILNUMBER := 1 TO 4 DO
                    BEGIN

                        CASE SIZE OF
                            1, 2, 3 : DRAWSAIL(4);
                            4, 5, 6 : DRAWSAIL(6);
                            7, 8 : DRAWSAIL(8)
                        END;

                        TURN(90)
                    END;
                TURN(-THETA);
                PENCOLOR(NONE)
              END
    END; (* DRAWMILL *)
```

Let us analyze the first case statement in more detail.

(a) The case statement

```
CASE SIZE OF
    1, 2 : DRAWBODY(4);
    3, 4, 5 : DRAWBODY(6);
    6, 7, 8 : DRAWBODY(8)
END
```

is equivalent to

```
IF SIZE = 1 THEN DRAWBODY (4) ELSE
  IF SIZE = 2 THEN DRAWBODY (4) ELSE
    IF SIZE = 3 THEN DRAWBODY (6) ELSE
      IF SIZE = 4 THEN DRAWBODY (6) ELSE
        IF SIZE = 5 THEN DRAWBODY (6) ELSE
          IF SIZE = 6 THEN DRAWBODY (8) ELSE
            IF SIZE = 7 THEN DRAWBODY (8) ELSE
              IF SIZE = 8 THEN DRAWBODY (8)
```

(b) **CASE** is always matched with an **END** which denotes the end of the statement.

(c) Between **CASE** and **OF** there is, in general, an expression (here, simply a variable) whose value determines the action of the case statement. Between **OF** and **END** there are one or more statements, each labelled with one or more constant values of the same type as the expression. The value of the expression is compared with the constants which label the statements. If a match is found, the statement with the matching label is executed.

(d) If no label is found to match the value of the expression, the entire case statement has no effect.

(e) The labelling constants

       - must all be different
       - must all be of the same type as the expression (this requirement will become apparent later)
       - need not be in any particular order.

(f) The statements may be of any kind (see the syntax diagram in section 6.1) including another case statement.

(g) Observe once again the use of the semicolon to separate rather than terminate statements; no semicolon is required after DRAWBODY(8).

EXERCISE 6A: Draw the syntax diagram of the case statement using the notes and examples above.

EXERCISE 6B: Express the case statement which draws the roof of the windmill in terms of a set of nested **IF ... THEN ... ELSE**'s.

EXERCISE 6C: Market forces suggest that the size 6 windmill be given size 7 sails. Modify the procedure accordingly.

EXERCISE 6D: Complete the following summary of conditional statements.

IF ... THEN ... ELSE ...	choose	1	from	2
IF ... THEN ...	choose		from	
CASE ... OF ...	choose		from	

6.3 A POSSIBLE AMBIGUITY

    Suppose that you have been asked to collect the admission charges at a disco, and have been given the following instructions from the organizer.

    "if age < 18 then if sex = female then admitfree else dontadmit"

    Your first customer is a pretty young girl, obviously under 18. You let her in free. Next is a troublesome-looking youth, also under 18. You don't like the look of him and so on the grounds that you think the instructions are

        IF age < 18 THEN
            IF sex = female THEN admitfree ELSE dontadmit

you attempt to keep him out. But the youth demands to see your instructions, and reckons they mean

        IF age < 18 THEN   IF sex = female THEN admitfree
        ELSE dontadmit

and he offers to pay for admission.

    Who is correct?

    If the instructions were in the English language, then there is an ambiguity and neither party could be said to be correct. The question of the troublesome-looking youth's admission would probably be resolved by just how troublesome he chose to be!

    If, however, the instructions were intended to be in the Pascal language, then the definition of the language anticipates such a situation and defines the meaning in favor of keeping the troublesome-looking youth out of the disco. The official definition of Pascal is somewhat less colorful the way it puts it.

"The syntactic ambiguity arising from the construct

    IF condition-1 **THEN** IF condition-2 **THEN** statement-1
                          ELSE statement-2

is resolved by interpreting the construct as equivalent to

    IF condition-1 **THEN**
      BEGIN
        IF condition-2 **THEN** statement-1 **ELSE** statement-2
      END"

In other words, **ELSE** is associated with the nearer preceding **IF**.

It is interesting to note that the programming language COBOL shares the same policy as Pascal, but that Algol 60 would regard the organizer's instructions on admission as being illegal. Algol 68 and Ada avoid the problem by insisting that, at the end of every if statement (of either kind) you write **fi** and **endif** respectively. This illustrates three different linguistic approaches to a common problem.

EXERCISE 6E: Rewrite the disco organizer's instructions in Ada,

        (a) so that they would admit the youth on payment
        (b) so that they would not admit the youth.

EXERCISE 6F: For each interpretation of the organizer's instructions, say what happens to adults (18 and over).

EXERCISE 6G: Rewrite the organizer's instructions in Pascal so that the youth would be allowed to pay for admission.

EXERCISE 6H: A program has b **BEGINs** and e **ENDs**. For each of the following statements, say whether it is true or false.

        (a) In every correct program b = e
        (b) In every correct program b $\leq$ e
        (c) If b $>$ e the program must be incorrect
        (d) If b = e the program must be correct.

6.4 SNOOKER

Figure 6.1 shows the path of a snooker ball as it bounces off the cushions of an otherwise empty table (with no pockets!). A program to draw this contains examples of the use of conditional statements. In order to keep this program simple and within the scope of material covered thus far, we will specify how far the ball travels before coming to rest. Other values which we have to specify are the dimensions of the table, the starting coordinates of the ball and the initial direction of the shot. The problem is presented in the form of exercises.

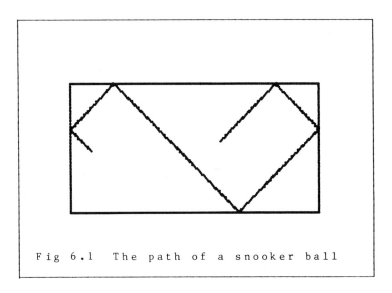

```
Fig 6.1   The  path  of  a  snooker  ball
```

EXERCISE 6J: If the outline program were written as

PROGRAM SNOOKERBALL;

USES TURTLEGRAPHICS;

BEGIN
  TRACKBALL(...)
END.

what should the parameters of TRACKBALL represent?

EXERCISE 6K: Given the outline procedure TRACKBALL

PROCEDURE TRACKBALL(TABLEX, TABLEY, X0, Y0,
           THETA, DIST : INTEGER);

  BEGIN
    DRAWTABLE;
    (* initialize ball *)
    (* draw path *)
  END; (* TRACKBALL *)

write the procedure DRAWTABLE assuming that it is nested within
the procedure TRACKBALL. The table should be centered at the
center of the screen, (139, 95). (See discussion of nested
procedures in section 4.1.)

EXERCISE 6L: Write down statements corresponding to the comment (* initialize
ball *) in the outline program in exercise 6K.

  The general idea behind the tracing of the path is to move the ball only
a small step at a time, regularly asking whether a cushion is about to be hit.
Thus the comment (* draw path *) can be developed into

```
FOR STEP := 1 TO DIST DO
    BEGIN
        (* check for a cushion *)
        MOVE(1)
    END
```

This introduces a new feature into the program we shall write. Hitherto we have always either known where the turtle was, or else been blissfully ignorant of its whereabouts. But here, unless we engage in some trigonometry, we need to be able to find out when it is about to hit a cushion. In appendix 1, you should have noticed that the turtlegraphics package provides three <u>functions</u> whose values always give the position of the turtle and its <u>direction</u>. These functions, which have no parameters, can, for the time being, be treated as though they were variables. They are

        TURTLEX   TURTLEY   TURTLEANG.

For example, the statements MOVETO(TURTLEX, TURTLEY) and TURNTO(TURTLEANG) never have any effect on the turtle.

EXERCISE 6M: Consider reflections off the top cushion (parallel to the x-axis). In figure 6.2, imagine the ball coming up from bottom left, hitting the cushion and leaving bottom right.

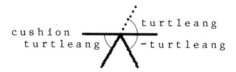

Fig 6.2   Reflection   at   a   cushion

        (a)   What is the y-coordinate of this cushion?
        (b)   What condition is satisfied when the ball is about to hit the cushion?
        (c)   Through what angle is the ball turned?

        Answer the same questions for a ball approaching the same cushion but from the bottom right.

EXERCISE 6N: What happens when the bottom cushion is hit from either side?

EXERCISE 6P: Now do a complete analysis of what happens when the ball hits either of the side cushions (parallel to the y-axis).

EXERCISE 6Q: Write down four if statements that embody the answers to the four exercises above.

EXERCISE 6R: Complete the program using 45° as the angle of the shot and 300 as the distance travelled.

The advice to use 45° in the last exercise draws attention to a deficiency of the Apple turtlegraphics package. As appendix 1 indicates, the screen may only have dots placed on it at the points of intersection of a 280 by 192 grid. The turtlegraphics package therefore illuminates the dots closest to the lines it is asked to draw. Unfortunately, after completing a line, it remembers, not the exact coordinates of its destination, nor even a good approximation to the coordinates of its destination, but rather the grid point where it drew the last dot. When drawing long lines, say of length 50, the positional error will be about 1%, but when drawing very short lines, for example, of length 1 in the snooker program, the error can be in the region of 41%. What is worse is the inability of the turtle to MOVE(1) at an angle other than 0, 45, 90, 135, 180, 225, 270, 315 degrees. When, at chapter 17, we have the means to understand this problem better, we shall return to it and program a way around it.

6.5 RECURSION

In section 2.9 where we discussed the for statement informally, we observed that

- the for statement was defined in terms of statement
- statement was defined in terms of the for statement

and we used the phrase mutual recursion to describe the definition of each in terms of the other. Another example of mutual recursion was given in section 5.5 by the Argyll sock program, where the prodedures CLOCK and ANTICLOCK were defined in terms of each other.

In section 4.3 we used the following syntax diagram to define a block.

block: [incomplete]

In this definition, we noted that a block was defined in terms of itself. This is simply called recursion.

At first sight we might be tempted to think that something defined in terms of itself (either directly or indirectly) would inevitably lead to an infinitely long definition that gets us precisely nowhere, rather like the assertion that "A rose is a rose is a rose ...". This definition of a rose gives no alternative to that of itself, whereas the definition of block does admit the possibility of a block which does not contain a procedure declaration and hence another block. Were this not so, all blocks, and hence all programs, would be infinitely long!

We have also encountered things defined in terms of themselves in some of the programs of chapter 5. It was first slipped in almost unnoticed in section 5.2 where we faced up to the provision of a token size 1 windmill, when one of negative or zero size was ordered. The version of the procedure that did this was

```
PROCEDURE DRAWMILL(SIZE, XO, YO, THETA : INTEGER);

    VAR SAILNUMBER : INTEGER;

    PROCEDURE DRAWBODY(S : INTEGER); ...;
    PROCEDURE DRAWROOF(S : INTEGER); ...;
    PROCEDURE DRAWSAIL(S : INTEGER); ...;

    BEGIN (* DRAWMILL *)
        IF SIZE <= 0 THEN DRAWMILL(1, XO, YO, THETA)
            ELSE
                BEGIN
                    MOVETO(XO, YO);
                    PENCOLOR(WHITE);
                    DRAWBODY(SIZE);
                    DRAWROOF(SIZE);
                    TURN(THETA);
                    FOR SAILNUMBER := 1 TO 4 DO
                        BEGIN
                            DRAWSAIL(SIZE);
                            TURN(90)
                        END;
                    TURN(-THETA);
                    PENCOLOR(NONE)
                END
    END; (* DRAWMILL *)
```

Recall that a procedure declaration is a "how to do it" kind of object. Then notice that amongst the statements constituting how to draw a windmill of size SIZE, is a statement saying "draw a windmill of size 1 now". Thus, the definition of DRAWMILL is given in terms of itself. However, note that not all traces of the procedure DRAWMILL need to make use of the recursive element of the definition. In fact recursion is only utilized in the event of a negative or zero value of the parameter SIZE.

The most important feature of this example is the natural way we wrote the procedure, and how closely it reflects the way the problem was posed. Compare the first line of the body of DRAWMILL with

"requests for negative and zero-sized windmills
should be met by drawing a windmill of size 1".

EXERCISE 6S: Imagine you are the turtle and you are in the main program, about to execute a procedure statement which calls the procedure DRAWMILL above. Without looking at the actual parameters, what is the maximum number of times you can enter the procedure DRAWMILL, before returning to the main program?

Recursion was next encountered in the programs which drew the flags of Computopia. Here again, the program closely followed the specification of the flag.

EXERCISE 6T: Look back at the program you wrote in response to exercise 5E.
              How many times was the procedure FLAG entered?

     In the case of the flag of Computopia (exercise 5E) the flag of order n is
defined in terms of the flag of order (n-1). The definition is only guaranteed
to terminate because

          - a flag of order less than or equal to zero is drawn by doing
             nothing, and
          - each successive entry to the procedure FLAG reduces the order
             of the flag to be drawn.

     The same principle was used to produce multiple frames round the windmill
and also the nested squares. In the case of the nested squares the drawing of
the picture closely reflects the nested procedure calls. As the procedure
FRAME keeps calling itself with decreasing S, the first side of each square is
drawn with decreasing length. When no further nested squares are to be started,
the smallest square is completed and the innermost procedure terminates,
allowing the second smallest square to be completed, and so on until the first
square has been completed.

     The Argyll sock program of section 5.5 uses mutual recursion. The
procedure CLOCK is defined in terms of what ANTICLOCK does, and ANTICLOCK is
defined in terms of what CLOCK does. This is reflected in the design itself,
for the clockwise (larger) diamonds do not have direct contact with each
other; only with the anticlockwise (smaller) diamonds.

EXERCISE 6U: Modify the basic windmill drawing program (in file USER:MILL5) so
              that a quarter size mini-windmill is drawn at the end of each
              sail, provided that the size of the mini-windmill is at least 1.
              (Use **DIV** to divide by 4.)

     Some tasks for which we write programs are clearly recursive, for they
are expressed in a recursive manner. The flags of Computopia and the
snowflakes of chapter 5 were clearly of this kind. Where tasks are explicitly
recursive, they should be programmed using recursion as the most natural, and
probably also the most readable way of expressing the solution. Other tasks
are not so obviously recursive, but analysis reveals some theme or themes
which repeat themselves in a way that lends itself to a recursive or mutually
recursive solution. The drawing of the Argyll sock pattern was an example of
this. (Try writing a non-recursive program to draw this pattern, in order to
appreciate the simplicity of the recursive solution.) It can require an
experienced eye to see whether recursion may be used, but it is hoped that,
even at this early stage in programming, that the reader will have gained
sufficient confidence in the use of recursion to regard it as a viable part of
the equipment with which to solve problems.

SOLUTIONS TO THE EXERCISES

6A: case statement:

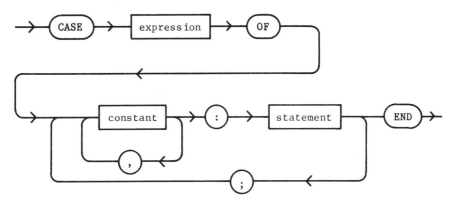

6B: IF SIZE = 1 **THEN** DRAWROOF (4) **ELSE**
  IF SIZE = 2 **THEN** DRAWROOF (6) **ELSE**
    IF SIZE = 3 **THEN** DRAWROOF (6) **ELSE**
      IF SIZE = 4 **THEN** DRAWROOF (6) **ELSE**
        IF SIZE = 5 **THEN** DRAWROOF (8) **ELSE**
          IF SIZE = 6 **THEN** DRAWROOF (8) **ELSE**
            IF SIZE = 7 **THEN** DRAWROOF (8) **ELSE**
              IF SIZE = 8 **THEN** DRAWROOF (10)

6C: Change the third case statement to

```
        CASE SIZE OF
          1, 2, 3 : DRAWSAIL(4);
             4, 5 : DRAWSAIL(6);
                6 : DRAWSAIL(7);
             7, 8 : DRAWSAIL(8)
        END
```

6D:

IF ... THEN ... ELSE ...	choose	1	from	2
IF ... THEN ...	choose	0 or 1	from	1
CASE ... OF ...	choose	1	from	many

6E: (a)   To admit the youth on payment

                    IF AGE < 18 **THEN**
                        IF SEX = FEMALE **THEN** ADMITFREE **ENDIF**

                    ELSE DONTADMIT **ENDIF**

           (b)   To keep him out

                    IF AGE < 18 **THEN**
                        IF SEX = FEMALE **THEN** ADMITFREE
                                        ELSE DONTADMIT **ENDIF ENDIF**

6F: First interpretation: not specified.
           Second interpretation: not admitted.

6G: IF AGE < 18 **THEN**
               BEGIN
                   IF SEX = FEMALE **THEN** ADMITFREE
               END
           ELSE DONTADMIT

6H: (a)   false
           (b)   true
           (c)   true
           (d)   false

6J: Parameters should represent

                    table length (x direction)
                    table width (y direction)
                    x0, y0 (starting position)
                    initial angle
                    total distance

           all being integers.

6K: **PROCEDURE** DRAWTABLE;

               BEGIN
                   MOVETO(139 - TABLEX **DIV** 2, 95 - TABLEY **DIV** 2);
                   PENCOLOR(WHITE);
                   MOVE(TABLEX);   TURN(90);
                   MOVE(TABLEY);   TURN(90);
                   MOVE(TABLEX);   TURN(90);
                   MOVE(TABLEY);   TURN(90);
                   PENCOLOR(NONE)
               END; (* DRAWTABLE *)

6L: MOVETO(X0, Y0);   TURNTO(THETA);   PENCOLOR(WHITE)

6M: (a)   95 + TABLEY **DIV** 2
           (b)   TURTLEY >= 95 + TABLEY **DIV** 2
           (c)   -2*TURTLEANG

           From the other side, the answers are the same as above.

6N: In both cases

        (a) 95 - TABLEY **DIV** 2
        (b) TURTLEY <= 95 - TABLEY **DIV** 2
        (c) -2*TURTLEANG

6P: On the left cushion, in both cases

        (a) x-coordinate is 139 - TABLEX **DIV** 2
        (b) TURTLEX <= 139 - TABLEX **DIV** 2
        (c) 180 - 2*TURTLEANG

        On the right cushion, in both cases

        (a) x-coordinate is 139 + TABLEX **DIV** 2
        (b) TURTLEX >= 139 + TABLEX **DIV** 2
        (c) 180 - 2*TURTLEANG

6Q: ```
        IF (TURTLEX >= 139 + TABLEX DIV 2) THEN TURN(180 - 2*TURTLEANG);
        IF (TURTLEX <= 139 - TABLEX DIV 2) THEN TURN(180 - 2*TURTLEANG);
        IF (TURTLEY >= 95 + TABLEY DIV 2) THEN TURN(-2*TURTLEANG);
        IF (TURTLEY <= 95 - TABLEY DIV 2) THEN TURN(-2*TURTLEANG)
        ```

6R:     ```
        PROGRAM SNOOKERBALL;

        USES TURTLEGRAPHICS;

        PROCEDURE TRACKBALL(TABLEX, TABLEY, X0, Y0, THETA, DIST : INTEGER);

            VAR STEP : INTEGER;

            PROCEDURE DRAWTABLE;

                BEGIN
                    MOVETO(139 - TABLEX DIV 2, 95 - TABLEY DIV 2);
                    PENCOLOR(WHITE);
                    MOVE(TABLEX);   TURN(90);
                    MOVE(TABLEY);   TURN(90);
                    MOVE(TABLEX);   TURN(90);
                    MOVE(TABLEY);   TURN(90);
                    PENCOLOR(NONE)
                END; (* DRAWTABLE *)

            BEGIN (* TRACKBALL *)
                DRAWTABLE;
                MOVETO(X0, Y0);   TURNTO(THETA);   PENCOLOR(WHITE);
                FOR STEP := 1 TO DIST DO
                  BEGIN
                    IF (TURTLEX >= 139 + TABLEX DIV 2) THEN TURN(180 - 2*TURTLEANG);
                    IF (TURTLEX <= 139 - TABLEX DIV 2) THEN TURN(180 - 2*TURTLEANG);
                    IF (TURTLEY >= 95 + TABLEY DIV 2) THEN TURN(-2*TURTLEANG);
                    IF (TURTLEY <= 95 - TABLEY DIV 2) THEN TURN(-2*TURTLEANG);
                    MOVE(1)
                  END;
                PENCOLOR(NONE)
            END; (* TRACKBALL *)

        BEGIN
            INITTURTLE;
            TRACKBALL(200, 100, 160, 100, 45, 300);
            READLN
        END.
        ```

6S: 2.

6T: 6. The parameter ORDER takes values 5, 4, 3, 2, 1, 0 on successive
         calls.

6U: **PROGRAM** MILLMILL;

         USES TURTLEGRAPHICS;

         PROCEDURE DRAWMILL(SIZE, XO, YO, THETA : INTEGER);

             VAR SAILNUMBER : INTEGER;

             PROCEDURE DRAWBODY(S : INTEGER); ...;
             PROCEDURE DRAWROOF(S : INTEGER); ...;

             PROCEDURE DRAWSAIL(S : INTEGER);

                 BEGIN
                     MOVE(6*S);
                     TURN(90);
                     MOVE(S);
                     IF S >= 4 **THEN**
                         BEGIN
                             DRAWMILL(S **DIV** 4, TURTLEX, TURTLEY, 40);
                             PENCOLOR(WHITE)
                         END;
                     TURN(90);
                     MOVE(5*S);
                     TURN(90);
                     MOVE(S);
                     TURN(90);
                     MOVE(-S)
                 END; (* DRAWSAIL *)

             BEGIN (* DRAWMILL *)
                 MOVETO(XO, YO);
                 PENCOLOR(WHITE);
                 DRAWBODY(SIZE);
                 DRAWROOF(SIZE);
                 TURN(THETA);
                 FOR SAILNUMBER := 1 **TO** 4 **DO**
                     BEGIN
                         DRAWSAIL(SIZE);
                         TURN(90)
                     END;
                 TURN(-THETA);
                 PENCOLOR(NONE)
             END; (* DRAWMILL *)

         BEGIN
             INITTURTLE;
             DRAWMILL(8, 139, 95, 30);
             READLN
         END.

CHAPTER 7
Towards Better Control

In a programming language, the decision making components and the loop-controlling mechanisms are often referred to as the control structures. In this chapter and the next, we extend the concept of a condition, introduced in chapter 5, to enable decisions to be made, and then consider two further ways of controlling loops. The for statement, which has already been used many times, is suitable for describing a loop when the number of repetitions is known at the outset, but as will shortly become apparent, this gives insufficient control in many situations.

7.1 MORE ELABORATE CONDITIONS

If you recall onto the screen the program USER:MILL7, you will see that this is the program that suppresses windmills of negative or zero size. Suppose we also wish to suppress windmills that are of size greater than 10. The natural way to express this is to replace

        IF SIZE > 0 THEN ...

in the procedure DRAWMILL by

        IF SIZE > 0 AND SIZE <= 10 THEN
            BEGIN
                .
                .
                .
            END

This makes good sense in English, but is not quite correct in Pascal, which insists that when AND, a Boolean operator, is used between two conditions, each condition be enclosed in parentheses. Thus, in Pascal it should be written

```
IF (SIZE > 0) AND (SIZE <= 10) THEN
    BEGIN
        .
        .
        .
    END
```

Make this modification and check that the program is correct.

Another Boolean operator is **OR** which says that if either condition (or both) be true, the ensuing statement is to be executed. As a somewhat artificial example of its use, suppose we wish to suppress windmills whose axis of rotation is in the range $100 < x0 < 180$ (that is, only draw windmills with $x0 \leq 100$ or $x0 \geq 180$) then we write

```
IF (X0 <= 100) OR (X0 >= 180) THEN
    BEGIN
        .
        .
        .
    END
```

The operators **AND** and **OR** can be combined, as in this example.

```
IF ((X0 <= 100) OR (X0 >= 180)) AND
   ((Y0 <= 70) OR (Y0 >= 130)) THEN
    BEGIN
        .
        .
        .
    END
```

The third Boolean operator is **NOT** which reverses the condition following it. The example above could have been written

```
IF NOT((X0 > 100) AND (X0 < 180)) AND
   NOT((Y0 > 70) AND (Y0 < 130)) THEN
    BEGIN
        .
        .
        .
    END
```

For the time being, use parentheses to ensure that the precedence of **AND** **OR** and **NOT** is in accordance with your requirements.

EXERCISE 7A: Where are windmills allowed to be drawn in the example above?

EXERCISE 7B: Modify the procedure DRAWMILL (the version in MILL5) so that only windmills whose axis of rotation is within the screen area are drawn.

EXERCISE 7C: Modify the procedure DRAWMILL so that only windmills completely within the screen area, are drawn. Assume that the sails are at an angle of 0° and that the SIZE is not negative.

EXERCISE 7D: Look again at exercise 6Q and using only 2 if statements, produce an equivalent solution.

7.2 THE REPEAT STATEMENT

The for statement introduced in chapter 1 is a useful means of specifying that an action or actions should be repeated several times. However, it should have been apparent from the examples so far that the number of times the action is to be repeated has to be known or be able to be calculated before the loop begins. Sometimes it is impossible and on other occasions it is difficult to calculate that number, but when the time comes to stop it is quite clear. As an example, a young baby, thought of as a processor of milk, is quite incapable of knowing at the outset of a feed how much milk it needs, but during the feed, internal mechanisms signal to it when to stop. Babies seem to be programmed to

REPEAT FEED **UNTIL** HADENOUGH

As an example of the use of this kind of control mechanism, we are going to tackle the problem of shading part of the screen with diagonal lines (see figure 7.1). Our immediate objective however, will be to draw a single line from the point (p, q) at 45° to the horizontal until it reaches the edge of the frame. Note the difference between this and the snooker program of the previous chapter in which the turtle travelled a given distance. In this case the length of the line to be drawn is not given, but with patience and trigonometry could be calculated. We shall take the lazier approach of asking the computer to draw a series of very short lines (as in the snooker program) until the edge of the frame is reached.

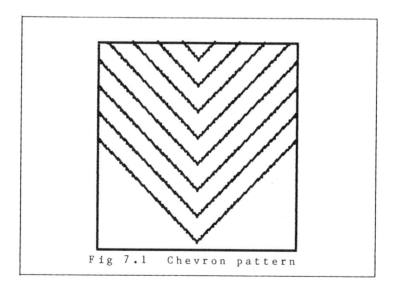

Fig 7.1   Chevron pattern

Get the program from the file DIAGONAL1 on the MACC: disk and display it on the screen. The procedure DRAWFRAME draws a fixed-size frame 160 by 160 centrally placed on the screen. The important section of the program is the **REPEAT ... UNTIL ...** in the procedure DRAWLINE. The condition following **UNTIL** is true on or outside the frame.

```
PROGRAM DIAGONAL1;

USES TURTLEGRAPHICS;

PROCEDURE DRAWFRAME;

    VAR SIDENUMBER : INTEGER;

    BEGIN
        PENCOLOR(NONE);
        MOVETO(139 - 80, 95 - 80);
        PENCOLOR(WHITE);
        FOR SIDENUMBER := 1 TO 4 DO
            BEGIN
                MOVE(160);
                TURN(90)
            END;
        PENCOLOR(NONE);
        MOVETO(139, 95)
    END; (* DRAWFRAME *)

PROCEDURE DRAWLINE(P, Q, THETA : INTEGER);

    BEGIN
        MOVETO(P, Q);
        PENCOLOR(WHITE);
        TURNTO(THETA);
        REPEAT
            MOVE(1)
        UNTIL (TURTLEX >= 139 + 80) OR (TURTLEX <= 139 - 80) OR
              (TURTLEY >= 95 + 80) OR (TURTLEY <= 95 - 80);
        PENCOLOR(NONE);
        MOVETO(P, Q)
    END; (* DRAWLINE *)

BEGIN
    INITTURTLE;
    DRAWFRAME;
    DRAWLINE(120, 30, 45);
    READLN
END.
```

Execute this program. If you wish for a further explanation of the repeat statement, execute the program XPLAIN7.1 on the MACC: disk. Now try it with the call

```
DRAWLINE(240, 30, 45)
```

and observe that an attempt to draw something occurs before the procedure discovers that the pen is outside the frame. This is a characteristic of the **REPEAT ... UNTIL** iteration. It always does it, at least once.

7.3 THE WHILE STATEMENT

Although we did not emphasize it, the model of the feeding baby implies that the baby will always take at least one mouthful. Those with experience in these matters will know that this does not correctly describe the behavior of all babies. Certain individuals appear to have had enough before some feeds begin. It would appear that they have been programmed

WHILE NOT HADENOUGH DO FEED

This suggests that the question be asked before the first, as well as every
other mouthful. Using another analogy, the use of REPEAT ... UNTIL
suggests a "shoot first and ask questions afterwards" policy, whereas the use
of WHILE ... DO suggests "ask first, and then, maybe, shoot". The program
DIAGONAL1 should be modified, changing the REPEAT ... UNTIL to WHILE ...
DO as in the following program.

```
PROGRAM DIAGONAL2;

USES TURTLEGRAPHICS;

PROCEDURE DRAWFRAME; ... END; (* DRAWFRAME *)

PROCEDURE DRAWLINE(P, Q, THETA : INTEGER);

    BEGIN
        MOVETO(P, Q);
        PENCOLOR(WHITE);
        TURNTO(THETA);
        WHILE (TURTLEX < 139 + 80) AND (TURTLEX > 139 - 80) AND
              (TURTLEY <  95 + 80) AND (TURTLEY >  95 - 80) DO
            MOVE(1);
        PENCOLOR(NONE);
        MOVETO(P, Q)
    END; (* DRAWLINE *)

BEGIN
    INITTURTLE;
    DRAWFRAME;
    DRAWLINE(120, 30, 45);
    READLN
END.
```

Execute it noting that its behavior appears to be the same as that of
DIAGONAL1. Now replace the call of DRAWLINE by

```
DRAWLINE(240, 30, 45)
```

and observe that it now makes no attempt to draw outside the frame. It has
"asked the question before shooting". Note also that the condition is the
converse of the previous condition. It is a condition for carrying on, not
one for stopping. If you wish for a further explanation of the while
statement, execute the program XPLAIN7.2 on the MACC: disk.

There is a subtle difference between the syntax of the while statement
and the repeat statement not apparent in the examples above. The while
statement causes the repetition of the statement following the DO. Thus if
several statements are to be repeated (as is usually the case) they must be
formed into a single compound statement, exactly as in the for statement.
The REPEAT of the repeat statement, on the other hand, together with its
UNTIL behave rather like the parentheses BEGIN and END, and all
statements between REPEAT and its matching UNTIL are repeated.

EXERCISE 7E: Develop one of the versions of this program, to produce the
              shaded picture in figure 7.1.

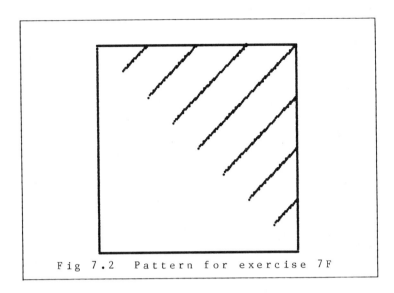

Fig 7.2   Pattern for exercise 7F

EXERCISE 7F: Write a program to draw the half-shaded frame shown in
              figure 7.2.

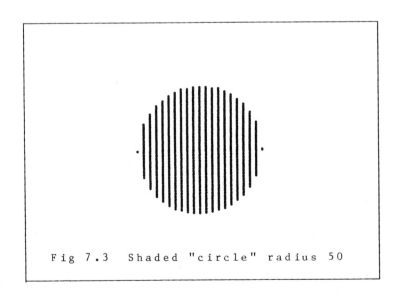

Fig 7.3   Shaded "circle" radius 50

EXERCISE 7G: Write a program to draw the shaded "circle" shown in figure 7.3.

7.4 CLIPPING AND COVERING

(This section may be omitted at the first reading.)

When displaying graphical information it is often desirable to clip the display by drawing only those parts which are within a defined rectangular area. For example, if the circle of figure 7.3 is clipped by the rectangle defined by

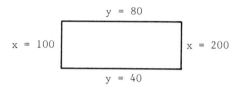

then figure 7.4 is obtained.

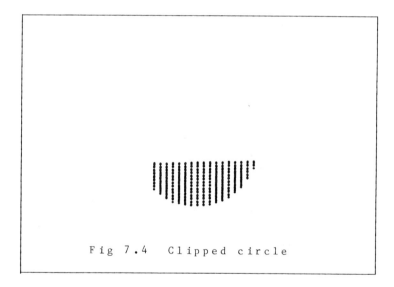

Fig 7.4   Clipped circle

The converse operation covers a rectangular area of a figure with the pencolor NONE, to enable a caption or other message to be displayed without interference from the graphical information.

In either case a rectangle can be drawn, to outline the area clipped or covered.

Clipping and covering can easily be applied to turtle drawn pictures by changing the pencolor to NONE in those parts of the screen where the picture is not to be drawn. This is not the most efficient way to implement clipping or covering but it does serve to illustrate another application of the more elaborate conditions introduced in section 7.2.

EXERCISE 7H: Modify the program written in response to exercise 7G so that a
               square of side 25 covers the center of the circle. Hint: replace
               the statement

                    MOVE(1)

               by

                    MYMOVE1

               and make the procedure MYMOVE1 ascertain whether the present
               position of the turtle is in a covered part of the screen or not,
               and hence use the appropriate pencolor.

     Clipping can also be achieved in Apple Pascal by means of the VIEWPORT
statement [Apple, 1980]. For a more detailed discussion of clipping and
covering see [Angell, 1981].

SOLUTIONS TO THE EXERCISES

7A: In any of the four corners of the screen, shaded in the diagram below.

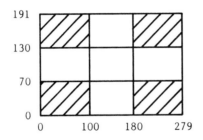

7B: **PROCEDURE** DRAWMILL(SIZE, XO, YO, THETA : INTEGER);

        VAR SAILNUMBER : INTEGER;

        PROCEDURE DRAWBODY(S : INTEGER); ...;
        PROCEDURE DRAWROOF(S : INTEGER); ...;
        PROCEDURE DRAWSAIL(S : INTEGER); ...;

        BEGIN (* DRAWMILL *)
           IF (XO >= 0) **AND** (XO <= 279) **AND**
                               (YO >= 0) **AND** (YO <= 191) **THEN**
              BEGIN
                MOVETO(XO, YO);   PENCOLOR(WHITE);
                DRAWBODY(SIZE);   DRAWROOF(SIZE);
                TURN(THETA);
                FOR SAILNUMBER := 1 **TO** 4 **DO**
                     BEGIN DRAWSAIL(SIZE);   TURN(90) **END**;
                TURN(-THETA);
                PENCOLOR(NONE)
              END
        END; (* DRAWMILL *)

```
7C:      PROCEDURE DRAWMILL(SIZE, X0, Y0, THETA : INTEGER);

              VAR SAILNUMBER : INTEGER;

              PROCEDURE DRAWBODY(S : INTEGER); ...;
              PROCEDURE DRAWROOF(S : INTEGER); ...;
              PROCEDURE DRAWSAIL(S : INTEGER); ...;

              BEGIN (* DRAWMILL *)
                  IF (X0 - 6*SIZE >= 0) AND (X0 + 6*SIZE <= 279) AND
                     (Y0 - 6*SIZE >= 0) AND (Y0 + 6*SIZE <= 191) THEN
                    BEGIN
                         ...
                    END
              END; (* DRAWMILL *)


7D:      Replace the four if statements by

              IF (TURTLEX >= 139 + TABLEX DIV 2) OR
                 (TURTLEX <= 139 - TABLEX DIV 2) THEN TURN(180 - 2*TURTLEANG);
              IF (TURTLEY >= 95 + TABLEY DIV 2) OR
                 (TURTLEY <= 95 - TABLEY DIV 2) THEN TURN(-2*TURTLEANG)


7E:      PROGRAM CHEVRON;

         USES TURTLEGRAPHICS;

         VAR Y : INTEGER;

         PROCEDURE DRAWFRAME; ... END; (* DRAWFRAME *)

         PROCEDURE DRAWLINE(P, Q, THETA : INTEGER);

              BEGIN
                  MOVETO(P, Q);
                  PENCOLOR(WHITE);
                  TURNTO(THETA);
                  REPEAT
                      MOVE(1)
                  UNTIL (TURTLEX >= 139 + 80) OR (TURTLEX <= 139 - 80) OR
                        (TURTLEY >= 95 + 80) OR (TURTLEY <= 95 - 80);
                  PENCOLOR(NONE);
                  MOVETO(P, Q)
              END; (* DRAWLINE *)
         BEGIN
              INITTURTLE;
              DRAWFRAME;
              FOR Y := 1 TO 8 DO
                  BEGIN
                      DRAWLINE(139, Y*20, 45);
                      DRAWLINE(139, Y*20, 135)
                  END;
              READLN
         END.
```

```
7F:     PROGRAM HALFSHADE;

        USES TURTLEGRAPHICS;

        VAR X : INTEGER;

        PROCEDURE DRAWFRAME; ... END; (* DRAWFRAME *)

        PROCEDURE DRAWLINE(P, Q, THETA : INTEGER);

            BEGIN
                MOVETO(P, Q);
                PENCOLOR(WHITE);
                TURNTO(THETA);
                REPEAT
                    MOVE(1)
                UNTIL (TURTLEX >= 139 + 80) OR (TURTLEX <= 139 - 80) OR
                      (TURTLEY >= 95 + 80) OR (TURTLEY <= 95 - 80);
                PENCOLOR(NONE);
                MOVETO(P, Q)
            END; (* DRAWLINE *)

        BEGIN
            INITTURTLE;
            DRAWFRAME;
            FOR X := 4 TO 10 DO
                DRAWLINE(X*20, (235 - 20*X), 45);
            READLN
        END.


7G:     PROGRAM CIRCLE;

        USES TURTLEGRAPHICS;

        VAR X : INTEGER;


        PROCEDURE DRAWLINE(P, Q, THETA : INTEGER);

            BEGIN
                MOVETO(P, Q);
                PENCOLOR(WHITE);
                TURNTO(THETA);
                REPEAT
                    MOVE(1)
                UNTIL SQR(TURTLEX - 139) + SQR(TURTLEY - 95) >= SQR(50);
                                        (* PYTHAGORAS' THEOREM *)

                PENCOLOR(NONE);
                MOVETO(P, Q)
            END; (* DRAWLINE *)

        BEGIN
            INITTURTLE;
            FOR X := 18 TO 38 DO
                BEGIN
                    DRAWLINE(X*5 - 1, 95, 90);
                    DRAWLINE(X*5 - 1, 95, -90);
                END;
            READLN
        END.
```

7H: In the program in the solution to exercise 7G, change MOVE(1) to
         MYMOVE1 and add the procedure

         PROCEDURE MYMOVE1;

                 BEGIN
                     IF (TURTLEX >= 152) **OR**
                        (TURTLEX <= 127) **OR**
                        (TURTLEY >= 108) **OR**
                        (TURTLEY <= 83) **THEN** PENCOLOR(WHITE)
                                        ELSE PENCOLOR(NONE);
                     MOVE(1)
                 END; (* MYMOVE1 *)

CHAPTER 8
Boolean-valued Expressions and Iterations

The use of conditions, in chapters 5 to 7, to provide the decision making mechanisms of conditional, repeat and while statements raises the apparently unrelated issue of the <u>type</u> of a variable. We postpone a more detailed discussion of type to chapters 11 and 12, but would note here that the concept of an expression, introduced in chapter 2 as a rule for calculating a value, is not necessarily to be limited to rules for calculating integer values. The type of a variable is the <u>range of values</u> it may take. On the Apple, the type INTEGER describes whole numbers in the range -32768 to +32767. We shall see that many other types may be used in Pascal, and in particular, it should be noted that conditions, such as

SIZE > 0

(SIZE > 0) **AND** (SIZE <= 10)

(XO <= 100) **OR** (XO >= 180)

NOT((XO > 100) **AND** (XO < 180)) **AND** **NOT**((YO > 70) **AND** (YO < 130))

are <u>expressions</u> whose values belong to the very restricted range

false   true

which (like the type INTEGER) is pre-defined, and is known by the identifier BOOLEAN.

8.1 THE BOOLEAN OPERATORS AND, OR, NOT

An important consequence of variables having types is the restriction it places on the kind of operation that may be performed on them. For example, (false + true) makes no sense in Pascal; the operator + can only be applied to the type INTEGER and to a type yet to be introduced. The operators which apply and only apply to the Boolean values false and true are **AND**, **OR** and **NOT**, known as Boolean operators.

The operator **AND** may be defined by a truth table.

A	B	A **AND** B
false	false	false
false	true	false
true	false	false
true	true	true

The second operator introduced in section 7.1 was **OR**, sometimes known as inclusive or, since it is true when either one or both operands is true. It too can be defined by a truth table.

A	B	A **OR** B
false	false	false
false	true	true
true	false	true
true	true	true

The third Boolean operator is **NOT** which is applied to one operand only. It may be defined by the truth table.

A	**NOT** A
false	true
true	false

Truth tables also provide a convenient means of verifying results in Boolean algebra. For example, the distributive property of **AND** and **OR**,

$$A \ \textbf{AND} \ (B \ \textbf{OR} \ C) \ = \ (A \ \textbf{AND} \ B) \ \textbf{OR} \ (A \ \textbf{AND} \ C)$$

may be verified by comparing the final columns in the truth tables representing each side of the identity.

A	B	C	B **OR** C	A **AND** (B **OR** C)
false	false	false	false	false
false	false	true	true	false
false	true	false	true	false
false	true	true	true	false
true	false	false	false	false
true	false	true	true	true
true	true	false	true	true
true	true	true	true	true

A	B	C	A AND B	A AND C	(A AND B) OR (A AND C)
false	false	false	false	false	false
false	false	true	false	false	false
false	true	false	false	false	false
false	true	true	false	false	false
true	false	false	false	false	false
true	false	true	false	true	true
true	true	false	true	false	true
true	true	true	true	true	true

EXERCISE 8A: Verify that

$$A \text{ OR } (B \text{ AND } C) = (A \text{ OR } B) \text{ AND } (A \text{ OR } C)$$

The operators **AND**, **OR** and **NOT** enable us to build up expressions whose values are either false or true. Just as we needed rules to determine the meaning and structure of the integer-valued expressions of section 2.5, we need similar rules for Boolean-valued expressions.

8.2   EXPRESSIONS OF TYPE BOOLEAN

As was hinted at the beginning of this chapter, Boolean-valued expressions bear a close family resemblence to integer-valued expressions. The relevant operators (**AND, OR, NOT**) have quite different meanings to the arithmetic operators (+, −, *, **DIV**), but strong analogies exist between the two sets of operators with regard to their operator precedence. It is not surprising therefore that this section will echo many of the thoughts of section 2.5.

8.2.1   Boolean Constants

There are only two Boolean values. They are false and true, and are represented as Boolean constants in a program by the identifiers

        FALSE   TRUE

For example, the statement

        REPEAT ... UNTIL FALSE

causes the loop to be repeated for ever or until the program is interrupted by pressing RESET.

8.2.2 <u>Boolean Expressions - How to Write Them</u>

Boolean operands (that is, the program elements that have values)
encountered so far are

- Boolean constants (represented by FALSE, TRUE), and
- conditions, introduced in section 5.1.

The Boolean operators are

- AND
- OR
- NOT

Boolean operators may only be applied to Boolean operands.

Pascal recognizes just 4 levels of <u>operator precedence</u>. The 4 levels
embrace the arithmetic, Boolean, relational and set operators (see chapter 14).
Their precedence, in order from the strongest to the weakest is

STRONGEST

NOT	logical not
* DIV / MOD AND	multiplication integer division real division - (chapters 17 and 18) remainder operator logical and
+ - OR	addition subtraction logical or
= <> < <= > >= IN	equals not equals less than less than or equals greater than greater than or equals membership of a set - (chapter 14)

WEAKEST

From this table, we see that **NOT** binds more strongly than **AND**. Thus,
we may write

        IF (SIZE > 0) **AND NOT** (SIZE > 10) **THEN** ...

but no further removal of parentheses is possible. If we were to remove the
second of the remaining set of parentheses, leaving

        IF (SIZE > 0) **AND NOT** SIZE > 10 **THEN** ...

then applying the rules of precedence, we would attempt to evaluate

        NOT SIZE

which is nonsense (**NOT** only applies to Boolean operands).

EXERCISE 8B: Show similarly that removal of the first set of parentheses would lead to nonsense.

EXERCISE 8C: The Boolean operator known as exclusive or (**xor**) differs from inclusive or, in that it is true if and only if both operands differ. Write down the truth table for **xor**. Note that **xor** is not a Pascal operand.

EXERCISE 8D: Express A **xor** B in terms of **AND**, **OR** and **NOT**.

EXERCISE 8E: By means of a truth table, verify de Morgan's rule,

    NOT (A AND B) = NOT A OR NOT B

Deduce the other form,

    NOT (A OR B) = NOT A AND NOT B.

EXERCISE 8F: The expression **NOT** (A **AND** B) is sometimes written A **nand** B. (Note that **nand** is not a Pascal operator.) Write down the truth table for **nand**. Similarly, **NOT** (A **OR** B) is written A **nor** B. Write down the truth table for **nor**.

EXERCISE 8G: How many, if any, of the parentheses in the following may be removed without changing the sense?

    (a) ((X > Y) OR (Y > Z)) AND (X > Z)
    (b) ((X0 <= 100) OR (X0 >= 180)) AND
                     ((Y0 <= 70) OR (Y0 >= 130))
    (c) NOT((X0 > 100) AND (X0 < 180)) AND
                     NOT((Y0 > 70) AND (Y0 < 130))

EXERCISE 8H: Explain why

    IF X > 0 AND < 10 THEN ...

is incorrect in Pascal, and give the correct form.

EXERCISE 8J: Simplify

    (a) (X < 0) AND FALSE
    (b) (X < 0) AND TRUE
    (c) (X < 0) OR FALSE
    (d) (X < 0) OR TRUE

EXERCISE 8K: Express the following in Pascal.

    "if x is greater than or equal to zero but not greater than ten then printdigit(x)"

8.2.3 Formal Syntax of Boolean-valued Expressions

The syntax of Boolean-valued expressions is closely related to that of integer-valued expressions. Following the approach of section 4.3 and referring only to material covered so far, the definition of a Boolean-valued simple expression is

simple expression: [incomplete]

term: [incomplete]

factor: [incomplete]

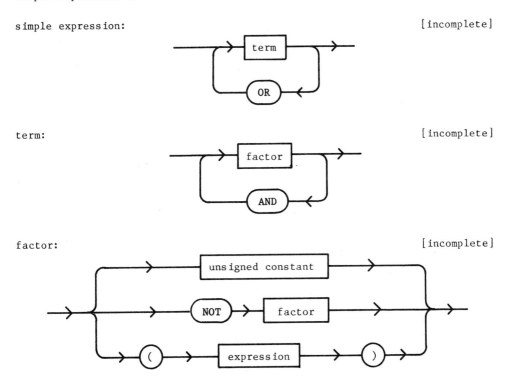

where an "expression" is what we have hitherto called a condition. See the syntax diagram in section 5.1. The diagram for "factor" above highlights the necessity for parentheses in expressions involving both Boolean operators and the comparison of integer-valued expressions. In the complete syntax diagrams of Pascal (see appendix 6 or [Jensen and Wirth, 1978]) the syntax of an expression is given in a single set of diagrams, embracing both those above and those in section 4.3. The combined syntax diagrams must be read in the spirit of Pascal's rigid attitude to type, and not interpreted as a licence to mix types freely.

8.2.4 The If Statement

This can now be described more completely by the syntax diagram

if statement:

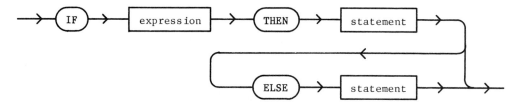

where it is understood that the expression must be Boolean-valued.

8.2.5 Programming Style

Excessively complex Boolean-valued expressions can be used to inject more confusion into programs than most other methods! Whereas an expression of type INTEGER is usually a representation of a mathematical formula, an expression of type BOOLEAN is usually a representation of a conditional clause in an English sentence. If a Boolean-valued expression cannot be readily understood as an English language conditional clause, it should be regarded as poor programming practice. (An exception to this is in the field of algebraic logic, where a Boolean-valued expression may well be used to represent a formula in formal logic.)

8.3 ITERATION

Iteration means doing something repeatedly. The ability to write down statements that are to be executed many times is one of the powerful features of computer programming. Now that we have encountered and used the three iterative forms in Pascal, namely the for statement, the repeat statement and the while statement, it is important that their proper use be understood.

We iterate in everyday life with two quite distinct ways of deciding when to stop. There are occasions on which we know at the outset how many times to do it, such as, "three coats of paint must be applied". There are occasions on which we do not know the number of times in advance, but there is a test to be applied, each time it is done, to determine whether or not to continue. For example, "apply further coats of paint until a satisfactory cover is achieved". Instances of each kind of iteration can be found in most recipe books. To cook a turkey, you might be recommended to "roast for 20 minutes plus 20 minutes per 0.5 kg", whereas to make soup (from a packet) you might be advised to "stir until the powder has dissolved". An iteration of the first kind (where you know how many times to do it at the commencement of the iteration, but as the turkey recipe illustrates, not necessarily at the time of writing the recipe) is dealt with in Pascal by the for statement which we first met in chapter 1. Iteration of the second kind (where some kind of test has to be applied on each cycle of the iteration) requires the repeat and while statements which we introduced in chapter 7. The remainder of this section gives more formal descriptions of these two statements.

8.3.1 The Repeat Statement

The syntax diagram of the repeat statement is

repeat statement:

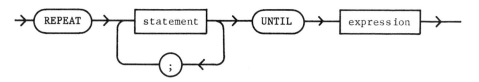

where it is understood that the expression is Boolean-valued. Note from the diagram that the reserved words **REPEAT** and **UNTIL** also serve as brackets in much the same way as **BEGIN** and **END** do in a compound statement.

The meaning of the repeat statement may be expressed as a <u>flow diagram</u>.

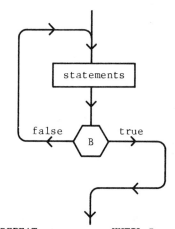

REPEAT statements **UNTIL** B

If nothing else, this emphasizes that the Boolean expression B is evaluated and tested after each execution of the statements. This forces the statements to be executed at least once. A rather more elegant recursive definition is

```
REPEAT statements UNTIL B  =  statements;
                              IF NOT B THEN
                                 REPEAT statements UNTIL B
```

EXERCISE 8L: Simplify

REPEAT S **UNTIL** TRUE

8.3.2 The While Statement

The syntax diagram of the while statement is

while statement:

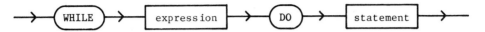

where it is understood that the expression is Boolean-valued. Note that the syntactic unit which is to be iterated is a single statement. This is different from the repeat statement. If several statements are to be iterated, they must be bracketed together into a compound statement.

The meaning of the while statement may be expressed as a flow diagram in which S stands for a single statement.

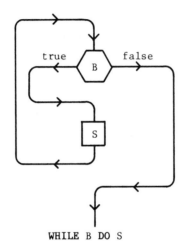

WHILE B DO S

This diagram shows clearly that the Boolean expression B is evaluated and tested before any execution of the statement S. This allows for the possibility that the statement S may be executed zero times. A rather more elegant recursive definition is

```
WHILE B DO S  =  IF B THEN
                    BEGIN
                       S;
                       WHILE B DO S
                    END
```

EXERCISE 8M: In your own words, distinguish between

WHILE X > 0 **DO** SOMETHING

and

IF X > 0 **THEN** SOMETHING

EXERCISE 8N: Express the following in terms of the repeat statement.

                   S; **WHILE NOT** B **DO** S

EXERCISE 8P: Express the following in terms of the while statement.

                   IF B **THEN REPEAT** S **UNTIL NOT** B

EXERCISE 8Q: What is the following trying to say?

                   WHILE TRUE **DO** S

EXERCISE 8R: Add pockets to the snooker table in exercise 6R, and test for
the ball being pocketed, rather than for a certain distance
travelled. The test will have to be rather severe in order to
keep the program to a reasonable length. Test for the
coordinates of the ball being equal to the coordinates of the
center of the pockets. See also exercise 7D. Remove the
parameter DIST from TRACKBALL and try your program with the call

               TRACKBALL(220, 100, 59, 55, 45)

8.3.3 The Syntax of Statement (yet again)

The syntax diagram describing statement can now be revised (but note that
it is still not complete.

statement: [incomplete]

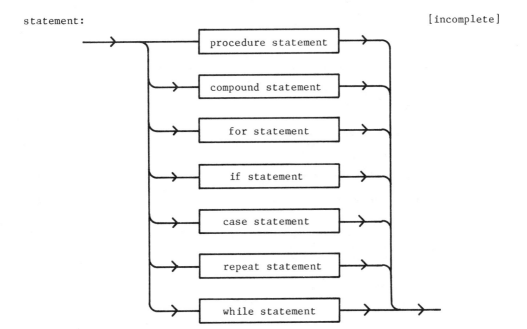

SOLUTIONS TO THE EXERCISES

8A:

A	B	C	B AND C	A OR (B AND C)
false	false	false	false	false
false	false	true	false	false
false	true	false	false	false
false	true	true	true	true
true	false	false	false	true
true	false	true	false	true
true	true	false	false	true
true	true	true	true	true

A	B	C	A OR B	A OR C	(A OR B) AND (A OR C)
false	false	false	false	false	false
false	false	true	false	true	false
false	true	false	true	false	false
false	true	true	true	true	true
true	false	false	true	true	true
true	false	true	true	true	true
true	true	false	true	true	true
true	true	true	true	true	true

8B: Consider

        IF SIZE > 0 AND NOT (SIZE > 10) THEN ...

The parenthesis (SIZE > 10) would be evaluated first, then
NOT (SIZE > 10). Call this value (which is false or true) B.
We now have to deal with

        IF SIZE > 0 AND B THEN ...

Next in the order of precedence is **AND,** and clearly

        0 **AND** B

is nonsense, since **AND** is only defined between the Boolean values
false and true.

8C:

A	B	A **xor** B
false	false	false
false	true	true
true	false	true
true	true	false

8D: **NOT** A **AND** B **OR** A **AND NOT** B

8E:

A	B	A AND B	NOT (A AND B)	NOT A	NOT B	NOT A OR NOT B
false	false	false	true	true	true	true
false	true	false	true	true	false	true
true	false	false	true	false	true	true
true	true	true	false	false	false	false

In

$$NOT (A AND B) = NOT A OR NOT B$$

substitute **NOT** A for A and **NOT** B for B. Then,

$$NOT (NOT A AND NOT B) = NOT NOT A OR NOT NOT B$$

$$NOT (NOT A AND NOT B) = A OR B.$$

Apply **NOT** to both sides.

$$NOT A AND NOT B = NOT (A OR B).$$

8F:

A	B	A **nand** B
false	false	true
false	true	true
true	false	true
true	true	false

A	B	A **nor** B
false	false	true
false	true	false
true	false	false
true	true	false

8G: (a)   none
       (b)   none
       (c)   none

8H: The strongest operator is **AND**, which appears between an integer
       constant and <. It should be

$$IF (X > 0) AND (X < 10) THEN ...$$

8J: (a)   FALSE
       (b) $X < 0$
       (c) $X < 0$
       (d)   TRUE

8K: "But not" means the same as "and not".

```
IF (X >= 0) AND NOT (X > 10) THEN PRINTDIGIT(X)
```

or,

```
IF (X >= 0) AND (X <= 10) THEN PRINTDIGIT(X)
```

8L: S

8M: WHILE X > 0 DO SOMETHING   means so long as X > 0 keep doing
                                      SOMETHING. Note that if this is to
                                      terminate, SOMETHING (presumably a
                                      procedure) must change the value of X.

        IF X > 0 THEN SOMETHING   means if X > 0, do SOMETHING only once.

8N: REPEAT S UNTIL B

8P: WHILE B DO S

8Q: Keep doing S for ever.

8R: PROGRAM SNOOKERBALL;   (* WITH POCKETS *)

        USES TURTLEGRAPHICS;

        PROCEDURE TRACKBALL(TABLEX, TABLEY, X0, Y0, THETA : INTEGER);

          PROCEDURE DRAWTABLE;

            PROCEDURE CORNERPOCKET;

```
              BEGIN
                TURN(-90);  MOVE(2);  TURN(90);  MOVE(4);
                TURN(90);   MOVE(4);  TURN(90);  MOVE(2);
                TURN(-90)
              END; (* CORNERPOCKET *)
```

            PROCEDURE SIDEPOCKET;

```
              BEGIN
                TURN(-90);  MOVE(2);  TURN(90);  MOVE(4);
                TURN(90);   MOVE(2);
                TURN(-90)
              END; (* SIDEPOCKET *)
```

```
            BEGIN (* DRAWTABLE *)
                MOVETO(141 - TABLEX DIV 2, 95 - TABLEY DIV 2);
                PENCOLOR(WHITE);
                MOVE(TABLEX DIV 2 - 4);   SIDEPOCKET;
                MOVE(TABLEX DIV 2 - 4);   CORNERPOCKET;
                MOVE(TABLEY - 4);         CORNERPOCKET;
                MOVE(TABLEX DIV 2 - 4);   SIDEPOCKET;
                MOVE(TABLEX DIV 2 - 4);   CORNERPOCKET;
                MOVE(TABLEY - 4);         CORNERPOCKET;
                PENCOLOR(NONE)
            END; (* DRAWTABLE *)
```

```
BEGIN (* TRACKBALL *)
  DRAWTABLE;
  MOVETO(X0, Y0);  TURNTO(THETA);  PENCOLOR(WHITE);
  REPEAT
    IF (TURTLEX >= 139 + TABLEX DIV 2) OR
       (TURTLEX <= 139 - TABLEX DIV 2) THEN TURN(180 - 2*TURTLEANG);
    IF (TURTLEY >= 95 + TABLEY DIV 2) OR
       (TURTLEY <= 95 - TABLEY DIV 2) THEN TURN(-2*TURTLEANG);
    MOVE(1)
  UNTIL (TURTLEX = 139 - TABLEX DIV 2) AND
                                (TURTLEY = 95 - TABLEY DIV 2) OR
        (TURTLEX = 139 - TABLEX DIV 2) AND
                                (TURTLEY = 95 + TABLEY DIV 2) OR
        (TURTLEX = 139 + TABLEX DIV 2) AND
                                (TURTLEY = 95 + TABLEY DIV 2) OR
        (TURTLEX = 139 + TABLEX DIV 2) AND
                                (TURTLEY = 95 - TABLEY DIV 2) OR
        (TURTLEX = 139) AND (TURTLEY = 95 + TABLEY DIV 2) OR
        (TURTLEX = 139) AND (TURTLEY = 95 - TABLEY DIV 2);
  PENCOLOR(NONE)
END; (* TRACKBALL *)

BEGIN
  INITTURTLE;
  TRACKBALL(220, 100, 59, 55, 45);
  READLN
END.
```

PART 2
Data Types

Now the party is over, and we must face up to the fact that computers are required to do tasks other than drawing pictures. It is the need to process numerical and textual information that leads to an awareness of data and restrictions on the kind of values that variables may take. Communication with the world outside (output and input) is introduced and hierarchical structures (arrays, records and sets) are developed from more elementary components.

CHAPTER 9
Conversing with Programs

Two characteristics of programming have so far been conspicuous by their absence. One, the ability to put letters, numbers and other symbols (collectively known as text) on the screen, was a consequence of the early graphical emphasis of this book. The other notable omission was the input statement which enables values (such as numbers and characters) to be "read" by the program whilst in execution, and hence modify its behavior. In chapters 1 to 8 we circumvented the need for input by having short main program sections containing mainly procedure calls, whose parameters we changed in order to change the program's behavior. Each change required recompilation of the program text. In this chapter, we will discover how to change a program's behavior without the need for recompilation. With suitable combinations of reading and writing activities we can endow our programs with a very limited but still useful conversational facade.

9.1 ADDING TEXT TO PICTURES

When drawing pictures on the screen we have used the concept of a turtle to focus attention on the current place of activity. At that point we have only drawn dots on the screen, forming lines and pictures. The turtlegraphics package makes provision for the "drawing" of characters (letters, digits, punctuation, etc.) in a 7 wide by 8 high grid of dots whose lower left-hand corner is at the current position of the turtle.

To see this in action, get the program USER:MILL5 onto the screen, and after DRAWMILL(12, 70, 100, 45) add the lines

```
MOVETO(105, 10);
WSTRING('A WINDMILL');
```

(Don't forget that typing JE in the Editor takes you directly to the end of the file being edited.) Execute the program (type QUR) and leave it in the workfile. What has happened is

- MOVETO(105, 10) has moved the turtle to (105, 10).

- WSTRING('A WINDMILL') has "written" the string of characters

A	in the rectangle bounded by (105, 10) and (111, 17)
a space	in the rectangle bounded by (112, 10) and (118, 17)
W	in the rectangle bounded by (119, 10) and (125, 17)
I	in the rectangle bounded by (126, 10) and (132, 17)
	.
	.
L	in the rectangle bounded by (168, 10) and (174, 17)

and left the turtle at (175, 10).

EXERCISE 9A: Modify the program now in the workfile so that the MOVETO
statement becomes successively

     (a)   MOVETO(250, 60)
     (b)   MOVETO(25, 60)

and in each case, deduce how the WSTRING statement behaves in
that situation.

EXERCISE 9B: Move the call for DRAWMILL after the WSTRING statement. (Delete
the line containing DRAWMILL(...), move the cursor down two
lines and Copy from the Buffer.) Explain the difference between
the effect of this and that of exercise 9A(b) above.

There is great freedom as to where you can put characters on the screen
using the WSTRING statement. To the program in USER:MILL5 add an integer
variable L and, after DRAWMILL(12, 70, 100, 45), the lines

```
FOR L := 1 TO 10 DO
    BEGIN
        MOVETO(7*L, 10+L);
        WSTRING('X')
    END
```

and then

```
FOR L := 1 TO 10 DO
    BEGIN
        MOVETO(10+L, 8*L);
        WSTRING('X')
    END
```

The flexibility that this demonstrates is entirely due to the turtlegraphics
package, of which WSTRING is a part. In the absence of that package where
WSTRING cannot be used (for example, in the Editor and as described in section
9.2 below) character placement is restricted to an 80 wide by 24 deep grid.

The actual parameter of the WSTRING statement, for example,

     'A WINDMILL'   and   'X'

is known as a string (or more precisely a string constant or string
literal). Strings are delimited by the quote mark (or apostrophe).
A quote mark appearing within a string would terminate it prematurely. To
denote a quote mark within a string, the quote mark is written twice, for
example,

'JOSEPHINE''S WINDMILL'

Modify the program in the workfile to caption your windmill with your own name, centrally placed near the bottom of the screen.

9.2   GENERAL OUTPUT OF TEXT

Programs that only draw captioned pictures may be useful during the process of learning to program, but otherwise they are fairly unrepresentative of the uses to which computers are generally put. As well as graphics, text and numerical information are also important. In recognition of this, Pascal provides special procedure statements to facilitate sending textual and numerical information to the screen. They are WRITE and WRITELN.

The Apple's handling of information displayed on the screen, whilst allowing relatively good quality graphics, does require careful consideration by the programmer. We therefore look in more depth into the Apple's screen.

9.2.1   Apple Graphics Screen Management

The Apple computer organizes its screen display from two separate areas of its memory. It is as though there are two independent internal screens, only one of which is visible at any time. That is why, when running the programs of chapters 1 to 8, you may have noticed that certain textual information which was on the screen at the start reappeared on completion of execution. In a turtlegraphics program the two modes of screen display are called textmode and grafmode. Initially, a program starts in textmode, and the execution of the INITTURTLE statement puts it into grafmode. On completion, it reverts to textmode. It is possible to force the Apple into either mode by the execution, in a program, of the statements

        TEXTMODE   or   GRAFMODE

In grafmode you will see only turtlegraphics-generated information, including anything produced by WSTRING. The screen modes set by CTRL-A and CTRL-Z have no effect upon a grafmode display. In textmode you will only see information produced by the WRITE and WRITELN statements which we are about to describe.

9.2.2   The WRITE and WRITELN Statements

Add to the program in the workfile, before the INITTURTLE statement,

        WRITE('PRESS RETURN TO SEE A WINDMILL');
        READLN;

The READLN statement has exactly the same purpose here as it has at the end of each program written so far. The program waits until you press RETURN and then continues. Execute this program. The WRITE statement displays its information starting at the current position of the cursor, and leaves the cursor one character position to the right of the last character displayed. Try to reconcile what you see on the screen with the program that produced it.

In textmode, the screen is regarded as 24 lines of 80 characters, the control functions CTRL-A and CTRL-Z being available to view the right-hand half. Like the WSTRING statement of the turtlegraphics package, WRITE does not "wrap around" from the end of one line to the next. Characters sent to the screen beyond column 80 are simply lost.

When a lot of text is to be put on the screen, it is often thought of in terms of lines of text. To send a line of text to the screen and then move the cursor to the beginning of the next line, use WRITELN (short for "write line"). When issued on the bottom line of the screen, WRITELN causes the whole screen to scroll up by one line. For example, in the program in the workfile, change the statements prior to INITTURTLE into something like

```
WRITELN('PRESS RETURN');
WRITELN('TO SEE A WINDMILL');
READLN;
```

and execute it. (If you are not convinced of the difference between WRITE and WRITELN, change the first WRITELN to WRITE in the program in the workfile and see the difference.)

The WRITELN statement may be used without an actual parameter to generate a blank line. Insert

```
WRITELN;
```

between the two WRITELN statements in the program in the workfile to see the effect.

WRITE and WRITELN are rather special procedures in that they can be given any number of parameters (denoting values to be displayed on the screen) provided, of course, that they are separated by commas. The procedures we invent in our programs do not and cannot have this property.

9.2.3 Numerical Information

Change the main program of the workfile into

```
BEGIN
    FOR MILLNUMBER := 1 TO 7 DO
        BEGIN
            INITTURTLE;
            DRAWMILL(MILLNUMBER*2, 139, 95, MILLNUMBER*10);
            READLN
        END
END.
```

add a suitable variable declaration for MILLNUMBER and execute it, remembering to press RETURN after admiring each artistic creation. Our next task is to modify this program to tell the user what size of windmill is about to appear. For this we will use the screen in textmode, and therefore add, before the INITTURTLE statement,

```
WRITELN('NEXT WINDMILL IS SIZE ', MILLNUMBER*2);
WRITELN('PRESS RETURN TO SEE IT.');
READLN;
```

The screen will certainly be in textmode on the first excursion through the
WRITELN statements, but on subsequent occasions it will be in grafmode due to
the INITTURTLE statement. To restore the screen to textmode after the windmill
has been drawn and viewed, add, after the final READLN, a semicolon and then
the line

        TEXTMODE

Execute the program. We have another example here of invariance with respect
to an external object, namely the mode of the screen. Each iteration of the
for statement leaves the screen in the mode in which it was found. However,
the important point about this program is the second parameter of the first
WRITELN statement, namely

        MILLNUMBER*2

It is an expression whose value is to be displayed. The WRITE and WRITELN
statements will accept any integer-valued expression (see section 2.5) as a
parameter and will print its value. Do not forget that a variable alone is
also an example of an expression.

EXERCISE 9C: Change the message to the forms

                    (a)   NEXT, IS A SIZE ... WINDMILL
                    (b)   NEXT, IS A WINDMILL OF DIAMETER ...
                    (c)   MILL NUMBER ... IS SIZE ...

               (Refer to the procedure DRAWSAIL in section 3.3 for information
               regarding the proportions of the windmill.)

EXERCISE 9D: To the picture of the windmill, add a reminder to press RETURN
               to continue.

9.3   INPUT

     Before we discuss the mechanism for input, let us describe a possible
"conversational" dialogue for an interactive windmill design program. The
user's replies are underlined.

        WHAT SIZE OF WINDMILL?
        5
        CENTERED WHERE? X Y = ?
        -20 10
        SAIL ANGLE?
        20

     The questions put by the computer, known as prompts, are generated
by WRITE or WRITELN statements. Your replies, which go in the opposite
direction into the computer, are taken in by the READ statement.

     The READ statement is necessarily different from the WRITE statement.
When writing to the screen, the values of the data being transmitted are
either known or able to be calculated by the evaluation of an expression. But
when information is transferred into the computer, the program text cannot

possibly anticipate the value to be supplied; all it can do is transfer the value it is given into a (named) variable. In other words,

- WRITE statement parameters say what value is to be transferred.
- READ statement parameters say where the transferred value is to be put.

Get the program in the file USER:MILL5 again and after the line **USES** TURTLEGRAPHICS; add the line

      VAR MILLSIZE, X, Y, T : INTEGER;

and replace the main program by

```
BEGIN
    WRITELN('WHAT SIZE OF WINDMILL?');
    READ(MILLSIZE);
    WRITELN('CENTERED WHERE? X   Y = ?');
    READ(X, Y);
    WRITELN('SAIL ANGLE?');
    READ(T);
    INITTURTLE;
    DRAWMILL(MILLSIZE, X, Y, T);
    READLN
END.
```

Execute the program and carefully reply to the questions as follows

7	followed by RETURN
170 80	followed by RETURN
20	followed by the SPACEBAR

Leave this program in the workfile.

The READ statement waits for you to type in the appropriate number of values of the appropriate type. Each value is put into the corresponding variable as soon as it has been keyed in. You cannot type an expression, as a value to be input. Leading spaces and RETURNS are ignored when reading a number. You must not use CTRL-I (TAB) whilst entering a number. Numbers keyed in are terminated by any non-digit (for example, SPACE and RETURN above) but the terminating character remains in the input stream as the next character to be read. For this reason, it is generally safe to use SPACE or RETURN as a terminator especially when the next item to be read is numeric. But if you had used RETURN to terminate the sail angle above, then that RETURN would have remained in the input stream, and would have immediately satisfied the READLN at the end of the program, denying you the opportunity to ponder the picture.

UCSD Pascal allows only certain errors to be corrected during the input of a number. You can backspace (←) over digits already typed in, but since non-digits terminate a number, they cannot be corrected. If a number is expected, and a non-digit is given as the first character, a fatal error is signalled. In this event, follow the instructions given on the screen, and when back at the outermost level of command, type U to restart the program. Take extra care, therefore, when entering data.

EXERCISE 9E: Modify the program in the previous exercise, so that it goes on for ever inviting you to specify more windmills. Press RESET when you've had enough.

EXERCISE 9F: Modify the program in the previous exercise so that it stops
               when a zero-sized windmill has been specified.

9.4   THE TYPE CHAR

By now it should be obvious (if only from your use of the Editor) that
the computer can handle characters. But how? The type CHAR, which we now
meet, is to an individual character as the type INTEGER is to a number. A
complete list of characters will be found in chapter 10, but for the time
being, think of a character as a letter, digit, space, punctuation mark, etc.

To see how character handling can improve the program produced in
response to exercise 9F, we will add a prompt after the windmill has been
drawn, asking whether another is required. Make the following changes to the
solution to that exercise.

- After the line beginning **VAR** near the beginning of the program,
  add

        REPLY : CHAR;

- After the statement TEXTMODE, add a semicolon, and then

        WRITELN('ANOTHER WINDMILL (Y/N)?');
        REPEAT READ(REPLY) **UNTIL** REPLY <> ' ';
        WRITELN

- Change **UNTIL** MILLSIZE = 0 into

        UNTIL REPLY = 'N'

This modification establishes a variable whose name is REPLY which can hold
an object of type CHAR. The READ statement embedded in the **REPEAT ...
UNTIL** absorbs any number of space characters (including any terminators of
numbers) and delivers into the variable REPLY the first non-space character
keyed. The outer **REPEAT ... UNTIL** loop ensures that the main program
continues until the variable REPLY has been given the letter 'N'.

EXERCISE 9G: Make this modification to the program in the workfile.

Note that we distinguish the character constant 'N' from an identifier N
by enclosing the former in quote marks. You can also think of a character
constant as a string constant of length one.

The reading of strings is less straightforward and is deferred until
chapter 13.

9.5   CHECKING THE INPUT

The program currently in the workfile should be one which repeatedly
draws windmills until you key 'N' in response to the prompt, "ANOTHER
WINDMILL (Y/N)?". If you were to key any other character it would continue

its relentless cycle and ask for details of yet another windmill. Before we
leave this program, we will study ways of checking more positively that the
input data you key in is correct. In the context of the present program, let
us assume that 'Y' and 'N' are the only acceptable replies. With the program
currently in the workfile replace

```
        WRITELN('ANOTHER WINDMILL (Y/N)?');
        REPEAT READ(REPLY) UNTIL REPLY <> ' ';
        WRITELN
```

by

```
        REPEAT
            WRITELN('ANOTHER WINDMILL (Y/N)?');
            REPEAT READ(REPLY) UNTIL REPLY <> ' ';
            WRITELN
        UNTIL (REPLY = 'Y') OR (REPLY = 'N')
```

Execute this and try it with correct and incorrect responses to the prompt
"ANOTHER WINDMILL (Y/N)?".

     The conversation is less than satisfactory, since the computer gives no
explanation following an invalid reply. If the computer is to reply in a more
helpful way when erroneous information is given (an essential aspect of a well-
engineered user interface) then the loop above should take care of the error
situation and the initial question should be posed once only, outside this
loop. One way to do this, and it is hoped that the reader will not regard
this as the most obvious, is

```
        WRITELN('ANOTHER WINDMILL (Y/N)?');
        REPEAT
            REPEAT READ(REPLY) UNTIL REPLY <> ' ';
            WRITELN;
            IF NOT ((REPLY = 'Y') OR (REPLY = 'N')) THEN
                    WRITELN('SORRY, YOU MUST TYPE Y OR N')
        UNTIL (REPLY = 'Y') OR (REPLY = 'N')
```

     This is still not very satisfactory, since the test for a valid reply has
to be applied twice. A better solution is presented in the next exercise
whose solution must be understood before proceeding.

EXERCISE 9H: Change the main program of the program in the workfile to the
              form

```
              BEGIN
                  REPEAT
                      .
                      .
                      WRITELN('ANOTHER WINDMILL (Y/N)?');
                      GETREPLY
                  UNTIL REPLY = 'N'
              END.
```

              Now write the procedure GETREPLY, using recursion to keep it as
              simple as possible. You should then have only one test for a
              valid reply. Save this version as USER:MILL9.

9.6 SPECIAL EFFECTS

Each character of type CHAR has a corresponding unique numeric code whose values are tabulated in chapter 10. You can refer to a character by a character constant or by its character code by means of the function CHR. For example, the code for 'A' is 65, so,

        WRITE('A')   and   WRITE(CHR(65))

are equivalent.

The codes of the characters you can see are in the range 32 to 127. The codes in the range 0 to 31 are called control codes and they cause special things to happen on the screen and on devices such as printers. A list of some relevant control codes for the screen is given in chapter 10. In this section two of the more useful control codes are introduced.

9.6.1 Reverse Video

Change the first prompt-issuing statement in the program in the workfile (assumed to be the solution to exercise 9H) to

        WRITELN(CHR(18), 'WHAT SIZE OF WINDMILL?', CHR(20));

and all other prompts similarly. (Remember the Editor's Copy from Buffer feature.) Execute the program.

EXERCISE 9J: Deduce what chr(18) and chr(20) appear to do.

9.6.2 Writing at a Given Position on the Screen

In textmode there is an analog of the MOVETO statement of the turtlegraphics package. It is called GOTOXY and it takes two parameters, different to those of MOVETO. The first gives the line number (0 is the top line and 23 is the bottom line) and the second gives the column number (0 is the leftmost and 79 the rightmost) of the character position to which the cursor is to be moved. Note that the y-axis points down the screen, not up.

When using the screen in this fashion, it is best to precede every writing statement by a GOTOXY indicating where it is to start. Since the UCSD p-System puts remarks such as RUNNING... at the top of the screen when starting a program, a user program making this kind of use of the screen should first clear the screen completely by executing the statement

        WRITE(CHR(12))

For a demonstration of the close control over the placement of characters on the screen, type in the following program and execute it.

```
PROGRAM MIDDLE;

BEGIN
    WRITE(CHR(12));
    GOTOXY(19, 11);   WRITE(CHR(92));
    GOTOXY(20, 12);   WRITE(CHR(92));
    GOTOXY(19, 12);   WRITE('/');
    GOTOXY(20, 11);   WRITE('/');

    GOTOXY(11, 23);   WRITE('X MARKS THE CENTER')
END.
```

GOTOXY is a UCSD Pascal feature and may not be found in other Pascal implementations.

EXERCISE 9K: Write a program to display the song "Ten Green Bottles" one
               verse at a time on the screen. Its first two and last verses are

```
              10 green bottles standing on the wall,
              10 green bottles standing on the wall,
              And if one green bottle should
                                    accident'ly fall,
              There'd be 9 green bottles
                                standing on the wall.

              9 green bottles standing on the wall,
              9 green bottles standing on the wall,
              And if one green bottle should
                                    accident'ly fall,
              There'd be 8 green bottles
                                standing on the wall.

                         .
                         .
                         .

              1 green bottles standing on the wall,
              1 green bottles standing on the wall,
              And if one green bottle should
                                    accident'ly fall,
              There'd be 0 green bottles
                                standing on the wall.
```

SOLUTIONS TO THE EXERCISES

9A: (a) After the end of a line text is lost. There is no "wrap around"
              onto the next line.
         (b) Text and graphics cannot both occupy the same character position on
              the screen.

9B: WSTRING sends a 7 by 8 grid of points to the screen most of which are
         in the black background color. On the other hand, traces left by the
         turtle as it moves only affect the points it passes through.

9C: (a) WRITELN('NEXT, IS A SIZE ', MILLNUMBER*2, ' WINDMILL')
        (b) WRITELN('NEXT, IS A WINDMILL OF DIAMETER ', MILLNUMBER*24)
        (c) WRITELN('MILL NUMBER ', MILLNUMBER, ' IS SIZE ', MILLNUMBER*2)

9D: This requires a display of text in grafmode. Therefore add

```
MOVETO(56, 10);
WSTRING('PRESS RETURN TO CONTINUE');
```

        immediately after the statement DRAWMILL(...).

9E: Main program becomes

```
BEGIN
    REPEAT
        WRITELN('WHAT SIZE OF WINDMILL?');
        READ(MILLSIZE);
        WRITELN('CENTERED WHERE? X  Y = ?');
        READ(X, Y);
        WRITELN('SAIL ANGLE?');
        READ(T);
        INITTURTLE;
        DRAWMILL(MILLSIZE, X, Y, T);
        READLN;
        TEXTMODE
    UNTIL FALSE
END.
```


9F: Replace **UNTIL** FALSE by **UNTIL** MILLSIZE = 0

        It still attempts to "draw" the zero-sized windmill which shows on the
        screen as a single dot.

9G: Main program is

```
BEGIN
    REPEAT
        WRITELN('WHAT SIZE OF WINDMILL?');
        READ(MILLSIZE);
        WRITELN('CENTERED WHERE? X  Y  = ?');
        READ(X, Y);
        WRITELN('SAIL ANGLE?');
        READ(T);
        INITTURTLE;
        DRAWMILL(MILLSIZE, X, Y, T);
        READLN;
        TEXTMODE;
        WRITELN('ANOTHER WINDMILL (Y/N)?');
        REPEAT READ(REPLY) UNTIL REPLY <> ' ';
        WRITELN
    UNTIL REPLY = 'N'
END.
```

9H: PROCEDURE GETREPLY;

```
        BEGIN
            REPEAT READ(REPLY) UNTIL REPLY <> ' ';
            WRITELN;
            IF NOT((REPLY = 'Y') OR (REPLY = 'N')) THEN
                BEGIN
                    WRITELN('SORRY, YOU MUST TYPE Y OR N');
                    GETREPLY
                END
        END; (* GETREPLY *)
```

9J: The control character CHR(18) switches to a form of reverse video, in
        which letters (only) are reversed. CHR(20) restores normal display.

        [The situation is rather more complicated than this. Lower-case
        letters can be entered from the keyboard (see chapter 10) and they may
        arrive from other sources but are only displayed in upper case on a
        standard 40-column display. If CHR(18) is sent to the screen, only
        upper-case letters are reversed and lower-case letters are shown as
        normal upper-case letters. The character CHR(20) restores the display
        of all letters to normal white-on-black upper-case characters.]

9K: PROGRAM TENGREENBOTTLES;

```
VAR BOTTLES : INTEGER;

BEGIN
  FOR BOTTLES := 10 DOWNTO 1 DO
    BEGIN
      WRITE(CHR(12));
      GOTOXY(0, 6);
      WRITE(BOTTLES, ' GREEN BOTTLES STANDING ON THE WALL,');
      GOTOXY(0, 8);
      WRITE(BOTTLES, ' GREEN BOTTLES STANDING ON THE WALL,');
      GOTOXY(0, 10);
      WRITE('AND IF ONE GREEN BOTTLE SHOULD');
      GOTOXY(20, 11);
      WRITE('ACCIDENT''LY FALL,');
      GOTOXY(0, 13);
      WRITE('THERE''D BE ', BOTTLES-1,' GREEN BOTTLES');
      GOTOXY(16, 14);
      WRITE('STANDING ON THE WALL.');
      GOTOXY(14, 22);
      WRITE('[PRESS RETURN TO CONTINUE');
      READLN
    END
END.
```

CHAPTER 10
Simple Output and Input

There is almost no limit to the variety of output and input devices that can be attached to a computer. For each kind of device, the data transferred to it and from it may take a different form and may need a different means of control. In this chapter, we consider only the relatively simple video screen for output, and the keyboard for input.

The output and input of text, introduced in the previous chapter, is performed by means of so-called standard procedures WRITE, WRITELN, READ and READLN. However, the actual parameters of these procedure calls are decidedly non-standard, and need to be considered in more detail.

10.1 OUTPUT

The standard procedures for the output of text are WRITE and WRITELN. WRITELN is similar to WRITE, except that it causes the cursor to be advanced to the start of the next line after the values of its parameters have been displayed. (Ex-FORTRAN programmers, beware!) The parameters are essentially either expressions or string constants.

Pascal allows (only in the cases of WRITE and WRITELN) two forms of parameter, one of which permits some control over how the value is to be displayed. The two forms are

x   and   x : e

where

x   stands for an expression or string constant, and

e   stands for an integer-valued expression (usually a constant) which denotes the field width, that is, the width in terms of character positions that the value is to occupy on the screen.

The interpretation of these parameters depends on the type of the expression x. In certain cases, which are noted, the interpretation is implementation specific and may therefore not be applicable to non-UCSD systems. In the examples which follow, we use the symbol # to denote a visible space on the screen.

10.1.1 Integers

The form x : e causes the value of the expression x to be displayed in the next e character positions on the screen. The value is right-justified within this field, and if negative, one extra position must be allowed for the minus sign. For example,

        FOR I := -1 TO 5 DO WRITE(I : 3)

sends

        #-1##0##1##2##3##4##5

to the screen, and

        FOR I := 1 TO 8 DO WRITE(I : I)

sends

        1#2##3###4####5#####6######7#######8

In UCSD Pascal, the form x (the colon and the field width expression omitted) causes numbers to be displayed with neither leading nor trailing spaces. Thus,

        FOR I := -1 TO 5 DO WRITE(I)

produces

        -1012345

If insufficient field width is allowed, UCSD Pascal does not suppress the output or otherwise warn you that this has happened. The value is displayed in full and subsequent output may be displaced to the right or even lost beyond the right-hand edge of the screen.

EXERCISE 10A: What you would expect to see displayed by the statement

        WRITE(D : 2, M : 3, Y : 5)

        if D, M and Y have the values 29, 2 and 2000 respectively?

10.1.2 String Constants

A string constant may be followed by a field width expression. In this case, if the string constant is shorter than the field width, the display is right-justified, and if it is longer, it is the left-most characters that are displayed. If the field width expression is omitted, it is assumed to be the length of the string. For example, the parameter

        'A WINDMILL'

is equivalent to

        'A WINDMILL' : 10

All four possibilities are demonstrated in the WRITE statement,

        WRITE('SHORT' : 7, 'TOO LONG' : 7, 'DEFAULT', 'JUST RIGHT' : 10)

which produces the output

        ##SHORTTOO#LONDEFAULTJUST#RIGHT

String constants may not be spread over more than one line. String constants of length 1 are equivalent to character constants (see section 10.3).

EXERCISE 10B: Write a program to display the multiplication tables up to
                16 x 16 in the form

```
              1   2   3   4   ......   16

         1    1   2   3   4   ......   16
         2    2   4   6   8   ......   32
         3    3   6   9  12   ......   48

         .                             .
         .                             .
         .                             .

        16   16  32  48  64   ......  256
```

EXERCISE 10C: Write down statements to display the digits 0 to 9, eight times
                across one complete line of the (80-column) screen.

EXERCISE 10D: Write a program to display a cluster of 4 asterisks (*) around
                the center of the (40 by 24) screen, without using GOTOXY.

EXERCISE 10E: What would be displayed by the following?

                FOR I := 1 TO 5 DO WRITELN('*****' : I)

10.2   INPUT

Input is the business of getting an external value into a variable, during the execution of the program. A program which requires input stops temporarily and waits until you have typed in a value (or values), transferring each value to the named variable (or variables). The value or values you type in are called <u>data</u>.

The two procedure statements which effect this process are

      READ(parameter, parameter, ..., parameter)
      READLN(parameter, parameter, ..., parameter)

In either statement, each parameter says where to place the next value as it is read. It is therefore not an expression; rather it must be the name of a variable which is to receive the value. It is essential that the value supplied as data is consistent with the type of the variable named to receive that value. The difference between READ and READLN is described later, in section 10.5.

10.2.1   Input of Integer Values

We need to be specific about what may and may not be supplied as input. A value of type INTEGER must conform to a Pascal integer constant as given in section 2.4, except that

   (a)   it may be preceded immediately by a + or a − sign,
   (b)   the number (and sign if included) may be preceded by any
         number of spaces or RETURNs, and
   (c)   it will be terminated by any character other than a digit.

Remember that the terminating character is still in the input stream after the number has been read.

No attempt to add field lengths to the parameters of a READ statement must be made (followers of FORTRAN please note).

EXERCISE 10F: What do the following (not very useful) statements display, when
                supplied with the data shown? (I, N and X are all integer
                variables.) Show spaces in the output explicitly.

                     READ(N);
                     FOR I := 1 TO N DO READ(X);
                     WRITELN(X : 6)

                Data:

                     4   2   135   200   −192

EXERCISE 10G: A program containing the statement READ(I, J, K) needs 3
                 integers as data. Which 2 of the following ways of entering
                 the data are equivalent to each other?

                      (a)   1234   5678   9012   RETURN

                      (b)   1234   56   78   9012   RETURN

                      (c)   1234   RETURN

                            5678   RETURN

                            9012   RETURN

10.2.2   Input of Strings

     The input of strings in standard Pascal is a relatively tricky task which
is deferred to chapter 13.

10.3   THE TYPE CHAR

     The type CHAR (short for character) which we met in the previous chapter
is predefined. It has, as its values, the basic character set of the computer.
Since different computers may have slightly different character sets, the
enumeration of the type CHAR may vary from one Pascal implementation to
another.

10.3.1   The Character Set for Apple Pascal

     The Apple Pascal character set is based on the standard ASCII
character set. The following table lists the visible characters and
corresponding internal integer coded representations. The management of the
Apple's screen in textmode causes codes 96 to 127 to be displayed as codes 64
to 95, forcing letters to be displayed in upper case only. However, in
grafmode, all 96 codes above have representations on the screen. Section
10.3.7 below describes a way of entering representations of lower-case letters.

Code	Char	Code	Char	Code	Char
32	space	64	@	96	grave
33	!	65	A	97	a
34	"	66	B	98	b
35	#	67	C	99	c
36	$	68	D	100	d
37	%	69	E	101	e
38	&	70	F	102	f
39	'	71	G	103	g
40	(	72	H	104	h
41	)	73	I	105	i
42	*	74	J	106	j
43	+	75	K	107	k
44	,	76	L	108	l
45	-	77	M	109	m
46	.	78	N	110	n
47	/	79	O	111	o
48	0	80	P	112	p
49	1	81	Q	113	q
50	2	82	R	114	r
51	3	83	S	115	s
52	4	84	T	116	t
53	5	85	U	117	u
54	6	86	V	118	v
55	7	87	W	119	w
56	8	88	X	120	x
57	9	89	Y	121	y
58	:	90	Z	122	z
59	;	91	[	123	{
60	<	92	\	124	|
61	=	93	]	125	}
62	>	94	^	126	~
63	?	95	_	127	delete

A constant of type CHAR is written in a program by placing the character in single quotes (thus making a string of one character). Examples are

    'A'   '[' '%' '7'

An exception is the single quotes sign (code 39) which is denoted by

    ''''

The type CHAR actually includes all characters whose codes range from 0 to 255. Those in the range 0 to 31 are control codes, some of which are described in section 10.3.2. Those in the range 128 to 255 generally duplicate those in the range 0 to 127.

10.3.2 The Function CHR

Characters of the set above may be represented in the text of a program in an alternative form. The function CHR converts a code of type INTEGER into the corresponding character of type CHAR. For example, CHR(65) is an alternative representation of 'A'.

An important use of the function CHR is for denoting control characters which lie outside the range of the table above. Control characters generally vary from one kind of computer to another. Those which can be used on the Apple in a WRITE statement to influence the screen (or the speaker) are

```
CHR(7)        bleep
CHR(8)        cursor left (backspace)
CHR(10)       cursor down (line feed)
CHR(11)       clear from cursor to end of screen
CHR(12)       clear screen
CHR(13)       carriage return (cursor to start of next line)
CHR(16)       clear to end of line
CHR(18)       reverse video on upper-case letters only
CHR(20)       cancel CHR(18)
CHR(25)       home (cursor to (0, 0))
CHR(28)       cursor right
CHR(31)       cursor up
```

Do not use these codes for data destined for any other device. Its control codes will almost certainly be quite different. As an example of the use of four of these codes, the following program causes the cursor to gyrate clockwise in the center of the screen.

```
PROGRAM SPIN;

BEGIN
    GOTOXY(20, 12);
    REPEAT
        WRITE(CHR(8), CHR(31), CHR(28), CHR(10))
    UNTIL FALSE
END.
```

EXERCISE 10H: What would appear on the screen as a result of

WRITE('1', CHR(10), CHR(8), '-', CHR(10), CHR(8), '2')

EXERCISE 10J: What should be added to the WRITE statement above, to return the cursor to the character position following the '1'?

10.3.3 Output of Values of Type CHAR

As for numbers and strings, two forms of parameter are allowed,

x : e   and   x   (which is equivalent to x : 1)

where x stands for an expression of type CHAR, and e stands for the field width expression of type INTEGER. The only expressions of type CHAR, covered so far, are

```
character constant
CHR(...)
```

Thus,

WRITE('P', 'Q', 'R' : 4)

would display

    PQ###R

the infilling of spaces being on the left. A useful application of this enables the production of a sequence of e spaces, where e is an expression. To produce (6*s - 1) spaces on the screen it is possible to write

    FOR I := 1 TO 6*S - 1 DO WRITE(' ')

but it is shorter to write

    WRITE(' ' : 6*S - 1)

    It is important to notice the difference between the representation of values as constants in a program and as external data.

Type	Program representation	Data representation
INTEGER	-1234	-1234
string	'DAY IS'	DAY IS (output only)
CHAR	'P'	P (input and output)

Whilst strings and character constants are enclosed in single quotes in programs to avoid confusion with identifiers, quotes are not necessary, and therefore are not used in their external representation.

10.3.4 Variables of Type CHAR

    These are declared in a similar way to those of type INTEGER. For example,

    VAR C1, C2, C3 : CHAR;

creates three variables called C1, C2 and C3 each of which can hold a single character. Variables of type CHAR may not be subjected to arithmetic or Boolean operators, but, as the rest of this chapter shows, they may be compared and operated on by special functions. They may also be used as parameters of WRITE statements (see section 10.3.3).

10.3.5 Order

    Values of type CHAR are ordered by their character codes. (See table in section 10.3.1). Thus, for example,

```
'%'  is greater than '$'
'-'  is greater than '+'
'8'  is greater than '7'
```

An interesting consequence of the definition of the type CHAR is that variables of type CHAR may be used to control a for statement. For example, in the context of section 10.3.4,

```
FOR C1 := '8' TO 'A' DO WRITE(C1)
```

displays

```
89:;<=>?@A
```

EXERCISE 10K: Write a program which prints out the alphabet

- on a single line,
- one letter to a line, and then
- backwards on a single line.

EXERCISE 10L: Describe the output of the following program.

```
PROGRAM EXERCISE10L;

VAR I, J : CHAR;

BEGIN
    FOR I := '0' TO '9' DO
        FOR J := '0' TO '9' DO WRITELN(I, J)
END.
```

EXERCISE 10M: If, in the program above, we had written

```
0 in place of '0' and
9 in place of '9'
```

would the program

(a)   still be correct or
(b)   be incorrect

Justify your answer, and if it was (b), correct the revised program.

10.3.6   Input of Values of Type CHAR

Suppose C is declared to be of type CHAR, and the statement

```
READ(C)
```

is encountered. The program waits until the next character is keyed. This character becomes the value of the variable C. For example, the following section of program reads the next non-space character from the keyboard and prints out whether it is a letter or not.

```
VAR C : CHAR;

BEGIN
     .
     .
     .
     REPEAT READ(C) UNTIL C <> ' ';
     IF (C >= 'A') AND (C <= 'Z') THEN WRITE(' LETTER')
                                  ELSE WRITE(' NOT A LETTER');
     .
     .
     .
END
```

The warnings of section 9.3 regarding the reading of alternate integer and character values should be heeded. In that section and in the example above we used

```
REPEAT READ(REPLY) UNTIL REPLY <> ' '
```

to absorb any number-terminating character as well as any other leading spaces, so that the variable REPLY was filled with a non-space character. Another approach is to insert a statement such as

```
READ(TERMINATOR)
```

after each number-reading statement, to absorb the terminating character in the variable TERMINATOR, and then use the simpler

```
READ(REPLY)
```

to read characters, remembering that this will not now ignore deliberately inserted leading spaces. A third approach is dealt with in section 10.5.

10.3.7 The Function ORD

(This section may be omitted at the first reading.)

The converse of the function CHR (which converts integer codes to characters) is ORD. It can be used to convert a character to its corresponding integer code. For example,

```
ORD('A')
```

has the value 65. This is particularly useful when reading from the keyboard characters corresponding to keys which do not appear in the table in section 10.3.1. The ESC key, for example, has the code 27, and so a program which does nothing until ESC is pressed, and then stops, is

```
PROGRAM NOTALOT;

VAR C : CHAR;

BEGIN
    REPEAT READ(C) UNTIL ORD(C) = 27
END.
```

There is little correspondence between the keyboard's control codes and the screen's control codes listed in section 10.3.2. The control codes (below in parentheses) which are generated by the Apple keyboard's special keys are

←	(8)	also produced by CTRL-H
ESC	(27)	also known as escape
RETURN	(32)	also produced by CTRL-M. See section 10.4
SPACEBAR	(32)	see section 10.4
→	(21)	also produced by CTRL-U
CTRL-K	(91)	[
SHIFT-M	(92)	]

The following control codes may be read, but their echo back to the screen, unless suppressed (see section 10.3.8) have the additional effects described.

CTRL-G	(7)	bleep
CTRL-J	(10)	line feed
CTRL-M	(13)	carriage return
CTRL-R	(18)	reverse video on upper-case letters
CTRL-T	(20)	cancel CTRL-R

The following control codes are intercepted before a Pascal program sees them.

CTRL-@	(0)	Permanently suspend program.
CTRL-A	(1)	Toggle to see other half of screen.
CTRL-E*	(5)	lower-case keyboard toggle. Type this once, and the keys 'A' to 'Z' are subsequently delivered as codes 97 to 122. Type it again and the keys 'A' to 'Z' once again deliver codes 65 to 90.
CTRL-F	(6)	Inhibit output toggle. Program continues but output is suppressed.
CTRL-S	(19)	Temporarily suspend program toggle.
CTRL-W*	(23)	The following key depression is interpreted as upper case and subsequent ones lower case.
CTRL-Z	(26)	Enter automatic cursor following mode.

Note that the starred codes also put the textmode screen into a mode in which upper-case letters are reversed and lower-case letters are normal white on black. This mode can also be set by sending CHR(18) to the screen or by typing CTRL-R at the outermost level of command.

To complete the list of control codes we list those which are safe for ordinary use in an Apple Pascal program on a standard Apple where the application needs characters other than those in the visible range (codes 32 to 127).

CTRL-B (2)	CTRL-D (4)	CTRL-G (7)	CTRL-I (9)
CTRL-L (12)	CTRL-N (14)	CTRL-O (15)	CTRL-P (16)
CTRL-Q (17)	CTRL-V (22)	CTRL-X (24)	CTRL-Y (25)

EXERCISE 10N: Modify the program NOTALOT in this section so that in response to each key depression it displays DIGIT 0 in response to key '0', DIGIT 1 for key '1', ... DIGIT 9 for '9', and NON-DIGIT in response to any other key. Hint: ORD('0') = 48.

10.3.8 Echo-suppressed Reading

(This section may be omitted at the first reading.)

When you press a key in response to a program waiting on a READ statement, the key pressed is normally echoed on the screen. The keyboard and the screen are in fact independent devices, as far as the computer is concerned, and it is the READ statement that causes the screen to echo the keyboard. The echo can be suppressed, if the READ statement is directed to read from the device called KEYBOARD. For example, if C is of type CHAR

        READ(KEYBOARD, C)

reads one character without echoing it on the screen. If you apply this to the READ statement in the program NOTALOT in the section above, you will have a program that does even less! It should not be inferred from this rather trivial example that echo-suppressed reading is a frivolous past-time. In the interests of security, it is sometimes necessary for users of a computer to identify themselves by typing a password, and in these circumstances, echo-suppression prevents passers-by reading the password from the screen.

The parameters of the READ and WRITE statements are far from standard, for it can be seen that if the first parameter is the name of a device, it is interpreted as the source or destination device for the transfer and not as a value or variable to be transferred. In the absence of a device being given as the first parameter, READ reads from the echoing keyboard and WRITE writes to the screen. We shall return to this first parameter when files are considered in detail in chapter 22.

10.4 END OF LINE

Referring back to the table of values of the type CHAR in section 10.3.1 and the control codes in section 10.3.7, it will be seen that no distinct value corresponds to the RETURN key. In UCSD Pascal, when end of line is encountered in the input, a space (CHR(32)) is seen by the READ statement. Data can be spread over several lines, with each end of line regarded as a space. If it is necessary to know whether a CHR(32) is a space, or in fact the end of a line, a special function, EOLN, whose value is either false or true, may be used. For example,

```
        READ(C);
        IF C = ' ' THEN
            IF EOLN THEN WRITE('THAT WAS END-OF-LINE')
                    ELSE WRITE('THAT WAS A SPACE')
```

This way of handling the end of a line is not in accordance with that of standard Pascal. See chapter 22.

10.5 READLN

This is the other input procedure mentioned earlier in this chapter. The procedure READLN does everything that READ does, but then it ignores all subsequent characters up to and including the end of the line. The next input statement is then ready to read from the beginning of the next line.

If all numeric input can be terminated by RETURN, then the use of READLN for numbers provides the third solution to the problem of absorbing the unwanted terminator.

EXERCISE 10P: Rewrite the main program part of the solution to exercise 9G using

        (a) the method of section 10.3.6.
        (b) the READLN statement.

SOLUTIONS TO THE EXERCISES

10A: 29##2#2000

10B:
```
PROGRAM TABLES;

PROCEDURE TABLE(ROWMAX, COLMAX : INTEGER);

    VAR ROW, COL : INTEGER;

    PROCEDURE HEADER(C : INTEGER);

        BEGIN
            WRITE(' ' : 4);
            FOR COL := 1 TO C DO WRITE(COL : 4);
            WRITELN;  WRITELN
        END; (* HEADER *)

    PROCEDURE PRINTROW(R : INTEGER);

        BEGIN
            WRITE(R : 2, ' ' : 2);
            FOR COL := 1 TO COLMAX DO WRITE(R*COL : 4);
            WRITELN
        END; (* PRINTROW *)

    BEGIN (* TABLE *)
        HEADER(COLMAX);
        FOR ROW := 1 TO ROWMAX DO PRINTROW(ROW)
    END; (* TABLE *)

BEGIN
    TABLE(16, 16)
END.
```

10C: **FOR** I := 1 **TO** 8 **DO** WRITE('0123456789')

Note that the string constant in

WRITE('01234567890123456789012345678901234567890123456789
           01234567890123456789012345678901234567890123456789')

spans more than one line and is therefore not acceptable.

10D: **PROGRAM** ASTERISKS;

VAR I : INTEGER;

BEGIN
    FOR I := 1 **TO** 11 **DO** WRITELN;
    FOR I := 1 **TO** 2 **DO** WRITELN(' ' : 19, '**')
END.

10E: *
      **
      ***
      ****
      *****

10F: ##-192

10G: (a) and (c) are equivalent. (b) represents four values.

10H: 1
      ─
      2

10J: WRITE(CHR(31), CHR(31))

10K: **PROGRAM** ALPHABETS;

VAR LETTER : CHAR;

BEGIN
    FOR LETTER := 'A' **TO** 'Z' **DO** WRITE(LETTER : 2);
    WRITELN;
    FOR LETTER := 'A' **TO** 'Z' **DO** WRITELN(LETTER);
    FOR LETTER := 'Z' **DOWNTO** 'A' **DO** WRITE(LETTER : 2)
END.

10L: 00
      01
      02
      .
      .
      .
      99

10M: 0, 1, ..., 9 are not representations of characters. They are
      representations of integers. To correct the program, declare

          VAR I, J : INTEGER;

10N: ```
PROGRAM ABITMORE;

VAR C : CHAR;

BEGIN
    REPEAT
        READ(C);
        IF (C >= '0') AND (C <= '9')
            THEN WRITELN(' DIGIT ', ORD(C) - 48)
            ELSE WRITELN(' NON-DIGIT')
    UNTIL ORD(C) = 27
END.
```

10P:    (a)  The main program is

```
BEGIN
    REPEAT
        WRITELN('WHAT SIZE OF WINDMILL?');
        READ(MILLSIZE);
        WRITELN('CENTERED WHERE? X   Y  = ?');
        READ(X, Y);
        WRITELN('SAIL ANGLE?');
        READ(T);   READ(REPLY);   (* IGNORE TERMINATOR *)
        INITTURTLE;
        DRAWMILL(MILLSIZE, X, Y, T);
        READLN;
        TEXTMODE;
        WRITELN('ANOTHER WINDMILL (Y/N)?');
        READ(REPLY)
    UNTIL REPLY = 'N'
END.
```

(b) The main program is

```
BEGIN
    REPEAT
        WRITELN('WHAT SIZE OF WINDMILL?');
        READLN(MILLSIZE);
        WRITELN('CENTERED WHERE? X   Y  = ?');
        READLN(X, Y);
        WRITELN('SAIL ANGLE?');
        READLN(T);
        INITTURTLE;
        DRAWMILL(MILLSIZE, X, Y, T);
        READLN;
        TEXTMODE;
        WRITELN('ANOTHER WINDMILL (Y/N)?');
        READ(REPLY)
    UNTIL REPLY = 'N'
END.
```
```

CHAPTER 11
New Data Types from Old

A variable is like a box which can hold one value at a time, but from time to time that value can change. We have not yet fully exploited the variable. Apart from the control variable in a for statement and the variables which are the parameters of a read statement, variables have been rather static objects. In this chapter we concentrate on how the values in a variable can be readily changed (the assignment statement), the use of variables with user-defined values (enumerated types) and restricted sets of values (subrange types), and how variables can be grouped together to form a composite structure called a record.

11.1 VARIABLES

Variables whose values we can determine at will serve as a form of memory. A variable is rather like a named scratch pad, whose sheets of paper are used but once and then discarded as the next value is to be remembered. The life cycle of a variable during program execution is

- Creation. On entering the block (see section 4.2) in which it is declared, a variable is created. Its value is said to be undefined (except in the case of a formal parameter when its value is initialized to the value of the actual parameter).

- Initialization. Initial value is given, maybe by for statement, READ statement, or the assignment statement introduced below.

- Utilization and Alteration. Value may be used (for example as an actual parameter, in a WRITE statement, for statement) and changed (for example in a for statement, assignment statement, READ statement) any number of times.

- Annihilation. On exit from the block in which it is declared the variable ceases to exist. On re-entry to that block, a new unitialized variable will be created.

   As an illustration of one of the more obvious uses of variables, we will
modify the program in USER:MILL9 (saved at exercise 9H) so that when the user
finally indicates that enough is enough, the screen displays something like

          YOU HAVE HAD 5 WINDMILLS
          YOU WILL BE CHARGED $8.25
          HAVE A GOOD DAY!

Windmills of size s cost 25*s cents.

EXERCISE 11A: (Difficult, and can be omitted at a first reading.) Using only
                material from chapters 1 to 10, write such a program.

   The main program of USER:MILL9 as saved, is assumed to be

          BEGIN
             REPEAT
                WRITELN('WHAT SIZE OF WINDMILL?');
                READ(MILLSIZE);
                WRITELN('CENTERED WHERE? X Y = ?');
                READ(X, Y);
                WRITELN('SAIL ANGLE?');
                READ(T);
                INITTURTLE;
                DRAWMILL(MILLSIZE, X, Y, T);
                READLN;
                TEXTMODE;
                WRITELN('ANOTHER WINDMILL (Y/N)?');
                GETREPLY
             UNTIL REPLY = 'N'
          END.

   We shall tackle the charging problem as a vehicle for the introduction of
the assignment statement. Modify USER:MILL9 as follows.

      - To the declaration of integer variables add two further variables
         of type INTEGER, namely

             MILLCOUNT, CHARGE

         This gives rise to the creation of two additional variables when
         the program is entered. All variables must be declared.

      - Immediately after the BEGIN of the main program, add

             MILLCOUNT := 0; CHARGE := 0;

         These statements initialize the variables.

      - Immediately after DRAWMILL(MILLSIZE, X, Y, T) add the assignment
         statements

             MILLCOUNT := MILLCOUNT + 1;
             CHARGE := CHARGE + 25*MILLSIZE;

         Each of these statements use and change the variables.

      – Immediately after the final **UNTIL** clause, add a semicolon and

```
WRITELN;
WRITELN('YOU HAVE HAD ', MILLCOUNT, ' WINDMILLS');
WRITELN('YOU WILL BE CHARGED $',
        CHARGE DIV 100, '.', CHARGE MOD 100);
WRITELN('HAVE A GOOD DAY!')
```

These statements use but do not change the variables.

EXERCISE 11B: Execute the modified program, check that it behaves sensibly.

11.2 THE ASSIGNMENT STATEMENT

    The statements which initialized, used and changed the values of the variables, namely

```
MILLCOUNT := 0
CHARGE := 0
MILLCOUNT := MILLCOUNT + 1
CHARGE := CHARGE + 25*MILLSIZE
```

are examples of the <u>assignment statement</u>, whose syntactic form is

assignment statement:

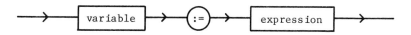

    The box "variable" will receive further consideration in chapter 12. For the present, it can safely be assumed to be synonymous with "identifier". The composite symbol

```
:=
```

is pronounced "becomes". The meaning of the assignment statement is as follows: first the expression on the right of the ":=" is evaluated; then this value is placed in the variable whose name appears to the left. Hence we can sensibly write

```
MILLCOUNT := MILLCOUNT + 1
```

as a means of adding 1 to the value already in MILLCOUNT. In terms of the scratch pad analogy,

    (a)   look at the number on the top sheet of the pad
    (b)   add 1 to it and make a mental note of the result
    (c)   tear off the top sheet
    (d)   write down the result of (b) on the sheet now on top.

Pascal insists that the variable and the expression are of either identical or compatible type. In the context of the material covered so far they must be of identical type, that is, both of type INTEGER or both of type CHAR.

EXERCISE 11C: Suppose the charging formula were "twice the cube of MILLSIZE" cents per windmill, plus a fixed overhead of 25 cents. How would the program be altered?

11.3 THE CONCEPT OF TYPE

We have used the word "type" informally to describe a property of a variable that describes the set of values it may take.

Imagine that at your front door there are two boxes. One is labelled "M" and the other "N". Now stretch your imagination and suppose each box is intelligent enough to sense what is about to be thrust past its flap, and reject or accept items at will. The box labelled "M" accepts only mail and the box labelled "N" accepts only newspapers. This is a picture of two variables: the variable labelled "M" is of type MAIL and the variable labelled "N" is of type NEWSPAPER. In Pascal we would declare them by

              VAR M : MAIL;
                  N : NEWSPAPER;

Next door, they have similarly constructed boxes but they have labelled them "POST" and "PAPERS" respectively. In Pascal they would be declared

              VAR POST : MAIL;
                  PAPERS : NEWSPAPER;

In Pascal, variables, like these boxes, are sensitive to the type of value they can hold. They can accept only values in the range specified by or implied by their type.

11.4 SUBRANGE TYPES

In Pascal, one type can be derived from another type by specifying a subrange of allowable values. Recall the windmill drawing program in USER:MILL9. The parameter THETA denoted the angle between the sails and the horizontal. Now we know that angles greater than or equal to $360°$ have an equivalent angle in the range $0°$ to $359°$. In fact, if T is any angle, then

         T   is equivalent to   T MOD 360

In other words, if we take due care, THETA can be restricted to the range 0 to 359 with no loss of generality. (In fact, if we continue to restrict ourselves to 4-sailed windmills, 0 to 89 would do, but since both 3- and

5-sailed windmills exist, we will keep all options open and stick to 0 to 359.)
To reflect this in the program USER:MILL9, make the following changes.

- Immediately after the line **USES** TURTLEGRAPHICS; add

    TYPE ANGLE = 0 .. 359;

  Make sure there are no spaces between the two dots.

- Change the heading of the procedure DRAWMILL to

    PROCEDURE DRAWMILL(SIZE, X0, Y0 : INTEGER; THETA : ANGLE);

  noting that parameters of different type are separated, not by a
  comma but by a semicolon.

Execute the program and try it with angles 30, 340, 380. Note that the program
does not accept 380. (It has, in fact, taken it into the variable named T, of
type INTEGER, but not into the variable named THETA of type 0 .. 359. The
message "S# 1, P# 1, ..." says that the trouble was spotted in Procedure 1 of
Segment 1, that is, the procedure DRAWMILL. Further information on the
interpretation of error messages of this kind will be found in appendix 5.)

    Fortunately, we have a simple remedy. In the main program, change the
call of DRAWMILL to

    DRAWMILL(MILLSIZE, X, Y, T **MOD** 360);

This ensures that the parameter THETA receives only numbers in the range
0 to 359 inclusive. Check that all is now well, even for negative angles.
Save this program as USER:MILL10.

EXERCISE 11D: Study the program USER:MILL10 and for each variable and
                parameter, assess whether it may be replaced by a variable or
                parameter of subrange type.

11.5   VARIABLES WITH NAMED VALUES

    Consider the following problem which, although it refers yet again to
windmills, typifies a very common situation in programming.

    Windmills of size 1, 2, 3 and 4 are to be drawn, but if the user of
    the program cannot tolerate any more, he or she can terminate the
    program early. The final message should be either

        "CONGRATULATIONS ON COMPLETING THE COURSE."

    or

        "YOU DID NOT COMPLETE THE COURSE. WE UNDERSTAND YOUR PROBLEM."

We will assume that the procedure GETREPLY is available, as before, and yields
only valid replies. In the context of what we have done so far, the main
program might be the following. (There is no need to create this version.)

```
BEGIN
    MILLSIZE := 1;
    REPEAT
        WRITE('DO YOU WANT THE NEXT WINDMILL OF SIZE ', MILLSIZE,
            ' (Y/N)?');
        GETREPLY;
        IF REPLY = 'Y' THEN
            BEGIN
                INITTURTLE;
                DRAWMILL(MILLSIZE, 139, 95, 45);
                READLN;
                TEXTMODE;
                MILLSIZE := MILLSIZE + 1
            END
    UNTIL (REPLY = 'N') OR (MILLSIZE > 4);
    WRITELN;
    IF REPLY = 'Y' THEN
        WRITELN('CONGRATULATIONS ON COMPLETING THE COURSE.')
    ELSE
        WRITELN('YOU DID NOT COMPLETE THE COURSE.   ',
                'WE UNDERSTAND YOUR PROBLEM.')
END.
```

This may seem satisfactory at first sight, but there are essentially three appearances of the condition

        REPLY = 'Y'

in the program, and we note that had this condition been more complex (such as (REPLY = 'Y') or (ORD(REPLY) = 25)) the complexity would have been replicated three times.

EXERCISE 11E: It is possible to remove one of the three appearances of this condition. What should be done? Does it really solve the problem?

A second unsavory aspect of this program relates to what follows the exit from the **REPEAT ... UNTIL** loop. You can come out of this loop either early or on completion of the four windmills, and the only representation of the state of affairs at the exit is the value of the two variables REPLY and MILLSIZE.

The program clearly operates in three distinct <u>states</u>, which can be identified with the state of the user or customer of this program. They are

        customer active
        customer retired early
        customer completed the course

In Pascal we can represent the state of affairs of the customer by the introduction of a new type in which the programmer enumerates all the values of that type,

        TYPE STATE = (ACTIVE, RETIRED, COMPLETED);

and, in the **VAR** section, a variable of this new <u>enumerated type</u>,

        CUSTOMER : STATE;

The reserved word **TYPE** marks the start of the <u>TYPE section</u> of a
program or block. It always precedes the **VAR** <u>section</u>. The identifier
STATE names a new type. (Recall from chapter 2 that the identifier INTEGER
names the type whose range of values is -32768 to +32767.) CUSTOMER is a
variable of this new type; namely a box into which only one of the named values

```
         ACTIVE
         RETIRED
         COMPLETED
```

may be placed. Assignment statements which can alter the value of the variable
CUSTOMER are

```
         CUSTOMER := ACTIVE
         CUSTOMER := RETIRED
         CUSTOMER := COMPLETED
```

but arithmetic is not defined over these values. For example, (ACTIVE + 1) has
no meaning, but conditions, such as

```
         CUSTOMER = COMPLETED
         CUSTOMER <> ACTIVE
```

may be used to make decisions depending on the value of the variable CUSTOMER.

A variable such as CUSTOMER used to describe the state of a process
(regardless of its type) is sometimes called a <u>state variable</u>. We can
rewrite the main program, so that CUSTOMER keeps track of the state of its
namesake. To simplify matters, we will continue to restrict windmills to those
centered at (139, 95) having their sails at an angle of 45°. Using the
program in USER:MILL9 as a basis, create the following program, execute it and
leave it in the workfile.

```
    PROGRAM MILL11;

    USES TURTLEGRAPHICS;

    TYPE STATE = (ACTIVE, RETIRED, COMPLETED);

    VAR CUSTOMER : STATE; ...;
    ...

    BEGIN (* MAIN PROGRAM *)
        MILLSIZE := 1;  CUSTOMER := ACTIVE;
        REPEAT
            WRITE('DO YOU WANT THE NEXT MILL OF SIZE ', MILLSIZE,
                ' (Y/N)?');
            GETREPLY;
            IF REPLY = 'Y' THEN
                BEGIN
                    INITTURTLE;
                    DRAWMILL(MILLSIZE, 139, 95, 45);
                    READLN;
                    TEXTMODE;
                    IF MILLSIZE = 4 THEN CUSTOMER := COMPLETED
                                    ELSE MILLSIZE := MILLSIZE + 1
                END
            ELSE
                    CUSTOMER := RETIRED
        UNTIL CUSTOMER <> ACTIVE;
```

```
                WRITELN;
                IF CUSTOMER = COMPLETED THEN
                    WRITELN('CONGRATULATIONS ON COMPLETING THE COURSE.')
                ELSE
                    WRITELN('YOU DID NOT COMPLETE THE COURSE.  ',
                            'WE UNDERSTAND YOUR PROBLEM.')
            END.
```

It should perhaps be pointed out that a similar program with

```
        TYPE STATE = 1 .. 3;
```

could be written, but that it would then contain statements such as

```
        CUSTOMER := 1
        IF CUSTOMER = 3 THEN ...
```

which, a few weeks after being written, would be rather obscure. The self-documenting property of enumerated types is of great importance in the construction of clear programs.

EXERCISE 11F: What is a more appropriate type for the variable MILLSIZE. Make
                this change to the program in the workfile and save this version
                as USER:MILL11.

It would be nice to see the value of the state variable CUSTOMER displayed, as its value changes. Unfortunately, Pascal does not allow enumerated type values to be displayed directly in a WRITE statement. However, with the aid of a procedure which uses a case statement, we can achieve the desired effect. To the program in USER:MILL11 add the procedure

```
        PROCEDURE DISPLAYSTATE(ST : STATE);

            BEGIN
                CASE ST OF
                    ACTIVE : WRITE('ACTIVE');
                    RETIRED : WRITE('RETIRED');
                    COMPLETED : WRITE('COMPLETED')
                END;
                WRITELN
            END; (* DISPLAYSTATE *)
```

and before each prompt to the user, add

```
        DISPLAYSTATE(CUSTOMER);
```

EXERCISE 11G: Execute the modified program and observe displayed values of the
                variable CUSTOMER. Save the program again as USER:MILL11.

EXERCISE 11H: In the procedure DISPLAYSTATE, the identifier ST is used in two
                places. By referring to exercise 6A, what is the syntactic form
                of its second appearance?

Statements such as DISPLAYSTATE(CUSTOMER) above, which are added to a program under development, are of great value in the process of debugging. They would normally be removed from an operational program. (See appendix 5.)

11.6 RECORDS

Windmills have been described by four values. Suppose we decide that the values are to be of the following types.

```
SIZE  : INTEGER;
X0    : INTEGER;
Y0    : INTEGER;
THETA : ANGLE;
```

We now consider how we can group 4 such values together, to form a composite object to which we can give a single name. We will modify the program in USER:MILL10 to draw a landscape with 3 windmills, a big one and a small one each of fixed specification,

	BIGMILL	SMALLMILL
SIZE	12	4
X0	210	40
Y0	120	70
THETA	20	75

and one other that completes the scene, to be determined by the user. To draw the big windmill, we would like to be able to write

        DRAWMILL(BIGMILL)

and to draw the small one,

        DRAWMILL(SMALLMILL)

and the third one,

        DRAWMILL(THIRDMILL)

The variables BIGMILL and SMALLMILL have to be thought of as constructions of elementary variables. A composite object in Pascal is said to be of structured type, and the method of structuring used here, in which items of different type are collected together, creates what are called records. To specify records of this form, develop the type section of the program in USER:MILL10 into

```
TYPE ANGLE = 0 .. 359;
     MILLSPEC = RECORD
                     SIZE  : INTEGER;
                     X0    : INTEGER;
                     Y0    : INTEGER;
                     THETA : ANGLE
                END;
```

and add to the VAR section

        BIGMILL, SMALLMILL, THIRDMILL : MILLSPEC;

MILLSPEC is a new type of object, namely a record, whose component parts, or
fields, are called SIZE, X0, Y0 and THETA. BIGMILL, SMALLMILL and
THIRDMILL are the names of three instances of such a record. To refer to a
particular field of a particular record, we write

   recordname.fieldname

where recordname and fieldname stand for the identifiers used to name the
particular record and the selected field respectively. For example, the THETA
field of the record BIGMILL would be referred to as

   BIGMILL.THETA

and the Y0 field of the record THIRDMILL would be referred to as

   THIRDMILL.Y0

To make the big windmill three times the size of the small windmill, write

   BIGMILL.SIZE := SMALLMILL.SIZE * 3

  We required that the procedure DRAWMILL take a single parameter of type
MILLSPEC, so change its heading to

   PROCEDURE DRAWMILL(MILLREC : MILLSPEC);

Note that the identifier MILLREC refers to not one value, but to a collection
of 4 values.
  Next we change the body of the procedure DRAWMILL. In the program
USER:MILL10, SIZE, X0, Y0 and THETA were formal parameters of the procedure
DRAWMILL. We have just changed them into field names of the record MILLREC.
Thus, for example,

MOVETO(X0, Y0)	becomes	MOVETO(MILLREC.X0, MILLREC.Y0)
DRAWBODY(SIZE)	becomes	DRAWBODY(MILLREC.SIZE)
TURN(THETA)	becomes	TURN(MILLREC.THETA)

The body of DRAWMILL should now be

```
BEGIN (* DRAWMILL *)
    MOVETO(MILLREC.X0, MILLREC.Y0);
    PENCOLOR(WHITE);
    DRAWBODY(MILLREC.SIZE);
    DRAWROOF(MILLREC.SIZE);
    TURN(MILLREC.THETA);
    FOR SAILNUMBER := 1 TO 4 DO
        BEGIN
            DRAWSAIL(MILLREC.SIZE);
            TURN(90)
        END;
    TURN(-MILLREC.THETA);
    PENCOLOR(NONE)
END; (* DRAWMILL *)
```

(Remember the Editor's Copy from Buffer command, and this change is easily
made.)

Finally, we have to change the main program. To establish the big windmill we add, at the beginning of the main program,

```
BIGMILL.SIZE   := 12;      BIGMILL.XO    := 210;
BIGMILL.YO     := 120;     BIGMILL.THETA := 20;
```

followed by a similar sequence to establish the small windmill. For the third windmill, defined by the user,

```
READ(MILLSIZE)      becomes    READ(THIRDMILL.SIZE)
READ(X, Y)          becomes    READ(THIRDMILL.XO, THIRDMILL.YO)
```

and READ(T) remains, but is followed by

```
THIRDMILL.THETA := T MOD 360;
```

The call for DRAWMILL is now replaced by the three calls

```
DRAWMILL(BIGMILL);
DRAWMILL(SMALLMILL);
DRAWMILL(THIRDMILL)
```

EXERCISE 11J: Make these changes, check that the program operates correctly and save it as USER:MILL12.

11.7   A SHORTHAND NOTATION

If you are concerned that the introduction of records has led to the lengthening of the names of variables, do not despair. The program in USER:MILL12 is textually longer than the version which did not use records by exactly 19 occurrences of MILLREC., BIGMILL., SMALLMILL. and THIRDMILL. We can use the with statement to shorten and clarify this program. The procedure DRAWMILL reverts to the more manageable

```
        PROCEDURE DRAWMILL(MILLREC : MILLSPEC);
        ...
        BEGIN (* DRAWMILL *)
            WITH MILLREC DO
              BEGIN
                MOVETO(X0, Y0);
                PENCOLOR(WHITE);

                DRAWBODY(SIZE);
                DRAWROOF(SIZE);
                TURN(THETA);
                FOR SAILNUMBER := 1 TO 4 DO
                    BEGIN
                        DRAWSAIL(SIZE);
                        TURN(90)
                    END;
                TURN(-THETA);

                PENCOLOR(NONE)
              END
        END; (* DRAWMILL *)
```

and the main program becomes

```
        BEGIN
            WITH BIGMILL DO
              BEGIN  SIZE := 12;  X0 := 210;  Y0 := 120;  THETA := 20  END;
            WITH SMALLMILL DO
              BEGIN  SIZE := 4;   X0 := 40;   Y0 := 70;   THETA := 75  END;
            REPEAT
                WITH THIRDMILL DO
                    BEGIN
                        WRITELN('WHAT SIZE OF WINDMILL?');
                        READ(SIZE);
                        WRITELN('CENTERED WHERE? X Y = ?');
                        READ(X0, Y0);
                        WRITELN('SAIL ANGLE?');
                        READ(T);
                        THETA := T MOD 360
                    END;
                INITTURTLE;
                DRAWMILL(BIGMILL);
                DRAWMILL(SMALLMILL);
                DRAWMILL(THIRDMILL);
                READLN;
                TEXTMODE;
                WRITELN('ANOTHER WINDMILL (Y/N)?');
                GETREPLY
            UNTIL REPLY = 'N'
        END.
```

At first sight, the with statement seems hardly a statement at all. In
its simplest form its two important parts are a record name, (such as MILLREC)
and a statement. It says that within the statement following the DO
(usually a compound statement as in all 4 cases above) fields of the record
denoted by the record name following the WITH may be referred to with the
record name (and the dot) omitted. The use of the with statement in record
processing should be regarded as normal.

Make these changes to the program in USER:MILL12, execute it, save it
again as USER:MILL12.

EXERCISE 11K: Why, in the program in USER:MILL12, is the sail angle not placed
               directly into the record THIRDMILL?

EXERCISE 11L: Can you argue that the variable MILLSIZE in the program in
USER:MILL11 is never given a value other than 1, 2, 3 or 4?

EXERCISE 11M: Can you reason that, provided that all procedure calls
terminate, the **REPEAT ... UNTIL** section of the program
in USER:MILL11 must terminate?

EXERCISE 11N: How does your argument in exercise 11M break down if

"**ELSE** MILLSIZE := MILLSIZE + 1"

became

"**ELSE** MILLSIZE := MILLSIZE + 2"?

SOLUTIONS TO THE EXERCISES

```
11A:    PROGRAM EXERCISE11A;

     USES TURTLEGRAPHICS;

     PROCEDURE COST(MILLCOUNT, CHARGE : INTEGER);

          VAR MILLSIZE, X, Y, T : INTEGER;
             REPLY : CHAR;

          PROCEDURE DRAWMILL(SIZE, X0, Y0, THETA : INTEGER); ...;
          PROCEDURE GETREPLY; ...;

          BEGIN (* COST *)
              WRITELN('WHAT SIZE OF WINDMILL?');
              READ(MILLSIZE);
              WRITELN('CENTERED WHERE? X Y = ?');
              READ(X, Y);
              WRITELN('SAIL ANGLE?');
              READ(T);
              INITTURTLE;
              DRAWMILL(MILLSIZE, X, Y, T);
              READLN;
              TEXTMODE;
              WRITELN('ANOTHER WINDMILL (Y/N)?');
              GETREPLY;
              IF REPLY = 'Y' THEN COST(MILLCOUNT + 1, CHARGE + MILLSIZE*25)
              ELSE
                  BEGIN
                      WRITELN;
                      WRITELN('YOU HAVE HAD ', MILLCOUNT + 1, ' WINDMILLS');
                      WRITELN('YOU WILL BE CHARGED $',
                              (CHARGE + MILLSIZE*25) DIV 100,
                              '.', (CHARGE + MILLSIZE*25) MOD 100);
                      WRITELN('HAVE A GOOD DAY!')
                  END
          END; (* COST *)

     BEGIN
         COST(0, 0)
     END.
```

```
11B:      PROGRAM EXERCISE11B;

          USES TURTLEGRAPHICS;

          VAR MILLSIZE, X, Y, T, MILLCOUNT, CHARGE : INTEGER;
              REPLY : CHAR;

          PROCEDURE DRAWMILL(SIZE, XO, YO, THETA : INTEGER); ...;
          PROCEDURE GETREPLY; ...;

          BEGIN
              MILLCOUNT := 0;   CHARGE := 0;
              REPEAT
                  WRITELN('WHAT SIZE OF WINDMILL?');
                  READ(MILLSIZE);
                  WRITELN('CENTERED WHERE? X Y = ?');
                  READ(X, Y);
                  WRITELN('SAIL ANGLE?');
                  READ(T);
                  INITTURTLE;
                  DRAWMILL(MILLSIZE, X, Y, T);
                  MILLCOUNT := MILLCOUNT + 1;
                  CHARGE := CHARGE + 25*MILLSIZE;
                  READLN;
                  TEXTMODE;
                  WRITELN('ANOTHER WINDMILL (Y/N)?');
                  GETREPLY
              UNTIL REPLY = 'N';

              WRITELN;
              WRITELN('YOU HAVE HAD ', MILLCOUNT, ' WINDMILLS');
              WRITELN('YOU WILL BE CHARGED $',
                        CHARGE DIV 100, '.', CHARGE MOD 100);
              WRITELN('HAVE A GOOD DAY!')
          END.
```

```
11C:      Replace  CHARGE := 0  by  CHARGE := 25  and
          replace  CHARGE := CHARGE + 25*MILLSIZE  by
                   CHARGE := CHARGE + 2*MILLSIZE*MILLSIZE*MILLSIZE  or by
                   CHARGE := CHARGE + 2*MILLSIZE*SQR(MILLSIZE)
```

11D: The main program variables MILLSIZE, X, Y and T have to be integers
        since they are used as parameters of the READ statement, and the
        programmer has no control over what will be given as input. Checking
        or transforming to another range (as we did for T) should be done after
        reading the number.

        The parameter SIZE could be of type 1 .. 8 if this restriction were
        required, and checking were done in the main program. Similarly
        XO and YO could be of type 0 .. 279 and 0 .. 191 if it were considered
        desirable to restrict the position of the axis of the sails.

        The parameter S of the procedures DRAWBODY, DRAWROOF and DRAWSAIL
        would follow the decision on the type of SIZE chosen for the procedure
        DRAWMILL.

11E: The second appearance of

          IF REPLY = 'Y' THEN

could be replaced by

          IF MILLSIZE > 4 THEN

No. Two instances of the condition (REPLY = 'Y') are still left behind, and we now have two instances of (MILLSIZE > 4).

11F: Add ONETOFOUR = 1 .. 4; after the line beginning **TYPE** and replace the declaration of MILLSIZE by MILLSIZE : ONETOFOUR;

It should be noted that we could not have used this subrange type in the first version of this program given at the beginning of this section. It used MILLSIZE > 4 as one terminating condition, and that in itself should have told us that that solution was less than satisfactory.

11G: The main program is

```
BEGIN
    MILLSIZE := 1;  CUSTOMER := ACTIVE;
    REPEAT
        DISPLAYSTATE(CUSTOMER);
        WRITE('DO YOU WANT NEXT MILL OF SIZE ',
            MILLSIZE, ' (Y/N)?');
        GETREPLY;
        IF REPLY = 'Y' THEN
            BEGIN
                INITTURTLE;
                DRAWMILL(MILLSIZE, 139, 95, 45);
                READLN;
                TEXTMODE;
                IF MILLSIZE = 4 THEN CUSTOMER := COMPLETED
                                ELSE MILLSIZE := MILLSIZE + 1
            END
        ELSE CUSTOMER := RETIRED
    UNTIL CUSTOMER <> ACTIVE;
    WRITELN;
    DISPLAYSTATE(CUSTOMER);
    IF CUSTOMER = COMPLETED THEN
        WRITELN('CONGRATULATIONS ON COMPLETING THE COURSE.')
    ELSE
        WRITELN('YOU DID NOT COMPLETE THE COURSE.  ',
            'WE UNDERSTAND YOUR PROBLEM.')
END.
```

11H: An expression.

```
11J:     PROGRAM EXERCISE11J;   (* MILL12 *)

         USES TURTLEGRAPHICS;

         TYPE ANGLE = 0 .. 359;
              MILLSPEC = RECORD
                              SIZE  : INTEGER;
                              X0    : INTEGER;
                              Y0    : INTEGER;
                              THETA : ANGLE
                         END;

         VAR MILLSIZE, X, Y, T : INTEGER;
             REPLY : CHAR;
             BIGMILL, SMALLMILL, THIRDMILL : MILLSPEC;

         PROCEDURE DRAWMILL(MILLREC : MILLSPEC); ...;
         PROCEDURE GETREPLY; ...;

         BEGIN
             BIGMILL.SIZE := 12;   BIGMILL.X0 := 210;
             BIGMILL.Y0 := 120;   BIGMILL.THETA := 20;

             SMALLMILL.SIZE := 4;   SMALLMILL.X0 := 40;
             SMALLMILL.Y0 := 70;   SMALLMILL.THETA := 75;

             REPEAT
                 WRITELN('WHAT SIZE OF WINDMILL?');
                 READ(THIRDMILL.SIZE);
                 WRITELN('CENTERED WHERE? X Y = ?');
                 READ(THIRDMILL.X0, THIRDMILL.Y0);
                 WRITELN('SAIL ANGLE?');
                 READ(T);
                 THIRDMILL.THETA := T MOD 360;

                 INITTURTLE;
                 DRAWMILL(BIGMILL);
                 DRAWMILL(SMALLMILL);
                 DRAWMILL(THIRDMILL);
                 READLN;
                 TEXTMODE;
                 WRITELN('ANOTHER WINDMILL (Y/N)?');
                 GETREPLY
             UNTIL REPLY = 'N'
         END.
```

11K: The reason is essentially that 2 distinct actions have to take place.
         First the data value has to be read into a suitable variable T and then
         the remaindering operation has to be applied before it is placed in the
         record where only a value in the range 0 to 359 will do. If we had
         written

              READ(THETA);

         then data values outside the range 0 to 359 would be faulted by the
         system (see section 11.4). If you were tempted to write

              READ(THETA MOD 360);

         go back and read section 9.3 carefully. Expressions cannot be
         parameters of a READ statement.

11L: We have to show that 1 <= MILLSIZE and MILLSIZE <= 4 throughout
       the program. There are only 2 statements which assign values to
       MILLSIZE.

                    MILLSIZE := 1   - (1)

               IF MILLSIZE = 4 **THEN** CUSTOMER := COMPLETED
                             ELSE MILLSIZE := MILLSIZE + 1   - (2)

       1 <= MILLSIZE is obviously true throughout.

       MILLSIZE <= 4 is initially true, and statement (2) is the only
       statement which can change the value of this condition (or
       <u>predicate</u> as it is sometimes called). The effect of statement (2)
       on the value of this ensures that MILLSIZE <= 4 is still true.

       In other words, 1 <= MILLSIZE and MILLSIZE <= 4 are invariant during
       the execution of the program.

11M: Consider the pair of variables {MILLSIZE, CUSTOMER}. On the first
       entry to the **REPEAT ... UNTIL** the value of this pair is
       {1, ACTIVE}. Let the body of the **REPEAT ... UNTIL** be entered with
       the value pair {m, ACTIVE}, where m ≠ 4. Then, depending on the
       value which REPLY receives, the value pair becomes either

               (i) {m, RETIRED}   or   (ii) {m+1, ACTIVE}

       In the first case, the **REPEAT ... UNTIL** terminates immediately,
       and in the second it does not. However, when m = 4 we have to consider
       the effect on the value pair {4, ACTIVE}. The body of the **REPEAT ...
       UNTIL** transforms this to either

               (i) {4, RETIRED}   or   (ii) {4, COMPLETED}

       and in either case the **REPEAT ... UNTIL** terminates.

11N: In the discussion above, replace "m+1" by "m+2". Then m takes only the
       values 1, 3, 5, ... and m is never 4. The value pair {4, ACTIVE} never
       occurs, and termination cannot be guaranteed.

CHAPTER 12
Types and Related Issues

In this chapter we consider more formally the concept of type (that is, the range of values which a variable may take) and how the programmer may introduce new types into a program in order to improve its security and its readability. These attributes are also to be found in the use of records, one of the so-called structured types. But first we return to the assignment statement, the basic mechanism for putting values into variables.

12.1   THE ASSIGNMENT STATEMENT

The assignment statement is an action statement. It causes the variable on the left-hand side to have its value changed to the value of the expression on the right. Since the right-hand side is an expression (a rule for calculating a value) the assignment statement is often used as the basis of numerical computation. However, the experience of chapters 1 to 10 should have demonstrated that a great deal of programming (including some numerical computation) can be achieved without it. We shall first deal more formally with the syntax and semantics (meaning) of the assignment statement, and then, as an example of its use in a numerical context, consider the problem of calculating the day of the week according to the Gregorian Calendar.

12.1.1   The Syntax

The syntax diagram for the assignment statement, as given in chapter 11, is

assignment statement:

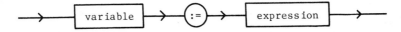

The box "variable" stands for the name of or description of a variable (sometimes called a reference to a variable). So far, most variables have been named by a single identifier, but towards the end of chapter 11 we encountered records, whose component fields were described by both record name and field name. Two examples were

      MILLREC.XO   THIRDMILL.SIZE

The composite symbol

        :=

implies the action of changing the value of the variable on the left. It is pronounced "becomes". The expression must produce one of the values which the variable on the left may take. The expression on the right-hand side can range from the very simple, such as

      BIGMILL.SIZE := 0
      CHARGE := 25
      CUSTOMER := ACTIVE

to the incoherently complex, but a good program, which should read like an essay, should aim to confine itself to expressions that reflect recognizable components in the solution of the problem.

12.1.2 The Semantics

It is common to find the variable on the left also referred to in the expression on the right. The precise meaning of the assignment statement is

- evaluate the expression on the right-hand side, and then
- put this value into the variable named on the left-hand side.

For example

      MILLNUMBER := MILLNUMBER + 1   add 1 to the value of MILLNUMBER
      I := I*2   double the value of I
      J := (J - 1) * (J + 1)   replace J by $(J^2 - 1)$.

EXERCISE 12A: In the context of the declaration **VAR** A, B, T : INTEGER; what does the sequence

          T := A;
          A := B;
          B := T

do to the variables A and B?

EXERCISE 12B: Suppose the variable C contains either the value 1 or the value 2. Write down a single assignment statement to replace the value of C by the other value. There are two ways to do this.

EXERCISE 12C: Write down a conditional statement which does the same thing as exercise 12B, and comment on the clarity of both solutions.

12.1.3 An Example: What Day of the Week is it?

Here is an interesting program which makes good use of expressions and assignment statements. It is also an example of a program which produces a useful result which, at least at first sight, appears to be difficult to obtain. The problem, however, is simple to state.

> For any correctly written date since 15 October 1582, determine which day of the week it falls on.

On 15 October 1582, the Gregorian calendar was introduced into Europe. This is the calendar we use today and which will continue to maintain calendar and solar time to within a day of each other until the year 4317 [Moyer, 1982]. The task does indeed look difficult. However, formulas exist, which are fairly easy to incorporate into a program. If we write the date as three integers

$$d \quad m \quad y$$

then, for January and February, we calculate

$$a = 365y + 31(m - 1) + d + \left[\frac{y - 1}{4} \right] - \left[\frac{3 \left[\frac{y + 99}{100} \right]}{4} \right]$$

and for March to December, we calculate

$$a = 365y + 31(m - 1) + d - \left[\frac{4m + 23}{10} \right] + \left[\frac{y}{4} \right] - \left[\frac{3 \left[\frac{y + 100}{100} \right]}{4} \right]$$

The variable "a" is an absolute day number, counting from 1 January 0000, on the assumption that the Gregorian calendar had been in existence since that date. Its actual value (724 042 on the day this chapter was written) is of very little significance. Now it is obvious that, provided that the formulas are correct,

a MOD 7

whose value is in the range 0 to 6, must relate to the day of the week. It turns out that the relationship is

a MOD 7	day of the week
0	Saturday
1	Sunday
2	Monday
3	Tuesday
4	Wednesday
5	Thursday
6	Friday

EXERCISE 12D: On which day of the week was this chapter written?

EXERCISE 12E: Any attempt to do arithmetic with results outside the range
                -32768 to 32767 in Apple Pascal produces an incorrect result.
                (The result is computed, mod 32768.) The formulas above yield
                values well outside this range. Show that, since all that we
                require is the remainder on dividing by 7, we can replace 365y
                by y in both formulas, without affecting the result.

    If you recall exercise 2L, you will see that we are now in a position to
write a procedure for displaying the day of the week. In outline, the
procedure will be

```
PROCEDURE DISPLAYDAY(D, M, Y : INTEGER);

BEGIN
    WRITE(D : 3, M : 3, Y : 5, ' IS ON A ');

    IF M <= 2 THEN (* calculate absolute day number using the
                      January February formula *)
              ELSE (* calculate absolute day number using the
                      March to December formula *)

    (* convert absolute day number (mod 7) to day of the week
       and display *)
END; (* DISPLAYDAY *)
```

Conversion of absolute day number (mod 7) to the day of the week suggests a
case statement. In full, the procedure is

```
PROCEDURE DISPLAYDAY(D, M, Y : INTEGER);

VAR ABSDAYNO : INTEGER;

BEGIN
    WRITE(D : 3, M : 3, Y : 5, ' IS ON A ');

    IF M <= 2 THEN ABSDAYNO := Y + 31*(M - 1) + D
                              + (Y - 1) DIV 4
                              - 3*((Y + 99) DIV 100) DIV 4

              ELSE ABSDAYNO := Y + 31*(M - 1) + D
                              - (4*M + 23) DIV 10 + Y DIV 4
                              - (3*(Y DIV 100 + 1)) DIV 4;

    CASE ABSDAYNO MOD 7 OF

        0: WRITE('SATURDAY');
        1: WRITE('SUNDAY');
        2: WRITE('MONDAY');
        3: WRITE('TUESDAY');
        4: WRITE('WEDNESDAY');
        5: WRITE('THURSDAY');
        6: WRITE('FRIDAY')

    END;
    WRITELN

END; (* DISPLAYDAY *)
```

A complete program with a simple user interface, to display the day of the week
for a sequence of dates, keyed in as three integers representing day, month,
year is

```
      PROGRAM GREGORY1;

      TYPE PROGSTATUS = (CARRYON, DONE);

      VAR DAYIN, MONTHIN, YEARIN : INTEGER;
          STATE : PROGSTATUS;

      PROCEDURE DISPLAYDAY(D, M, Y : INTEGER); ... END; (* DISPLAYDAY *)

      BEGIN
          STATE := CARRYON;
          REPEAT
             WRITELN('ENTER DAY  MONTH  YEAR  (0 0 0 TO STOP)');
             READ(DAYIN, MONTHIN, YEARIN);

             IF (DAYIN = 0) AND (MONTHIN = 0) AND (YEARIN = 0) THEN
                STATE := DONE
             ELSE DISPLAYDAY(DAYIN, MONTHIN, YEARIN)

          UNTIL STATE <> CARRYON
      END.
```

Now for a number of reasons this program leaves us with a less than satisfactory feeling within. Whether it is correct or not depends entirely on the correctness of the formulas quoted at the beginning of the section. It is not a particularly good example of programming as an exercise in solving problems since the heart of the program is embodied in the two formulas, which are no more, no less than an arithmetical model of the Gregorian calendar. However, for this reason, it is a good example of the use of expressions and assignment statements. Another more obvious deficiency is the omission of any check against even an obviously illegal date such as 32 13 1984. (See exercise 16G.)

EXERCISE 12F: Verify the correctness of the two formulas.

EXERCISE 12G: Write out, in full, a procedure DISPLAYDAY which does not use the variable ABSDAYNO and which has no assignment statement.

12.2   ENUMERATED TYPES

Enumerated types (sometimes called scalar types) were introduced in the previous chapter and were used in the program GREGORY1 as a means of describing the set of states a program could be in. Since the values of such types are expressed as identifiers, the program becomes clearer to the reader. Enumerated types have other applications in that they can more naturally represent certain non-numeric data.

An enumerated type has been used from the very beginning of this course. If you refer to appendix 1, section 1, you will see that the color of the pen is already defined in the turtlegraphics package by

```
      TYPE SCREENCOLOR = (NONE, WHITE, BLACK, REVERSE, RADAR, BLACK1,
                          GREEN, VIOLET, WHITE1, BLACK2, ORANGE, BLUE,
                          WHITE2);
```

Hence your programs have been able to use these values as actual parameters

without further definition. Note also in appendix 1 that the procedure
PENCOLOR has a formal parameter of type SCREENCOLOR.

   The definition of an enumerated type involves the introduction of
several identifiers which, like other identifiers, must be unique within that
block. The syntax diagram of an enumerated type definition is

enumerated type definition:

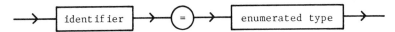

enumerated type:

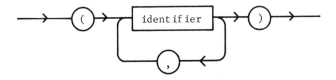

For example,

         STATE = (ACTIVE, RETIRED, COMPLETED);

introduces 4 new identifiers, one of which, STATE, is the name of the new type,
the remaining 3 being the complete set of values of that type. Another
example is

         DAYNAME = (SUNDAY, MONDAY, TUESDAY, WEDNESDAY, THURSDAY,
                    FRIDAY, SATURDAY);

which introduces 8 new identifiers. Variables of these types may be declared
thus.

         VAR D1, D2, D3 : DAYNAME;
             CUSTOMER : STATE;

Examples of the use of variables of this type are

         D1 := MONDAY
         D2 := D1
         IF D3 = THURSDAY THEN GETUPAT(07, 30)
         CUSTOMER := COMPLETED

But beware, arithmetic operations are not allowed on enumerated types, so any
attempt such as

         D3 := D1 + 1

will be faulted at compile time.

   Even though a variable, declared to be of an enumerated type, does not
have a numerical value, it does have an ordering with respect to other values
of its own type. The ordering is implied in the type definition. In our
examples,

```
SUNDAY < MONDAY < TUESDAY < ... < SATURDAY
ACTIVE < RETIRED < COMPLETED
```

This ordering may be exploited in a number of ways: in a condition,

IF D1 > WEDNESDAY **THEN** WRITE('TOO LATE.')

to control a for statement,

FOR D3 := MONDAY **TO** FRIDAY **DO** CALCULATEWAGES

and in two special functions,

```
SUCC(...)
PRED(...)
```

for obtaining the next-to-the-right value (the successor), and the next-to-the-left value (the predecessor) respectively. The sequence of statements

```
D1 := THURSDAY;
D2 := SUCC(D1);
D3 := PRED(MONDAY)
```

would give the following values to the variables.

```
D1      THURSDAY
D2      FRIDAY
D3      SUNDAY
```

Any attempt to obtain the successor of the last enumerated value or the predecessor of the first enumerated value (for example, SUCC(SATURDAY) or PRED(SUNDAY)) will cause the program to fail during execution.

EXERCISE 12H: In the context above,

        (a) what is the value (if any) of

```
SUCC(TUESDAY)          PRED(SATURDAY)
PRED(ACTIVE)           SUCC(COMPLETED)
```

        (b) for which values of D1 are each of the following conditions valid?

```
D1 = SUCC(PRED(D1))
D1 = PRED(SUCC(D1))
```

EXERCISE 12J: In the program GREGORY1 in section 12.1.3, suppose there were a variable DAYOFWEEK of type DAYNAME available to the procedure DISPLAYDAY. Modify the procedure to assign the appropriate value to this variable.

EXERCISE 12K: Suppose a program, which uses the turtlegraphics package, contains

FOR COLOR := NONE **TO** WHITE2 **DO** ...

how should the identifier COLOR be declared?

EXERCISE 12L: In the context of type definitions in this section, are
                 the values of these conditions true or false?

                     (a)   MONDAY > TUESDAY
                     (b)   BLACK > WHITE
                     (c)   ACTIVE > RETIRED

12.3 SUBRANGE TYPES

     Subrange types, introduced to describe the limited range of values of an
angle in the previous chapter, are an aid to the production of clearer and
more reliable programs. Highly efficient compilers may be able to economize
on the memory used by a variable of subrange type, but as the cost of memory
drops, this becomes of less importance. However, if a variable is known to
have only a limited range of allowable values, then by specifying it as a
subrange type, the compiler is given the opportunity to check that only
allowable values ever find their way into that variable. Unfortunately, in
Apple Pascal, the trap into which the program falls if unacceptable values are
assigned is fatal and the program cannot recover. Hence, subrange types are
more useful for ensuring the internal consistency of a program than for the
validation of input data. A further benefit of subrange variables is that,
like variables of enumerated type, they inform the human reader of a program
just what range of values such a variable may take.

     Subrange types can be constructed from the types

     -   INTEGER
     -   CHAR
     -   any already defined enumerated type.

The syntax of a subrange type definition is

subrange type definition:

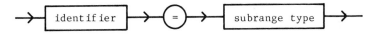

subrange type:

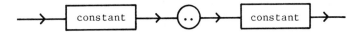

where "constant" is an integer constant, a character constant or an already
defined enumerated type value. Examples are

         ANGLE = 0 .. 359
         UPPERCASE = 'A' .. 'Z'
         WEEKDAY = MONDAY .. FRIDAY

Variables of a subrange type are declared in the usual way in the **VAR**
section, for example,

```
VAR PHI, PSI : ANGLE;
    CAP : UPPERCASE;
    WD : WEEKDAY;
```

EXERCISE 12M: Write down subrange type definitions for

        (a)   the decimal digits 0 to 9
        (b)   the integers −1, 0 and +1
        (c)   the upper-case letters I, J, K, L, M, N.

Every subrange type has an associated base type from which it is derived. For example,

Subrange type	Base type
0 .. 359	INTEGER
'A' .. 'Z'	CHAR
'0' .. '9'	CHAR
MONDAY .. FRIDAY	(SUNDAY, MONDAY, TUESDAY, WEDNESDAY, THURSDAY, FRIDAY, SATURDAY)

An assignment statement involving subrange types is syntactically valid if the base types on each side are identical. However, it is at program execution time that values are checked. Thus the following program will compile satisfactorily, but will not execute beyond the first WRITELN statement.

```
PROGRAM RANGEDEMO;

TYPE SMALLINT = 12 .. 31;
     BASETYPE = (A, B, C, D, E, F);
     SUBTYPE = B .. E;

VAR I : INTEGER;
    S : SMALLINT;
    BAS : BASETYPE;
    SUB : SUBTYPE;

BEGIN
    I := 13;    S := I;
    BAS := D;   SUB := BAS;   BAS := A;
    WRITELN('SHOULD GET HERE');
    S := 0;
    WRITELN('SHOUDN''T GET HERE');
    SUB := A;       WRITELN('OR HERE');
    SUB := BAS;     WRITELN('OR HERE')
END.
```

Formal parameters receive their initial values from the corresponding actual parameters by means of the assignment mechanism, and are therefore subject to the same constraints.

EXERCISE 12N: Given the type definitions of sections 12.2 to 12.3, determine
whether each of the following assignment statements

  (a) fails to compile
  (b) compiles but will not execute
  (c) compiles and will always execute
  (d) compiles but successful execution is value dependent.

   (i) PHI := 360
   (ii) CAP := A
   (iii) CAP := 'Z'
   (iv) Dl := WD
   (v) WD := Dl
   (vi) SUBTYPE := B
   (vii) BAS := SUB
   (viii) S := I

12.4 TYPE DEFINITIONS

The concept of type in a programming language such as Pascal is a deeply
rooted abstract property of the language. It pervades almost every discussion
of data and enjoys a status similar to that of the variable, in that types may
be introduced and named at will by the programmer. We shall see that types may
also be used anonymously.

Readers who have a knowledge of languages which do not exhibit type
strongly (such as BASIC, FORTRAN and BCPL) are well advised to be sure to
understand the concept before leaving this chapter.

12.4.1 Named Types

As seen in the previous chapter, new types may be introduced in a special
section which begins with the reserved word **TYPE**. The **TYPE** section is part
of a block, rather than part of the program, enabling types to be introduced
solely for the benefit of a procedure body. In the example of section 11.4
where the type ANGLE was used in the procedure heading, the **TYPE** section had to
be external to the procedure and, in that case, at the main program level.

In Pascal types fall into three syntactic classes: simple types,
structured types (such as records) and pointer types (chapters 19 to 24).
If we gather together the type definitions from sections 12.2 and 12.3 we can
depict a type definition as

type definition: [incomplete]

simple type:

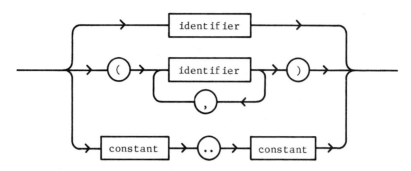

Remember that INTEGER and CHAR which are predeclared identifiers are included in the uppermost option of this diagram. The outline syntax diagram of a block can be extended.

block: [incomplete]

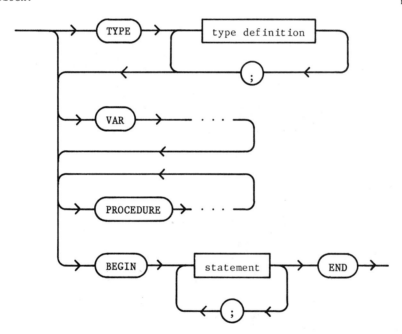

As can be seen from the diagram, the **TYPE** section may contain the definitions of several new types.

```
TYPE DAYNAME = (SUNDAY, MONDAY, TUESDAY, WEDNESDAY, THURSDAY,
               FRIDAY, SATURDAY);
     ANGLE = 0 .. 359;
     WEEKDAYNAME = MONDAY .. FRIDAY;
```

Types and Related Issues 199

12.4.2 Unnamed Programmer-defined Types

The type definition of section 12.4.1 has two purposes. It introduces a new type of object into the program, and it names the new type. It is useful (and sometimes essential) to name a new type if there are several declarations of variables of that type. It is essential to name a new type, as in the program in the file USER:MILL10, where the new type is used as a formal parameter. Pascal insists (as a concession to the process of compilation) that the declaration of the formal parameters (SIZE, X0, Y0, THETA) are made in terms of named types. Hence we may not write

        PROCEDURE DRAWMILL(SIZE, X0, Y0 : INTEGER; THETA : 0 .. 359);

However, if it is neither useful nor essential to name a type, then the new type may appear explicitly in a variable declaration. The program in the file USER:MILL11 is one which demonstrates this well. It may be written beginning

        PROGRAM MILL11;

        USES TURTLEGRAPHICS;

        VAR X, Y, T : INTEGER;
            REPLY : CHAR;
            CUSTOMER : (ACTIVE, RETIRED, COMPLETED);
            MILLSIZE : 1 .. 4;
        ...

However, remember that a declaration such as

        CUSTOMER : (ACTIVE, RETIRED, COMPLETED);

does more than may at first meet the eye! Not only does it introduce the variable whose name is CUSTOMER and which may take one of the listed values, it also introduces the names ACTIVE, RETIRED and COMPLETED into the vocabulary of this program, and any subsequent attempt to repeat their declaration in this block will be interpreted as a second attempt to introduce the names ACTIVE, RETIRED and COMPLETED. For example

        VAR CUSTOMER : (ACTIVE, RETIRED, COMPLETED);
            EMPLOYEE : (ACTIVE, RETIRED);

is faulted, since the second declaration is regarded as an attempt to re-declare the names ACTIVE and RETIRED. On the other hand,

        EMPLOYEE : ACTIVE .. RETIRED;

is quite correct for the second declaration, since it declares EMPLOYEE to be a subrange of a previously defined (but not named) type.

EXERCISE 12P: Eliminate the **TYPE** section from the program GREGORY1 in section 12.1.3. Why is it not possible to do the same to the program in USER:MILL12 in sections 11.6 and 11.7?

12.4.3 Enumerated Types Make Programs Clearer

By now, it should have become apparent that relatively little of the data which can be processed by a computer is actually of type INTEGER. The use of a variable to describe the state of a program in section 11.5 demonstrated the documentary benefit of non-numerical values in a program. As a further example, consider two chess playing programs, identical except that in one the pieces are denoted by integer representations,

1	stands for	pawn
2	stands for	rook
3	stands for	knight
4	stands for	bishop
5	stands for	queen
6	stands for	king

and in the other, by variables of the type defined by

        TYPE PIECE = (PAWN, ROOK, KNIGHT, BISHOP, QUEEN, KING);

Equivalent assignments to the variable PIECEMOVED in the two programs would be

        PIECEMOVED := 4;   where PIECEMOVED is of type INTEGER
        PIECEMOVED := BISHOP; where PIECEMOVED is of type PIECE

Clearly, the second version is more expressive, exemplifying the contribution to clarity made by enumerated types (whether named or unnamed).

12.5 THE TYPE BOOLEAN

The values false and true to which conditions evaluate are the enumerated values of a predefined type called BOOLEAN. You should not attempt to define the type BOOLEAN in your program, but its definition is as though you had written

        BOOLEAN = (FALSE, TRUE);

in the **TYPE** section. Thus FALSE and TRUE are the values of type BOOLEAN. This is the third predefined type we have encountered, the others being INTEGER and CHAR.

12.5.1 Declaration of Boolean Variables

To declare variables A, B and C to be of type BOOLEAN, write

        A, B, C : BOOLEAN;

in the **VAR** section of the program. Boolean variables may not be used as parameters of READ or WRITE statements in UCSD Pascal, although standard Pascal does admit them in a WRITE statement.

12.5.2 Assignment Statement

In order to assign a Boolean value to a Boolean variable the assignment statement is used in which both sides must be of type BOOLEAN. Three examples, in the context of the declarations above, are

```
A := TRUE
B := A
C := PIECEMOVED <> KING
```

If the left-hand side of an assignment statement is of type BOOLEAN, then the right-hand side must also be an expression of type BOOLEAN (see section 8.2).

12.5.3 A Warning

A perhaps unfortunate consequence of the enumerative definition of the type BOOLEAN is that the values represented by the constants FALSE and TRUE are ordered (see section 12.2). Thus it is not incorrect to write the following expressions where A and B are of type BOOLEAN.

```
A  = B        A <> B
A >= B        A <= B
A >  B        A <  B
```

From the ordering in the definition, FALSE < TRUE, and therefore

```
A  = B    has the value true if A and B are both true or both false
A >= B    has the value false only if A is false and B is true
A >  B    has the value true only if A is true and B is false.
```

Unbridled use of the relational operators, whilst not ambiguous, can lead to less readable programs.

EXERCISE 12Q: Produce truth tables (as in section 8.1) which express the meaning of the six relational operators when used as Boolean operators.

EXERCISE 12R: Perhaps you will be convinced of the hazards above if, for Boolean A, B and C and integer X and Y, you can decide whether

```
A = B AND C
```

is allowed or not, and if allowed, what it means. Then do the same with

```
X = Y AND C    and    A = B = C
```

12.5.4 Boolean Parameters

As an example of the use of a parameter of type BOOLEAN, recall the snowflake in exercise 5R. An interesting variant is produced if the mirror image of each segment is drawn, the turns in DRAWSEGMENT being +60, -120, +60 in place of -60, +120, -60. If we add a third parameter to DRAWFLAKE and DRAWSEGMENT, whose value is to be interpreted as true for the original snowflake and false for the introverted one, the program becomes

```
PROGRAM SNOWFLAKE;

USES TURTLEGRAPHICS;

PROCEDURE DRAWFLAKE(ORDER, SEGLENGTH : INTEGER; NORMAL : BOOLEAN);

    VAR SEGNUMBER : INTEGER;

    PROCEDURE DRAWSEGMENT(N, S : INTEGER; NORMAL : BOOLEAN);

        VAR SIGN : -1 .. +1;

        BEGIN
          IF N = 1 THEN MOVE(S)
            ELSE
              BEGIN
                IF NORMAL THEN SIGN := 1 ELSE SIGN := -1;
                DRAWSEGMENT(N - 1, S DIV 3, NORMAL); TURN(-60*SIGN);
                DRAWSEGMENT(N - 1, S DIV 3, NORMAL); TURN(120*SIGN);
                DRAWSEGMENT(N - 1, S DIV 3, NORMAL); TURN(-60*SIGN);
                DRAWSEGMENT(N - 1, S DIV 3, NORMAL)
              END
        END; (* DRAWSEGMENT *)

    BEGIN (* DRAWFLAKE *)
        IF ORDER > 0 THEN
            FOR SEGNUMBER := 1 TO 3 DO
                BEGIN
                    DRAWSEGMENT(ORDER, SEGLENGTH, NORMAL); TURN(120)
                END
    END; (* DRAWFLAKE *)

BEGIN
    INITTURTLE;
    MOVETO(59, 48);
    PENCOLOR(WHITE);
    DRAWFLAKE(4, 162, FALSE);
    READLN
END.
```

EXERCISE 12S: Change the Boolean parameter in the program above to one of type

                    (NORMAL, INTROVERTED)

12.6   RECORDS

    Pascal maintains a distinction between elementary data items on the one
hand, which it calls <u>unstructured types,</u> and composite data items on the
other, which it calls <u>structured types.</u> Unstructured types include the
predefined or <u>primitive types</u> (INTEGER, CHAR, BOOLEAN and the still to
be discussed REAL), enumerated types and subrange types. We have encountered
one structured type so far, the record, in section 11.6 where we collected 4
miscellaneous values describing a windmill into a single entity. We now
consider records in more detail.

12.6.1   Record Types and Record Variables

    Consider the example of a date, expressed as three numbers. To define a
new type called DATE which collectively represents 3 integers of a date, we
write

```
          TYPE DAYINT = 1 .. 31;
               MONTHINT = 1 .. 12;
               DATE = RECORD
                         DAY : DAYINT;
                         MONTH : MONTHINT;
                         YEAR : INTEGER
                      END;
```

or (in the spirit of section 12.4.2) a shorter version in which the types
1 .. 31 and 1 .. 12 are not named

```
          TYPE DATE = RECORD
                         DAY : 1 .. 31;
                         MONTH : 1 .. 12;
                         YEAR : INTEGER
                      END;
```

We have defined a <u>record type</u> called DATE consisting of 3 <u>fields</u>
whose names (or <u>field identifiers</u>) are DAY, MONTH and YEAR. We have not
yet created a <u>record variable</u> (or <u>record</u>) by virtue of this
definition, but rather we have said what shape and size (that is, type) such a
record would be, were one to be created.
    Records of type DATE are declared in the **VAR** section, by

          TODAY, TOMORROW, YESTERDAY, NEXTYEAR : DATE;

This example creates 4 instances of record variables, all of the same structure
as described in the definition of the type DATE.

EXERCISE 12T: Add to the record type MILLSPEC (section 11.6) a fifth field
                called MILLNAME which can hold a single letter that could be
                used to label the windmill on the screen. Write down the new
                definition of MILLSPEC.

12.6.2 Referencing a Record Field

The identifier TODAY describes a record consisting of 3 fields. A particular field is selected by appending to the record identifier a dot, called the field selector symbol, followed by the name of that field.

```
TODAY.DAY
TOMORROW.MONTH
```

These forms are known as field designators and may be used in expressions, or as variables to which values are assigned.

```
TODAY.DAY := 14;  TODAY.MONTH := 8;  TODAY.YEAR := 1983;
TOMORROW.DAY := TODAY.DAY + 1
```

EXERCISE 12U: Write down a statement that displays the single letter of exercise 12T, at the current position of the cursor.

12.6.3 Complete Records

Complete records may be handled as entities. For example, the pair of assignment statements

```
NEXTYEAR := TODAY;
NEXTYEAR.YEAR := NEXTYEAR.YEAR + 1
```

set NEXTYEAR to a date exactly one year ahead of TODAY. The first statement is valid because both sides are of the type DATE. It may be tempting, but it is nonetheless wrong, to write

```
TODAY := 1
```

in an attempt to set DAY, MONTH and YEAR fields all to the value 1, for the left-hand side is of type DATE whilst the right-hand side is of type INTEGER.

Complete records may also be specified as parameters as in the version of DRAWMILL in section 11.6. Note that the types of the actual and formal parameters must be the identical identifier, for example, MILLSPEC in the program of section 11.6.

EXERCISE 12V: At the end of the main program in section 11.7, add a statement which would replace the record SMALLMILL by THIRDMILL if THIRDMILL represented a smaller windmill than SMALLMILL.

12.6.4 Nested Record Structures

Record types may be nested but the requirement for all identifiers within a block to be distinct remains. For example, part of a personal record type may be defined by

```
TYPE DATE = RECORD
                DAY : 1 .. 31;
                MONTH : 1 .. 12;
                YEAR : INTEGER
            END;

     IDEN = RECORD
                DATEOFBIRTH : DATE;
                SEX : (FEMALE, MALE)
            END;
```

or equivalently

```
TYPE IDEN = RECORD
                DATEOFBIRTH : RECORD
                                  DAY : 1 .. 31;
                                  MONTH : 1 .. 12;
                                  YEAR : INTEGER
                              END;
                SEX : (FEMALE, MALE)
            END;
```

provided that the type DATE is not referred to elsewhere. Variables of type IDEN are declared by

```
VAR HISREC, HERREC : IDEN;
```

To refer to the month of the date of birth of the record HERREC, write

```
HERREC.DATEOFBIRTH.MONTH
```

To refer to the sex of HISREC, write

```
HISREC.SEX
```

Records may be nested to any depth (subject to the availability of space) but, for the sake of clarity, nesting should be limited to that which may be readily understood.

EXERCISE 12W: Reorganize the record MILLSPEC of exercise 12T so that it has 4 fields named

SIZE, ORIGIN, THETA, MILLNAME

and ORIGIN is itself a record of the two coordinates. How would you then reference the x-coordinate of the origin of the third mill?

12.6.5 The With Statement

We noted in section 11.7 that the with statement seemed not to be much like a statement at all. If anything it seems more like a declaration. The general form is with statement:

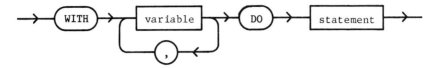

Note that "variable" is again used in the sense of section 12.1.1 as either an
identifier or a reference to the field of a record. Remembering that records
may be defined in terms of records, this means that the variable in a with
statement may refer to a complete record (as in the example of section 11.7)
or to a subrecord as in the following example.

```
        WITH HERREC.DATEOFBIRTH DO
            BEGIN
                READ(YEAR);
                YEAR := YEAR + 5;
                READ(MONTH, DAY)
            END
```

which is equivalent to

```
        READ(HERREC.DATEOFBIRTH.YEAR);
        HERREC.DATEOFBIRTH.YEAR := HERREC.DATEOFBIRTH.YEAR + 5;
        READ(HERREC.DATEOFBIRTH.MONTH, HERREC.DATEOFBIRTH.DAY)
```

    The effect of the with statement is as though the statement becomes a
block in which all the field identifiers associated with each variable named
between WITH and DO are explicitly declared. In circumstances to be
explained in chapters 19 and 20, it will be seen that the with statement can
have a dynamic quality, justifying its classification as a statement.

EXERCISE 12X: The assignment statement and the with statement complete the
                members of the class "statement", as far as this course is
                concerned. Draw the final form of the syntax diagram for
                "statement".

12.6.6 An Application of Records

    The full benefit of records will not be appreciated until towards the end
of the book, but the following application of record structures to the polygon
drawing program of exercise 3P produces a better structured program. A
polygon (not necessarily convex) drawn by that program could be expressed as
a record of the type defined by

```
        TYPE POLYTYPE = RECORD
                        ORDER : 3 .. 60;
                        EXTANGLE : 0 .. 359;
                        SIDE : 0 .. 220
                    END;
```

(No polygon of side greater than 220 can fit in the screen.) If we add to this
the coordinates of the starting vertex of the polygon (which must be on the
screen) and the way it is to be drawn, clockwise or anticlockwise, we get

```
TYPE POLYTYPE = RECORD
                    ORDER : 3 .. 60;
                    EXTANGLE : 0 .. 359;
                    SIDE : 0 .. 220;
                    COORD : RECORD
                                X : 0 .. 279;
                                Y : 0 .. 191
                            END;
                    CLOCKWISE : BOOLEAN
            END;
```

The corresponding main program is an adaptation of the solution to exercise 3P. In outline, the program is

```
PROGRAM POLYRECS;

USES TURTLEGRAPHICS;

TYPE POLYTYPE = RECORD
                    ORDER : 3 .. 60;
                    EXTANGLE : 0 .. 359;
                    SIDE : 0 .. 220;
                    COORD : RECORD
                                X : 0 .. 279;
                                Y : 0 .. 191
                            END;
                    CLOCKWISE : BOOLEAN
            END;

VAR POLYGON : POLYTYPE;

BEGIN
    WITH POLYGON DO
        BEGIN
            ORDER := 24;
            EXTANGLE := 105;
            SIDE := 80;
            WITH COORD DO
                BEGIN
                    X := 100;
                    Y := 60
                END;
            CLOCKWISE := TRUE
        END;
    INITTURTLE;
    DRAWNCPOLYGON(POLYGON);
    READLN
END.
```

The procedure DRAWNCPOLYGON can be rewritten

```
PROCEDURE DRAWNCPOLYGON(POLY : POLYTYPE);

    VAR SIDENUMBER : 1 .. 60;

    BEGIN
        WITH POLY DO
            BEGIN
                WITH COORD DO MOVETO(X, Y);
                PENCOLOR(WHITE);
                IF NOT CLOCKWISE THEN EXTANGLE := -EXTANGLE;
                FOR SIDENUMBER := 1 TO ORDER DO
                    BEGIN
                        MOVE(SIDE);
                        TURN(EXTANGLE)
                    END;
                PENCOLOR(NONE)
            END;
    END; (* OF DRAWNCPOLYGON *)
```

EXERCISE 12Y: Write a main program section incorporating a call for DRAWNCPOLYGON which draws the picture in figure 1.3.

SOLUTIONS TO THE EXERCISES

12A: The values in the variables A and B are exchanged using the temporary variable T.

12B: C := 3 - C   or   C := 2 DIV C .

12C: IF C = 1 THEN C := 2 ELSE C := 1

        or

```
CASE C OF
    1:   C := 2;
    2:   C := 1
END
```

These are undoubtedly clearer since they say what values C is expected to have. The expressions in exercise 12B do not indicate that C is only expected to have the value 1 or 2.

12D: Wednesday.

12E: The difference between 365y and y is 364y. Factorize 364.

$$364 = 2^2 * 7 * 13 = 7k \text{ (say)}$$

Therefore, replacing 365y by y makes a difference of (7 * something), and therefore makes no difference to a MOD 7.

12F: First, the common part of the formulas

$$365y + 31(m-1) + d$$

calculates the absolute day number ignoring leap years, and assuming all completed months have 31 days.

As far as dates in January and February are concerned, the second assumption is true: January has 31 days. Therefore only leap years need to be allowed for.

January and February in year y are only affected by leap years up to year (y-1). Leap years generally occur every 4th year, hence the term

$$+ \left[\frac{y - 1}{4} \right]$$

Leap years, however, do not occur on years which are multiples of 100 and not multiples of 400. For example, 1900 was not a leap year but 2000 will be. Thus for 3 out of every 4 centuries up to year (y-1) we must subtract one day. Hence

$$- \left[\frac{3 \left[\frac{y - 1}{100} \right]}{4} \right]$$

but this subtracts 1 for the years 1600, 1800, 1900, ..., and so to make it work on the years 1700, 1800, 1900, 2100, ..., we must add 100 to y, giving

$$- \left[\frac{3 \left[\frac{y + 99}{100} \right]}{4} \right]$$

For the months March to December, the year y does count for leap year adjustment. Here y is replaced by (y+1) in the leap year adjustments giving

$$+ \left[\frac{y}{4} \right] \quad - \quad \left[\frac{3 \left[\frac{y + 100}{100} \right]}{4} \right]$$

This leaves the enigmatic month adjustment, best explained by a table. It assumes a 28 day February. Note that dates in March are affected by the number of days in February, not March.

Month	Adjustment relative to 31	m	Cumulative adjustment
March	-3	3	-3
April	0	4	-3
May	-1	5	-4
June	0	6	-4
July	-1	7	-5
August	0	8	-5
September	0	9	-5
October	-1	10	-6
November	0	11	-6
December	-1	12	-7

Without delving into the theory of numbers, we can use an empirical approach to find a formula relating the cumulative adjustment to m.

The cumulative adjustment column can be thought of as an infinite column of numbers in the sequence 2 even, 3 odd, 2 even, 3 odd, ...
Thus we can see the pattern

m	Adjustment
0	-2
5	-4
10	-6
15	-8
.	.
.	.
.	.

which we can model with

$$\text{Adjustment} = -\left(\frac{2*m}{5} + 2 \right)$$

Using integer division,

$$\text{Adjustment} = -\left[\frac{2*m + 10}{5} \right]$$

is nearly correct but gets the values for m = 7, 12, 17 ..., wrong by one. A further adjustment of 0.3 inside the brackets gets the adjustment correct, namely

$$-\left[\frac{2*m + 10}{5} + \frac{3}{10} \right] = -\left[\frac{4m + 23}{10} \right]$$

12G: **PROCEDURE** DISPLAYDAY(D, M, Y : INTEGER);

```
    BEGIN
        WRITE(D : 3, M : 3, Y : 5, ' IS ON A ');

        IF M <= 2 THEN
            CASE (Y + 31*(M - 1) + D
                  + (Y - 1) DIV 4
                  - 3*((Y + 99) DIV 100) DIV 4) MOD 7 OF

            0: WRITE('SATURDAY');
            1: WRITE('SUNDAY');
            2: WRITE('MONDAY');
            3: WRITE('TUESDAY');
            4: WRITE('WEDNESDAY');
            5: WRITE('THURSDAY');
            6: WRITE('FRIDAY')

        END
```

```
            ELSE
              CASE (Y + 31*(M - 1) + D
                        - (4*M + 23) DIV 10 + Y DIV 4
                        - (3*(Y DIV 100 + 1)) DIV 4) MOD 7 OF

                  0: WRITE('SATURDAY');
                  1: WRITE('SUNDAY');
                  2: WRITE('MONDAY');
                  3: WRITE('TUESDAY');
                  4: WRITE('WEDNESDAY');
                  5: WRITE('THURSDAY');
                  6: WRITE('FRIDAY')

              END;

          WRITELN

      END; (* DISPLAYDAY *)
```

12H: (a)   WEDNESDAY   FRIDAY
               not defined   not defined

        (b)   MONDAY, TUESDAY, ..., SATURDAY
               SUNDAY, MONDAY, ..., FRIDAY

12J: Add, before or after the case statement, another case statement

```
        CASE ABSDAYNO MOD 7 OF

            0: DAYOFWEEK := SATURDAY;
            1: DAYOFWEEK := SUNDAY;
            2: DAYOFWEEK := MONDAY;
            3: DAYOFWEEK := TUESDAY;
            4: DAYOFWEEK := WEDNESDAY;
            5: DAYOFWEEK := THURSDAY;
            6: DAYOFWEEK := FRIDAY

        END;
```

12K: **VAR** COLOR : SCREENCOLOR;

12L: (a) false
        (b) true
        (c) false

12M: In the **TYPE** section

        (a) DECDIGS   = '0' .. '9'
        (b) SIGN   = -1 .. 1
        (c) IMPLICINTS = 'I' .. 'N'

        (The names given to these types are quite arbitrary.)

12N: (i) b   (ii) a   (iii) c   (iv) c
        (v) d   (vi) a   (vii) c   (viii) d

12P: The program begins

         PROGRAM GREGORY1;

         VAR DAYIN, MONTHIN, YEARIN : INTEGER;
              STATE : (CARRYON, DONE);

         . . .

         The procedure DRAWMILL has a parameter of type MILLSPEC. The type
         of this parameter, given in the procedure heading, must be expressed
         as an identifier.

12Q:

A	B	A = B	A <> B	A >= B	A <= B	A > B	A < B
false	false	true	false	true	true	false	false
false	true	false	true	false	true	false	true
true	false	false	true	true	false	true	false
true	true	true	false	true	true	false	false

12R: Syntactically A = B **AND** C is correct. A = B **AND** C might mean
         either

             (A = B) **AND** C   or   A = (B **AND** C)

         both of which make some sense. However, the order of precedence given
         in section 8.2.2 indicates that the equivalent meaning is

             A = (B **AND** C)

         The order of precedence also implies that

             X = Y **AND** C   means   X = (Y **AND** C)

         which is clearly nonsense, since Y is an integer and C a Boolean.

         Applying the left-to-right rule to the "equals" operators,

             A = B = C   means   (A = B) = C

         It is syntactically valid, but it does not mean what it seems to mean.
         It does not mean "If A, B and C are all the same, then true, otherwise
         false". However, as small compensation,

             (A = B) = C   is the same as   A = (B = C)

```
12S:     PROGRAM SNOWFLAKE;

         USES TURTLEGRAPHICS;

         TYPE FLAKEKIND = (NORMAL, INTROVERTED);

         PROCEDURE DRAWFLAKE(ORDER, SEGLENGTH : INTEGER; KIND : FLAKEKIND);

             VAR SEGNUMBER : INTEGER;

             PROCEDURE DRAWSEGMENT(N, S : INTEGER; KIND : FLAKEKIND);

                 VAR SIGN : -1 .. +1;

                 BEGIN
                   IF N = 1 THEN MOVE(S)
                     ELSE
                       BEGIN
                         IF KIND = NORMAL THEN SIGN := 1 ELSE SIGN := -1;
                         DRAWSEGMENT(N - 1, S DIV 3, KIND); TURN(-60*SIGN);
                         DRAWSEGMENT(N - 1, S DIV 3, KIND); TURN(120*SIGN);
                         DRAWSEGMENT(N - 1, S DIV 3, KIND); TURN(-60*SIGN);
                         DRAWSEGMENT(N - 1, S DIV 3, KIND)
                       END
                 END; (* DRAWSEGMENT *)

             BEGIN (* DRAWFLAKE *)
                 IF ORDER > 0 THEN
                     FOR SEGNUMBER := 1 TO 3 DO
                       BEGIN
                           DRAWSEGMENT(ORDER, SEGLENGTH, KIND); TURN(120)
                       END
             END; (* DRAWFLAKE *)

         BEGIN
             INITTURTLE;
             MOVETO(59, 48);
             PENCOLOR(WHITE);
             DRAWFLAKE(4, 162, INTROVERTED);
             READLN
         END.


12T:     MILLSPEC = RECORD
                       SIZE  : INTEGER;
                       XO    : INTEGER;
                       YO    : INTEGER;
                       THETA : ANGLE;
                       MILLNAME : 'A' .. 'Z'
                    END
```

12U: Assuming you used the field selector MILLNAME in exercise 12T, the
         statement is WRITE(MILLREC.MILLNAME)

```
12V:     IF THIRDMILL.SIZE < SMALLMILL.SIZE THEN SMALLMILL := THIRDMILL
```

```
12W:    MILLSPEC = RECORD
                        SIZE : INTEGER;
                        ORIGIN : RECORD
                                      XO : INTEGER;
                                      YO : INTEGER
                                 END;
                        THETA : ANGLE;
                        MILLNAME : 'A' .. 'Z'
                   END

        THIRDMILL.ORIGIN.XO
```

12X: statement: [incomplete]

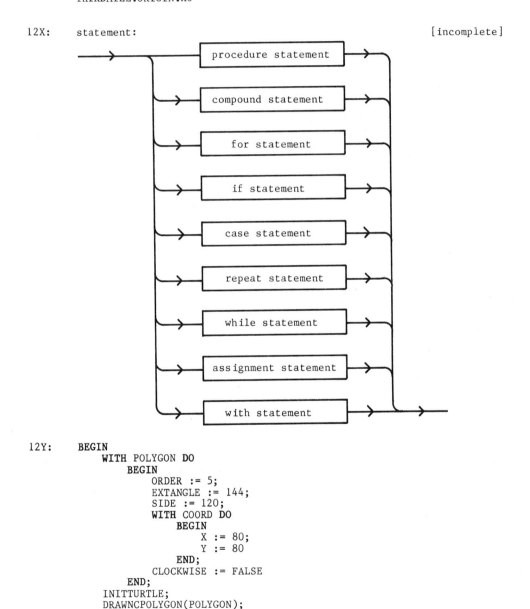

```
12Y:    BEGIN
            WITH POLYGON DO
                BEGIN
                    ORDER := 5;
                    EXTANGLE := 144;
                    SIDE := 120;
                    WITH COORD DO
                        BEGIN
                            X := 80;
                            Y := 80
                        END;
                    CLOCKWISE := FALSE
                END;
            INITTURTLE;
            DRAWNCPOLYGON(POLYGON);
            READLN
        END.
```

CHAPTER 13
Little Boxes, All the Same

The nice thing about designing a record structure is that you can bundle all sorts of different types of objects together into a new composite or structured type. Sometimes we wish to collect together a number of objects of the same type, and frequently the number of such objects is so large that the separate naming of the objects (such as we were able to do for the fields of a record) is both impracticable and undesirable. Collections of objects of the same type are called arrays, their components are called elements and individual elements are identified by the evaluation of one (or more) expressions, known as subscripts.

13.1 ARRAYS OF WINDMILLS

You can have arrays of almost anything in Pascal provided all components are of the same type. In this section we will emphasize this generality by using a number of different ways of making arrays of windmills, and it is hoped that the reader who has used an array of windmills will have no difficulty with the more commonly occurring arrays of characters and integers.

13.1.1 Windmills Selected by a Letter

We shall pick up the landscape designing program USER:MILL12 saved in chapter 11, and use an array to hold a collection of windmills, or more precisely, a collection of objects of type MILLSPEC. The program will operate in two phases.

> Phase 1: Windmills of various sizes and locations are defined by the
> user, using a dialogue similar to that in USER:MILL12.
> One by one, windmills are displayed on the screen and their
> specification placed in an array. When no more are to be
> designed, the program enters phase 2.

Phase 2: The user may select windmills from those already designed
          in phase 1 and have them added to the display on the
          screen.

The following changes should be made to the program USER:MILL12.

- To the definition of the type MILLSPEC add a fifth field,

  CAPTION : CHAR

  so that we can later identify a windmill by a single letter.

- Remove all references to BIGMILL and SMALLMILL. (There will
  be no pre-defined windmills in this program.) Change
  THIRDMILL to MILL.

- Add a prompt and a READ statement before the other prompts to
  enable the user to identify a windmill by a single letter, which
  is then placed in MILL.CAPTION.

Test the program at this stage. It should merely deal with the dialogue,
and draw windmills until you ask for no more.

Observe that the main program you have just executed has only one record
variable of the type MILLSPEC (called MILL) which is used repeatedly for each
windmill drawn. We are now going to declare a collection of variables all of
type MILLSPEC, so that each windmill specification may be kept in it for later
use. We will call the collection MILLDESIGN. To represent this in the program
add, in the **VAR** section somewhere near to the declaration of MILL,

MILLDESIGN : **ARRAY** ['A' .. 'Z'] OF MILLSPEC;

(The character [is keyed as CTRL-K and] is keyed as SHIFT-M.) This
declaration introduces the name MILLDESIGN as that of a composite object which
accommodates 26 components or elements, each being of the record type MILLSPEC.
The individual elements within MILLDESIGN are known as

MILLDESIGN['A']
MILLDESIGN['B']
...
MILLDESIGN['Z']

After the statement that draws the windmill (DRAWMILL(MILL)) add the following
statement that places the specification of the windmill just drawn into the
array MILLDESIGN:

MILLDESIGN[MILL.CAPTION] := MILL

This completes phase 1. Test the program again, being careful to identify a
windmill only with a letter. Its behavior, as far as the screen is concerned,
should be the same as before. Note carefully what the assignment statement
MILLDESIGN[MILL.CAPTION] := MILL does.

- MILL.CAPTION is the field of a record that is of type CHAR.
  Suppose you had typed W as the caption letter, then MILL.CAPTION
  has the value 'W'. Therefore, MILLDESIGN[MILL.CAPTION] is the
  element MILLDESIGN['W']. Think of the value of MILL.CAPTION as
  selecting the element MILLDESIGN['W'] from the composite object
  MILLDESIGN. For reasons that will be given in chapter 14, the
  selectors [MILL.CAPTION] and ['W'] are often called subscripts.

-   Having established the destination of the assignment, it then causes the windmill specification in the record MILL to be copied into that part of MILLDESIGN known as MILLDESIGN['W']. Recall from section 12.6.3 that complete records can be copied using the assignment statement.

EXERCISE 13A: What happens if you caption another windmill with a previously used letter?

EXERCISE 13B: Deliberately reply to the first question with a digit in place of a letter. Whereabouts in your program is the error detected?

The final set of additions comprise phase 2, and will enable you to create a landscape from the windmills saved in the array MILLDESIGN in phase 1. Add the following at the end of the main program.

```
(* PHASE 2 *)

INITTURTLE;
REPEAT
    TEXTMODE;
    WRITE('CAPTION LETTER OF NEXT WINDMILL? ');
    REPEAT READ(REPLY) UNTIL REPLY <> ' ';

    GRAFMODE;
    DRAWMILL(MILLDESIGN[REPLY]);
    (* THE STATEMENT ABOVE SELECTS THE ELEMENT OF MILLDESIGN,
        DENOTED BY THE VALUE OF THE VARIABLE REPLY. THIS ELEMENT IS A
        RECORD. THEN IT PASSES THIS RECORD AS A PARAMETER ON TO THE
        PROCEDURE DRAWMILL *)
    READLN;

    TEXTMODE;
    WRITELN('ANOTHER WINDMILL (Y/N)?');
    GETREPLY
UNTIL REPLY = 'N'
```

EXERCISE 13C: Complete this version of the program and save it as USER:MILL13.

The array MILLDESIGN has the capacity for 26 windmills, and the program accesses the array in random order illustrating one of the useful features of arrays. It also emphasizes the need to initialize all variables before they are used, including fields of records and elements of arrays. To see what happens when uninitialized elements of arrays are referred to, reply to the prompt "CAPTION LETTER OF NEXT WINDMILL?" with a letter other than one originally used to caption the windmill in phase 1. The result should be quite unpredictable. (You may have to press RESET to continue.) The next version of the program puts this right.

13.1.2 A More Robust Program

The reason for the unpredictable behavior of the program USER:MILL13 when supplied with a reference to an undefined windmill is that not all

elements of the array MILLDESIGN have been initialized (see section 11.1).
To make the program more robust, we shall, at the outset of phase 1, make every
element of the array describe a zero-sized windmill. Then in phase 2, we will
check the size of a windmill before attempting to add it to the landscape.

To initialize the size of all windmills in the array add, before the first
REPEAT of the main program in USER:MILL13,

        FOR ID := 'A' **TO** 'Z' **DO** MILLDESIGN[ID].SIZE := 0;

and declare ID to be of type CHAR. Note that this has not initialized every
field of the elements of the array MILLDESIGN. This will not be necessary
since phase 2 of the program will be disciplined to ignore zero-sized windmills
(see exercises 13D to F).

EXERCISE 13D: Write a section of program which initializes each integer field
                of the array MILLDESIGN to the value 0.

EXERCISE 13E: Modify phase 2 to ignore any attempt to draw zero-sized
                windmills. Test the program and leave it in the workfile.

EXERCISE 13F: Modify phase 1 of the program in the workfile (exercise 13E) to
                ensure that zero-sized windmills are never placed in the array
                by the dialogue section. Test the program and save it as
                USER:MILL14.

13.1.3 Windmills Selected by Number

We made random use of the array MILLDESIGN in the previous sections of
this chapter. The array accommodated up to 26 windmill specifications,
captioned 'A', 'B', ..., 'Z', and every windmill in the array had a unique
caption letter (see exercise 13A). Suppose we wish to remove this restriction,
and allow for more than 26 windmills in the array (say 100), and suppose we are
now content to have the windmills numbered (according to the sequence of their
initial design in phase 1) rather than be identified by a letter. The program
in USER:MILL14 will do as a starting point. Make the following changes.

-   The declaration of MILLDESIGN becomes

        MILLDESIGN : **ARRAY** [1 .. 100] **OF** MILLSPEC;

    and in place of ID we need an integer variable

        MILLCOUNT : 1 .. 100;

    The individual elements of MILLDESIGN will now be known as

        MILLDESIGN[1]
        MILLDESIGN[2]
        ...
        MILLDESIGN[100]

-   The statement that places the specification of the windmill just
    drawn into the array becomes

        MILLDESIGN[MILLCOUNT] := MILL

- The variable MILLCOUNT needs to be initialized to 1 outside and incremented inside the **REPEAT** ... **UNTIL** of phase 1. (Be careful where you do this.) At the end of phase 1, MILLCOUNT should say how many windmills are actually in the array.

- There is no need to initialize the array in this approach since the only part of the array used is from MILLDESIGN[1] to MILLDESIGN[MILLCOUNT].

- In phase 2, reference to the caption letter must be replaced by reference to MILLNUMBER which should be of type INTEGER. Check that MILLNUMBER is in the range 1 to MILLCOUNT inclusive.

EXERCISE 13G: Make these modifications, check the program and save it as USER:MILL15.

EXERCISE 13H: It is important during phase 1 that MILLCOUNT does not exceed 100. Why? Using a state variable, modify the program in USER:MILL15 so that this cannot happen. Why are we not so concerned about MILLCOUNT becoming less than 1?

13.2   THE CONST SECTION

Suppose, in the program USER:MILL15 in exercise 13H, you are asked to make provision for 8 rather than 100 windmills. This involves the changing of 3 appearances of the number 100 into the number 8. Admittedly this is easily done with the Editor in this case, but in another program perhaps not all occurrences of 100 would necessarily relate to the maximum number of windmills allowed. (See, for example, the program USER:MILL9 in section 11.1.) It would make sense to be able to refer to all occurrences of the maximum number of windmills permitted, by a name (identifier) which stands for the value chosen. If the limit is 100, and the name is say, MAXMILLS, we express this in the program by declaring the identifier before the **TYPE** section in what is called the **CONST** section.

```
PROGRAM MILL15;

USES TURTLEGRAPHICS;

CONST MAXMILLS = 100;

TYPE ...
```

and by utilizing MAXMILLS in the declarations

```
VAR ...
     MILLDESIGN : ARRAY [1 .. MAXMILLS] OF MILLSPEC;
     MILLNUMBER, MILLCOUNT : 1 .. MAXMILLS;
```

In the main program we can refer to MAXMILLS thus,

```
IF MILLCOUNT < MAXMILLS THEN ...
```

as though it were a variable, except that it may not, of course, have its value changed by, for example, appearing on the left-hand side of an assignment statement. Make these modifications to the program in USER:MILL15 and save it again under the same filename.

13.3   STRINGS

In sections 9.1 and 10.1.2 we considered string constants. We conclude this chapter with an application of records and arrays, that permits us to handle strings of characters in standard Pascal and without reference to the UCSD Pascal type STRING. It also shows that records can have arrays as fields (in contrast to the arrays which had records as elements in earlier sections of this chapter.) We conclude with references to the basic string facilities of standard Pascal and to UCSD Pascal strings.

13.3.1   Strings Implemented by Records

Consider the type definition

```
TYPE STRING80 = RECORD
                    LENGTH : 0 .. 80;
                    CH : ARRAY [1 .. 80] OF CHAR
                END;
```

A variable declared to be of type STRING80 will consist of the LENGTH field (call its value n, an integer in the range 0 to 80), followed by 80 characters, only the first n of which are significant. A variable of this type, whose LENGTH field is zero, represents an empty string. We shall now design a set of procedures to operate on record variables of type STRING80.

First, the procedure to display the string S at the current cursor position consists of a simple iteration in which each of the first S.LENGTH elements of the array S.CH is displayed in subscript order.

```
PROCEDURE WRITESTRING(S : STRING80);

    VAR I : 0 .. 80;

    BEGIN
        FOR I := 1 TO S.LENGTH DO WRITE(S.CH[I])
    END; (* WRITESTRING *)
```

EXERCISE 13J: What does WRITESTRING do with an empty string?

EXERCISE 13K: Write a program which sets up a variable of type STRING80 with the string HELLO, and uses the procedure WRITESTRING to display

HELLO, HELLO, HELLO,

and save it as USER:STRING1.

The reading of strings is less straightforward. It is complicated by the question of what terminates a string. Sometimes we want a space, or maybe a punctuation mark to terminate a string; on other occasions the quote symbol (′), or even the delimiter which marked the start (as in the Find and Replace operations of the Editor). In each case the procedure will be slightly different. In the first example below we will ignore leading spaces and then consider a string to consist of all non-space characters up to but excluding next space character. The procedure could be further complicated by the nature of parameters in Pascal, which we have yet to discuss in chapters 15 and 16. We will therefore write a procedure with no parameters; the string being read will be placed in a variable INSTRING : STRING80 declared at the main program level. In chapter 15 we shall improved on this. Our first attempt ignores the possibility of a string of more than 80 characters.

```
PROCEDURE READSTRING1;

    VAR CHARCOUNT : 0 .. 80;
        C : CHAR;

    BEGIN
        REPEAT READ(C) UNTIL C <> ′ ′;      (* IGNORE LEADING SPACES  *)

        CHARCOUNT := 0;                      (*                        *)
        REPEAT                               (*                        *)
            CHARCOUNT := CHARCOUNT + 1;      (*     SET UP THE ARRAY    *)
            INSTRING.CH[CHARCOUNT] := C;     (*        INSTRING.CH      *)
            READ(C)                          (*                        *)
        UNTIL C = ′ ′;                       (*                        *)

        INSTRING.LENGTH := CHARCOUNT         (* SET UP INSTRING.LENGTH *)
    END; (* READSTRING1 *)
```

In the discussion of variables in section 2.2 it was stated that a variable may be used throughout the part of the text in which it is declared. The variable INSTRING is declared at the main program level, and is therefore also available within the body of the procedure READSTRING1. From the point of view of READSTRING1, we say that INSTRING is non-local, and in contrast, CHARCOUNT and C are both local being declared within READSTRING1. (For a more complete discussion of this topic see section 15.3.)

EXERCISE 13L: Modify the procedure to continue to read but otherwise ignore any characters after the 80th. Call it READSTRING2. Add this procedure to the program in USER:STRING1 which should have all reference to HELLO removed, and be modified so that it reads a string and then displays the string it has just read. Enclose the main program in a **REPEAT ... UNTIL** FALSE loop, and key CTRL-@ to terminate the program. Save the program again as USER:STRING1.

EXERCISE 13M: Modify the procedure READSTRING2 so that it reads strings represented by the sequence

- an arbitrary number of spaces (to be ignored)
- a quote symbol (′)
- up to 80 characters excluding the quote symbol
- a quote symbol

Note that your strings may now contain spaces (but not quote symbols). Name the procedure READSTRING3 and save the program again as USER:STRING1.

EXERCISE 13N: Modify READSTRING3 so that the first non-space character
                encountered becomes the string delimiter (in place of the
                quote symbol). For example, the input sequence

                    /MARY'S WINDMILL/

                represents the string

                    MARY'S WINDMILL

                Call this procedure READSTRING4, and save the program again
                as USER:STRING1. Note the flexibility that this offers. Almost
                any string you are likely to want to input can be enclosed by a
                delimiter chosen from the set of characters not represented in
                the string.

EXERCISE 13P: Modify the procedure WRITESTRING so that it displays strings
                backwards. There is no need to save this version.

EXERCISE 13Q: Modify only the main program in USER:STRING1 so that the number
                of times 'E' occurs in INSTRING is displayed. The display might
                look like

                    /EVEREST/ HAS 3 E'S
                    /MARY'S WINDMILL/ HAS 0 E'S
                    /E/ HAS 1 E'S
                    // HAS 0 E'S

                There is no need to save this version.

EXERCISE 13R: Modify only the main program in USER:STRING1 so that it displays
                the position of the first space in the string INSTRING. For
                example the display might look like

                    /STRINGS ARE FUN/ - FIRST SPACE AT 8
                    /NO, THEY ARE NOT/ - FIRST SPACE AT 4
                    /RUBBISH/ - NO SPACES
                    // - NO SPACES

                Save this program as USER:STRING2.

        Did you notice in the exercises above that mistakes could not be corrected
by use of the ← key? This key has no mysterious powers to correct errors;
it simply delivers the control code 8 as described in section 10.3.7. In fact
it could even be used as a delimiter! We will now modify the procedure
READSTRING4 so that, provided it has not been used as a delimiter, ← may be
used to remove the last character keyed. It may be used repeatedly, but will
not remove the initial delimiter.

        First, how do we recognize ← ? From section 10.3.7, we see that if C
has been produced by the key ← then

            ORD(C) = 8

Next we have to decide what to do when ← is pressed.

        -   If there is nothing to delete (CHARCOUNT = 0) do nothing, but
        -   if there is something to delete, reduce CHARCOUNT by 1 (there
            is no need to remove the offending character from the array CH).
            Remove the character on the screen and step the cursor back by
            WRITE(CHR(8), ' ', CHR(8))

EXERCISE 13S: Make these modificationsto the program in USER:STRING2, using
               the **CONST** section to define BS as a constant with the value
               8. Name the procedure READSTRING5, test it and save the
               program again as USER:STRING2.

The procedure READSTRING5 represents a modest but acceptable approach to
the reading of general strings of characters. The improvements promised in
chapter 15 will relate to the way the procedure is called, not to its inner
working.

13.3.2 Strings in Standard Pascal

Standard Pascal provides only the most elementary form of strings. They
are essentially fixed length arrays of type CHAR. The string constant, which
was introduced in sections 9.1 and 10.1.2, is in fact a constant of this type.
For example, the string constant

        'A WINDMILL'

is a constant of the type

        PACKED ARRAY [1 .. 10] **OF** CHAR;

(You should not concern yourself over the reserved word **PACKED**. It
indicates to the compiler that the array should be represented in the memory of
the computer as economically as possible. See appendix 9.) What is important
is that if assignment or any of the six comparisons is to be performed between
a string constant and an array reference, then the array must have exactly the
same number of elements as the number of characters in the string constant.
Comparison of packed arrays of CHAR are made lexicographically according to the
character set given in section 10.3.1.

The following program illustrates these points.


```
PROGRAM STRINGDEMO;

CONST MAX = 10;

VAR DEMOSTRING : PACKED ARRAY [1 .. MAX] OF CHAR;
    I : 1 .. MAX;

BEGIN
    DEMOSTRING := 'A WINDMILL';
    FOR I := 1 TO MAX DO WRITELN(DEMOSTRING[I]);
    IF DEMOSTRING > 'A WINDSOCK' THEN
        WRITELN('WE''RE IN TROUBLE!')
END.
```


To appreciate the restrictions imposed, change MAX to something other
than 10, or change one of the string constants to something longer or shorter
than MAX. Note that the program is faulted at compile time even when there is
sufficient room in the array for the string constant. This is an example of
what is called strong typing of the language Pascal.

Our STRING80 strings are more flexible than this. However, they could
benefit from the economy of space if the field CH were declared

224   Little Boxes, All the Same

```
CH : PACKED ARRAY [1 .. 80] OF CHAR;
```

and so in future we shall use this form.

13.3.3 Strings in UCSD Pascal

In many respects, strings are more important than integers in computing. Consider, for example, the Editor. It is almost entirely concerned with strings of text; similarly the Compiler, which takes your programs in Pascal and converts them to a form more amenable to interpretation by the computer, works principally with strings.

In recognition of this, UCSD Pascal has a pre-declared type called STRING (not compatible with our STRING80 nor with PACKED ARRAY [...] OF CHAR) which, together with a number of special procedures, allows fairly comprehensive string handling. For further details of UCSD Pascal strings, see appendix 7.

SOLUTIONS TO THE EXERCISES

13A: The record of the previous windmill with that caption letter is replaced by the more recent one.

13B: In the main program

       - READ(REPLY) is OK
       - CAPTION := REPLY is OK
       - the call and execution of DRAWMILL(MILL) is OK, hence the windmill is drawn.
       - but MILLDESIGN[MILL.CAPTION] := MILL fails since the value of MILL.CAPTION is not one of the range of values allowed for the subscripts of MILLDESIGN.

13C:
```
BEGIN    (* PHASE 1 *)
  REPEAT
    WITH MILL DO
      BEGIN
        WRITELN('IDENTIFY WINDMILL BY SINGLE LETTER:');
        REPEAT READ(REPLY) UNTIL REPLY <> ' ';
        CAPTION := REPLY;
        WRITELN;
        WRITELN('WHAT SIZE OF WINDMILL?');
        READ(SIZE);
        WRITELN('CENTERED WHERE? X Y = ?');
        READ(XO, YO);
        WRITELN('SAIL ANGLE?');
        READ(T);
        THETA := T MOD 360
      END;
    INITTURTLE;
    DRAWMILL(MILL);  READLN;  TEXTMODE;
    MILLDESIGN[MILL.CAPTION] := MILL;
    WRITELN('ANOTHER WINDMILL (Y/N)?');   GETREPLY
  UNTIL REPLY = 'N';
```

```
              (* PHASE 2 *)

              INITTURTLE;
              REPEAT ... UNTIL REPLY = 'N'
         END.


13D:     FOR ID := 'A' TO 'Z' DO
              WITH MILLDESIGN[ID] DO
                   BEGIN
                       SIZE := 0;
                       X0 := 0;
                       Y0 := 0;
                       THETA := 0
                   END


13E:     In phase 2 replace

                   DRAWMILL(MILLDESIGN[REPLY])

         by

                   IF MILLDESIGN[REPLY].SIZE <> 0 THEN
                       DRAWMILL(MILLDESIGN[REPLY])


13F:     In phase 1 replace

                   MILLDESIGN[MILL.CAPTION] := MILL

         by

                   IF MILL.SIZE <> 0 THEN MILLDESIGN[MILL.CAPTION] := MILL


13G:     BEGIN   (* PHASE 1 *)
              MILLCOUNT := 1;
              REPEAT
                WITH MILL DO
                  BEGIN ... END;

                INITTURTLE;
                DRAWMILL(MILL);  READLN;  TEXTMODE;
                MILLDESIGN[MILLCOUNT] := MILL;
                MILLCOUNT := MILLCOUNT + 1;
                WRITELN('ANOTHER WINDMILL (Y/N)?');  GETREPLY
              UNTIL REPLY = 'N';
              MILLCOUNT := MILLCOUNT - 1;

              (* PHASE 2 *)

              REPEAT
                INITTURTLE;
                WRITE('NUMBER OF NEXT WINDMILL? ');
                READLN(MILLNUMBER);
                IF (MILLNUMBER >= 1) AND (MILLNUMBER <= MILLCOUNT) THEN
                    BEGIN
                        GRAFMODE;
                        DRAWMILL(MILLDESIGN[MILLNUMBER]);  READLN;  TEXTMODE
                    END;
                WRITELN('ANOTHER WINDMILL (Y/N)?');  GETREPLY
              UNTIL REPLY = 'N'

         END.
```

13H: Because MILLCOUNT is of type 1 .. 100.

```
VAR STATE : (ACCEPTING, FINISHED, FULLUP);
  .
  .
BEGIN     (* PHASE 1 *)
  STATE := ACCEPTING;
  MILLCOUNT := 1;
  REPEAT
    WITH MILL DO
      BEGIN ... END;

    INITTURTLE;
    DRAWMILL(MILL);  READLN;  TEXTMODE;
    MILLDESIGN[MILLCOUNT] := MILL;
    IF MILLCOUNT < 100 THEN
        BEGIN
            MILLCOUNT := MILLCOUNT + 1;
            WRITELN('ANOTHER WINDMILL (Y/N)?');  GETREPLY;
            IF REPLY = 'N' THEN STATE := FINISHED
        END
    ELSE
        STATE := FULLUP
  UNTIL STATE <> ACCEPTING;
  IF STATE <> FULLUP THEN MILLCOUNT := MILLCOUNT - 1;
```

Either MILLCOUNT is undefined or (MILLCOUNT $\geq$ 1) is invariant
throughout the section of program above. To show this, all we have to
do is show that, on exit from the repeat statement, MILLCOUNT is
greater than 1. On entry to the repeat statement MILLCOUNT = 1, and
each time before the UNTIL is reached either MILLCOUNT $\geq$ 100
or MILLCOUNT has been incremented by 1.

13J: FOR I := 1 TO 0 DO ... implies that there will be no execution of
the WRITE statement.

13K: PROGRAM EXERCISE13K;

```
TYPE STRING80 = RECORD
                    LENGTH : 0 .. 80;
                    CH : ARRAY [1 .. 80] OF CHAR
                END;

VAR MESSAGE : STRING80;

PROCEDURE WRITESTRING(S : STRING80); ...;

BEGIN     (* MAIN PROGRAM *)
    WITH MESSAGE DO
        BEGIN
            CH[1] := 'H';
            CH[2] := 'E';
            CH[3] := 'L';
            CH[4] := 'L';
            CH[5] := 'O';
            CH[6] := ',';
            CH[7] := ' ';
            LENGTH := 7
        END;
    WRITESTRING(MESSAGE);  WRITESTRING(MESSAGE);  WRITESTRING(MESSAGE)
END.
```

```
13L:    PROGRAM EXERCISE13L;

        TYPE STRING80 = RECORD
                            LENGTH : 0 .. 80;
                            CH : ARRAY [1 .. 80] OF CHAR
                        END;

        VAR INSTRING : STRING80;

        PROCEDURE WRITESTRING(S : STRING80); ...;

        PROCEDURE READSTRING2;

            VAR CHARCOUNT : 0 .. 80;
                C : CHAR;

            BEGIN
                REPEAT READ(C) UNTIL C <> ' ';
                CHARCOUNT := 0;
                REPEAT
                    IF CHARCOUNT < 80 THEN
                        BEGIN
                            CHARCOUNT := CHARCOUNT + 1;
                            INSTRING.CH[CHARCOUNT] := C
                        END;
                    READ(C)
                UNTIL C = ' ';
                INSTRING.LENGTH := CHARCOUNT
            END; (* READSTRING2 *)

        BEGIN
            REPEAT
                READSTRING2;
                WRITELN;
                WRITESTRING(INSTRING);
                WRITELN
            UNTIL FALSE
        END.


13M:    PROCEDURE READSTRING3;

            VAR CHARCOUNT : 0 .. 80;
                C : CHAR;

            BEGIN
                REPEAT READ(C) UNTIL C <> ' ';
                CHARCOUNT := 0;
                IF C <> '''' THEN WRITE('NOT A STRING')
                    ELSE
                      BEGIN
                        READ(C);
                        WHILE C <> '''' DO
                          BEGIN
                            IF CHARCOUNT < 80 THEN
                              BEGIN
                                CHARCOUNT := CHARCOUNT + 1;
                                INSTRING.CH[CHARCOUNT] := C
                              END;
                            READ(C)
                          END
                      END;
                INSTRING.LENGTH := CHARCOUNT
            END; (* READSTRING3 *)
```

```
13N:    PROCEDURE READSTRING4;

            VAR CHARCOUNT : 0 .. 80;
                C, DELIMITER : CHAR;

            BEGIN
                REPEAT READ(DELIMITER) UNTIL DELIMITER <> ' ';
                CHARCOUNT := 0;
                READ(C);
                WHILE C <> DELIMITER DO
                    BEGIN
                        IF CHARCOUNT < 80 THEN
                            BEGIN
                                CHARCOUNT := CHARCOUNT + 1;
                                INSTRING.CH[CHARCOUNT] := C
                            END;
                        READ(C)
                    END;
                INSTRING.LENGTH := CHARCOUNT
            END; (* READSTRING4 *)


13P:    PROCEDURE WRITEBACK(S : STRING80);

            VAR I : 0 .. 80;

            BEGIN
                FOR I := S.LENGTH DOWNTO 1 DO WRITE(S.CH[I])
            END; (* WRITEBACK *)


13Q:    PROGRAM EXERCISE13Q;

        TYPE STRING80 = RECORD
                            LENGTH : 0 .. 80;
                            CH : ARRAY [1 .. 80] OF CHAR
                        END;

        VAR INSTRING : STRING80;
            CHCOUNT, ECOUNT : 0 .. 80;
          .
          .
        BEGIN
            REPEAT
                READSTRING4;
                ECOUNT := 0;
                FOR CHCOUNT := 1 TO INSTRING.LENGTH DO
                    IF INSTRING.CH[CHCOUNT] = 'E' THEN ECOUNT := ECOUNT + 1;
                WRITELN(' HAS ', ECOUNT, ' E''S')
            UNTIL FALSE
        END.
```

```
13R:    PROGRAM EXERCISE13R;

        TYPE STRING80 = RECORD
                          LENGTH : 0 .. 80;
                          CH : ARRAY [1 .. 80] OF CHAR
                        END;

        VAR INSTRING : STRING80;
            STATE : (STILLLOOKING, FOUNDONE, ATEND);
            CHCOUNT : 0 .. 80;
        ...
        BEGIN
            REPEAT
                READSTRING4;
                WITH INSTRING DO
                  BEGIN
                    IF LENGTH = 0 THEN STATE := ATEND
                                  ELSE STATE := STILLLOOKING;
                    CHCOUNT := 1;
                    WHILE STATE = STILLLOOKING DO
                        IF CH[CHCOUNT] = ' ' THEN STATE := FOUNDONE
                        ELSE IF CHCOUNT < LENGTH THEN CHCOUNT := CHCOUNT + 1
                                                 ELSE STATE := ATEND
                  END;
                IF STATE = ATEND THEN WRITELN(' - NO SPACES')
                   ELSE WRITELN(' - FIRST SPACE AT ', CHCOUNT)
            UNTIL FALSE
        END.


13S:    PROCEDURE READSTRING5;

        CONST BS = 8;        (* FOR BOTH KEYBOARD AND SCREEN *)

        VAR CHARCOUNT : 0 .. 80;
            C, DELIMITER : CHAR;

        BEGIN
            REPEAT READ(DELIMITER) UNTIL DELIMITER <> ' ';
            CHARCOUNT := 0;
            READ(C);
            WHILE C <> DELIMITER DO
              BEGIN
                IF CHARCOUNT < 80 THEN
                  BEGIN                  (* NECESSARY - SEE SECTION 6.3 *)
                    IF ORD(C) = BS THEN
                      BEGIN
                        IF CHARCOUNT > 0 THEN
                          BEGIN
                            CHARCOUNT := CHARCOUNT - 1;
                            WRITE(CHR(BS), ' ', CHR(BS))
                          END
                      END
                    ELSE
                      BEGIN
                        CHARCOUNT := CHARCOUNT + 1;
                        INSTRING.CH[CHARCOUNT] := C
                      END
                  END;
                READ(C)
              END;
            INSTRING.LENGTH := CHARCOUNT
        END; (* READSTRING5 *)
```

CHAPTER 14
Arrays and Sets

The array, introduced in the previous chapter, was seen as a homogeneous collection of objects called <u>elements</u>. Whilst each element was of the same type, their values were generally different. Selection of a particular element from the collection was by means of the value of an expression, known as a <u>subscript</u>. Before we look more formally at the array, we would do well to compare and contrast the array and the record, the two collective structured data types encountered so far.

	Array	Record
Whole collection named by	an identifier	an identifier
Nature of collection	homogeneous	heterogeneous
Component	element	field
Component type	any	any
Component selection	value of subscript	name of field

EXERCISE 14A: In the previous chapter, what was the name of the array of records and what was the name of the type which was a record of an array?

14.1 A SIMPLE APPLICATION OF AN ARRAY

The arrays of the previous chapter represented fairly natural collections of homogeneous objects in the real world, namely windmills and characters.

Another aspect of the array is that it removes the need to invent different identifiers for every variable used in a program. The following program, for reading 10 numbers from the input and displaying them in the reverse order, does not use an array but it does require many differently named variables.

```
PROGRAM REVERSE1;

VAR FIRST, SECOND, THIRD, FOURTH, FIFTH,
    SIXTH, SEVENTH, EIGHTH, NINTH, TENTH : INTEGER;

BEGIN
    READ(FIRST, SECOND, THIRD, FOURTH, FIFTH,
        SIXTH, SEVENTH, EIGHTH, NINTH, TENTH);
    WRITELN(TENTH : 8, NINTH : 8, EIGHTH : 8, SEVENTH : 8, SIXTH : 8,
            FIFTH : 8, FOURTH : 8, THIRD : 8, SECOND : 8, FIRST : 8)
END.
```

The program becomes unacceptably monotonous if, instead of reversing 10 numbers, we have to reverse 100 numbers!

EXERCISE 14B: (May be omitted at first reading.)

Write a program to solve this problem, using only the facilities covered in chapters 1 to 12, which eliminates the monotony of the program above.

The numbers which have to be reversed constitute a homogeneous collection, since they are all of type INTEGER. If we declare an array named NUM replacing the 10 separately named variables, and a variable I with which to select elements of the array, we can write the program

```
PROGRAM REVERSE2;

VAR I : 1 .. 10;
    NUM : ARRAY [1 .. 10] OF INTEGER;

BEGIN
    FOR I := 1 TO 10 DO READ(NUM[I]);
    FOR I := 10 DOWNTO 1 DO WRITE(NUM[I] : 8);
    WRITELN
END.
```

In detail, the declaration of the array in the third line is saying

NUM	is the name of the collection of variables
:	is the usual separator between an identifier and its type
ARRAY	says we are defining a homogeneous collection
1 .. 10	describes the subrange in which subscripts must lie, 1 being the smallest and 10 the largest.
[ ]	are brackets enclosing the subscript subrange
OF	is another separator
INTEGER	says what type of variable each element of the collection is
;	terminates the declaration.

The latter part of the declaration of NUM, namely

ARRAY [1 .. 10] OF INTEGER

is, in effect, a new unnamed type in the spirit of section 12.4.2. It is
distinguished from

             the primitive types INTEGER, BOOLEAN, CHAR
             enumerated types
             subrange types

(known as unstructured types) by being called a structured type.
The other references to NUM in the main program are in the statements

             READ(NUM[I])
             WRITE(NUM[I] : 8)

In the READ statement, the current value of I selects which element of the
array is to receive the next number keyed in. In the WRITE statement, the
current value of I selects the element whose value is to be displayed.

EXERCISE 14C: Modify the program REVERSE2 to read 100 numbers and display them
                in reverse order.

     We can, of course, name the type **ARRAY** [1 .. 10] **OF** INTEGER in the
TYPE section as in section 12.4.1, and so the following program is equivalent
to REVERSE2 above.

             PROGRAM REVERSE3;

             TYPE A10 = **ARRAY** [1 .. 10] **OF** INTEGER;

             VAR I : 1 .. 10;
                 NUM : A10;

             BEGIN
                 FOR I := 1 **TO** 10 **DO** READ (NUM[I]);
                 FOR I := 10 **DOWNTO** 1 **DO** WRITE(NUM[I] : 8);
                 WRITELN
             END.

EXERCISE 14D: How might the program saved as USER:MILL13 in section 13.1.1 be
                modified so that the array type is named?

EXERCISE 14E: How should the program REVERSE3 be modified to make use of a
                constant which says how many numbers are to be reversed?

14.2 **ARRAYS IN MATHEMATICS**

     If you were to explain the action of the tedious program (REVERSE1) to a
mathematician he or she would probably think of it as

             read x_i for i := 1, 2, ..., 10
             display x_i for i := 10, 9, ..., 1

The symbol x would be regarded as the name of not one variable, but 10 variables, probably called a <u>vector</u>. The variable i, used to refer to particular elements of the vector, is called a <u>subscript</u> because of its physical position below the main line of text. Our mathematician would also be familiar with integer constants used as subscripts, as in x_1, x_2, ..., x_{10}. Apart from these minor notational differences, the concepts are those of the array in Pascal.

In a programming language, we have to write statements as physically linear strings of characters, and hence a different notation is adopted. In Pascal (as in most programming languages) we write

X[i]	for	x_i
X[1], X[2], ..., X[10]	for	x_1, x_2, ..., x_{10}

14.3 <u>FORMAL DESCRIPTION OF A SIMPLE ARRAY DECLARATION</u>

Arrays in Pascal have been described as homogeneous collections of variables. Whilst this is true, it tends to obscure the fact that the collection itself is a variable. In fact it is a variable of an array type, and as we saw in section 14.1 that type may be named or unnamed.

To introduce an array type into a program or block, its definition must appear in the **TYPE** section. The general form of the definition of an array type is

array type definition:

array type: [incomplete]

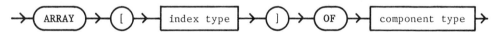

The <u>index type</u>, values of which are used to select a particular element of the array, must be both enumerable and reasonably bounded. This places a restriction on the index type, namely that it can only be one of

- an enumerated type
- a subrange type
- CHAR
- BOOLEAN

Observe that the type INTEGER is not included, for if it were, it would imply an array whose subscripts run from −32768 to 32767. For the Apple with even 64K bytes of memory, that is just too much! Subranges of integers are, of course, allowed.

In contrast, there is almost no restriction on the <u>component type</u>, that is, the kind of object that can be collected into an array. In terms of what has been covered so far, the component type can be

```
      -  INTEGER
      -  enumerated type
      -  subrange type
      -  BOOLEAN
      -  CHAR
      -  record
      -  another array type (see section 14.5)
```

    The following examples of array declarations illustrate the variety of
structures which can be built using arrays in Pascal. They assume the
following type definitions.

```
    TYPE MILLSPEC = RECORD ... END;
         WAGES    = RECORD ... END;
         SUIT     = (CLUBS, DIAMONDS, HEARTS, SPADES);
         DAYNAME  = (SUNDAY, MONDAY, TUESDAY, WEDNESDAY,
                     THURSDAY, FRIDAY, SATURDAY);
         WEEKDAY  = MONDAY .. FRIDAY;
```

Examples of declarations written in the **VAR** section are

```
      -  MILLDESIGN : ARRAY ['A' .. 'Z'] OF MILLSPEC;
```

           26 records as described in section 13.1

```
      -  CARD : ARRAY [1 .. 52] OF SUIT;
```

           52 variables each of type SUIT, referred to as CARD[1],
           CARD[2], ..., CARD[52]

```
      -  TRICKS : ARRAY [SUIT] OF 0 .. 13;
```

           4 variables each of type 0 .. 13, referred to as
           TRICKS[CLUBS], TRICKS[DIAMONDS], TRICKS[HEARTS],
           TRICKS[SPADES]

```
      -  OVERTIME : ARRAY [DAYNAME] OF WAGES;
```

           7 records referred to as OVERTIME[SUNDAY],
           OVERTIME[MONDAY], ..., OVERTIME[SATURDAY]

```
      -  PAY : ARRAY [WEEKDAY] OF WAGES;
```

           5 records referred to as PAY[MONDAY], PAY[TUESDAY], ...,
           PAY[FRIDAY]

```
      -  COUNT : ARRAY [BOOLEAN] OF INTEGER;
```

           2 integer variables referred to as COUNT[FALSE],
           COUNT[TRUE]

```
      -  BIT : ARRAY [0 .. 15] OF BOOLEAN;
```

           16 Boolean variables referred to as BIT[0], BIT[1], ...,
           BIT[15]

```
      -  HISTOGRAM : ARRAY [CHAR] OF INTEGER;
```

           256 integer variables referred to as HISTOGRAM[CHR(0)],
           HISTOGRAM[CHR(1)], ..., HISTOGRAM[CHR(255)]

EXERCISE 14F: Declare an array of integers called A, with subscripts in the
               range 1 to 20.

EXERCISE 14G: Declare an array of DAYNAME called EARLYCLOSING with subscripts
               in the range 1 to 100.

EXERCISE 14H: Declare an array of decimal digits called LONGINT with
                subscripts in the range 0 to 999.

EXERCISE 14J: Declare an array of integers, called GOALS denoting the number
                of goals scored for and against a team.

14.4   FORMAL DESCRIPTION OF AN ARRAY REFERENCE

The term array reference describes any appearance of a subscripted
variable in a statement. In its simplest form, the syntax diagram is

array reference: [incomplete]

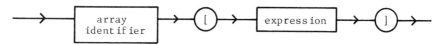

An array reference (sometimes called a subscripted variable) may be
used in two different contexts.

-   As an operand in an expression (see section 2.5) where it is the
    value of the element that is used. Note that this creates a
    mutually recursive definition, and allows subscripts to be
    subscripted, as for example

        X[K[I]]   or in mathematics, X_{k_i}

    Other examples of the use of subscripted variables in expressions
    are

        A[I] * B[I]   D[2*(J - K)]
        X[I + 1]   Y[X[M] + 2]
        MILLDESIGN[MILL.CAPTION]

-   As the left-hand side variable in an assignment statement, where
    it is used as a reference to a particular element, as in

        X[I] := X[I] * W[I]   INSTRING.CH[CHARCOUNT] := C

    The second and third programs for reversing numbers contained an
    implicit assignment to a subscripted variable in the statement

        READ(NUM[i])

An expression used as a subscript must yield a value within the range of
values denoted by the index type of the array declaration. Failure to comply
with this causes the program execution to terminate.

EXERCISE 14K: (a) Declare an array which can hold the value of each of the
                     following British currency notes and coins: £20, £10, £5,
                     £1, 50p, 20p, 10p, 5p, 2p and 1p; and write a program to
                     put the appropriate values (in pence) into that array in
                     descending order of monetary value. (Warning: this is not
                     a very exciting program.)

(b) Write a procedure DISPLAYCHANGE for displaying the best way
     of giving change from a financial transaction specified in
     pence. For example, the procedure statement

     DISPLAYCHANGE(51, 500)

     should cause to be displayed the change given when £5 is
     given for goods costing 51p, namely

```
     0 of 2000p
     0 of 1000p
     0 of  500p
     4 of  100p
     0 of   50p
     2 of   20p
     0 of   10p
     1 of    5p
     2 of    2p
     0 of    1p
```

     or, better still,

```
     4 of  100p
     2 of   20p
     1 of    5p
     2 of    2p
```

     The procedure should make reference to the array declared
     at (a) in the main program.

(c) Develop the program and procedure above into a program
     which asks the user for the cost and amount given, and
     displays the change, as above.

EXERCISE 14L: Make improvements to the program to check that enough money has
               been tendered, and to display the note and coin values more
               conventionally.

14.5 ARRAYS OF ARRAYS

    The 1981 British Rail timetable showed the following train schedule from
London to Colchester.

London Liverpool Street	07 00
Ilford	–
Romford	–
Shenfield	07 22
Ingatestone	07 26
Chelmsford	07 34
Hatfield Peveral	07 41
Witham	07 46
Kelvedon	07 51
Marks Tey	07 56
Colchester	08 04

Suppose we already have in the **TYPE** section

```
TIME = RECORD
            STOPS : BOOLEAN;
            HOURS : 0 .. 23;
            MINS  : 0 .. 59
       END;
```

then we could construct a type to represent a schedule such as this by

```
SCHEDULE = ARRAY [1 .. 11] OF TIME;
```

EXERCISE 14M: Declare an array called EARLYTRAIN of type SCHEDULE, and write
                down statements which assign values to certain fields to
                indicate that this train departs from Marks Tey at 07 56, and
                that it does not stop at Romford.

EXERCISE 14N: Suggest an alternative to the index type 1 .. 11, and repeat
                exercise 14M with it.

There are in fact 62 trains each weekday from London to Colchester of
which the one quoted above is the fifth of the day. To represent the complete
timetable for this service, we would naturally write in the **TYPE** section,
after the definition of SCHEDULE,

```
TIMETABLE = ARRAY [1 .. 62] OF SCHEDULE;
```

which is quite correct in Pascal. However to see what it means, we may
substitute for the component type SCHEDULE, and get (still correctly)

```
TIMETABLE = ARRAY [1 .. 62] OF ARRAY [1 .. 11] OF TIME;
```

Suppose we have a variable declared by

```
VAR LONCOL81 : TIMETABLE;
```

and suppose further, that some kind person has filled this array with the
entire timetable, how would we then refer, say, to the departure time of the
fifth train from Marks Tey? From the first type definition given for the
timetable above, this particular train schedule is

```
LONCOL81[5]
```

But this is itself an array of elements of type TIME. Marks Tey is the tenth
station down the line, so the time of departure from Marks Tey is referred to
as

```
LONCOL81[5][10]
```

But this is a record, and the departure is given as 2 fields, one for hours and
another for minutes. The departure time is therefore referred to as

```
LONCOL81[5][10].HOURS
LONCOL81[5][10].MINS
```

EXERCISE 14P: Write down a statement which displays whether or not the
                30th train of the day stops at Ingatestone.

The discussion above shows how elegantly the concept of a two-dimensional
array is derived from the freedom to build arrays of almost anything. It
extends to arrays of any number of dimensions.

EXERCISE 14Q: Given the type (WEEKDAYS, SATURDAYS, SUNDAYS) declare a
                variable that represents the complete timetable of train
                journeys from London to Colchester, and write down references to
                the time of departure from London of the first train on a
                Sunday.

The notation above does use rather a lot of square brackets, and is not
consistent with other programming languages such as FORTRAN, COBOL and BASIC.
An abbreviated form of type definition and reference may be used for arrays
of more than one dimension. Wherever

        ARRAY [INDEXTYPE1] **OF ARRAY** [INDEXTYPE2] **OF** ...

occurs it may be replaced by

        ARRAY [INDEXTYPE1, INDEXTYPE2] **OF** ...

Thus the definition of the type TIMETABLE may be shortened to

        TIMETABLE = **ARRAY** [1 .. 62, 1 .. 11] **OF** TIME;

and the references to the departure time of the fifth train from Marks Tey may
be written

        LONCOL81[5, 10].HOURS
        LONCOL81[5, 10].MINS

It should be emphasized that these are merely alternative ways of writing type
definitions and array references. The programs they produce are identical and
either form of reference may be used with either form of definition. Most
books use the latter forms, and we shall henceforth do likewise.

EXERCISE 14R: (a) How should the syntax diagram for array reference in
                     section 14.4 be modified to account for array references
                     such as LONCOL81[5][10]?

                (b) How should the syntax diagram for array type (section 14.3)
                     and array reference of (a) above be modified so that they
                     describe the abbreviated forms for arrays of multiple
                     dimensions?

14.6 AN EXAMPLE OF THE USE OF ARRAYS

As an example of array processing, we shall refer to the array of the previous section and consider the problem of finding the fastest scheduled train between pairs of stations on the London to Colchester line. We shall again make the assumption that the array representing the timetable has been given appropriate values. (In practice, a large volume of data such as this would be held externally on a file and at the beginning of the program the array would be initialized from this file. Files will not be covered until chapter 22.)

We assume (see exercise 14N) that there is a type defined by

```
STATION = (LONDONLIVERPOOLSTREET,
           ILFORD,
           ROMFORD,
           SHENFIELD,
           INGATESTONE,
           CHELMSFORD,
           HATFIELDPEVERAL,
           WITHAM,
           KELVEDON,
           MARKSTEY,
           COLCHESTER);
```

so that we can define the type TIMETABLE as

```
TIMETABLE = ARRAY [1 .. 62, STATION] OF TIME;
```

Our task is to write a procedure to display the fastest schedule as

FASTEST TRAIN FROM CHELMSFORD TO COLCHESTER TAKES 21 MINUTES.

```
CHELMSFORD           09 02
HATFIELD PEVERAL       -
WITHAM                 -
KELVEDON               -
MARKS TEY              -
COLCHESTER           09 23
```

We further assume that a procedure named WRITESTATION has been provided (see section 11.5).

The problem of finding the fastest train is an example of a very common operation in programming. It sometimes causes difficulty with those new to programming, because the human brain has become so well adapted to searching for the biggest or the smallest, that it is often done entirely in the subconscious. The process has to be broken down into elementary stages before we can express it in Pascal. Essentially the search goes thus:

- Regard the first as the best-time-so-far.
- Examine all from the second to the last, and for each of these, if a faster one is found it becomes the new best-time-so-far.
- At the end, the best-time-so-far is the one we seek.

It is very tempting to try to simplify this process by the trick of initializing the best time so far to some very large number (which, it is asserted, cannot possibly occur in the comparison) in place of the first step above. Then the remainder of the process can examine all elements to be searched, assuming that the first time through, the best time so far will be bettered. This practice is to be deprecated, since there may be occasions when, with the passage of time, the assertion turns out to be false.

As we shall see, our problem is not as simple as this, for not all trains stop at every station. The first train examined in the process above may not stop at the two relevant stations and thus render the search incorrect. We will first make the assumption that all trains stop everywhere, and derive a simple solution, and then address the more realistic problem where they don't.

14.6.1 The Simpler Solution

In the preceding discussion, the number 62 has received undue publicity. It would be far clearer to the reader if it were a constant.

        CONST TRAINSPERDAY = 62;

Thus the program outline is

        PROGRAM ALLSTOP;

        CONST TRAINSPERDAY = 62;

        TYPE STATION = (LONDONLIVERPOOLSTREET, ILFORD, ROMFORD, SHENFIELD,
                        INGATESTONE, CHELMSFORD, HATFIELDPEVERAL, WITHAM,
                        KELVEDON, MARKSTEY, COLCHESTER);

            TIME = RECORD
                        HOURS : 0 .. 23;
                        MINS : 0 .. 59;
                        STOPS : BOOLEAN
                    END;

            TIMETABLE = ARRAY [1 .. TRAINSPERDAY, STATION] OF TIME;

        VAR LONCOL81 : TIMETABLE;
            I : 1 .. TRAINSPERDAY;
            J : STATION;

        PROCEDURE DISPLAYFASTEST(START, FINISH : STATION); ...;

        BEGIN (* MAIN PROGRAM *)
            ...
            DISPLAYFASTEST(LONDONLIVERPOOLSTREET, COLCHESTER)
        END.

The search process outlined above is represented by the procedure DISPLAYFASTEST which, in the interests of simplicity, is given enumerated type values as parameters. (You can provide a READSTATION procedure of your own if you wish.) In DISPLAYFASTEST we clearly need a variable to count through the schedules. We call this N, and the variable to keep track of the the value of N corresponding to the best train found so far will be called BESTN. The best time itself will be represented by the variable BESTTIMESOFAR. These are the obvious variables which closely relate to the the analysis of the searching process above. However, implicit in the analysis is a further variable, used to represent transient values, kept in the memory of the human interpreter of that analysis. To represent this, we use a variable called SCHEDULETIME.

Using the principles of top-down design, our first attempt at the procedure is

```
PROCEDURE DISPLAYFASTEST(START, FINISH : STATION);

    VAR BESTN : 1 .. TRAINSPERDAY;
        N, BESTTIMESOFAR, SCHEDULETIME : INTEGER;

    BEGIN
        N := 1;
        CALCTIME;  UPDATEFASTESTSOFAR;
        FOR N := 2 TO TRAINSPERDAY DO
          BEGIN
            CALCTIME;
            IF SCHEDULETIME < BESTTIMESOFAR THEN UPDATEFASTESTSOFAR
          END;
        displayschedule
    END; (* DISPLAYFASTEST *)
```

This requires two procedures, CALCTIME and UPDATEFASTESTSOFAR. (We will refine "displayschedule" in the body of the procedure DISPLAYFASTEST, rather than make it into a procedure.) Consider the procedure CALCTIME, the values it uses and where it leaves the result of its labors. We anticipated above the need for a temporary resting place for its results and declared SCHEDULETIME in the procedure DISPLAYFASTEST for just that purpose. Provided we nest CALCTIME within DISPLAYFASTEST, it has access to SCHEDULETIME as a non-local variable. The values which CALCTIME uses are found in the array LONCOL81 which, being declared at the outer level of the program, are available in CALCTIME. Similarly the procedure UPDATEFASTESTSOFAR uses non-local variables. The simplest way to calculate the scheduled time is to convert both times to minutes since midnight, and subtract taking due care with trains that run through midnight. We have

```
    PROCEDURE CALCTIME;

        VAR STARTMINS, FINISHMINS : INTEGER;

        BEGIN
            WITH LONCOL81[N, START] DO STARTMINS := HOURS*60 + MINS;
            WITH LONCOL81[N, FINISH] DO FINISHMINS := HOURS*60 + MINS;
            SCHEDULETIME := (FINISHMINS - STARTMINS) MOD (24*60)
        END; (* CALCTIME *)
```

and to update the best time so far, and the schedule to which it refers,

```
    PROCEDURE UPDATEFASTESTSOFAR;

        BEGIN
            BESTTIMESOFAR := SCHEDULETIME;
            BESTN := N
        END; (* UPDATEFASTESTSOFAR *)
```

We can now write the procedure DISPLAYFASTEST as follows.

```
PROCEDURE DISPLAYFASTEST(START, FINISH : STATION);

    VAR BESTN : 1 .. TRAINSPERDAY;
        N, BESTTIMESOFAR, SCHEDULETIME : INTEGER;
        S : STATION;

    PROCEDURE WRITESTATION(STN : STATION); ...;
    PROCEDURE UPDATEFASTESTSOFAR; ...;
    PROCEDURE CALCTIME; ...;

    BEGIN  (* DISPLAYFASTEST *)
        N := 1;
        CALCTIME;
        UPDATEFASTESTSOFAR;
        FOR N := 2 TO TRAINSPERDAY DO
          BEGIN
            CALCTIME;
            IF SCHEDULETIME < BESTTIMESOFAR THEN UPDATEFASTESTSOFAR
          END;
        WRITELN;
        WRITE('THE FASTEST TRAIN BETWEEN ');
        WRITESTATION(START); WRITE(' AND '); WRITESTATION(FINISH);
        WRITELN;
        WRITELN(' TAKES ', BESTTIMESOFAR, ' MINUTES.');
        WRITELN;
        FOR S := START TO FINISH DO
          BEGIN
            WRITESTATION(S);
            WITH LONCOL81[BESTN, S] DO
              BEGIN
                IF (HOURS >= 0) AND (HOURS <= 23)
                    THEN WRITELN('   ', HOURS : 2, MINS : 3)
                    ELSE WRITELN('     -')
              END
          END
    END; (* DISPLAYFASTEST *)
```

EXERCISE 14S: Assemble the complete program. If you wish to test it, use the following extract of 4 schedules from the London Liverpool Street to Colchester timetable.

London Liverpool Street	07 00	07 15	08 30	09 30
Ilford	-1 00	-1 00	-1 00	-1 00
Romford	-1 00	-1 00	-1 00	-1 00
Shenfield	07 22	-1 00	-1 00	-1 00
Ingatestone	07 26	-1 00	-1 00	-1 00
Chelmsford	07 34	07 51	09 02	-1 00
Hatfield Peveral	07 41	-1 00	-1 00	-1 00
Witham	07 46	08 01	-1 00	-1 00
Kelvedon	07 51	-1 00	-1 00	-1 00
Marks Tey	07 56	-1 00	-1 00	-1 00
Colchester	08 04	08 15	09 23	10 20

where -1 00 indicates that a train does not stop. The data may be read by lines, starting 07 00 07 15 08 30 ...

14.6.2 The More Realistic Solution

(This section may be omitted at the first reading since there is little more to be learned about arrays here.)

We still have to examine every element of the array LONCOL81 but what we do with each element rather depends on what has happened before. Another state variable,

```
        STATE : (LOOKINGFORFIRST, TRYINGTOIMPROVE);
```

reflects the two distinct phases of the search, and gives useful information at the end of the search, as to whether any train had been found. In outline the procedure DISPLAYFASTEST looks like

```
        PROCEDURE DISPLAYFASTEST(START, FINISH : STATION);

            VAR STATE : (LOOKINGFORFIRST, TRYINGTOIMPROVE);
                BESTN, N : 1 .. TRAINSPERDAY;
                BESTTIMESOFAR, SCHEDULETIME : INTEGER;
                S : STATION;

            PROCEDURE WRITESTATION(STN : STATION); ...;
            PROCEDURE UPDATEFASTESTSOFAR; ...;
            PROCEDURE CALCTIME; ...;

            BEGIN (* DISPLAYFASTEST *)
                STATE := LOOKINGFORFIRST;
                FOR N := 1 TO TRAINSPERDAY DO
                  BEGIN
                    IF train N stops at both stations THEN
                      CASE STATE OF
                        LOOKINGFORFIRST:
                            BEGIN
                              CALCTIME;
                              UPDATEFASTESTSOFAR;
                              STATE := TRYINGTOIMPROVE
                            END;
                        TRYINGTOIMPROVE:
                            BEGIN
                              CALCTIME;
                              IF SCHEDULETIME < BESTTIMESOFAR THEN
                                    UPDATEFASTESTSOFAR
                            END
                      END (* CASE AND IF *)
                  END (* FOR *);

                CASE STATE OF
                  LOOKINGFORFIRST:   noschedule;
                  TRYINGTOIMPROVE:   displayschedule
                END
            END; (* DISPLAYFASTEST *)
```

EXERCISE 14T: Complete this version of the program.

The use of an enumerated type to represent the stations by their names should be viewed with caution. In this particular example, it certainly adds clarity, but it also imposes inflexibility on the program. It would be next to useless as it stands for studying the London to Cambridge schedules. A general timetable processing program should therefore keep the names of its stations as the values of the elements of another array.

14.7 WHOLE ARRAY REFERENCES

It was noted in section 12.6.3 that complete records can be handled as entities in assignment and as parameters. The same is true for arrays. The definition of arrays of more than one dimension in terms of an array of arrays means that slices of arrays may also be handled as entities. (A <u>slice</u> of an n-dimensional array is an (n-1)-dimensional array.)

Recall the declaration of the train timetable of the previous section, which, in its non-abbreviated form, is included in

        TYPE SCHEDULE = **ARRAY** [STATION] **OF** TIME;
             TIMETABLE = **ARRAY** [1 .. 62] **OF** SCHEDULE;

        VAR LONCOL81, LONCOL82 : TIMETABLE;
            EXCURSION : SCHEDULE;

We have added two additional arrays: LONCOL82 representing another full timetable, and EXCURSION, representing just one train schedule. Both the following assignments are allowed.

        LONCOL82 := LONCOL81
        EXCURSION := LONCOL81[5]

However, even though it may appear reasonable to do so, neither arithmetic nor comparison may be performed on whole arrays or slices.

14.8 THE CONST SECTION

The **CONST** section of a program, or block, allows constant values to be referred to by name. It has already been used in a few examples to improve the readability of a program, but more importantly it improves the maintainability, since a constant used in several places has its value written only once. The **CONST** section precedes the **TYPE** section and takes the form

CONST section:

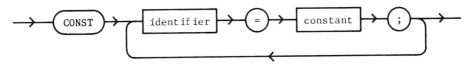

constant:

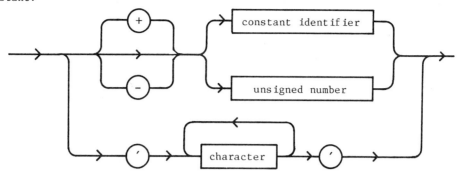

From the latter diagram, it can be seen that constants may be numbers, character constants or string constants. But beware, expressions are not allowed as constants, and whilst it is tempting to write

       CONST BACKSPACE = CHR(8);

this is not allowed. The best we can do is to name the value 8 as we did in exercise 13S.

    As an example of the use of a string constant, the program given as the solution to exercise 13C might have the CONST section

       CONST MORE = 'ANOTHER WINDMILL (Y/N)?';

and, in place of each WRITELN('ANOTHER WINDMILL (Y/N)?'), there would be WRITELN(MORE).

14.9 SETS

    The set is one of the most primitive concepts in mathematics and logic. A set is a possibly empty, unordered collection of distinguishable elements. The essential relationship between an element and a set is that of membership.

14.9.1 A Little Set Theory

    In mathematics, a set is usually denoted by either an identifier, or by a list denoting its elements as in

       d = {0, 1, 2, 3, 4, 5, 6, 7, 8, 9}
       p = {2, 3, 5, 7, 11, 13, 17, 19}
       e = {0, 2, 4, 6, 8}

The empty set may be denoted by

          { }

and in Mathematics (but not Pascal) sets of sets are still sets. For example

          S = {d, p, e}

    Three operators on sets yield a set as the result. The <u>intersection</u>
of sets a and b, written

          a /\ b

is the set of all elements common to sets a and b. (A more common symbol for
the intersection operator is an inverted sanserif upper-case U.) The
<u>union</u> of sets a and b, written

          a \/ b

is the set of all elements in a, or in b or in both a and b. (A more common
symbol for the union operator is a sanserif upper-case U.) The
<u>difference</u> between sets a and b, written

          a - b

is the set of all elements in a which are not also in b. Examples of these
operators are

          p /\ d   = {2, 3, 5, 7}
          p /\ e   = {2}
          d \/ e   = d
          s /\ { } = { } for any set s
          s \/ { } = s   for any set s
          e - p   = {0, 4, 6, 8}

Five operators on sets yield a Boolean result. The <u>membership</u> operator,
which we write as

          x ¢ a

is true if and only if x is an element of the set a. (Text books generally use
a curly lower-case e which looks like the Greek letter epsilon.) The
<u>inclusion</u> operator, which is sometimes written as

          a ≤ b

is true if and only if, for all x for which x ¢ a is true, x ¢ b is also
true. In other words, it is true if and only if a is a subset of b. The
operator may be reversed

          a ≥ b

to mean the converse of the above. That is, it is true if and only if b is a
subset of a. The operator which tests for the <u>equality</u> of two sets a and b
is written

```
      a = b
```

and is true if and only if a is the same set as b. The converse operator
denotes <u>inequality</u>. Thus

```
      a ≠ b
```

is true if and only if a is a different set from b. For example, each of the
following is true.

```
      3 ¢ d          e ≤ d        e \/ d = d        {0, 1} = {1, 0}
```

There is an algebra of sets which is closely related to Boolean algebra.
A detailed discussion is outside the scope of this book.

EXERCISE 14U: In the context of the definitions in this section, are the
                following true or false?

```
      p ≥ {19}                  {0} = {}

      {2} ¢ p /\ e              {2} ≤ p /\ e
```

14.9.2 <u>Sets in Pascal</u>

Sets are essentially arrays of Booleans, whose values denote presence or
absence of the corresponding element. However, the form that sets take in a
Pascal program is quite different from that of arrays. Sets are represented by
either <u>set denotations</u> in which specific elements are listed or implied,
or by variables of a type which has been defined to be a <u>set type</u>.
Examples of set denotations are

```
      [0, 1, 2, 3, 4, 5, 6, 7, 8, 9]
      [0 .. 9]                      (same as the set above)
      ['0' .. '9']                  (not the same as the set above)
      ['Y', 'N']
      [SPADES, CLUBS]
      [CLUBS, SPADES]               (same as the set above)
      [N - I .. N + I]              (set of integers N - I to N + I)
      []                            (the empty set)
```

A restriction in Apple Pascal limits the total membership of a set to 512
elements and restricts integer members to the values 0 to 511.

To declare an identifier to be of a set type, we first define the
base type, which you can think of as enumerating a "full house" or one
of each. For example, in the declarations

```
      TYPE SUBJECT = (ART, BIOLOGY, CHEMISTRY, COMPUTING, ECONOMICS,
                      ELECTRONICS, GOVERNMENT, HISTORY, LAW,
                      LINGUISTICS, LITERATURE, MATHEMATICS, PHILOSOPHY,
                      PHYSICS, SOCIOLOGY);

           SCHEME  = SET OF SUBJECT;
```

SUBJECT is the base type, and SCHEME is a set type. A variable of the set type
SCHEME is declared in the usual way.

```
VAR S1, S2, S3 : SCHEME;
    A, B, C : SCHEME;
    X, Y, Z : SUBJECT;
```

Think of the variables S1, S2, and S3 as representing the schemes of three students. Assignment of a set denotation to a set variable is allowed. For example

```
S1 := [MATHEMATICS, COMPUTING, ELECTRONICS];
S2 := [ECONOMICS, GOVERNMENT, COMPUTING];
S3 := [COMPUTING, MATHEMATICS, ELECTRONICS]
```

give set values to the variables S1, S2 and S3. Incidentally, S1 = S3.

Operations on sets in Pascal, corresponding to those in mathematics, are

Operator	Mathematics	Pascal
Intersection	a /\ b	A * B
Union	a \/ b	A + B
Difference	a - b	A - B
Membership	x ¢ a	X IN A
Inclusion	a ≤ b	A <= B
	a ≥ b	A >= B
Equality	a = b	A = B
Inequality	a ≠ b	A <> B

there being three levels of operator precedence, the strongest at the top of the table and the weakest at the bottom. (See also, table in section 8.2.2.) Examples of the use of these operators in Pascal are

```
IF X IN (S1 * S2) THEN ...

    meaning  IF (X IN S1) AND (X IN S2) THEN ...

IF A <= S2 THEN ...

IF X IN (S1 + S2*S3) THEN ...

    meaning  IF (X IN S1) OR (X IN (S2*S3)) THEN ...

IF D IN ['0' .. '9'] THEN ...
```

The last example illustrates a common use of sets to improve readability. The variable D is of type CHAR and the set denotation does not require the declaration of a set variable.

EXERCISE 14V: Write down if statements which

        (a)   test whether the variable C of type CHAR is an upper-case letter
        (b)   test whether the variable C of type CHAR is either an upper-case letter or a decimal digit
        (c)   test whether integer I is in the range 0 to 15
        (d)   test whether schemes S1 and S2 are disjoint
        (e)   improve the procedure GETREPLY of exercise 9N.

14.9.3 Formal Syntax for Sets

As hinted in the previous section, set denotations, which represent specific instances of sets (almost set constants) may be written using the subrange notation. This is expressed in the diagram

set denotation:

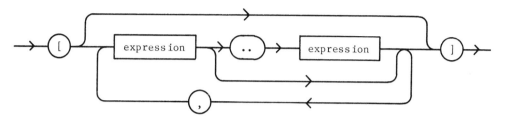

The declaration of a set is described by the diagram

set type:

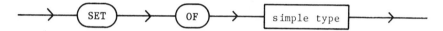

where the box "simple type" stands for the base type of the set which must be an enumerated type, INTEGER, CHAR or BOOLEAN, or a subrange of one of these. Sets of structured types and reals are forbidden. Further examples of valid sets are

```
TYPE DECDIG = SET OF '0' .. '9';
     CAPS = SET OF 'A' .. 'Z';
     HUE = SET OF (RED, BLUE, GREEN);

VAR ALPHA1, ALPHA2, ALPHABET : CAPS;
    ODDDIG, EVENDIG : DECDIG;
    C : CHAR;
    H1, H2 : HUE;

ALPHA1 := [];
ALPHA2 := ['A', 'E', 'I', 'O', 'U'];
ALPHABET := ['A' .. 'Z'];

EVENDIG := ['0', '2', '4', '6', '8'];
ODDDIG := ['1', '3', '5', '7', '9'];

IF C IN EVENDIG THEN ...
    ELSE IF C IN ODDDIG THEN ...
        ELSE IF C IN ALPHA2 THEN ...
            ELSE ...;

H1 := [RED, BLUE];
H2 := H1 - [BLUE];
H1 := H1 * H2;

IF C IN ['0' .. '9', 'A' .. 'Z'] THEN ...
```

EXERCISE 14W: Write down an alternative to the last example above, which
                tests whether the character C is either a letter or a decimal
                digit.

14.9.4 Example of the Use of Sets

We have to write a section of program to validate a student's choice of options. Suppose a student has to choose 5 options from 2 lists such that

3 options are from List A and
2 options are from List B.

The problem is that some options are in both List A and List B. The same option may not be chosen from both lists. Furthermore, if Computing has been chosen, the procedure REGISTERUSER has to be called. We assume the definitions and declarations

```
TYPE SUBJECT = (ART, BIOLOGY, CHEMISTRY, COMPUTING, ECONOMICS,
                ELECTRONICS, GOVERNMENT, HISTORY, LAW,
                LINGUISTICS, LITERATURE, MATHEMATICS, PHILOSOPHY,
                PHYSICS, SOCIOLOGY);

     SCHEME  = SET OF SUBJECT;

VAR LISTA, LISTB, CHOICEA, CHOICEB, OPTIONS : SCHEME;
```

Assuming that LISTA, LISTB, CHOICEA and CHOICEB have all been initialized, the program fragment to validate the student's chosen options is

```
IF (CHOICEA <= LISTA) AND (CHOICEB <= LISTB) THEN
    IF CHOICEA * CHOICEB = [] THEN
        BEGIN
            OPTIONS := CHOICEA + CHOICEB;
            IF COMPUTING IN OPTIONS THEN REGISTERUSER
        END
    ELSE WRITE('CHOICES NOT DISJOINT')
ELSE WRITE('OPTION NOT IN LIST')
```

SOLUTIONS TO THE EXERCISES

14A: The array of records was called MILLDESIGN
        The type which was a record of an array was STRING80

14B: PROGRAM RECURSIVEREVERSE;

```
PROCEDURE RDPRTREV(I : INTEGER);

    VAR X : INTEGER;

    BEGIN
        READ(X);
        IF I > 1 THEN RDPRTREV(I - 1);
        WRITE(X : 8)
    END; (* RDPRTREV *)

BEGIN
    RDPRTREV(10);  WRITELN
END.
```

14C: **PROGRAM** REVERSE2;

```
VAR I : 1 .. 100;
    NUM : ARRAY [1 .. 100] OF INTEGER;

BEGIN
    FOR I := 1 TO 100 DO READ(NUM[I]);
    FOR I := 100 DOWNTO 1 DO WRITE(NUM[I] : 8);
    WRITELN
END.
```

14D: Add the **TYPE** section

```
        TYPE MILLTYPE : ARRAY ['A' .. 'Z'] OF MILLSPEC;
```

and in the **VAR** section, declare MILLDESIGN by

```
        MILLDESIGN : MILLTYPE;
```

(Any meaningful and otherwise unused identifier will do in place of MILLTYPE.)

14E: **PROGRAM** REVERSE3;

```
CONST N = 10;

TYPE A10 = ARRAY [1 .. N] OF INTEGER;

VAR I : 1 .. N;
    NUM : A10;

BEGIN
    FOR I := 1 TO N DO READ (NUM[I]);
    FOR I := N DOWNTO 1 DO WRITE(NUM[I] : 8);
    WRITELN
END.
```

14F: A : **ARRAY** [1 .. 20] **OF** INTEGER;

14G: EARLYCLOSING : **ARRAY** [1 .. 100] **OF** DAYNAME;

14H: LONGINT : **ARRAY** [0 .. 999] **OF** 0 .. 9;   (suitable for arithmetic)
        LONGINT : **ARRAY** [0 .. 999] **OF** '0' .. '9';   (suitable for display)

14J: GOALS : **ARRAY** [BOOLEAN] **OF** INTEGER;

        or, if there is a type (FORGOALS, AGAINSTGOALS) we may declare

        GOALS : **ARRAY** [FORGOALS .. AGAINSTGOALS] **OF** INTEGER;

14K: (a) **PROGRAM** EX14KA;

             (* USES IDENTIFIER TOKEN FOR THE ARRAY OF NOTE AND COIN VALUES. *)

             CONST NNC = 10;   (* NUMBER OF DIFFERENT NOTES AND COINS *)

             VAR TOKEN : **ARRAY** [1 .. NNC] **OF** INTEGER;

             BEGIN
                 (* INITIALIZE THE ARRAY OF NOTE AND COIN VALUES *)
                 TOKEN[1] := 2000;   TOKEN[2] := 1000;
                 TOKEN[3] := 500;   TOKEN[4] := 100;
                 TOKEN[5] := 50;   TOKEN[6] := 20;
                 TOKEN[7] := 10;   TOKEN[8] := 5;
                 TOKEN[9] := 2;   TOKEN[10] := 1

             END.

        (b) See procedure DISPLAYCHANGE in (c) below.

        (c) **PROGRAM** EX14KC;

             (* USES IDENTIFIER TOKEN FOR THE ARRAY OF NOTE AND COIN VALUES. *)

             CONST NNC = 10;   (* NUMBER OF DIFFERENT NOTES AND COINS *)

             VAR TOKEN : **ARRAY** [1 .. NNC] **OF** INTEGER;
                 PRICE, TENDERED : INTEGER;

             PROCEDURE DISPLAYCHANGE(COST, OFFERED : INTEGER);

                 VAR CHANGE : INTEGER;
                     I : 1 .. NNC;

                 BEGIN
                     CHANGE := OFFERED - COST;

                     (* START WITH £20 NOTES AND WORK DOWN TO 1P. *)
                     FOR I := 1 **TO** NNC **DO**

                         (* CHECK IF THERE ARE ANY OF THIS TOKEN TO GIVE *)
                         IF CHANGE **DIV** TOKEN[I] <> 0 **THEN**
                           BEGIN

                             (* DISPLAY NUMBER OF THIS TOKEN *)
                             WRITELN(CHANGE **DIV** TOKEN[I], ' OF ', TOKEN[I]);

                             (* WORK OUT HOW MUCH IS STILL TO BE GIVEN *)
                             CHANGE := CHANGE **MOD** TOKEN[I]
                           END
                 END; (* DISPLAYCHANGE *)

             BEGIN
                 (* INITIALIZE THE ARRAY OF NOTE AND COIN VALUES *)
                 TOKEN[1] := 2000;   TOKEN[2] := 1000;
                 TOKEN[3] := 500;   TOKEN[4] := 100;
                 TOKEN[5] := 50;   TOKEN[6] := 20;
                 TOKEN[7] := 10;   TOKEN[8] := 5;
                 TOKEN[9] := 2;   TOKEN[10] := 1;

```
(* THE FOLLOWING DIALOGUE HAS BEEN KEPT VERY SIMPLE. *)

      REPEAT
            WRITE('ENTER PRICE OF GOODS: ');    READLN(PRICE);
            WRITE('ENTER AMOUNT TENDERED: ');   READLN(TENDERED);
            DISPLAYCHANGE(PRICE, TENDERED)
      UNTIL (PRICE = 0) AND (TENDERED = 0)
END.
```

14L: The body of DISPLAYCHANGE should begin

```
      BEGIN
            CHANGE := OFFERED - COST;

            IF CHANGE < 0 THEN WRITELN('INSUFFICIENT MONEY OFFERED')
            ELSE
                  (* START WITH £20 NOTES AND WORK DOWN TO 1P. *)
                  FOR I := 1 TO NNC DO ...
```

and the statement

```
      WRITELN(CHANGE DIV TOKEN[I], ' OF ', TOKEN[I])
```

is replaced by

```
      WRITE(CHANGE DIV TOKEN[I], ' OF ');
      IF TOKEN[I] DIV 100 > 0 THEN
            WRITELN(TOKEN[I] DIV 100, ' POUND NOTE')
      ELSE WRITELN(TOKEN[I], 'P')
```

14M: VAR EARLYTRAIN : SCHEDULE;
            .
            .
```
      WITH EARLYTRAIN[10] DO
        BEGIN
            STOPS := TRUE;
            HOURS := 07;
            MINS  := 56
        END;
      WITH EARLYTRAIN[3] DO STOPS := FALSE;
```

14N: TYPE STATION = (LONDONLIVERPOOLSTREET, ILFORD, ROMFORD, SHENFIELD,
                        INGATESTONE, CHELMSFORD, HATFIELDPEVERAL, WITHAM,
                        KELVEDON, MARKSTEY, COLCHESTER);
            .
            .
```
      WITH EARLYTRAIN[MARKSTEY] DO
        BEGIN
            STOPS := TRUE;
            HOURS := 07;
            MINS  := 56
        END;
      WITH EARLYTRAIN[ROMFORD] DO STOPS := FALSE;
```

14P: IF LONCOL81[30][5].STOPS THEN WRITE('STOPS AT INGATESTONE')
                                 ELSE WRITE('DOESN''T STOP AT INGATESTONE')

14Q: Assuming no more than 62 trains per day on any kind of day

        LC81ALL : **ARRAY** [WEEKDAYS .. SUNDAYS] **OF** TIMETABLE;

        or

        LC81ALL : **ARRAY** [WEEKDAYS .. SUNDAYS] **OF ARRAY** [1 .. 62] **OF**
                                                  ARRAY [1 .. 11] **OF** TIME;

        LC81ALL[SUNDAY][1][1].HOURS
        LC81ALL[SUNDAY][1][1].MINS.

14R: (a) array reference: [incomplete]

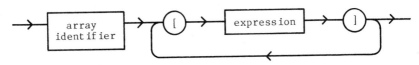

        (b) array type:

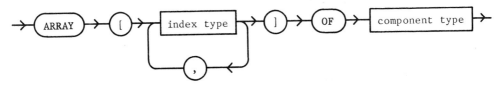

             array reference:

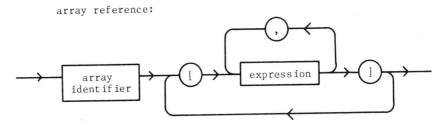

14S: **PROGRAM** ALLSTOP;

        CONST TRAINSPERDAY = 4;

        TYPE STATION = (LONDONLIVERPOOLSTREET, ILFORD, ROMFORD, SHENFIELD,
                     INGATESTONE, CHELMSFORD, HATFIELDPEVERAL, WITHAM,
                     KELVEDON, MARKSTEY, COLCHESTER);

            TIME = **RECORD**
                        HOURS : 0 .. 23;
                        MINS : 0 .. 59;
                        STOPS : BOOLEAN
                   END;

            TIMETABLE = **ARRAY** [1 .. TRAINSPERDAY, STATION] **OF** TIME;

        VAR LONCOL81 : TIMETABLE;
            I : 1 .. TRAINSPERDAY;
            J : STATION;

```
PROCEDURE DISPLAYFASTEST(START, FINISH : STATION);

    VAR BESTN : 1 .. TRAINSPERDAY;
        N, BESTTIMESOFAR, SCHEDULETIME : INTEGER;
        S : STATION;

    PROCEDURE WRITESTATION(STN : STATION);

        BEGIN
          CASE STN OF
            LONDONLIVERPOOLSTREET: WRITE('LONDON LIVERPOOL STREET');
            ILFORD:                WRITE('ILFORD                 ');
            ROMFORD:               WRITE('ROMFORD                ');
            SHENFIELD:             WRITE('SHENFIELD              ');
            INGATESTONE:           WRITE('INGATESTONE            ');
            CHELMSFORD:            WRITE('CHELMSFORD             ');
            HATFIELDPEVERAL:       WRITE('HATFIELD PEVERAL       ');
            WITHAM:                WRITE('WITHAM                 ');
            KELVEDON:              WRITE('KELVEDON               ');
            MARKSTEY:              WRITE('MARKS TEY              ');
            COLCHESTER:            WRITE('COLCHESTER             ')
          END
        END; (* WRITESTATION *)

    PROCEDURE UPDATEFASTESTSOFAR; ...;
    PROCEDURE CALCTIME; ...;

    BEGIN ... END; (* DISPLAYFASTEST *)

BEGIN
    FOR J := LONDONLIVERPOOLSTREET TO COLCHESTER DO
      FOR I := 1 TO TRAINSPERDAY DO
        WITH LONCOL81[I, J] DO
          BEGIN
            READ(HOURS);   READ(MINS);
            STOPS := (HOURS >= 0) AND (HOURS <= 23)
          END;
    DISPLAYFASTEST(LONDONLIVERPOOLSTREET, COLCHESTER)
END.


14T:    As for exercise 14S, except for

PROCEDURE DISPLAYFASTEST(START, FINISH : STATION);
    ...
    BEGIN (* DISPLAYFASTEST *)
      STATE := LOOKINGFORFIRST;
      FOR N := 1 TO TRAINSPERDAY DO
        BEGIN
          IF LONCOL81[N, START].STOPS AND LONCOL81[N, FINISH].STOPS THEN
            CASE STATE OF
              LOOKINGFORFIRST:
                BEGIN
                  CALCTIME; UPDATEFASTESTSOFAR; STATE := TRYINGTOIMPROVE
                END;
              TRYINGTOIMPROVE:
                BEGIN
                  CALCTIME;
                  IF SCHEDULETIME < BESTTIMESOFAR
                                      THEN UPDATEFASTESTSOFAR
                END
          END (* CASE AND IF *)
        END (* FOR *);
```

```
            CASE STATE OF
              LOOKINGFORFIRST:
                BEGIN
                  WRITE('NO SERVICE BETWEEN ');
                  WRITESTATION(START); WRITE(' AND '); WRITESTATION(FINISH)
                END;
              TRYINGTOIMPROVE:
                BEGIN
                  WRITELN;  WRITE('THE FASTEST TRAIN BETWEEN ');
                  WRITESTATION(START); WRITE(' AND '); WRITESTATION(FINISH);
                  WRITELN;  WRITELN(' TAKES ', BESTTIMESOFAR, ' MINUTES.');
                  WRITELN;
                  FOR S := START TO FINISH DO
                    BEGIN
                      WRITESTATION(S);
                      WITH LONCOL81[BESTN, S] DO
                        BEGIN
                          IF (HOURS >= 0) AND (HOURS <= 23)
                            THEN WRITELN('  ', HOURS : 2, MINS : 3)
                            ELSE WRITELN('    -')
                        END
                    END (* FOR *)
                END
            END (* CASE *)
          END; (* DISPLAYFASTEST *)
```

14U: true   false
        false (note that 2 ¢ p /\ e is true)   true

14V: (a) IF C IN ['A' .. 'Z'] THEN ...

        (b) IF (C IN ['A' .. 'Z']) OR (C IN ['0' .. '9'] THEN ...

        (c) IF I IN [0 .. 15] THEN ...

        (d) IF S1*S2 = [] THEN ...

        (e) The if statement becomes

                IF NOT (REPLY IN ['Y', 'N']) THEN ...

        (See table in section 8.2.2 and note on precedence in section 14.9.2
        to appreciate the need for the parentheses.)

14W: IF C IN ['0' .. '9'] + ['A' .. 'Z'] THEN ...

        or IF C IN ['0' .. '9'] + ALPHABET THEN ...

        or IF (C IN ['0' ..'9']) OR (C IN ALPHABET) THEN ...

        but not IF C IN ['0' .. '9', ALPHABET] THEN ...

CHAPTER 15
Loose Ends

In this chapter, three substantial loose ends will be tied up. First we investigate a different kind of parameter-passing mechanism which will, amongst other things, deal with the problem of the procedures READSTRING1 to READSTRING5 (section 13.3). Then we discover how to write our own bespoke functions, which can be used in much the same way as the pre-declared functions, SQR, SUCC, PRED, etc. Finally we delve more deeply into the question of whereabouts in the text of a program you can refer to an object declared at the head of a block.

15.1 VARIABLE PARAMETERS

The first thing we now have to get used to is thinking of the familiar parameters of chapters 1 to 14 as value parameters. Value parameters can be of any type, so we shall use concepts such as "value parameter of type CHAR", remembering that depending on the context it will be either a formal parameter or an actual parameter that is referred to. Recall from section 11.1 that a formal (value) parameter of a procedure is like a variable which is initialized to the value of the corresponding actual parameter at the time of the call. But there has been something decidedly odd about these "variables". They have never varied! In no instance of a body of a procedure has a formal (value) parameter appeared on the left-hand side of an assignment statement, or in a READ statement. Yet value parameters are variables and there is no reason why they should not vary.

15.1.1 Demonstration Programs

The following program is on the MACC: disk in the file VALUEPARAM.TEXT. It shows the effect (or rather the lack of effect) of changing the value of such parameters. Compile and execute it, noting especially the last set of values it displays.

```
PROGRAM VALUEPARAM;

VAR P, Q : INTEGER;

PROCEDURE MISC(A, B : INTEGER);

    (* MAKES MISCELLANEOUS CHANGES TO THE PARAMETERS *)

    BEGIN
        WRITELN;  WRITELN('JUST AFTER ENTRY TO MISC,');
        WRITELN('  A = ', A, ' AND B = ', B);
        A := -A;
        WRITELN;  WRITELN('THINK OF A NUMBER DIFFERENT FROM ', B);
        READLN(B);
        WRITELN;  WRITELN('JUST BEFORE EXIT FROM MISC,');
        WRITELN('  A = ', A, ' AND B = ', B)
    END; (* MISC *)

BEGIN
    P := 5;  Q := 15;
    WRITELN;  WRITELN('BEFORE THE CALL,');
    WRITELN('  P = ', P, ' AND Q = ', Q);
    MISC(P, Q);
    WRITELN;  WRITELN('AFTER THE CALL,');
    WRITELN('  P = ', P, ' AND Q = ', Q)
END.
```

After execution keep this program in the workfile.

EXERCISE 15A: Write down what you consider to have been the effect of

    (a) A := -A   on the value of P
    (b) READLN(B)   on the value of Q

From the program above, it is clear that the value parameters A and B allow only one-way communication with the world outside. From the standpoint of the procedure they are "listening" parameters - they cannot talk back to the place from which the procedure was called.

The procedure WRITESTRING in section 13.3 had a parameter S. Place yourself in this procedure and you will realize that S is a "listening" parameter. It receives the string to be written, and then displays it on the screen. If, on the other hand, the procedure READSTRING1 were to have a parameter, then it clearly would need to be a "talking" parameter, for that procedure, having read a sequence of characters, has to communicate them back to the part of the program whence the procedure was called. Such "talking" parameters exist in Pascal and are called <u>variable parameters</u>, but as you will see from the next demonstration, they can listen as well.

Change name of the program in the workfile from VALUEPARAM to VARPARAM, and change the procedure heading to

PROCEDURE MISC(VAR A, B : INTEGER);

to indicate that A and B are each to be of the listening and talking kind, execute the program again, and note the values it displays. Each appearance of A and B within the body of MISC is now interpreted as a reference to the corresponding actual parameter, namely P and Q respectively. For example, the statement "A := -A" is interpreted as, "get the value of the variable that A (on the right) refers to (that is, the value of P), negate it and assign this value to the variable that A (on the left) refers to".

EXERCISE 15B: Which of the parameters A and B behave differently now?

EXERCISE 15C: Change the name of the program to BOTHKINDS and change the
                procedure heading to

                    PROCEDURE MISC(**VAR** A : INTEGER;
                                      B : INTEGER);

                execute the program and explain the difference between its
                operation and the program in exercise 15B.

     If you are still uncertain of the difference between value and variable
parameters, execute the program in the file XPLAIN15.1 on the MACC: disk.   This
takes you step by step through a program very similar to BOTHKINDS.

15.1.2 Readstring Revisited

     The procedure READSTRING5 (the latest version being the solution to
exercise 13S in section 13.3.1 and saved as USER:STRING2) is less than
satisfactory. Whereas the standard procedures for reading data (READ and
READLN) require the programmer to say where the data is to be put, the
READSTRING procedures do not. READSTRING5 clearly should have a variable
parameter so that it can "talk back" to the place it was called from and
deliver the good news to any suitable variable (that is, one of type STRING80).

EXERCISE 15D: Make the appropriate change to READSTRING5, call it READSTRING6
                and modify the program in USER:STRING2 accordingly.   Check that
                it works correctly and save it as USER:STRING3.

     The solution to exercise 15D can be improved again with the aid of a
further variable parameter. The main program would be more explicit if it were


```
        BEGIN
          REPEAT
            READSTRING6(ANYSTRING);
            LOCATE(' ', ANYSTRING, POS);
            IF POS = 0 THEN WRITELN(' - NO SPACES')
              ELSE WRITELN(' - FIRST SPACE AT CHARACTER POSITION ', POS)
          UNTIL FALSE
        END.
```


In other words, the procedure LOCATE returns, via the variable parameter POS,
the position of the first space.

EXERCISE 15E: Turn the character searching program in exercise 15D into one
                which searches for a given string. Add a procedure whose
                heading is

                    PROCEDURE LOCATE(C : CHAR; S : STRING80;
                                  VAR POS : INTEGER);

                Test it, check that it behaves correctly even on empty strings,
                and save it as USER:STRING4.

This is not the whole story by any means. There are restrictions on the
form of actual parameter that can be used with a variable parameter and these
will be detailed in chapter 16.

15.2 FUNCTIONS

There is another way of transmitting a value back to the place of the
call. We have encountered it already, from the receiving end, where we have
used pre-declared functions such as

        SQR SUCC PRED CHR ORD

in expressions such as

        SUCC(PRED(D1))   ORD('A')   CHR(20)
        SQR(TURTLEX - 139) + SQR(TURTLEY - 95) >= SQR(50)

Each occurrence of the function reference in an expression stands for a value
which is to be calculated by some already provided value-producing section of
program hidden from the ordinary programmer. In Pascal, we can define our own
functions in much the same way as we define our own procedures. Without
further delay, let us improve the solution to exercise 15E which searches for
the first occurrence of the character C in the string S.

15.2.1 User-defined Functions

In the program in USER:STRING4, change the procedure LOCATE into the
function

```
FUNCTION LOCATION(C : CHAR; S : STRING80) : INTEGER;

VAR STATE : (STILLLOOKING, FOUNDONE, ATEND);
    CHCOUNT : 0 .. 80;

BEGIN
  WITH S DO
    BEGIN
      CHCOUNT := 1;
      IF LENGTH = 0 THEN STATE := ATEND
                    ELSE STATE := STILLLOOKING;
      WHILE STATE = STILLLOOKING DO
          IF CH[CHCOUNT] = C THEN STATE := FOUNDONE
          ELSE IF CHCOUNT < LENGTH THEN CHCOUNT := CHCOUNT + 1
                                   ELSE STATE := ATEND
    END;
  IF STATE = ATEND THEN LOCATION := 0 ELSE LOCATION := CHCOUNT
END; (* LOCATION *)
```

and replace the main program by

```
BEGIN
    REPEAT
        WRITELN;  WRITELN('ENTER STRING:');  READSTRING(S);
        WRITELN;  WRITELN('ENTER CHARACTER:');  READ(C);
        WRITELN;
        IF LOCATION(C, S) <> 0 THEN
            WRITELN('CHARACTER FOUND AT ', LOCATION(C, S))
        ELSE WRITELN('NOT FOUND')
    UNTIL FALSE
END.
```

Execute the program and save it as USER:STRING5. Note four things.

- We have changed the name LOCATE (a verb in the imperative mood, suggesting action) of the procedure into LOCATION (a noun, suggesting a value) for the function.
- The first line of the function ends in : INTEGER to denote the type of value it will produce.
- The last statement of the body of the function is an assignment to the name of the function. This gives the function its value.
- In the main program we have used

    LOCATION(C, S)

    as a value to be compared and as a value to be displayed. In both cases, it merely stands for a value.

In the example above, the function LOCATION produces a value of type INTEGER, and is therefore said to be of type INTEGER. Functions can be defined which deliver values of type other than INTEGER. (See section 16.1.1.)

EXERCISE 15F: To the program in USER:STRING5, add a function to select the character following the first occurrence of the character C in the string S. If the character C is not present, or it occurs only as the last character of S, or S is the empty string, it should return the character DELETE. Note that ORD(DELETE) = 127. The function might begin

```
FUNCTION NEXTCHAR(C : CHAR; S : STRING80) : CHAR;

    BEGIN
        IF S.LENGTH < 2 THEN
        ...
```

How could it be called from the main program? Do not save this program.

EXERCISE 15G: What type of value is delivered by the predefined function CHR?

15.2.2 Recursive Functions

(This section may be omitted at the first reading.)

The following development of the function LOCATION shows how easy it is to describe certain iterative processes using recursion. Suppose the function has to find the Nth occurrence of character C in S. The first line appears to be

> **FUNCTION** NLOC(N : INTEGER; C : CHAR; S : STRING80) : INTEGER;

We can now focus on what to do about assigning a value to the name of the function, which in the function LOCATION was done by

> **IF** STATE = ATEND **THEN** LOCATION := 0 **ELSE** LOCATION := CHCOUNT

Again we have 2 cases to consider.

- If the value of STATE is ATEND, the value of NLOC must be 0 regardless of the value of N, and there is no more to be done.

- If the value of STATE is not ATEND then the value of NLOC does depend on N. If N is 1 it must be CHCOUNT but if N > 1, then the value of NLOC must be NLOC(N-1, C, S). However, the search must continue from the place we have already reached in the string. This means another parameter denoting the starting point of the search which replaces the variable CHCOUNT in the previous version of the function.

EXERCISE 15H: Starting with USER:STRING5, call the extra parameter I and change the function LOCATION into NLOC beginning

> **FUNCTION** NLOC(N, I : INTEGER; C : CHAR; S : STRING80)
> : INTEGER;

Make suitable changes to the main program, execute it, and save it as USER:STRING6.

EXERCISE 15J: From the following definition of the factorial function

$$n! \;=\; \left\{ \begin{array}{ll} 1 & \text{if } n = 1 \\ n * (n - 1)! & \text{if } n > 1 \end{array} \right.$$

write a function FACTORIAL(N : INTEGER) : INTEGER; and hence a program for displaying the factorials from 1! to 7!.

15.3 SCOPE

The scope of an identifier in a program (in any programming language) is that part of the text in which it may be referred to. It is therefore a concept of space rather than one of time. In Pascal it relates to

> constants
> types (including field identifiers)
> variables
> procedures
> functions

We have used the term "declaration" for the introduction of an identifier, whether it be in connection with a type definition, constant definition, variable, procedure or function declaration, or parameter information.

The rules of scope in Pascal are as follows.

1. No identifier may be declared more than once in any block except for the re-declaration of that identifier for some other purpose in a nested block.

2. A declaration is valid for the whole of the block in which it is declared, together with all nested blocks in which it is NOT re-declared for some other purpose.

3. Any identifier referred to in a program (except one which is pre-declared) must be declared in the block in which it appears or in some block which embraces that block.

As early as section 3.3 (the program MILL4) we had an example of the same identifier used for three different purposes. The identifier S was used as the parameter of three different procedures. In each case the scope of S was restricted to the body of the procedure it was declared in. The three scopes did not intersect and the program would have had the same meaning had the identifiers been S1, S2 and S3 respectively.

However, identifiers may be re-declared inside nested procedures or functions with different effect. This we have intentionally avoided so far. To see the effect, compile and execute the program in the file SCOPEDEMO.TEXT on the MACC: disk.

```
PROGRAM SCOPEDEMO;

VAR A, B, C, D : INTEGER;

PROCEDURE P(VAR A : INTEGER);

    VAR B : INTEGER;

    BEGIN
        B := 12;
        WRITELN;  WRITELN('ENTERED P AND INITIALIZED B,');
        WRITELN('  A = ', A, ' AND B = ', B);
        A := 11;  D := 14;
        WRITELN;  WRITELN('JUST BEFORE EXIT FROM P,');
        WRITELN('  A = ', A, ' AND B = ', B)
    END; (* P *)

BEGIN
    A := 1;  B := 2;  C := 3;  D := 4;
    WRITELN;  WRITELN('BEFORE THE CALL OF P,');
    WRITELN('  A = ', A, '  B = ', B, '  C = ', C, ' AND D = ', D);
    P(C);
    WRITELN;  WRITELN('AFTER THE CALL OF P,');
    WRITELN('  A = ', A, '  B = ', B, '  C = ', C, ' AND D = ', D)
END.
```

The identifiers A and B have been reused inside the procedure P as the names of a parameter and a local variable respectively. The values displayed by this program show that the outer variables A and B remain unaffected by the actions upon the inner variables bearing the same names. The only effects of P on the world outside are through its variable parameter and the the non-local variable D to which it makes reference.

EXERCISE 15K: List each distinct variable and parameter in the program above, and say in which parts of the program it may be referred to.

There are important implications for the authors of large programs. A procedure (or function) which refers only to its parameters and local variables can be implanted in a program without fear of identifier clashes, by virtue of rule 2. Thus the operation of the implanted procedure will be unaffected by its new surroundings except for any deliberate effects of its parameters. However, the converse is not so comfortable! Since a procedure may refer to non-local variables, it is quite possible for an implanted procedure to alter non-local variables in its new environment. Thus the security of the environment may well be affected by the inclusion of a new procedure.

15.4 A CALENDAR

The generation of a calendar for any year in the range 1583 to 4317 provides an opportunity to use functions and exploit the rules of scope. It also shows how the use of enumerated types improves the readability of the program.

It is presented as a sequence of exercises. In order to keep the program as simple as possible, the layout is not very beautiful. This can be improved at your leisure if you feel suitably moved.

The year in question is to be entered and verified in a dialogue with the computer. Then the heading, say CALENDAR FOR 1983 is displayed, then the 12 months, one below the other. Let us therefore start by defining some types which seem to be appropriate.

```
TYPE DAYINT = 1 .. 31;
     YEARINT = 1583 .. 4317;
     DAYNAME = (SUNDAY, MONDAY, TUESDAY, WEDNESDAY, THURSDAY,
               FRIDAY, SATURDAY);
     MONTHNAME = (JANUARY, FEBRUARY, MARCH, APRIL, MAY, JUNE, JULY,
               AUGUST, SEPTEMBER, OCTOBER, NOVEMBER, DECEMBER);
```

EXERCISE 15L: Write a main program section containing the dialogue, the heading "CALENDAR FOR ..." and suitable calls of a procedure DISPLAYMONTH.

EXERCISE 15M: Outline the procedure DISPLAYMONTH which produces a month in the following format.

```
                        JANUARY

        SUN   MON   TUE   WED   THU   FRI   SAT
                                              1
         2     3     4     5     6     7     8
         9    10    11    12    13    14    15
        16    17    18    19    20    21    22
        23    24    25    26    27    28    29
        30    31
```

Note that a month consists of

- the name of the month;
- abbreviated day names;
- the integers 1 to 28, 29, 30 or 31 carefully placed.

EXERCISE 15N: Write a procedure to display the name of the month.

EXERCISE 15P: Write a procedure to display the abbreviated day names.

Before we can start to put the integers in their correct places, we need
to know two things about the month:

- the day of the week of the first of the month
- the number of days in the month.

EXERCISE 15Q: Write down statements to determine the day of the week of the
first of the month and to display the appropriate number of
leading blanks (5 per day) on the first line of the month.

EXERCISE 15R: Assuming we know the number of days in the month, (and the day
of the first of the month) write down statements to display the
dates

                1   2   3   ...

After a Saturday, the date should be followed by WRITELN.

EXERCISE 15S: Write a function DAYOFWEEK which returns a value of type
DAYNAME. See section 12.1.3. The month will probably be passed
as a parameter of type MONTHNAME. If so you will need to use
the predeclared function ORD to convert from type MONTHNAME to
type INTEGER or 1 .. 12.

EXERCISE 15T: Assuming we know whether a year is a leap year or not, write a
function DAYSINMONTH which delivers a value of type DAYINT.
What kind of object is ideal for representing whether or not a
given year is a leap year or not?

EXERCISE 15U: Write a function to determine whether or not a given year is a
leap year or not. According to the Gregorian calendar, a year
is a leap year if it is divisible by 4 and not divisible by 100,
except that years divisible by 400 are leap years.

EXERCISE 15V: Assemble and execute the complete program. Save it as
USER:CALENDAR.

The program which is produced by this very modular, top-down approach is
certainly not the shortest way to achieve this result. One weakness is that
it contains the essence of the Gregorian calendar in two different functions,
DAYOFWEEK and LEAP. (See exercise 15W.) However it remains a flexible
program. For example, it is a trivial clerical matter to produce a French
calendar. It is less trivial, but not too difficult to present the months
side by side across a full width screen. And after the year 4317, when some
modification becomes necessary, it should require only localized changes.

EXERCISE 15W: Rewrite the function LEAP so that it uses the function
DAYSOFWEEK as its only source of information about the Gregorian
calendar.

SOLUTIONS TO THE EXERCISES

15A: (a) no effect   (b) no effect

15B: Both of them.

15C: The parameter B has reverted to a value parameter, and it no longer
        communicates back to the main program.

15D: **PROGRAM** EXERCISE15D;

```
TYPE STRING80 = RECORD
                    LENGTH : 0 .. 80;
                    CH : PACKED ARRAY [1 .. 80] OF CHAR
                END;

VAR ANYSTRING : STRING80;
    STATE : (STILLLOOKING, FOUNDONE, ATEND);
    CHCOUNT : 0 .. 80;

PROCEDURE READSTRING6(VAR ST : STRING80);

    CONST BS = 8;

    VAR CHARCOUNT : 0 .. 80;
        C, DELIMITER : CHAR;

    BEGIN
        REPEAT READ(DELIMITER) UNTIL DELIMITER <> ' ';
        CHARCOUNT := 0;
        READ(C);
        WHILE C <> DELIMITER DO
            BEGIN
                IF CHARCOUNT < 80 THEN
                    BEGIN
                        IF ORD(C) = BS THEN
                            BEGIN
                                IF CHARCOUNT > 0 THEN
                                    BEGIN
                                        CHARCOUNT := CHARCOUNT - 1;
                                        WRITE(CHR(BS), ' ', CHR(BS))
                                    END
                            END
                        ELSE
                            BEGIN
                                CHARCOUNT := CHARCOUNT + 1;
                                ST.CH[CHARCOUNT] := C
                            END
                    END;
                READ(C)
            END;
        ST.LENGTH := CHARCOUNT
    END; (* READSTRING6 *)
```

```
      BEGIN  (* MAIN PROGRAM *)
        REPEAT
           READSTRING6(ANYSTRING);
           WITH ANYSTRING DO
             BEGIN
               IF LENGTH = 0 THEN STATE := ATEND ELSE STATE := STILLLOOKING;
               CHCOUNT := 1;
               WHILE STATE = STILLLOOKING DO
                     IF CH[CHCOUNT] = ' ' THEN STATE := FOUNDONE
                   ELSE IF CHCOUNT < LENGTH THEN CHCOUNT := CHCOUNT + 1
                                            ELSE STATE := ATEND
             END;
           IF STATE = ATEND THEN WRITELN(' - NO SPACES')
                 ELSE WRITELN(' - FIRST SPACE AT ', CHCOUNT)
        UNTIL FALSE
      END.


15E:    PROGRAM EXERCISE15E;

        TYPE STRING80 = RECORD
                            LENGTH : 0 .. 80;
                            CH : PACKED ARRAY [1 .. 80] OF CHAR
                          END;

        VAR S : STRING80;
            C : CHAR;
            P : 0 .. 80;

        PROCEDURE READSTRING6(VAR ST : STRING80);

           (* AS IN EXERCISE 15D *)

        PROCEDURE LOCATE(C : CHAR; S : STRING80; VAR P : INTEGER);

           VAR STATE : (STILLLOOKING, FOUNDONE, ATEND);
               CHCOUNT : 0 .. 80;

           BEGIN
             WITH S DO
               BEGIN
                 CHCOUNT := 1;
                 IF LENGTH = 0 THEN STATE := ATEND ELSE STATE := STILLLOOKING;
                 WHILE STATE = STILLLOOKING DO
                       IF CH[CHCOUNT] = C THEN STATE := FOUNDONE
                     ELSE IF CHCOUNT < LENGTH THEN CHCOUNT := CHCOUNT + 1
                                              ELSE STATE := ATEND
               END;
             IF STATE = ATEND THEN P := 0 ELSE P := CHCOUNT
           END; (* LOCATE *)

        BEGIN
          REPEAT
             WRITELN;  WRITELN('ENTER STRING:');  READSTRING(S);
             WRITELN;  WRITELN('ENTER CHARACTER:');  READ(C);
             LOCATE(C, S, P);
             WRITELN;  IF P <> 0 THEN WRITELN('CHARACTER FOUND AT ', P)
                              ELSE WRITELN('NOT FOUND')
          UNTIL FALSE
        END.
```

```
15F:      FUNCTION NEXTCHAR(C : CHAR; S : STRING80) : CHAR;

              BEGIN
                 IF S.LENGTH < 2 THEN NEXTCHAR := CHR(127)
                 ELSE
                    IF LOCATION(C, S) IN [1 .. S.LENGTH - 1]
                       THEN NEXTCHAR := S.CH[LOCATION(C, S) + 1]
                       ELSE NEXTCHAR := CHR(127)
              END; (* NEXTCHAR *)
```

and it could be called from the main program thus.

```
              BEGIN
                 REPEAT
                    READSTRING6(S);
                    WRITELN(' - CHARACTER FOLLOWING FIRST SPACE IS: ',
                          NEXTCHAR(' ', S))
                 UNTIL FALSE
              END.
```

```
15G:      CHAR
```

```
15H:      FUNCTION NLOC(N, I : INTEGER; C : CHAR; S : STRING80) : INTEGER;

              VAR STATE : (STILLLOOKING, FOUNDONE, ATEND);

              BEGIN
                 WITH S DO
                   BEGIN
                     IF I > LENGTH THEN STATE := ATEND
                                   ELSE STATE := STILLLOOKING;
                     WHILE STATE = STILLLOOKING DO
                        IF CH[I] = C THEN STATE := FOUNDONE
                        ELSE IF I < LENGTH THEN I := I + 1 ELSE STATE := ATEND
                   END;
                 IF STATE = ATEND THEN NLOC := 0 ELSE
                    IF N > 1 THEN NLOC := NLOC(N-1, I+1, C, S)
                             ELSE NLOC := I
              END; (* NLOC *)

          BEGIN          (* MAIN PROGRAM SET UP FOR THIRD SPACES *)
              REPEAT
                 READSTRING6(S);
                 IF NLOC(3, 1, ' ', S)  = 0 THEN
                    WRITELN(' - INSUFFICIENT SPACES')
                 ELSE WRITELN(' - THIRD SPACE AT ', NLOC(3, 1, ' ', S))
              UNTIL FALSE
          END.
```

```
15J:      PROGRAM SHRIEK;

          VAR I : INTEGER;

          FUNCTION FACTORIAL(N : INTEGER) : INTEGER;

              BEGIN
                 IF N = 1 THEN FACTORIAL := 1
                          ELSE FACTORIAL := N * FACTORIAL(N - 1)
              END; (* FACTORIAL *)

          BEGIN
              FOR I := 1 TO 7 DO WRITELN(I : 2, FACTORIAL(I) : 6)
          END.
```

15K: In order of appearance

identifier	scope
A	main program only
B	main program only
C	main program and procedure
D	main program and procedure
A (variable parameter)	procedure only
B	procedure only

15L: PROGRAM CALENDAR;

(* OUTLINE PROGRAM PRODUCES CALENDAR FOR ANY YEAR FROM 1583 TO 4317 *)

TYPE ...

VAR YEAR : INTEGER;
    YEAROK : BOOLEAN;
    MONTH : MONTHNAME;

PROCEDURE DISPLAYMONTH(MONTH : MONTHNAME; YEAR : YEARNAME); ...;

```
BEGIN  (* MAIN PROGRAM *)
    REPEAT
      WRITELN('PLEASE ENTER THE YEAR FOR WHICH CALENDAR IS REQUIRED');
      READ(YEAR);
      IF (YEAR < 1583) OR (YEAR > 4317) THEN
         BEGIN
            WRITELN('YEAR MUST BE IN RANGE 1583 TO 4317. TRY AGAIN');
            YEAROK := FALSE
         END
      ELSE YEAROK := TRUE
    UNTIL YEAROK;

    WRITELN(' CALENDAR FOR ' , YEAR : 5);

    FOR MONTH := JANUARY TO DECEMBER DO DISPLAYMONTH(MONTH, YEAR)
END.
```

15M: PROCEDURE DISPLAYMONTH(MONTH : MONTHNAME; YEAR : YEARINT);

```
    VAR DATE : DAYINT;

    BEGIN
        WRITELN; WRITELN;
        MONTHHEADER(MONTH);
        WRITELN;
        DODAYNAMES;
        WRITELN;

        do leading blanks;

        FOR DATE := 1 TO DAYSINMONTH(MONTH, YEAR) DO
            put date in proper place

    END; (* DISPLAYMONTH *)
```

```
15N:    PROCEDURE MONTHHEADER(MONTH : MONTHNAME);

            PROCEDURE WRITEMONTH(MONTH : MONTHNAME);
                BEGIN
                    CASE MONTH OF
                        JANUARY:       WRITE(' JANUARY ');
                        FEBRUARY:      WRITE(' FEBRUARY');
                        MARCH:         WRITE('  MARCH  ');
                        APRIL:         WRITE('  APRIL  ');
                        MAY:           WRITE('   MAY   ');
                        JUNE:          WRITE('  JUNE   ');
                        JULY:          WRITE('  JULY   ');
                        AUGUST:        WRITE(' AUGUST  ');
                        SEPTEMBER:     WRITE('SEPTEMBER');
                        OCTOBER:       WRITE(' OCTOBER ');
                        NOVEMBER:      WRITE('NOVEMBER ');
                        DECEMBER:      WRITE('DECEMBER ')
                    END (* CASE *)
                END; (* WRITEMONTH *)

            BEGIN  (* MONTHHEADER *)
                WRITE(' ' : 14);  WRITEMONTH(MONTH);
                WRITELN
            END; (* MONTHHEADER *)


15P:    PROCEDURE DODAYNAMES;

            VAR DAY : DAYNAME;

            PROCEDURE WRITEDAY(DAY : DAYNAME);
                BEGIN
                    CASE DAY OF
                        SUNDAY:       WRITE('SUN');
                        MONDAY:       WRITE('MON');
                        TUESDAY:      WRITE('TUE');
                        WEDNESDAY:    WRITE('WED');
                        THURSDAY:     WRITE('THU');
                        FRIDAY:       WRITE('FRI');
                        SATURDAY:     WRITE('SAT')
                    END (* CASE *);
                    WRITE('   ')
                END; (* WRITEDAY *)

            BEGIN  (* DODAYNAMES *)
                WRITE('   ');
                FOR DAY := SUNDAY TO SATURDAY DO WRITEDAY(DAY);
                WRITELN
            END; (* DODAYNAMES *)


15Q:    FIRST := DAYOFWEEK(1, MONTH, YEAR);
        IF FIRST <> SUNDAY THEN (* DO LEADING BLANKS *)
            FOR DAY := SUNDAY TO PRED(FIRST) DO WRITE('      ')
```

```
15R:    DAY := FIRST;
        FOR DATE := 1 TO DAYSINMONTH(MONTH, YEAR) DO
            BEGIN
                IF DAY = SATURDAY THEN
                    BEGIN
                        WRITELN(DATE : 5);   DAY := SUNDAY
                    END
                ELSE
                    BEGIN
                        WRITE(DATE : 5);   DAY := SUCC(DAY)
                    END
            END (* FOR *)


15S:    FUNCTION DAYOFWEEK(D : DAYINT; MONTH : MONTHNAME; Y : YEARINT)
                                                        : DAYNAME;

            VAR ABSDAYNO : INTEGER; (* ABSOLUTE DAY NUMBER *)
                M : 1 .. 12;  (* MONTH NUMBER *)

            BEGIN
                M := ORD(MONTH) + 1;
                IF MONTH <= FEBRUARY THEN
                    ABSDAYNO := Y + 31*(M-1) + D
                                + (Y-1) DIV 4
                                - 3*((Y+99) DIV 100) DIV 4

                ELSE ABSDAYNO := Y + 31*(M-1) + D
                                - (4*M + 23) DIV 10 + Y DIV 4
                                - (3*(Y DIV 100 + 1)) DIV 4;

                CASE ABSDAYNO MOD 7 OF
                    0 : DAYOFWEEK := SATURDAY;
                    1 : DAYOFWEEK := SUNDAY;
                    2 : DAYOFWEEK := MONDAY;
                    3 : DAYOFWEEK := TUESDAY;
                    4 : DAYOFWEEK := WEDNESDAY;
                    5 : DAYOFWEEK := THURSDAY;
                    6 : DAYOFWEEK := FRIDAY
                END (* CASE *)
            END; (* DAYOFWEEK *)


15T:    FUNCTION DAYSINMONTH(MONTH : MONTHNAME; YEAR : YEARINT) : DAYINT;

            BEGIN
                IF (MONTH = FEBRUARY) THEN
                    IF LEAP(YEAR) THEN DAYSINMONTH := 29
                                  ELSE DAYSINMONTH := 28
                ELSE
                    IF (MONTH = APRIL) OR (MONTH = JUNE) OR
                       (MONTH = SEPTEMBER) OR (MONTH = NOVEMBER)
                    THEN DAYSINMONTH := 30
                    ELSE DAYSINMONTH := 31

            END; (* DAYSINMONTH *)

        Boolean


15U:    FUNCTION LEAP(YEAR : YEARINT) : BOOLEAN;

            BEGIN
                LEAP := (YEAR MOD 4 = 0) AND NOT (YEAR MOD 100 = 0)
                                            OR (YEAR MOD 400 = 0)
            END; (* LEAP *)
```

15V: Program and procedure structure is as follows.

```
PROGRAM CALENDAR;

TYPE DAYINT = 1 .. 31;
     YEARINT = 1583 .. 4317;
     DAYNAME = (SUNDAY, MONDAY, TUESDAY, WEDNESDAY, THURSDAY,
                FRIDAY, SATURDAY);
     MONTHNAME = (JANUARY, FEBRUARY, MARCH, APRIL, MAY, JUNE, JULY,
                  AUGUST, SEPTEMBER, OCTOBER, NOVEMBER, DECEMBER);

VAR YEAR : INTEGER;
    YEAROK : BOOLEAN;
    MONTH : MONTHNAME;

PROCEDURE DISPLAYMONTH(MONTH : MONTHNAME; YEAR : YEARINT);

    VAR FIRST, DAY : DAYNAME;
            DATE : DAYINT;

    PROCEDURE MONTHHEADER(MONTH : MONTHNAME);

        PROCEDURE WRITEMONTH(MONTH : MONTHNAME);
            BEGIN ... END; (* WRITEMONTH *)

        BEGIN ... END; (* MONTHHEADER *)

    PROCEDURE DODAYNAMES;

        VAR DAY : DAYNAME;

        PROCEDURE WRITEDAY(DAY : DAYNAME);
            BEGIN ... END; (* WRITEDAY *)

        BEGIN ... END; (* DODAYNAMES *)

    FUNCTION DAYOFWEEK(D : DAYINT; MONTH : MONTHNAME; Y : YEARINT)
                                                    : DAYNAME;

        VAR ABSDAYNO : INTEGER; (* ABSOLUTE DAY NUMBER *)
            M : 1 .. 12; (* MONTH NUMBER *)

        BEGIN ... END; (* DAYOFWEEK *)

    FUNCTION DAYSINMONTH(MONTH : MONTHNAME; YEAR : YEARINT) : DAYINT;

        FUNCTION LEAP(YEAR : YEARINT) : BOOLEAN;
            BEGIN ... END; (* LEAP *)

        BEGIN ... END; (* DAYSINMONTH *)

    BEGIN ... END; (* DISPLAYMONTH *)

(* MAIN PROGRAM *)

BEGIN ... END.
```

15W:
```
FUNCTION LEAP(YEAR : YEARINT) : BOOLEAN;

    BEGIN
        LEAP := DAYOFWEEK(29, FEBRUARY, YEAR) <>
                DAYOFWEEK(1, MARCH, YEAR)
    END; (* LEAP *)
```

CHAPTER 16
Functions and Parameters

A common objective is shared by the two apparently unrelated topics covered in this chapter. That objective is the transmission of values between sections of programs. More specifically, it is concerned with the return of values from a called to a calling section of program.

16.1 FUNCTIONS

If procedures are thought of as enhancing the statement repertoire of a program, then functions enhance the computational power of expressions. Functions bear a close resemblance to procedures, so it is important to understand both the similarities and the subtle differences.

16.1.1 User-declared Functions

Like programmer-defined procedures, programmer-defined functions are declared in the declaration part of a block, be it in a program, a procedure declaration, or a function declaration. In chapter 15, we had examples of functions declared in each of these contexts. The function LOCATION was declared in the program STRING5 (section 15.2.1); DAYOFWEEK was declared in the procedure DISPLAYMONTH; and LEAP was declared within the function DAYSINMONTH (exercise 15V).

The declaration of a function is similar to that of a procedure in that it

- introduces a new identifier as the name of the function
- takes parameters in much the same way as a procedure
- describes the meaning of the function in terms of statements.

The syntax diagram of a function declaration is

function declaration:

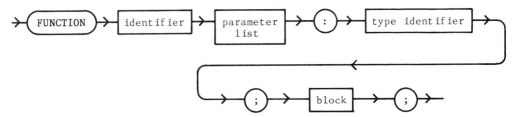

Unlike procedures, functions deliver values of given type, and are "called" from within expressions by what is known as a function reference. Referring back to section 4.3 it will be seen from the (incomplete) syntax diagram for "factor" how function references find their way into expressions. In that diagram the path through SQR represented the only function reference we had encountered at that time. The full syntax diagram for a function reference is

function reference:

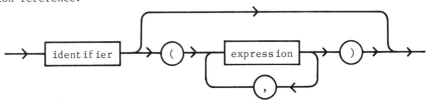

Within an expression, this syntactic unit always delivers a single value whose type is that of the function. The type of a function, always denoted by an identifier, may be one of the so-called primitive types (INTEGER, REAL, BOOLEAN and CHAR), an enumerated type or a subrange of any of these (but not a structured type). Two other types which functions may deliver will be revealed in chapters 17 and 19.

Function declarations are written along with procedure declarations. Within any block, function and procedure declarations follow the **VAR** section and precede the **BEGIN ... END**. They may be declared in arbitrary sequence, from the point of view of the syntax, but if, as is often the case, a procedure or function P1 refers to another procedure or function P2 in the same block, then P2 must precede P1, as for example the procedure RECTANGLE preceded the procedure FRAME in the program HOUSE2 in section 4.1. In other words, the scope of a procedure or function declaration is the union of

    (a)   the block which is its own body (thus admitting recursion)

    (b)   the bodies of any further procedures or functions declared after it at the same textual level (a concession to the compiler)

    (c)   the **BEGIN ... END** of the block in which the procedure or function is declared.

(You should recall that the scope of a variable is only (c) above.)

EXERCISE 16A: Draw a revised syntax diagram for a block based on that in section 4.2.

Some examples of functions and corresponding function references are given below. Note the variety of types of these functions.

- A function to return the greater of its two parameters is

        FUNCTION GREATER(X, Y : INTEGER) : INTEGER;

            BEGIN
                IF X > Y **THEN** GREATER := X **ELSE** GREATER := Y
            END; (* GREATER *)

    and within the scope of this function you can refer to it in statements such as

        T := GREATER(V[I], V[J])

        WRITELN(GREATER(C, D))

- A function to determine whether its parameter is an even integer yields a Boolean value.

        FUNCTION EVEN(I : INTEGER) : BOOLEAN;

            BEGIN
                EVEN := I **MOD** 2 = 0
            END; (* EVEN *)

    Examples of statements containing references to this function are

        IF NOT EVEN(N) **THEN** N := N + 1

        IF EVEN(I) **AND** EVEN(J) **THEN** K := (I + J) **DIV** 2

    Note that function references, since they are components of expressions, may appear as, or as part of, an actual parameter expression, as in

        IF EVEN(GREATER(A, B)) **THEN** ...

- A function to convert an integer in the range 0 to 6 into the name of the day of the week yields a value of an enumerated type.

        TYPE DAYNAME = (SUNDAY, MONDAY, TUESDAY, WEDNESDAY,
                        THURSDAY, FRIDAY, SATURDAY);
              DOWINT = 0 .. 6;

        FUNCTION INTTONAME(N : DOWINT) : DAYNAME;

            BEGIN
                CASE N **OF**

                    0: INTTONAME := SATURDAY;
                    1: INTTONAME := SUNDAY;
                    2: INTTONAME := MONDAY;
                    3: INTTONAME := TUESDAY;
                    4: INTTONAME := WEDNESDAY;
                    5: INTTONAME := THURSDAY;
                    6: INTTONAME := FRIDAY

                END
            END; (* INTTONAME *)

Note that the type of the function must be written as an identifier. It is tempting, but unfortunately wrong, to write the function heading as

```
FUNCTION INTTONAME(N : DOWINT) :
                    (SUNDAY, MONDAY, TUESDAY, WEDNESDAY,
                     THURSDAY, FRIDAY, SATURDAY);
```

An example of its use is

```
IF INTTONAME(6) <> FRIDAY THEN
    WRITELN('FUNCTION INTTONAME MUST BE WRONG')
```

- The following recursive function obtains the Highest Common Factor (HCF) of its two non-negative integer parameters by an ancient algorithm, ascribed to Euclid.

```
FUNCTION HCF(P, Q : INTEGER) : INTEGER;

    BEGIN
        IF Q = 0 THEN HCF := P
            ELSE HCF := HCF(Q, P MOD Q)
    END; (* HCF *)
```

It could be used in a section of program such as

```
FOR I := 1 TO 10 DO
    FOR J := 1 TO I DO
        WRITELN('HCF OF ', I, ' AND ', J, ' IS ', HCF(I, J))
```

EXERCISE 16B: In section 2.5.1 we stated that expressions were made up from

- operators (such as +, -)
- operands   (variables, constants)
- parentheses

Can you now be more specific about what is meant by "operand" in the context of integer-valued expressions?

EXERCISE 16C: How may the program developed in section 14.6.1 to find the best train in a timetable of schedules be improved by the use of a function in place of a procedure?

EXERCISE 16D: Suppose we have defined compass directions

```
TYPE DIR = (N, NE, E, SE, S, SW, W, NW);
```

Avoiding the use of case and if statements, write a function DEGREES, to convert a variable of type DIR into an integral number of degrees. For example,

```
DEGREES(NE) =  45
DEGREES(N)  =   0
DEGREES(W)  = 270
```

EXERCISE 16E: The following function seems at first sight to be the obvious way to compute Fibonacci numbers, that is, the sequence $\{f_i\}$

```
0  1  1  2  3  5  8  13  21  ...
```

where

$$f_0 = 0, \quad f_1 = 1$$

$$f_i = f_{i-1} + f_{i-2} \qquad \text{for } i \geq 2.$$

```
FUNCTION FIB(N : INTEGER) : INTEGER;

   BEGIN
      IF (N = 0) OR (N = 1) THEN FIB := N
                            ELSE FIB := FIB(N-1) + FIB(N-2)
   END; (* FIB *)
```

Verify that the calculation of f_N requires $2f_{N+1} - 1$ calls upon the function. (Hint: use induction on N.)

If, on a computer, it takes an average of 50 microseconds for each call of the function, estimate, in a suitable unit of time, how long it would take to evaluate f_{50} by this method.

Hint:
$$f_N = \left[\frac{1}{\text{sqrt}(5)} \left(\frac{\text{sqrt}(5)+1}{2} \right)^N + 0.5 \right]$$

Rewrite the function using iteration instead of recursion.

EXERCISE 16F: A little known relationship between the Fibonacci numbers and the Highest Common Factor function is that for any two non-negative integers i and j

$$f_{\text{HCF}(i, j)} = \text{HCF}(f_i, f_j)$$

Write a program which enables this relationship to be verified.

EXERCISE 16G: Make improvements to the program GREGORY1 in section 12.1.3, to incorporate better types and better validation of the date. The program CALENDAR in section 15.4 contains some useful material.

Since a function may produce a value of the same type as one of its parameters (which we assume to be a value parameter), it is possible for a function reference to appear in the actual parameter expression of a call for itself. For example, the statement

```
M := GREATER(GREATER(A, B), GREATER(C, D))
```

is readily seen to put the greatest of A, B, C and D into the variable M. It is tempting to consider this as another form of recursion, but in Pascal it is not. The expressions GREATER(A, B) and GREATER(C, D) are evaluated before the outer function is entered, and at all times during program execution, there is only one instance of the function in existence.

EXERCISE 16H: A celebrated example of recursion which has no known practical
               use (save to exercise the mind) is Ackerman's function. It is
               as easy to define in Pascal as it is in mathematics.

             FUNCTION A(M, N : INTEGER) : INTEGER;

                 BEGIN
                 IF M = 0 THEN A := N + 1
                         ELSE IF N = 0 THEN A := A(M-1, 1)
                                       ELSE A := A(M-1, A(M, N-1))
                 END; (* ACKERMAN *)

          Evaluate A(2, 3) without the use of the computer.

16.1.2 The Standard Pre-declared Functions

    We have used many of the standard pre-declared functions elsewhere. It
should be noted in the table below that although the pre-declared functions
are described as "standard" functions, this relates to their provision in all
Pascal systems rather than their nature. With the exception of ODD and CHR,
their respect for the strong typing of Pascal is anything but standard. For
example, SUCC and PRED are very weakly typed, since they admit any enumerated
type (including CHAR and BOOLEAN) as parameter, and return a value of the same
type.

Name	Type of parameter	Type of result	Description
ODD	INTEGER	BOOLEAN	true if parameter is odd, otherwise false
EOLN	none so far, but see chapter 22	BOOLEAN	true if last character read was the end of line space (not standard Pascal)
ORD	any enumerated type	INTEGER	result is the ordinal number of the value of the parameter in the set it is defined in. Starts at 0
CHR	INTEGER	CHAR	converts integer value to corresponding character
SUCC	any enumerated type	same as parameter	next value in enumeration
PRED	any enumerated type	same as parameter	previous value in enumeration
SQR	INTEGER or REAL (see chapter 17)	same as parameter	square of parameter

    Further standard pre-defined functions will be given in chapters 18
and 22. Examples of the uses of the functions above are

```
WHILE NOT EOLN DO READ(C)        (* ignores all characters up to the
                                    end of the line *)
IF ORD(CHR(I)) <> I THEN WRITE('SOMETHING''S WRONG')

IF ODD(4) THEN WRITE('SOMETHING ELSE IS WRONG')

IF I*I <> SQR(I) THEN WRITE('WE HAVE MAJOR PROBLEMS')
```

16.1.3 Comparison between Procedures and Functions

The principal differences between functions and procedures can be summarized in the following table.

	Function	Procedure
Basic objective	To generate a value	To perform some action(s)
Where used	As a component of an expression (and therefore must have a value)	As a statement (and therefore, may do nothing)
How declared	Use reserved word **FUNCTION**	Use reserved word **PROCEDURE**
	The type of the result must be specified in the heading	Has no type
	There must be at least one assignment to the name of the function on each execution	Has no value

16.1.4 Side Effects

The purpose of a function is to compute a value, and generally speaking functions should do no more than this. They should refrain from making any changes to the world outside. The proper name for such behavior is a side effect. There are 3 kinds of side effect, all to be avoided in a function.

- Output
- Assignment to a non-local variable
- Use of a variable parameter

Side effects are generally benign in procedures, but assignment to non-local variables should be avoided, unless there is good cause, since it impairs the readability of a program. The reason for the difference in attitude is that the notion of sequence is strong in the context of statements, but weak in the context of expressions. Procedures are called by procedure statements, and the sequence in which statements are executed is well defined. On the other hand,

functions are "called" from expressions, but the order in which the operands
of an expression are evaluated is not defined. As an example, the expression

     SQR(3) + SQR(4)

could be evaluated in the sequence

          evaluate SQR(3),   evaluate SQR(4),   add them together

or, in the sequence

          evaluate SQR(4),   evaluate SQR(3),   add them together

Since the standard function SQR has no side effects the result is always the
same. However, suppose SQR had the side effect of displaying its parameter,
then in the first instance, it would display

     34

and in the second

     43

     Side effects in functions therefore inhibit portability (that is, the
ease with which a program may be moved from one computer to another) and impair
the human reader's confidence in understanding a program.

16.2 PARAMETERS

     We have been deliberately vague on certain aspects of procedures and
functions. In section 11.1 it was noted that a formal parameter was really a
variable which has its initial value set to the value of the corresponding
actual parameter at the time the call is made. Whilst this is the case for
value parameters, we now have variable parameters to consider. It is important
to be clear how these two kinds of parameter differ.

16.2.1 Value Parameters

     More precisely, the call of a procedure or a function with value
parameters is as follows.

     1. It is essential that the actual parameters and the formal
         parameters match each other in number, type and order. Type
         matching should be in accordance with the rules for the
         assignment statement, namely, that for a corresponding pair of
         formal and actual parameters, an assignment statement of the form

              formal parameter := actual parameter

is legal. (For other kinds of parameter see sections 16.2.3 and 16.2.4.) Most mismatches will be found during compilation.

2. On entry to a function, a special kind of variable is created to accept the value of the function. Initially, the value of this variable is undefined. Within the function, a value can only be placed into this variable, that is, it may only appear as the left-hand side of an assignment statement. During execution of the function, there must be at least one such assignment to the name of the function.

3. For each formal parameter a variable is created, and initially assigned the value of the corresponding actual parameter at the time the call is made. This variable may be written to, but in none of the examples thus far have we done so. It is the emphasis on values being transferred that gives rise to the term "value parameter" (or call by value).

4. For each local identifier, a new variable is created, and the value is left undefined.

5. The body or statement part of the function or procedure is executed.

6. On exit, the variables created for the parameters and the local identifiers are destroyed. In the case of a function, the value in the special variable is used as the value of the function designator in the expression in which it appeared and then it too is destroyed.

In the case of a recursive function or procedure, each call or invocation involves a fresh application of rules 2 to 6, and a fresh set of variables (parameters and locals) is created for each call.

16.2.2 Variable Parameters

Variable parameters are dealt with differently to value parameters. Variable parameters are permitted in both functions and procedures but as their use in a function opens the way for another form of side effect, it is to be discouraged. The following rules should be read in conjunction with those in section 16.2.1.

1. Additionally, an assignment statement of the form

    actual parameter := formal parameter

    must be legal for each parameter of each call. (The significance of this will become apparent when the type REAL is introduced in chapter 17.)

2. No change.

3. At entry to a procedure, a special variable is reserved for each variable parameter. Into this special variable is placed a reference to the variable which is the actual parameter of that call. If the variable is subscripted then the reference is to the element specified at the time of the call.

4. No change.

5. During execution, all occurrences of a formal variable parameter
are interpreted as occurrences of the actual parameter via the
specially reserved variable. Thus, the actual parameter may be
changed by the procedure.

6. No change.

The procedure GETREPLY of exercise 9H provides an example of the use of a
variable parameter. As it stands, it leaves its result in the non-local
variable REPLY. If it were to pass its result back through a parameter it
would have to be a variable parameter.

```
PROCEDURE GETREPLY(VAR C : CHAR);

    BEGIN
        REPEAT READ(C) UNTIL C <> ' ';
        WRITELN;
        IF NOT((C = 'Y') OR (C = 'N')) THEN
            BEGIN
                WRITELN('SORRY, YOU MUST TYPE Y OR N');
                GETREPLY(C)
            END
    END; (* GETREPLY *)
```

As another example of the need for and use of variable parameters,
consider the following procedure to interchange the values of any two integer
variables.

```
PROCEDURE SWAP(VAR A, B : INTEGER);

    VAR T : INTEGER;

    BEGIN
        T := A;
        A := B;
        B := T
    END; (* SWAP *)
```

It could, for example, be called by any of the following procedure statements.

```
IF X > Y THEN SWAP(X, Y)

SWAP(NUM[I], NUM[J])

SWAP(BIGMILL.THETA, SMALLMILL.THETA)
```

A procedure such as this can be used in sorting (or arranging) the
elements of an array of integers.

EXERCISE 16J: What is achieved by the sequence of statements

```
IF X > Y THEN SWAP(X, Y);
IF Y > Z THEN SWAP(Y, Z);
IF X > Y THEN SWAP(X, Y)
```

The restriction in rule 1 above cannot be over-emphasized. It prohibits
the use of non-variables (such as constants and most expressions) as actual
parameters where the corresponding formal parameter is a variable parameter.
It is not an unreasonable rule in view of rule 5, for if the formal parameter
appears on the left-hand side of an assignment statement, then the assignment
has to be interpreted as one to the actual parameter. You can only assign a

value to something that can receive a value. Therefore the actual parameter must be a variable.

In Apple Pascal, a variable parameter may not be used as the control variable of a for statement.

EXERCISE 16K: Explain why and how the procedure SWAP would fail, if either or both formal parameters were value parameters.

EXERCISE 16L: Read rule 3 in this section carefully, and then determine what the following program displays.

```
PROGRAM SELFCHECK;

TYPE D7 = 1 .. 7;

VAR A : ARRAY [D7] OF CHAR;
    M : D7;

PROCEDURE P(VAR I : D7; VAR J : CHAR; K : CHAR);

    BEGIN
        A[M - 3] := A[M];
        I := I + 1;     A[I - 1] := A[I - 2];
        A[M] := J;
        M := M - 4;     J := A[I];
        I := I + 3;     A[M + 3] := K
    END; (* P *)

BEGIN
    A[1] := 'T';   A[2] := 'O';   A[3] := 'R';  A[4] := 'C';
    A[5] := 'H';   A[6] := 'E';   A[7] := 'S';
    M := 4;
    P(M, A[M + 2], A[M - 3]);
    WRITELN;
    FOR M := 1 TO 7 DO WRITE(A[M]);
    WRITELN
END.
```

16.2.3 Array and Record Parameters

Arrays and records are collections of fixed numbers of elements. A procedure or a function may have parameters of array or record type. But since an array type embodies both the index type and the component type (section 14.3) correspondence between formal and actual parameter types has to recognize both types. The index types must be identical, but the basic component types only have to agree to within the conditions laid down for unstructured types.

A record type embodies a structure of types representing its constituent fields. The structures must be identical, and the basic fields must match to within their base types.

Since the formal parameters must be given as type identifiers it is always safe to adopt the practice of restricting actual parameters of structured type to be declared as of the same named type.

The constraint on the index type of arrays is one of the most severe restrictions in Pascal. It means that a procedure written to operate on an array of a given index type can only operate on an array of that index type. For example, the following procedure, which reverses the elements of an array of 10 integers, cannot even be used to reverse arrays of fewer than 10

integers. Neither can it be used to reverse arrays of 10 integers whose index
type is other than 1 .. 10.

```
CONST N = 10;

TYPE A = ARRAY [1 .. N] OF INTEGER;

PROCEDURE REVERSE(VAR NUM : A);

    VAR I : 1 .. N;

    BEGIN
        FOR I := 1 TO N DIV 2 DO SWAP(NUM[I], NUM[N+1-I])
    END; (* REVERSE *)
```

If other than 10 integers are to be reversed, the constant N has to be given a
different value, and the program has to be re-compiled. In this particular
instance, this may not seem to be too great an inconvenience, but the problem
becomes severe if, in a program, several arrays of different index type have to
be reversed. A separate procedure for each index type is required.

    This limitation has been recognized by those who have drafted recent
proposals for an international standard for Pascal [ISO, 1981]. An optional
feature, known as conformant array parameters, but not implemented in
Apple Pascal, permits the formal parameter to be specified in a way that allows
the upper and lower bounds of each dimension of an array to be available to the
procedure or function. In the example quoted above, we could write

```
PROCEDURE REVERSE(VAR NUM : ARRAY [LOWER .. UPPER] OF INTEGER);

    VAR I, SIZE : INTEGER;

    BEGIN
        SIZE := UPPER - LOWER + 1;
        FOR I := 1 TO SIZE DIV 2 DO
            SWAP(NUM[LOWER + I - 1], NUM[UPPER - I + 1])
    END; (* REVERSE *)
```

For a fuller account of conformant array parameters, see [Welsh and Elder,
1982].

    If an array or record parameter is specified as a value parameter, then
every element of the array or field of the record is treated as though it were
a value parameter. This means

(a)   space for a local copy of the complete array or record has to be
      made at procedure or function entry, and then

(b)   a whole array or complete record transfer of the actual
      parameter structure into the space created at (a) is made.

    Such copying can be time- and space-consuming, and should only be
considered if there is a need to make local changes to the structure within the
function or procedure. It is usual therefore to specify array or record
parameters as variable parameters.

EXERCISE 16M: Write a function whose value is the greatest element in an

                    ARRAY [1 .. 20] OF INTEGER

EXERCISE 16N: (For those who can remember some linear algebra.)

A function is to be written to evaluate the determinant of a
(square) matrix. Should the array representing the matrix be a
value or variable parameter?

16.2.4 Function and Procedure Parameters (Not in Apple Pascal)

Suppose you wish to write a procedure to tabulate a function for a given
range of values. You may go to quite some trouble to make the layout pretty,
and then find that it was so successful that you are asked to make it
tabulate other functions. It is clear that, not only should the range of
tabulation be expressed as parameters, but that the function to be tabulated
should also be a parameter. Suppose there are several functions to be
tabulated, for example,

```
FUNCTION CUBE(I : INTEGER) : INTEGER;

    BEGIN
        CUBE := I*I*I
    END; (* CUBE *)


FUNCTION FIBONACCI(N : INTEGER) : INTEGER;

    VAR I, NEXT, PREV, THIS : INTEGER;

    BEGIN
        IF N <= 1 THEN FIBONACCI := N
        ELSE
            BEGIN
                PREV := 0;  THIS := 1;
                FOR I := 2 TO N DO
                    BEGIN
                        NEXT := THIS + PREV;
                        PREV := THIS;  THIS := NEXT
                    END;
                FIBONACCI := NEXT
            END
    END; (* FIBONACCI *)
```

it would be nice to be able to write

```
TABULATE(CUBE, 1, 10);
TABULATE(FIBONACCI, 0, 20)
```

To keep the program as simple as possible, we will keep the layout simple.
The procedure TABULATE requires three parameters, one of which has to
describe an integer function of one integer parameter. In Pascal this is a
third kind of parameter. (The other two were value parameters and variable
parameters.) It may be written

```
        PROCEDURE TABULATE(FUNCTION F(X : INTEGER) : INTEGER;
                           A, B : INTEGER);

            VAR I : INTEGER;

            BEGIN
                WRITELN;
                FOR I := A TO B DO WRITELN(I : 8, F(I) : 8)
            END; (* TABULATE *)
```

The new kind of parameter, **FUNCTION** F(X : INTEGER) : INTEGER is called
a function parameter. In this context, the identifier X is merely a
dummy and actual function parameters are not constrained to use the same
identifier. Any reference in the procedure TABULATE to the function parameter
F is interpreted as a reference to the function named as the actual parameter
of the call. The complete program to tabulate both functions is

```
        PROGRAM TWOTABS;

        FUNCTION CUBE(I : INTEGER) : INTEGER;

            BEGIN
                CUBE := I*I*I
            END; (* CUBE *)

        FUNCTION FIBONACCI(N : INTEGER) : INTEGER;

            VAR I, NEXT, PREV, THIS : INTEGER;

            BEGIN
                IF N <= 1 THEN FIBONACCI := N
                ELSE
                    BEGIN
                        PREV := 0;  THIS := 1;
                        FOR I := 2 TO N DO
                            BEGIN
                                NEXT := THIS + PREV;
                                PREV := THIS;  THIS := NEXT
                            END;
                        FIBONACCI := NEXT
                    END
            END; (* FIBONACCI *)

        PROCEDURE TABULATE(FUNCTION F(X : INTEGER) : INTEGER;
                           A, B : INTEGER);

            VAR I : INTEGER;

            BEGIN
                WRITELN;
                FOR I := A TO B DO WRITELN(I : 8, F(I) : 8)
            END; (* TABULATE *)

        BEGIN
            TABULATE(CUBE, 1, 10);
            TABULATE(FIBONACCI, 0, 20)
        END.
```

Certain restrictions apply to function parameters. The first two are
common sense.

1. In the declaration of the formal function parameter, the type of
    function and its parameters are given (for example,
    FUNCTION F(X : INTEGER) : INTEGER) and all corresponding
    actual parameters must also be of this pattern. For example,

    > CUBE(I : INTEGER) : INTEGER

    > FIBONACCI(N : INTEGER) : INTEGER

2. The parameters of the actual function parameters must agree in
    number, order and type. (For example, CUBE and FIBONACCI are
    both functions of a single integer variable.)

3. The parameters of function parameters must be value parameters.

EXERCISE 16P: Write a procedure which prints out the truth table of any
                Boolean function of 3 Boolean parameters. See, for example,
                exercise 8A. The procedure's heading might be

    > **PROCEDURE** TRUTHTABLE(**FUNCTION** L(P, Q, R : BOOLEAN)
    >   : BOOLEAN);

The use of <u>procedure parameters</u> (the fourth kind of parameter) is
less common but the rules above basically still apply.

16.2.5 The Syntax of the Parameter List

Parameters of different type and kind are separated from each other in the
parameter list by semicolons. For this purpose, value, variable, function and
procedure parameters are regarded as being of different kinds. Think of one
or more parameters of the same type and kind as forming a group. Groups are
separated by semicolons, and parameter identifiers within the group are
separated by commas. There is no limit to the number of groups, so the
ordering of parameters remains the choice of the programmer. For example, if
it is desirable that the parameters of a procedure X be declared in the order
A, B, RC, RD, RE, F, where A, B and F are integer value parameters, and RC,
RD and RE are integer variable parameters, they would be declared as

> **PROCEDURE** X(A, B : INTEGER; **VAR** RC, RD, RE : INTEGER; F : INTEGER);

Ignoring procedure and function parameters the syntax diagram is

parameter list: [incomplete]

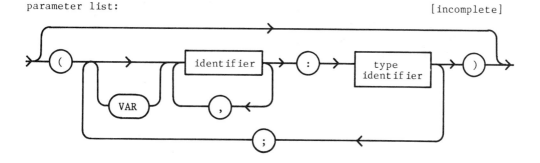

SOLUTIONS TO THE EXERCISES

16A: block: [incomplete]

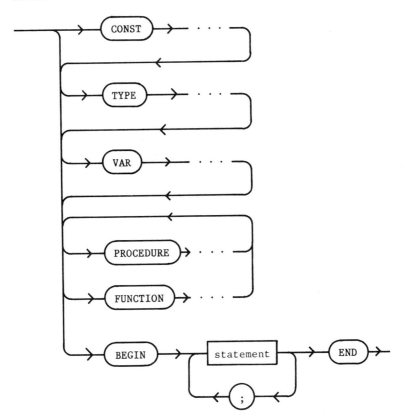

16B: An operand in an expression of type INTEGER can be a constant, a
        variable (including an array element or a record field) or a function
        reference.

16C: The procedure CALCTIME has only one purpose: to produce a value in
        SCHEDULETIME. It should be written as a function named SCHEDULETIME
        thus removing the need for a variable of that name. The procedure
        UPDATEFASTESTSOFAR remains a procedure, but it should be given, as a
        parameter, the value to be updated. Thus the body of the procedure
        DISPLAYFASTEST could begin

```
BEGIN (* DISPLAYFASTEST *)
    N := 1;
    UPDATEFASTESTSOFAR(SCHEDULETIME);
    FOR N := 2 TO TRAINSPERDAY DO
        IF SCHEDULETIME < BESTTIMESOFAR THEN
            UPDATEFASTESTSOFAR(SCHEDULETIME);
    ...
```

16D: **FUNCTION** DEGREES(D : DIR) : INTEGER;

```
        BEGIN
            DEGREES := ORD(D)*45
        END (* OF DEGREES *);
```

16E: If $n > 1$ then the number of calls C_n of FIB is 1 to get into it for the first time, plus C_{n-1} for the first recursive call, plus C_{n-2} for the second recursive call.

Therefore, $\qquad C_n = C_{n-1} + C_{n-2} + 1 \qquad\qquad -- (1)$

Assume as the inductive hypothesis, that for all n in $2 \le n \le N-1$

$$C_n = 2f_{n+1} - 1$$

From (1) and the inductive hypothesis,

$$C_N = 2f_N - 1 + 2f_{N-1} - 1 + 1$$
$$= 2(f_N + f_{N-1}) - 1$$
$$= 2f_{N+1} - 1$$

It is trivial to check that the formula is true for $N = 0$ and $N = 1$. Therefore the inductive hypothesis is true for all N.

$$f_{51} = 2.037 \times 10^{10}$$

Therefore, time = 50 (2 x 2.037 x 10^{10} - 1) microseconds
$$= 23.57 \text{ days.}$$

A more satisfactory function will be found in section 16.2.4 of the text.

16F: **PROGRAM** EX16F;

VAR I, J : INTEGER;

FUNCTION FIBONACCI(N : INTEGER) : INTEGER; ...; (* BETTER TO USE THE
VERSION IN SECTION 16.2.4 *)
FUNCTION HCF(P, Q : INTEGER) : INTEGER; ...;

```
BEGIN
  FOR I := 1 TO 12 DO
    FOR J := 1 TO I DO
      WRITELN(I:4, J:4,
        HCF(FIBONACCI(I), FIBONACCI(J)):6, FIBONACCI(HCF(I, J)):6)
END.
```

```
16G:     PROGRAM GREGORY2;

         TYPE DAYINT = 1 .. 31;
              MONTHINT = 1 .. 12;
              YEARINT = 1583 .. 4317;
              DAYNAME = (SUNDAY, MONDAY, TUESDAY, WEDNESDAY, THURSDAY,
                         FRIDAY, SATURDAY);
              MONTHNAME = (JANUARY, FEBRUARY, MARCH, APRIL, MAY, JUNE, JULY,
                           AUGUST, SEPTEMBER, OCTOBER, NOVEMBER, DECEMBER);

         VAR DAY : DAYINT; MONTH : MONTHINT; YEAR : YEARINT;

         FUNCTION DAYOFWEEK(D : DAYINT; M : MONTHINT; Y : YEARINT)
                                                    : DAYNAME; ...;
         PROCEDURE WRITEDAY(DAY : DAYNAME); ...;
         PROCEDURE WRITEMONTH(MONTH : MONTHINT); ...;

         PROCEDURE GETDATE(VAR D : DAYINT; VAR M : MONTHINT; VAR Y : YEARINT);

            VAR DIN, MIN, YIN : INTEGER;

            FUNCTION DAYSINMONTH(MONTH : MONTHINT; YEAR : YEARINT) : DAYINT;

               FUNCTION LEAP(YEAR : YEARINT) : BOOLEAN;

                  BEGIN
                      LEAP := DAYOFWEEK(29, 2, YEAR) <> DAYOFWEEK(1, 3, YEAR)
                  END; (* LEAP *)

               BEGIN (* DAYSINMONTH *)
                  IF (MONTH = 2) THEN
                      IF LEAP(YEAR) THEN DAYSINMONTH := 29
                                    ELSE DAYSINMONTH := 28
                  ELSE IF (MONTH = 4) OR (MONTH = 6) OR
                          (MONTH = 9) OR (MONTH = 11)
                       THEN DAYSINMONTH := 30
                       ELSE DAYSINMONTH := 31
               END; (* DAYSINMONTH *)

            BEGIN (* GETDATE *)
               READ(DIN, MIN, YIN);
               WRITELN;
               IF (YIN < 1583) OR (YIN > 4317) THEN
                   BEGIN
                       WRITE('YEAR OUT OF RANGE 1583 TO 4317.');
                       WRITELN('  PLEASE TRY AGAIN');
                       GETDATE(D, M, Y)
                   END
               ELSE
                   IF NOT (MIN IN [1 .. 12]) THEN
                       BEGIN
                           WRITE('MONTH OUT OF RANGE 1 TO 12.');
                           WRITELN('  PLEASE TRY AGAIN');
                           GETDATE(D, M, Y)
                       END
                   ELSE
                       IF NOT (DIN IN [1 .. DAYSINMONTH(MIN, YIN)]) THEN
                           BEGIN
                               WRITE('DAY IS INVALID.');
                               WRITELN('  PLEASE TRY AGAIN');
                               GETDATE(D, M, Y)
                           END
                       ELSE
                           BEGIN
                               D := DIN;  M := MIN;  Y := YIN
                           END
            END; (* GETDATE *)
```

```
BEGIN
    REPEAT
        WRITELN;  WRITELN('ENTER DATE AS 3 INTEGERS, DAY MONTH YEAR');
        GETDATE(DAY, MONTH, YEAR);
        WRITE(DAY, ' ');
        WRITEMONTH(MONTH);
        WRITE(' ', YEAR, ' IS A ');
        WRITEDAY(DAYOFWEEK(DAY, MONTH, YEAR)); WRITELN;
    UNTIL FALSE
END.
```

16H: 9

16J: The values in X, Y and Z satisfy

$$X \leq Y \leq Z$$

In other words, the values of X, Y and Z are "sorted" in increasing
value.

16K: Both A and B appear on the left-hand side of assignment statements
which cause the actual parameter to be given new values. Therefore
both must be variable parameters. If either is a value parameter, the
actual parameters finish up equal, and if both are value parameters,
the actual parameters finish up unchanged.

16L: CORRECT

16M: TYPE A20 = ARRAY [1 .. 20] OF INTEGER;

FUNCTION MAX(A : A20) : INTEGER;

```
    VAR I, MAXSOFAR : INTEGER;

    BEGIN
        MAXSOFAR := A[1];
        FOR I := 2 TO 20 DO
            IF A[I] > MAXSOFAR THEN MAXSOFAR := A[I];
        MAX := MAXSOFAR
    END; (* MAX *)
```

16N: The usual method of finding the determinant of a square matrix is to
change it to a triangular form. This implies changing the values of
the elements of the matrix. Since what is required by the caller of
such a function is merely a number, and an unaltered matrix, use of a
value parameter neatly achieves the desired result without the
programmer having explicitly to save a copy of the original matrix.

16P: Not Apple Pascal. The procedure shown below assumes a procedure
        WRITEBOOL, which displays the value of its Boolean parameter. It makes
        no attempt to present the values in a neatly ruled table.

```
PROCEDURE TRUTHTABLE(FUNCTION L(P, Q, R : BOOLEAN) : BOOLEAN);

    VAR A, B, C : BOOLEAN;

    BEGIN
        FOR A := FALSE TO TRUE DO
            FOR B := FALSE TO TRUE DO
                FOR C := FALSE TO TRUE DO
                    BEGIN
                        WRITEBOOL(A);
                        WRITEBOOL(B);
                        WRITEBOOL(C);
                        WRITEBOOL(L(A, B, C));
                        WRITELN
                    END
    END; (* TRUTHTABLE *)
```

CHAPTER 17
Experimenting with Reals

In one or two places so far, we have been somewhat embarrassed by the restriction of numerical values to the integers. In exercises 3M and 3N, the 7-sided regular polygon presented difficulties and in exercise 14K we conveniently ignored the halfpenny. But, in section 6.4 the problem was severe, and our snooker shots were restricted to a set of only eight not very interesting directions. Otherwise our avoidance of non-integers was perhaps more due to the careful planning of the chosen examples than good luck. For the present, we shall start by regarding non-integers, or values of type REAL, as values in between consecutive integers and in chapter 18 give a more formal account.

17.1   THE NUMBERS IN BETWEEN

It is the operation of division that gives rise to non-integers. So far we have only used a special kind of division DIV, which throws away remainders and does not in general enable a value to be divided into equal parts. The operator DIV always produces an integer result. The operator which does a much better job of dividing into equal parts is

Its operator precedence (see section 8.2.2) is the same as that of DIV. We use it in the following program to investigate the numbers in between the integers. Compile and execute the following program which is in the file REAL1.TEXT on the MACC: disk.

```
PROGRAM REAL1;

VAR X : REAL;  I : INTEGER;

BEGIN
    X := 0;
    FOR I := 1 TO 20 DO
        BEGIN
            WRITELN(I : 7, ' ', X);
            X := (3 + X)/4
        END
END.
```

Whilst the program is compiling, note that X is a variable that takes values
of type REAL, and that the interval 0 to 1 is successively quartered. You
should also note that the expression

$$(3 + X)/4$$

contains a mixture of operands of type INTEGER and REAL. This is one of
Pascal's few concessions to its policy of strong typing. Whenever real and
integer values are mixed in an expression, the result is real.

There are three important points to be noticed from the program just
executed.

- Pascal's output procedure has used two different ways of
  displaying real values on the screen. In the form with an 'E',
  'E' means "times 10 to the power of". For example, 7.50000E-1
  denotes 0.75.

- Real values seem to be expressed to an accuracy of only 6
  significant figures.

- There comes a point where it is no longer possible to divide the
  interval into quarters. There would appear to be no more numbers
  in between.

The last two observations are a direct consequence of the way these
numbers are represented internally. There will be more on this in chapter 18.
The important thing to understand is that values of the type REAL are not
continuous and they will, in general, only be approximations to the values
in the world outside which they represent. This will be developed in section
17.3.

EXERCISE 17A: The program contains a mixed assignment statement. Which one
                is it? Do you think a mixed assignment statement of the form

                    integer variable := real expression

                would be allowed?

EXERCISE 17B: (Can be omitted at a first reading). Rewrite the program REAL1
                using a recursive procedure.

17.2 THE NUMBERS OUT BEYOND

Compile and execute the following program in in the file REAL2.TEXT on the MACC: disk. (The function FIBONACCI is from section 16.2.4.)

```
PROGRAM REAL2;

VAR I : INTEGER;

FUNCTION FIBONACCI(N : INTEGER) : INTEGER;

    VAR I, NEXT, PREV, THIS : INTEGER;

    BEGIN
        IF N <= 1 THEN FIBONACCI := N
        ELSE
            BEGIN
                PREV := 0;   THIS := 1;
                FOR I := 2 TO N DO
                    BEGIN
                        NEXT := THIS + PREV;
                        PREV := THIS;   THIS := NEXT
                    END;
                FIBONACCI := NEXT
            END
    END; (* FIBONACCI *)

BEGIN
    FOR I := 1 TO 30 DO
        BEGIN
            WRITE(I : 9, FIBONACCI(I) : 11);
            IF NOT ODD(I) THEN WRITELN
        END
END.
```

This program gets into trouble as soon as the values it attempts to display exceed the range of integers.

EXERCISE 17C: (a) What is f_{24}, the 24th Fibonacci number?

(b) What is the difference between f_{24} and the value of FIBONACCI(24) produced by the program REAL2?

(c) Express the answer to (b) as a power of 2.

The exercise above should remind you that standard integer arithmetic on the Apple is restricted to the range

$$-2^{15} \quad \text{to} \quad 2^{15} - 1 \qquad (-32768 \quad \text{to} \quad 32767)$$

and that any attempt to compute a value outside this range is evaluated modulo 2^{16} and then adjusted to the range above.

Starting with the program REAL2, change the type of the variables NEXT, PREV and THIS to REAL, and change the type of the function FIBONACCI to REAL and observe the difference that this makes.

EXERCISE 17D: Write down the value of f_{30}.

With the program currently in the workfile, extend the upper limit of the for statement from 30 to 200. This attempts to exceed the range of values of the type REAL and will cause an error. You should then see that the overall range of real values extends to about 3.4×10^{38} and that the number of significant figures remains at six.

EXERCISE 17E: Run the program again, and using CTRL-S, stop the display so that you can deduce which is the largest Fibonacci number that this program displays precisely.

At the other end of the scale, as numbers approach zero, there is a limit to the smallness of a number of type REAL. Make the following change to the program in MACC:REAL1.TEXT.

change	X := 0;	to	X := 1;
change	(3 + X)/4	to	(0 + X)/4
change	20	to	70

and execute it.

EXERCISE 17F: What appears to be the closest we can approach to zero without actually getting there?

Similar limits apply to negative values. A full summary of the range and precision of real values appears in chapter 18.

17.3 A CAUTIONARY TALE

Since values of type REAL are, in general, only approximations to the numbers they represent, it follows that two different but mathematically equivalent computations may yield two different approximations to the mathematically precise value. The program in the file MACC:REAL3.TEXT would, on an ideal computer, give no output. However, execute it and see what happens.


```
PROGRAM REAL3;

VAR I : INTEGER;

BEGIN
    FOR I := 2 TO 100 DO
        BEGIN
        IF I * (1/I) > 1 THEN WRITELN(I, ' GREATER');
        IF I * (1/I) < 1 THEN WRITELN(I, ' LESS')
        END
END.
```

EXERCISE 17G: What can you say about the computer's calculated value of

                41 * (1/41)

     Whilst you may not be tempted to write such expressions as the one above,
the following fragment of program seems more plausible.

```
VAR X : REAL;
    .
    .
    .
X := 5;
REPEAT
    WRITELN(X, '  ', 1/X);
    X := X + 5.0
UNTIL X = 105.0
```

and it may terminate on most computers (including the Apple). If it does
terminate, the reason is probably that great care has been taken to represent
whole number values in real variables, precisely. Nevertheless, it is bad
programming practice to make assumptions about the precise value of a real
variable.

EXERCISE 17H: If X = 105.0 is replaced by X >= 100.0 will it prevent any
                computer executing the loop indefinitely? Will the loop
                necessarily be executed the same number of times on all
                computers? How should the program fragment above be written?

     A more general problem is that of dividing a real interval [A, B] into N
equal sized subintervals. The following for statement successively gives the
variable T the (N+1) approximations to the points of division.

```
H := (B - A)/N;
FOR I := 0 TO N DO
    BEGIN
        T := A + I*H;
        ...
    END
```

EXERCISE 17J: Write a similar sequence of statements where the interval
                [A, B] is to be divided into the smallest number of equally
                sized subintervals of size not greater than G.

17.4 STANDARD REAL FUNCTIONS

     Commonly used arithmetic, trigonometric and logarithmic functions are
provided amongst the standard functions of Apple Pascal. The trigonometric
and logarithmic functions are in a unit called TRANSCEND and therefore programs
requiring them must include this unit name in the uses section, for example,

        USES TRANSCEND;   or   USES TURTLEGRAPHICS, TRANSCEND;

17.4.1 Trigonometric Functions

All angles are in radians. The type of the actual parameter expression denoted by x may be integer or real. The result is always real.

ATAN(x)	$\tan^{-1}x$ in the range	$-\dfrac{pi}{2}$ to $\dfrac{pi}{2}$
COS(x)	cos x	x is in radians
SIN(x)	sin x	x is in radians

In standard Pascal, the function for $\tan^{-1}x$ is called ARCTAN. Although $\tan^{-1}$ can take an infinite argument, ATAN cannot. Thus, ATAN(x/0) will cause overflow before ATAN is entered.

17.4.2 Logarithmic and Exponential Functions

The type of the actual parameter expression may be integer or real. The result is always real.

EXP(x)	e^x
LN(x)	$\log_e x$

17.4.3 Miscellaneous Arithmetic Functions

ABS(x)	$\lvert x \rvert$ which may be expressed as IF X < 0 THEN ABS := -X ELSE ABS := X x may be of type real or integer, and the result is of the same type.
SQR(x)	x^2 x may be of type real or integer, and the result is of the same type
SQRT(x)	square root of x x may be of type real or integer. The result is always of type real

17.4.4 Transfer Functions

There are two ways of converting a real value to an integer value

- ignore the fractional part
- round to the nearest integer.

To ignore the fractional part of a real value, we write the function reference

    TRUNC(x)

Thus

    TRUNC(3.8) = 3
    TRUNC(-3.8) = -3

To round to the nearest integer, we write

    ROUND(x)

where ROUND(x) is defined to be

    TRUNC(x + 0.5)   for x >= 0
    TRUNC(x - 0.5)   for x < 0

Thus

    ROUND(3.8) = 4
    ROUND(4.2) = 4
    ROUND(4.5) = 5
    ROUND(-3.5) = -4

    If the value of the result of one of these functions is outside the range of integer values, an execution error is signalled.

EXERCISE 17K: Write down an expression whose value is an approximation to pi, the ratio of the circumference of a circle to its radius.

EXERCISE 17L: Use the computer to find out the approximate difference between pi and

            (a) 22/7
            (b) 3.142

EXERCISE 17M: Assuming the variable PI has the value of the expression in exercise 17K, write down an expression for sin 31°.

EXERCISE 17N: (a) Write a function FRAC(x) which delivers the fractional part of the real number x. That is

                FRAC(3.8) = 0.8
                FRAC(-3.8) = -0.8

            (b) Write a function MYTRUNC(x) which truncates the real number x towards minus infinity. That is

                MYTRUNC(3.8) = 3
                MYTRUNC(-3.8) = -4
                MYTRUNC(-3.0) = -3

EXERCISE 17P: Using the formula

$$a^2 = b^2 + c^2 - 2 \, b \, c \, \cos A$$

write down an assignment statement which finds "a", the third side of a triangle, given two sides, "b" and "c", and the included angle "A".

17.5 A BETTER TURTLE

In chapter 6 we discovered a limitation of the Apple turtle. The resolution of the graphics is such that only the points of intersection of a 280 by 192 grid may be illuminated. Whilst this does allow reasonable diagrams to be drawn, it cannot define with sufficient accuracy the coordinates at which the turtle finishes after an arbitrary MOVE. For example, if the turtle is at (0, 0) and its heading is 45°, then MOVE(1) should send it to (0.7071, 0.7071), approximately. It is obviously sensible to illuminate the dot at (1, 1) as a result of this move, but it is not very sensible to move the turtle there as well. This is especially so when a program instructs the turtle to make a large number of small moves.

We can overcome this ourselves by keeping track of where the turtle ought to be, or at least a better approximation than the grid of points whose coordinates are integers. Let the better approximation be (REALX, REALY), a pair of real variables which provide about 6 significant figures of accuracy. In order to make use of REALX and REALY we should write our own procedures say MYMOVE and MYMOVETO, to keep them as accurately updated as possible. We can give these procedures real parameters, and therefore improve their resolution. The procedure MYMOVETO is

```
PROCEDURE MYMOVETO(X, Y : REAL);

    BEGIN
        REALX := X;
        REALY := Y;
        MOVETO(ROUND(REALX), ROUND(REALY))
    END; (* MYMOVETO *)
```

EXERCISE 17Q: Write the procedure MYMOVE. Remember that this requires some trigonometry, and that the trigonometric functions assume their parameters are in radians.

Strictly speaking we should also write MYINITTURTLE but it will suffice to add

```
REALX := TURTLEX;
REALY := TURTLEY;
```

after INITTURTLE. Replace all MOVE and MOVETO statements by MYMOVE and MYMOVETO respectively, and reset REALX and REALY after any other turtle-moving statement (such as WSTRING).

EXERCISE 17R: Making use of the procedures MYMOVE and MYMOVETO, modify the program in MACC:DIAGONAL1.TEXT so that it responds sensibly to the call DRAWLINE(120, 30, -25).

17.6 CONVEX REGULAR POLYGONS OF GIVEN RADIUS

The convex polygons we drew in section 3.8.1 were specified by the number of sides (n) of the polygon and the length of a side (s). For a side length of 30, polygons of up to 20 sides fit onto the screen, but for higher order polygons, it is more convenient to specify the overall "diameter" or "radius" of the polygon. To calculate the side length given the "radius" (that is, the distance from the center to a vertex) we need to indulge in a little trigonometry, and hence use reals. Figure 17.1 shows one segment, that is, one n^{th} of the polygon.

Fig 17.1   Segment of a polygon.

Let O be the center of the polygon, s the side length and r the "radius". If the polygon has n sides, then the external angle, 2t, is given by

$$2t \;=\; \frac{360}{n} \quad \text{degrees}$$

$$=\; \frac{360}{n} \times \frac{pi}{180} \quad \text{radians}$$

Therefore $t \;=\; \dfrac{pi}{n}$ radians.

$$\frac{s}{2} \;=\; r \sin(t)$$

Hence $s \;=\; 2\ r\ \sin(t)$
or $s \;=\; 2\ r\ \sin(pi/n)$

Since, with the aid of MYMOVE, the turtle can now move a real distance, we can write

        MYMOVE(2*R*SIN(PI/N))

to draw one side.

EXERCISE 17S: Write a procedure DRAWPOLY2, along the lines of that in section 12.6.6, in which the record type POLYTYPE has the field SIDE replaced by RADIUS, and (X, Y) represents the center of the polygon. You will need to use the MYMOVE and MYMOVETO procedures of section 17.5. For a radius 60, experimentally find a value of n which draws an acceptable circle centered at (139, 95). Save this program as USER:POLYX.

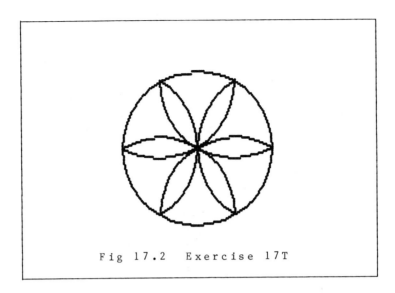

Fig 17.2   Exercise 17T

EXERCISE 17T: Write a procedure which begins

PROCEDURE ARC(X, Y : REAL; R, THETA1, THETA2 : INTEGER);

which draws an approximate arc of a circle of radius R, centered
at (X, Y), from heading THETA1 to heading THETA2 (anticlockwise),
and hence write a program to draw the pattern in figure 17.2.
(Hint: use polygons of order 36 and "circles" of radius 60.)

SOLUTIONS TO THE EXERCISES

17A: X := 0

To assign a real value to an integer variable, you would first have
to convert (or coerce) the real value to either the nearest
integer or the integer part of the value on the right hand side.
Because the form of the assignment statement does not make it clear
which is meant, Pascal disallows this form of mixed assignment
statement.

17B: PROGRAM EX17B;

    VAR I : INTEGER;

    PROCEDURE DISPLAYLEFT(A, B : REAL);

```
        (* DISPLAYS THE LEFT END OF THE INTERVAL, THEN QUARTERS IT *)
        BEGIN
            IF I <= 24 THEN
                BEGIN
                    WRITE(I : 7, '   ', A);
                    I := I + 1;
                    DISPLAYLEFT((A + 3*B)/4, B)
                END
        END; (* DISPLAYLEFT *)

    BEGIN
        I := 1;
        DISPLAYLEFT(0, 1)
    END.
```

17C: (a) 46368

    (b) 65536

    (c) 2^{16}

17D: 832040

17E: f_{30}

17F: About 1.0×10^{-38}

17G: It is ever so slightly less than zero.

17H: Yes.

No. X will get a value approximately equal to 100, but not necessarily equal to 100. Thus, a computer which gives X a value ever so slightly over 100 will stop after displaying the line beginning 95 ..., but a computer which gives X a value equal to 100, or ever so slightly less than 100 will stop after displaying the line beginning 100 ...

Always use integer variables for counting. The fragment should be

```
    VAR X : REAL;
        I : INTEGER;
        .
        .
        X := 5;
        FOR I := 1 TO 20 DO
            BEGIN
                WRITELN(X, '   ', 1/X);
                X := X + 5.0
            END
```

17J:
```
M := TRUNC((B - A)/G) + 1;
H := (B - A)/M;
FOR I := 0 TO M DO
     BEGIN
          T := A + I*H;
          ...
     END
```

17K: `4*ATAN(1)`

17L:
```
PROGRAM EX17L;

USES TRANSCEND;

VAR PI : REAL;

BEGIN
     PI := 4*ATAN(1);
     WRITELN(PI - 22/7, ' ', PI - 3.142)
END.
```

        (a) 0.00126   (b) 0.00041

        Note that the program above displays more significant digits than are
        shown above (0.00126362 and 0.000406504 respectively). Since the extra
        digits displayed correspond to decimal digits after the sixth, they
        must be of no value whatsoever. Subtraction of reals is always a
        potentially dangerous operation!

17M: `SIN(31*PI/180)`

17N: (a)
```
FUNCTION FRAC(X : REAL) : REAL;

     BEGIN
          FRAC := X - TRUNC(X)
     END; (* FRAC *)
```

        (b)
```
FUNCTION MYTRUNC(X : REAL) : INTEGER;

     BEGIN
          IF (X >= 0) OR (X = TRUNC(X)) THEN MYTRUNC := TRUNC(X)
                                        ELSE MYTRUNC := TRUNC(X) - 1
     END; (* MYTRUNC *)
```

17P: First note that the formula has an upper-case "A" and a lower-case
        "a", which are different. We call upper-case "A" ANGLEA and assume
        that ANGLEA is in degrees. The statement is

        `A := SQRT(SQR(B) + SQR(C) - 2*B*C*COS(ANGLEA*PI/180))`

17Q:
```
PROCEDURE MYMOVE(D : REAL);

     VAR T : REAL;

     BEGIN
          T := TURTLEANG*PI/180;
          REALX := REALX + D*COS(T);
          REALY := REALY + D*SIN(T);
          MOVETO(ROUND(REALX), ROUND(REALY))
     END; (* MYMOVE *)
```

```
17R:     PROGRAM DIAGONAL3;

         USES TURTLEGRAPHICS, TRANSCEND;

         CONST PI = 3.141593;

         VAR REALX, REALY : REAL;

         PROCEDURE MYMOVE(D : REAL);

             VAR T : REAL;

             BEGIN
                 T := TURTLEANG*PI/180;
                 REALX := REALX + D*COS(T);
                 REALY := REALY + D*SIN(T);
                 MOVETO(ROUND(REALX), ROUND(REALY))
             END; (* MYMOVE *)

         PROCEDURE MYMOVETO(X, Y : REAL);

             BEGIN
                 REALX := X;
                 REALY := Y;
                 MOVETO(ROUND(REALX), ROUND(REALY))
             END; (* MYMOVETO *)

         PROCEDURE DRAWFRAME;

             VAR SIDENUMBER : INTEGER;

             BEGIN
                 PENCOLOR(NONE);
                 MYMOVETO(139 - 80, 95 - 80);
                 PENCOLOR(WHITE);
                 FOR SIDENUMBER := 1 TO 4 DO
                     BEGIN
                         MYMOVE(160);
                         TURN(90)
                     END;
                 PENCOLOR(NONE);
                 MYMOVETO(139, 95)
             END; (* DRAWFRAME *)

         PROCEDURE DRAWLINE(P, Q, THETA : INTEGER);

             BEGIN
                 MYMOVETO(P, Q);
                 PENCOLOR(WHITE);
                 TURNTO(THETA);
                 REPEAT
                     MYMOVE(1)
                 UNTIL (TURTLEX >= 139 + 80) OR (TURTLEX <= 139 - 80) OR
                       (TURTLEY >=  95 + 80) OR (TURTLEY <= 95  - 80);
                 PENCOLOR(NONE);
                 MYMOVETO(P, Q)
             END; (* DRAWLINE *)

         BEGIN
             INITTURTLE;
             REALX := TURTLEX;
             REALY := TURTLEY;
             DRAWFRAME;
             DRAWLINE(120, 30, -25);
             READLN
         END.
```

17S: Polygons of order 36 produce fair circles. The following program can
        be used to experiment. The procedure DRAWPOLY2 draws convex or non-
        convex polygons.

```
PROGRAM EX17S;

USES TURTLEGRAPHICS, TRANSCEND;

CONST PI = 3.141593;

TYPE POLYTYPE = RECORD
                    ORDER : 3 .. 60;
                    EXTANGLE : 0 .. 359;
                    RADIUS : 1 .. 96;
                    COORD : RECORD
                                X : 0 .. 279;
                                Y : 0 .. 191
                            END
               END;

VAR POLYGON : POLYTYPE;
    REALX, REALY : REAL;

PROCEDURE MYMOVE(D : REAL); ...;
PROCEDURE MYMOVETO(X, Y : REAL); ...;

PROCEDURE DRAWPOLY2(POLY : POLYTYPE);

    VAR SIDENUMBER : 1 .. 60;

    BEGIN
        WITH POLY DO
            BEGIN
                WITH COORD DO MYMOVETO(X, Y);
                MYMOVE(RADIUS);
                TURN(90 + EXTANGLE DIV 2);
                PENCOLOR(WHITE);
                FOR SIDENUMBER := 1 TO ORDER DO
                    BEGIN
                        MYMOVE(2 * RADIUS * SIN(EXTANGLE*PI/360));
                        TURN(EXTANGLE)
                    END;
                PENCOLOR(NONE);
                TURN(-(90 + EXTANGLE DIV 2));
                MYMOVE(-RADIUS)
            END (* WITH *)
    END; (* DRAWPOLY2 *)

BEGIN
    REPEAT
        WITH POLYGON DO
            BEGIN
                TEXTMODE;
                WRITE('ENTER NUMBER OF SIDES: ');
                READLN(ORDER);
                INITTURTLE;
                REALX := TURTLEX;  REALY := TURTLEY;
                EXTANGLE := 360 DIV ORDER;  RADIUS := 60;
                WITH COORD DO
                    BEGIN
                        X := 139;  Y := 95
                    END
            END;
        DRAWPOLY2(POLYGON);  READLN
    UNTIL FALSE
END.
```

```
17T:    PROGRAM EX17T;

        USES TURTLEGRAPHICS, TRANSCEND;

        CONST ORDER = 36;
              RADIUS = 60;
              PI = 3.141593;

        VAR ARCNUMBER : INTEGER;
            REALX, REALY : REAL;

        PROCEDURE MYMOVE(D : REAL); ...;
        PROCEDURE MYMOVETO(X, Y : REAL); ...;

        PROCEDURE ARC(X, Y : REAL; R, THETA1, THETA2 : INTEGER);

            VAR SIDENUMBER : INTEGER;

            BEGIN
                PENCOLOR(NONE);  MYMOVETO(X, Y);
                TURNTO(THETA1);  MYMOVE(R);
                TURNTO(THETA1 + 90);
                PENCOLOR(WHITE);
                TURN(ROUND(180/ORDER));
                FOR SIDENUMBER := 1 TO ROUND(ORDER*(THETA2 - THETA1)/360) DO
                    BEGIN
                        MYMOVE(2*R*SIN(PI/ORDER));
                        TURN(ROUND(360/ORDER))
                    END;
                PENCOLOR(NONE);
                MYMOVETO(X, Y);
                TURNTO(0)
            END; (* ARC *)

        BEGIN
            INITTURTLE;
            REALX := TURTLEX;  REALY := TURTLEY;
            ARC(139, 95, RADIUS, 0, 360);
            FOR ARCNUMBER := 1 TO 6 DO
                ARC(139 + RADIUS*COS(ARCNUMBER*60*PI/180),
                     95 + RADIUS*SIN(ARCNUMBER*60*PI/180),
                     RADIUS, ARCNUMBER*60 + 120, ARCNUMBER*60 + 240);
            READLN
        END.
```

CHAPTER 18
The Type REAL

Numbers other than integers, that is, the so-called <u>reals</u>, have been left to this late stage for three reasons. They are not <u>essential</u> to the learning of the art of programming; they are commonly misunderstood because they are not so simple to handle on a computer as may appear at first; and their precise meaning varies from one computer to another.

18.1   THE SEMANTICS OF REAL NUMBERS

In mathematics, the simplest numbers are the integers. They constitute an infinite set ranging from minus infinity to plus infinity. However, integers on a (finite) computer are of necessity a finite subset of the mathematical integers, and you will recall that on the Apple the range of integers is restricted to

$$-2^{15} \quad \text{to} \quad 2^{15} - 1 \qquad (-32768 \quad \text{to} \quad +32767)$$

The next type of number encountered in mathematics is the <u>rational number</u>

$$\frac{p}{q}$$

where p and q are both integers. Rationals also appear in the guise of decimal numbers with a finite number of digits. The rationals are generally adequate for science, engineering and commerce, because they have the useful property that they fill any finite interval to any arbitrary denseness. In other words, no matter how small an interval may be selected, there is always a rational number in it. (In fact there are infinitely many rationals in it!) In spite of this, there are numbers which are not rationals, such as the square root of 2 and pi, known as <u>irrational numbers</u> respectively of the <u>algebraic</u> and <u>transcendental</u> kinds and between any pair of rationals there is an infinity of irrationals! In mathematics, the aggregation of rational and irrational numbers is known as the <u>real numbers</u>.

Unfortunately, the real numbers of computing are not the real numbers of mathematics. The reals of computing are, in fact, merely a subset of the rational numbers. The precise definition of the reals of computing varies from one computer to another, rather than from one language to another, reflecting their hardware rather than linguistic origin.

Roughly speaking, real values in Apple Pascal are in one of the ranges

$$-3.4 \times 10^{+38} \quad \text{to} \quad -1.3 \times 10^{-38}$$

$$0$$

$$+1.3 \times 10^{-38} \quad \text{to} \quad +3.4 \times 10^{+38}$$

subject to the limitation that they can be expressed in about 7 significant (decimal) digits.

An immediate consequence of this informal definition is that the reals of computing are anything but dense. In the case of Apple Pascal, the nearest reals to 1.000000 are approximately 0.9999999 and 1.000001, whilst the nearest reals to $3.300000 \times 10^{+38}$ are approximately $3.299999 \times 10^{+38}$ and $3.300001 \times 10^{+38}$, leaving gaps of about 10^{+32} on either side.

Thus the reals of computing are merely a subset of the rationals of mathematics, yet they have to serve as approximations to both rational and irrational numbers. Since arithmetic cannot be performed precisely, care has to be taken to minimize the build-up of errors, this being one of the principal concerns of numerical analysis and outside the scope of this book.

EXERCISE 18A: Suppose X and XDASH are real variables. Write down a condition whose value is true if X and XDASH differ by less than 0.0001.

EXERCISE 18B: For similar variables X and XDASH, write down a condition whose value is true if they differ by less than

      (a)   1%
      (b)   0.001%

What is (approximately) the smallest percentage difference that it is sensible to test for on the Apple?

EXERCISE 18C: Is the following fair?

      IF SIN(ATAN(1)) <> 1/SQRT(2) **THEN**
          WRITE('THE COMPUTER IS WRONG')

18.2   DECLARING A REAL VARIABLE

Like the types CHAR and INTEGER, the type REAL is predefined. All we have to do to declare X to be real is to write in the **VAR** section

    X : REAL;

or to declare A to be an array of real component type, write something like

A : **ARRAY** [1 .. 20] OF REAL;

Reals may not be used as an index type, nor may subranges of reals be defined. A formal parameters may be of type REAL. If it is a value parameter, the corresponding actual parameter may be of type REAL or INTEGER, but if it is a variable parameter, the actual parameter must be of type REAL.

18.3 REAL QUANTITIES IN EXPRESSIONS

18.3.1 Unsigned Real Numbers

In section 2.4 we described the form for writing numbers of type INTEGER in a program. This is the corresponding section for numbers of type REAL. Roughly speaking, real numbers are numbers with a decimal point, and optionally a decimal exponent part to express scaling by a power of 10. Numbers may not begin with a decimal point. Examples are

3.141593	1.414214	0.000001	1.0E-6
3.0E9	654321.0	3E09	2E0
987654321.0	(acceptable, but not represented in the Apple to this precision.)		

but not

.7071   .5E-3   3.   3.E1

The syntax diagram is

unsigned real number:

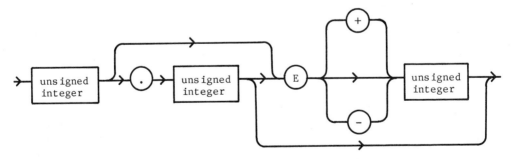

Note that it is the form of a number, not its value, that denotes its type. For example 2.0 and 2E0 both represent the real quantity 2.

18.3.2 The Real Division Operator (/)

Whereas the integer division operator **DIV** gives an integer result for integer operands only, the real division operator / gives a real result for any combination of integer and real operands. Thus, each of

      3/4   3.0/4   3/4.0   3.0/4.0

has the value 0.75, whereas you will recall that 3 **DIV** 4 has the value 0. Each of

      3.0 **DIV** 4   3 **DIV** 4.0   3.0 **DIV** 4.0

is invalid.

18.3.3 Mixed Expressions

It was a characteristic of some early programming languages that integer and real operands should not be mixed in expressions. This gave rise to much frustration amongst programmers, but as an understanding of compilers deepened it became an unnecessary restriction. Pascal, in common with most post-1960 languages, relaxes its strong typing principles and allows mixed expressions. The type of the result of an arithmetic operation is determined according to the following tables.

*, +, -	INTEGER	REAL
INTEGER	INTEGER	REAL
REAL	REAL	REAL

/	INTEGER	REAL
INTEGER	REAL	REAL
REAL	REAL	REAL

DIV, MOD	INTEGER	REAL
INTEGER	INTEGER	INVALID
REAL	INVALID	INVALID

= <> < > <= >=	INTEGER	REAL
INTEGER	BOOLEAN	BOOLEAN
REAL	BOOLEAN	BOOLEAN

EXERCISE 18D: Write down Pascal expressions for

(a)

$$\frac{-b + \sqrt{b^2 - 4ac}}{2a}$$

(b) $2\sin^2(\frac{A}{2})$

18.4 ASSIGNMENT STATEMENT

In chapter 17 we avoided the issue of type in the assignment statement. For example, we wrote

    X := 0

which contained a mixture of types, real on the left and integer on the right. We must now be more precise about just what types are allowed on either side of the assignment operator (:=). The variable on the left-hand side must be of the same base type as the expression on the right, except that if the type of the left-hand variable is real, the expression may be integer (or a subrange of integer). The reference to "base type" means that the type of the expression and the type of the left-hand variable may each be subranges of the same base type.

EXERCISE 18E: If X is a real variable, and I an integer, and a programmer incorrectly writes

        I := X

what are the two most likely ways in which it should be corrected. Explain the difference.

18.5 DISPLAYING REAL VALUES

The definition of the language Pascal allows compilers some freedom in their handling of exceptional cases in the output of data. This section may not apply to Pascal implementations other than those based on UCSD Pascal.

The WRITE and WRITELN statements permit two styles of output for real values, namely fixed-point and floating-point.

18.5.1 Fixed-point Output

The parameter is written as

x : e$_1$: e$_2$

where

x	is an expression of type REAL, the value of which is displayed
e$_1$	is an expression of type INTEGER, but more usually an integer constant, denoting the field width
e$_2$	is an expression of type INTEGER, but more usually an integer constant, denoting the number of decimal places to which the result is to be rounded. In Apple Pascal if e$_2$ = 0, the output is in floating-point style (see section 18.5.2).

The value is displayed right-justified. For example,

WRITELN(4*ATAN(1) : 11 : 4)

causes the display of

#####3.1416

where # stands for a space.

18.5.2 Floating-point Output

The parameter is written as

x : e$_1$

where

x	is an expression of type REAL, the value of which is displayed
e$_1$	is an expression of type INTEGER, but more usually an integer constant, denoting the field width.

In Apple Pascal, floating-point format is always to 6 significant digits. Since values are held internally to about 7 significant decimal digits, the sixth digit displayed is rounded and should, subject to the reliability of any numerical processes used, be correct. If the decimal exponent of the displayed value is 0, the exponent part is omitted entirely giving the appearance of a fixed-point number. For example,

```
WRITELN(0.01234567 : 12, 1.234567 : 12, 1234.567 : 12)
```

displays

```
##1.23457E-2#####1.23457###1.23457E3
```

In Apple Pascal, if neither e_1 nor e_2 is specified, a real value
is displayed in floating-point format using the minimum possible field width.

EXERCISE 18F: If PI has the value 3.141593, what is displayed by

```
WRITELN(PI:8:3, 100*PI:12, PI:12, '*', PI, '*')
```


EXERCISE 18G: Write a program to tabulate SIN(X) for X taking the values
               0, 1, 2, ..., 90 degrees.

EXERCISE 18H: Write a program to display negative powers of 2 from 2^{-1} to
               2^{-27} inclusive.

18.6 INPUT OF REALS

Real values in the input data should conform to the numbers described in
section 18.3.1, but they may be signed and they may begin with a decimal point.
Integer values (see section 10.2.1) may be read into real variables, but real
values may not be read into integer variables.

18.7 PSEUDO-RANDOM NUMBER GENERATORS

A thorough mathematical and algorithmic discussion of the generation
and analysis of sequences of pseudo-random numbers may be found in chapter 3
of [Knuth, 1969]. In case you think that the best way to produce random
numbers is by a randomly written program, read Knuth's own confession in
section 3.1. In this section we only consider simple generators, able to be
written in Pascal for computers based on 8-bit microprocessors.

Pseudo-random numbers are sequences of numbers which appear to be random,
and which satisfy certain statistical tests. They are produced by
deterministic processes, which use the previously produced value to create the
next value in the sequence. An initial value called a seed starts it off.
They are definitely not truly random, for two reasons.

  - The function itself defines a relationship between a number and
    its successor in the sequence.
  - For a given seed, the sequence of numbers is always the same.

The reproducibility of the sequences so generated makes this method appropriate for the debugging stages of program development.

18.7.1 Sequences of Integers

The method of linear congruences provides a simple method of producing sequences of pseudo-random integers. In general, such sequences are produced by recurrence relations of the form

$$x_{n+1} = (a\ x_n + c)\ \text{mod}\ m$$

where a is called the multiplier, c the increment and m the modulus. The relation

$$x_{n+1} = (26317\ x_n + 1)\ \text{mod}\ 65536$$

produces a sequence of 65536 different integers in the range

$$-2^{15} \quad \text{to} \quad 2^{15} - 1.$$

However, the principal virtue of this method is its extreme simplicity and the length of the sequence. It does not stand up well to the normal tests for randomness, and should not be used for any serious investigations. Inspection of the recurrence relation shows that the sequence alternates between odd and even values. What is worse is that this is but one instance of a more general deficiency. The remainders on dividing by any 2^n are of period 2^n. (See [Knuth, 1969] section 3.2.1.1.) An alternative generator is given below in section 18.7.3.

The modulus of 65536 $(= 2^{16})$ is chosen because all arithmetic in Apple Pascal is performed modulo 2^{16}. This leads to a very simple function.

```
FUNCTION RANDOM1(X : INTEGER) : INTEGER;

    BEGIN
        RANDOM1 := 26317*X + 1
    END;  (* RANDOM1 *)
```

Note that it is the responsibility of the user of this function to preserve the previous result and to feed it back as the next actual parameter. RANDOM1 should be called in a context such as

```
    REPEAT
        .
        .
        P := RANDOM1(P);
        .
        .
    UNTIL ...
```

where P (an integer variable) is not otherwise changed in the loop. The initial value of P (the seed) is normally read from data at the beginning of the program.

EXERCISE 18J: How may RANDOM1 be used to produce random integers

(a)   within the range 0 to 6
(b)   within the range 1 to 7?

18.7.2 Sequences of Reals

Sometimes it is necessary to produce random real values in the range 0 to 1. The function above can be adapted to this requirement.

```
FUNCTION RANDOM2(VAR X : INTEGER) : REAL;

    BEGIN
        X := 26317*X + 1;
        RANDOM2 := ABS(X/32767)
    END; (* RANDOM2 *)
```

Observe here that since this function takes an integer parameter but returns a real value, the result of one execution of the function cannot be used as the parameter for the next. Instead, we use the property of the **VAR** parameter to change the value of the actual parameter. This is an example of a side effect in a function and, in the light of what was said in section 16.1.4, is not particularly good practice.

18.7.3 A More Random Pseudo-random Number Generator

The limitations of the simple generator used in sections 18.7.1 and 18.7.2 are overcome by using a generator whose mathematical basis is more secure. However two prices have to be paid: one is that a much shorter sequence is produced; the other relates to the implementation of the algorithm. The recurrence relation

$$x_{i+1} = 4047 * x_i \ (\text{mod } 8191)$$

generates the integers 1, 2, ..., 8190. The corresponding function is similar to the function given in section 18.7.1, but is complicated by the need to perform 4-digit by 4-digit integer multiplication yielding an 8-digit result. To do this we have to employ the long integers of Apple Pascal. (See [Clark and Koehler, 1982] and [Apple, 1980a].)

```
FUNCTION RANDOM3(X : INTEGER) : INTEGER;

    VAR LB, LP : INTEGER[8];    (* MAKES PROVISION FOR INTEGERS
                                   OF UP TO 8 DECIMAL DIGITS *)

    BEGIN
        LB := 4047;
        LP := LB*X;
        RANDOM3 := TRUNC(LP - LP DIV 8191 * 8191)
    END; (* RANDOM3 *)
```

EXERCISE 18K: It is possible to estimate the value of pi by the following method.

(a) Consider the unit square whose corners are at (0, 0), (0, 1), (1, 1) and (1, 0), inscribed in which is the quadrant of the circle of unit radius centered at (0, 0).

(b) Choose points (x, y) randomly in the unit square. (That is, choose each of x and y randomly chosen in the interval 0 to 1.)

(c) Count the fraction f of the points which lie within or on the quadrant of the circle. This fraction is an approximation to the area of the quadrant. Therefore 4f is an approximation to the area of the unit circle, and hence to pi.

Write a program to estimate pi by this method.

EXERCISE 18L: Write a program to test the randomness of the numbers produced by the generator above, using the "Chi-square" test [Knuth, 1969], section 3.3.1. Suppose n numbers (observations)

$$x_1, x_2, \ldots, x_n,$$

are obtained from the generator. Divide the observations into 13 categories, say, determined by the remainders on dividing the subscripts by 13. Let the number of observations in each category be

$$Y_1, Y_2, \ldots, Y_{13}$$

Then calculate

$$V = \frac{1}{n} \sum_{s=1}^{s=13} \left(\frac{Y_s^2}{P_s} \right) - n$$

where P_s is the probability of an observation falling in category s. In this case, 13 divides 8190 exactly, therefore all P_s are 1/13.

If V lies between 6 and 16 the observations are regarded as passing this test for randomness. Do several tests with different seeds and values of n.

SOLUTIONS TO THE EXERCISES

18A: ABS(X - XDASH) < 0.0001

18B: (a) ABS((X - XDASH)/X) < 0.01

        (b) ABS((X - XDASH)/X) < 0.00001

        Seven significant digits implies a minimum resolution of 1 in 9999999
        which is 0.00001%.

18C: No. But bearing in mind that each side of the relation is
        approximately 0.7, it would be fair to write

                IF ABS(SIN(ATAN(1)) - 1/SQRT(2)) > 0.0000007 THEN
                   WRITE('THE COMPUTER IS WRONG')

18D: (a) (-B + SQRT(SQR(B) - 4*A*C))/(2*A)

        (b) 2*SQR(SIN(A/2))

18E: I := ROUND(X)

        I := TRUNC(X)

        See section 17.4.4 for descriptions of the two functions.

18F: ###3.142###3.14159E2#####3.14159*#3.14159*

18G: PROGRAM EX18G;

        USES TRANSCEND;

        VAR ANGLE : INTEGER;
            DEGTORAD : REAL;

        BEGIN
            DEGTORAD := ATAN(1)/45;
            FOR ANGLE := 0 TO 90 DO
                WRITELN(ANGLE : 4, SIN(ANGLE*DEGTORAD) : 12)
        END.

18H: PROGRAM EX18H;

        VAR EXPONENT : INTEGER;
            POWEROF2 : REAL;

        BEGIN
            POWEROF2 := 1;   (* 2^0 *)
            FOR EXPONENT := -1 DOWNTO -27 DO
                BEGIN
                    POWEROF2 := POWEROF2 / 2;
                    WRITELN(EXPONENT : 4, POWEROF2 : 12)
                END
        END.

18J: Declare

            VAR RAND0TO6 : 0 .. 6;
                RAND1TO7 : 1 .. 7;

        and call the function by

        (a) P := RANDOM1(P);
             RAND0TO6 := P **MOD** 7

        (b) P := RANDOM1(P);
             RAND1TO7 := (P **MOD** 7) + 1

18K: We adapt the function RANDOM3 to produce real values in the range 0
        to 1. The program shows very slow convergence to nearly 3 significant
        figures.

        PROGRAM PI;

        VAR SEED : INTEGER;

        FUNCTION RANDOM4(**VAR** X : INTEGER) : REAL;

            VAR LB, LP : INTEGER;

            BEGIN
                LB := 4047;
                LP := LB * X;
                X := TRUNC(LP - LP **DIV** 8191 * 8191);
                RANDOM4 := ABS(X/8191)
            END; (* RANDOM4 *)

        PROCEDURE ESTIMATEPI;

            VAR X, Y : REAL;
                INTERVAL, TRYNUMBER, NUMBERIN : INTEGER;

            BEGIN
                NUMBERIN := 0; INTERVAL := 0;
                FOR TRYNUMBER := 1 **TO** 8190 **DO**
                    BEGIN
                        INTERVAL := INTERVAL + 1;
                        X := RANDOM4(SEED);
                        Y := RANDOM4(SEED);
                        IF X*X + Y*Y <= 1 **THEN** NUMBERIN := NUMBERIN + 1;
                        IF INTERVAL = 500 **THEN**
                            BEGIN
                                INTERVAL := 0;
                                WRITELN((NUMBERIN/TRYNUMBER)*4 : 8 : 5)
                            END
                    END;
                WRITE((NUMBERIN/8190)*4 : 8 : 5)
            END; (* ESTIMATEPI *)

        BEGIN
            WRITE('ENTER SEED '); READ(SEED); WRITELN;
            ESTIMATEPI
        END.

```
18L:      PROGRAM CHI2;

          CONST K = 13;

          VAR N, OBS, P, S : INTEGER;
              V : REAL;
              Y : ARRAY [1 .. K] OF INTEGER;

          FUNCTION RANDOM3(X : INTEGER) : INTEGER; ...;

          BEGIN
              REPEAT
                  WRITE('SEED? ');   READLN(P);
                  WRITE('N? ');   READLN(N);
                  FOR S := 1 TO K DO Y[S] := 0;
                  FOR OBS := 1 TO N DO
                      BEGIN
                          P := RANDOM3(P);
                          S := P MOD K + 1;
                          Y[S] := Y[S] + 1
                      END;
                  V := 0;
                  FOR S := 1 TO K DO V := V + SQR(Y[S]);
                  V := V*K/N - N;
                  WRITELN('CHI-SQUARED = ', V)
              UNTIL FALSE
          END.
```

PART 3
More Structured Types

The final part of this book explores some applications of the two remaining types that Pascal offers. Pointers lead to a new kind of data object (one with value, but no name) whose creation is under the direct control of the program, thus permitting the modelling of dynamic structures in the world outside. Lists, queues, trees and graphs are discussed in some detail, culminating in a solution to one of the fundamental problems of computer science, the shortest path problem. In the midst of this, the other remaining type is introduced, namely the file. This exemplifies yet another property of data, for here we find a type of data whose values both precede and survive the duration of the program's execution.

CHAPTER 19
Objects Anonymous

In everyday life we name things to distinguish them from other similar
things. We name objects in programs for the same reason, and we have so far
accepted the discipline that all objects must be named at the time the program
is written, that is, before the program is executed. In this chapter, we
explore the usefulness of unnamed objects in applications where there is
uncertainty regarding the total number of such objects the program will have to
cater for.

19.1 SECOND THOUGHTS ON NAMING

Whilst the naming of objects in a program was at first seen as providing
the programmer with descriptive freedom, we shall now see that naming is also a
restrictive practice. Consider the following argument.

- If all objects in a program have to be named, then each name must
  be given in a declaration. (We think of an array declaration here
  as merely a shorthand for naming each element separately. The
  number of elements still has to be determined at program writing
  time.)

- Therefore, the number and variety of objects used in a program is
  limited to those which have been written down in declarations by
  the programmer at program writing time.

EXERCISE 19A: There is a flaw in the argument above. What is it?

Although the reasoning above is not quite watertight, it emphasizes the
restrictive aspect of naming. By and large, named objects have to be
anticipated at program writing time. In more advanced applications we
sometimes wish to avoid such restrictions on the maximum number of objects of
a certain type. Typical of such situations is the one in which several lists
of various kinds are maintained, and whereas there is not enough space to hold
the maximum size of each kind of list, there is room to hold any practical

combination of list sizes. For example, consider a program used to allocate
students to laboratory sessions and tutorial classes. It might have

```
 1  list of registered but unallocated students
24  lists of laboratory sessions
50  lists of tutorial classes
```

One can easily imagine, at the beginning of the academic year, that the list
of registered but unallocated students rapidly builds up, followed by a steady
transfer of students from that list to the other 2 kinds of list. As students
are transferred from one list, the space they occupied should be made available
for other growing lists. Dynamically varying structures such as these do not
lend themselves to the rigors of naming we have become accustomed to. How
then may we create and refer to unnamed objects?

     The basic mechanism is a <u>pointer</u>. The first newly created unnamed
object is pointed to by a named object, whose type is a pointer. If the newly
created object is a record, it may contain within it a field, or fields, which
are also of a pointer type and may be used to point to subsequent newly created
unnamed objects. The only constraint is that every unnamed object be
accessible via pointers from some named object of a pointer type. Detached
unnamed objects become completely inaccessible, and are a potential source of
trouble.

     Un-named objects are placed in a part of memory which is called the
<u>heap</u>. In spite of its name, it is carefully organized, and its use must
not be haphazard. Unfortunately, in current Apple Pascal, the heap is less
than satisfactorily managed, but this will not prevent us from the study of
unnamed objects.

19.2 AN EXAMPLE - A REMINDER LIST

     When forgetful people find themselves beseiged with more tasks to do than
they can find the immediate time for, they make reminder lists, and as and
when the tasks are completed, they strike them off the list. We shall develop
a program to do this, which will be completed in chapter 22.

     A restriction that we have to live with (until chapter 22) is that the
reminder list can only survive whilst the program is being executed. When
program execution begins, the reminder list is empty and when execution
terminates it is lost whether empty or not.

19.2.1 The Program in Outline

The program should respond to our wishes in 4 different ways.

Key pressed	Response
A	Add another task to the reminder list
D	Display the entire reminder list
R	Remove a specified task from the reminder list
S	Stop.

We can immediately sketch out the program as follows.

```
PROGRAM REMLIST1;

VAR REPLY : CHAR;

BEGIN
    INITIALIZE;
    PROMPT;
    GETREPLY(REPLY);
    WHILE REPLY <> 'S' DO
        BEGIN
            CASE REPLY OF
                'A' : ADDTASK;
                'D' : DISPLAYTASKS;
                'R' : REMOVETASK
            END;
            PROMPT;
            GETREPLY(REPLY)
        END
END.
```

For alternative ways of handling the dialogue and terminating condition, see chapter 11.

EXERCISE 19B: Write the procedures PROMPT and GETREPLY in which the variable
                parameter is guaranteed to be 'A', 'D', 'R' or 'S'. (See
                section 16.2.2.) Add dummy procedures for INITIALIZE, ADDTASK,
                DISPLAYTASK and REMOVETASK. Check that the dialogue works and
                save it as USER:REMLIST2.

     We are now left with four procedures to be written. These in turn depend
on the outcome of two design issues; how to represent a task and how to
represent a list of anonymous (unnamed) tasks.

19.2.2 Structure of a Task

     For the purpose of being reminded what has to be done, we might as well
use plain text to describe a task. In order to be able to refer to a
particular task, we shall also identify it with a number in the range 1 to
9999 and give it a priority in the range 0 to 99. The priority of a task will
be more or less ignored until the program is developed further in chapter 22.
Thus we could define a new type provisionally as the record

```
TYPE TASKSPEC = RECORD
                    IDEN : 1 .. 9999;
                    PRIORITY : 0 .. 99;
                    MESSAGE : STRING70
                END;
```

(STRING70 is a shorter version of the STRING80 type introduced in section 13.3.
The message length of 70 characters enables one reminder per line to be
displayed on a full width screen by the procedure DISPLAYTASK.)

19.2.3 Pointers

From the discussion in 19.1, we see that one named pointer is essential as an initial reference point. Call this TASKLIST. Initially, the list of tasks is empty, and so we can depict it as

$$\text{TASKLIST} \boxed{\textbf{NIL}}$$

where TASKLIST is the name of a pointer variable whose value is **NIL**. In other words, the pointer TASKLIST is not pointing anywhere. To represent this variable in your program, add to the outermost block the type definitions STRING70 and TASKSPEC, and to the **VAR** section add

        TASKLIST : ^TASKSPEC;

This says that TASKLIST is pointer variable which can point to an object of type TASKSPEC. Finally add the statement

        TASKLIST := **NIL**

to the empty body of INITIALIZE. Execute the program again to ensure that the dialogue still functions, and leave the program in the workfile.

In section 19.1, we noted that an unnamed object generally points to another so that access may be made by following pointers. A record of type TASKSPEC must have a field to enable it to point to another record of the same type. This is achieved by adding a field called NEXT to the record type TASKSPEC.

        TYPE TASKSPEC = **RECORD**
                        NEXT : ^TASKSPEC;
                        IDEN : 1 .. 9999;
                        PRIORITY : 0 .. 99;
                        MESSAGE : STRING70
                END;

The field NEXT is defined to be one which can hold a pointer which can (only) point to another record of type TASKSPEC.

We can thus envisage a sequence of records each pointing to the next.

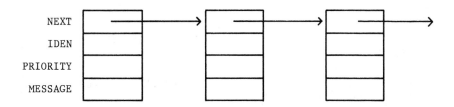

Sequences such as these are called <u>linked linear lists</u>, but we shall loosely refer to them as just <u>lists</u>.

19.2.4 Adding to the List

We next develop the procedure ADDTASK. If tasks are to be uniquely
identified by a number in the IDEN field, a suitable variable has to be
accessible to all the procedures that handle tasks. Therefore, add to the
VAR section of the outermost block

        TASKNUMBER : 1 .. 9999;

In outline, the procedure ADDTASK will be something like

        PROCEDURE ADDTASK;

            BEGIN
                create a new record;
                initialize it;
                link it into TASKLIST
            END; (* ADDTASK *)

19.2.4.1 Creating a New Record

The creation of a named variable is effected by the entry to a program,
procedure or function, at the head of which it is declared. Creation of an
unnamed variable (here, and in most cases, a record) is effected by the calling
of a standard procedure named NEW. It takes as an actual parameter a
variable which must be of a pointer type. When called, it does three things.

- From the actual parameter (a pointer) it decides what type of
  object is being pointed to.

- It creates a new object of this type on the heap.

- It gives the actual parameter a value which points to the newly
  created record, thus ensuring that it can be accessed.

We must therefore have a pointer variable, of the type which points to a record
of type TASKSPEC, which we can use as the actual parameter of the call to the
procedure NEW. Call this P, and add, local to ADDTASK, the declaration

        VAR P : ^TASKSPEC;

Creation of the new record is therefore effected by

        NEW(P)

What we now have, as a result of executing NEW(P) is a record variable,
pointed to by P, all of whose fields are undefined. In the next section we set
about filling those fields with relevant values.

19.2.4.2 Following Pointers

Pointers are of little use unless they can be followed. If P is any
pointer variable, then

```
P^
```

is the object it points to. Note that the symbol ^ is used in a different
sense here from its use in denoting a pointer type, where it precedes the type
of the thing to be pointed at (section 19.2.3). Here it is placed after a
variable of pointer type and is used, not in a delaration but in the context of
an expression. For example, a statement which puts the task number into the
IDEN field of the record pointed to by P is

```
P^.IDEN := TASKNUMBER
```

and another which reads the next number from the input to the PRIORITY field of
the same record is

```
READ(P^.PRIORITY)
```

If P points to a record then it is possible to use it in a with statement
(see sections 11.7 and 12.6.5) and the two statements above can be written as

```
WITH P^ DO
     BEGIN
          IDEN := TASKNUMBER;
          READ(PRIORITY)
     END
```

EXERCISE 19C: Complete the elaboration of the initialization of the newly
                created record. It will be necessary to add a statement to
                increment the variable TASKNUMBER each time it is used to
                identify a task. (Do not forget to initialize TASKNUMBER in the
                procedure INITIALIZE.) Also add dialogue to obtain the message
                itself, and a priority value. Do not attempt to link the new
                record into the list yet. Test these developments, but do not
                expect a list of reminders to be created yet.

In the program fragment representing the initialization of the record, the
with statement is rather more than a mere shorthand notation. For example,
each time the assignment statement

```
IDEN := TASKNUMBER
```

is executed, it assigns to quite different variables depending on the value of
P. The with statement has a dynamic effect on the statements within its scope,
supporting its categorization as a statement.

19.2.4.3 Linking it into the List

Before we can consider how to link the newly created record into the list,
we must study the structure of the list in more detail than we did in section
19.2.3. For reasons that will become apparent later we always make the NEXT
field of the last task in the list point back to the first. Various kinds of
lists can be pictured: an empty list

```
TASKLIST    | NIL |
```

a list with 1 task

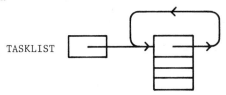

and a list with several tasks

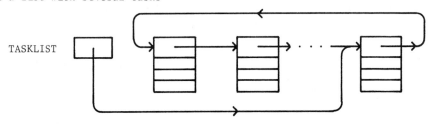

The mechanics of adding a new task to a list depend on whether the list is
empty to start with. We assume that the new task is pointed to by a pointer P.
If the list is empty, then the process may be pictured

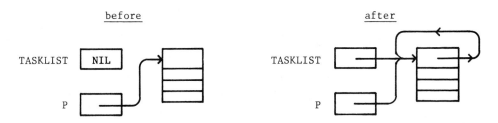

and may be described in Pascal by

```
TASKLIST := P;
TASKLIST^.NEXT := P
```

If the list is not empty, then the process may be pictured

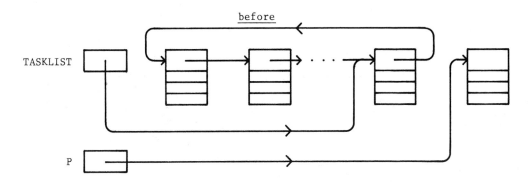

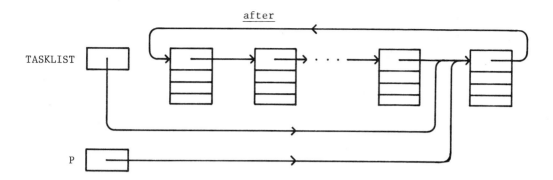

and may be described in Pascal by

```
P^.NEXT := TASKLIST^.NEXT;
TASKLIST^.NEXT := P;
TASKLIST := P
```

Combining the two cases, we can write a procedure which links the record pointed to by P into the list pointed to by TASKLIST.

```
PROCEDURE LINK;

    BEGIN
        IF TASKLIST = NIL THEN TASKLIST := P
                              ELSE P^.NEXT := TASKLIST^.NEXT;
        TASKLIST^.NEXT := P;
        TASKLIST := P
    END; (* LINK *)
```

Note that in the case of linking a record into an empty list, the third statement (TASKLIST := P) of the procedure changes nothing, but that it is not worth making it a conditional statement.

EXERCISE 19D: Complete the procedure ADDTASK. Save the present version of the program as USER:REMLIST3.

19.2.5 Displaying the List of Tasks

In order to convince yourself that things have indeed been added to the list, you need to complete the procedure DISPLAYTASKS. The procedure has to check whether there is anything to display, and therefore the outline of DISPLAYTASKS will be

```
PROCEDURE DISPLAYTASKS;

    BEGIN
        IF TASKLIST = NIL THEN WRITELN('NO REMINDERS')
            ELSE
                BEGIN
                    display all reminders
                END
    END; (* DISPLAYTASKS *)
```

In order to display each reminder we need a pointer whose values point
successively to each task in the list. This pointer may be local to
DISPLAYTASKS and if we call it P, the inner compound statement above becomes

```
BEGIN
    WRITELN('LIST OF REMINDERS');   WRITELN;
    P := TASKLIST;
    REPEAT
        WRITE(P^.IDEN : 4);
        WRITE(' [', P^.PRIORITY : 2, '] ');
        WRITESTRING(P^.MESSAGE);   WRITELN;
        P := P^.NEXT
    UNTIL P = TASKLIST
END
```

Note how the circular nature of the list facilitates its processing.

EXERCISE 19E: Develop the procedure DISPLAYTASKS in line with the guidance
                above. For the procedure WRITESTRING adapt the one in section
                13.3. Save it as USER:REMLIST4.

19.2.6 Removing a Task from the List

If we are to allow ourselves the luxury of removing any task from the list
this part of the program becomes more difficult. It happens to be easiest to
remove the task that has been in the list longest. Lists in which the First In
is always First Out are called queues (or FIFO lists). We will therefore,
in the interests of simplicity, regard the list as a queue. In any non-empty
queue the last item added is called the tail and the item which has been
in the queue longest is called the head. Thus our procedure REMOVETASK
will disconnect the head (leaving a pointer P pointing to it) and then display
it.

```
PROCEDURE REMOVETASK;

    VAR P : ^TASKSPEC;

    BEGIN
        disconnect (unlink) the head;
        IF there was a task THEN
            BEGIN
                display the disconnected task;
                dispose of this record
            END
    END; (* REMOVETASK *)
```

First we consider the disconnection of the head of the queue. There are
three cases to consider in the procedure that disconnects the head: if the
queue is empty then P is given the value NIL; if the queue consists only of
a single task, then the disconnection of the head will leave the queue empty;
and if the queue has more than one task, it is left non-empty.

If the queue is about to become empty, that is, if TASKLIST =
TASKLIST^.NEXT, the disconnection may be pictured

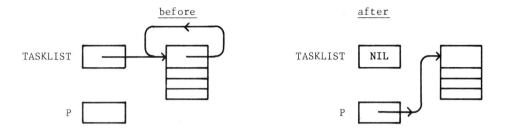

and may be described in Pascal by

```
P := TASKLIST^.NEXT;     (* P := TASKLIST; WOULD DO *)
TASKLIST := NIL
```

If the queue is not about to become empty, then the disconnection may be pictured

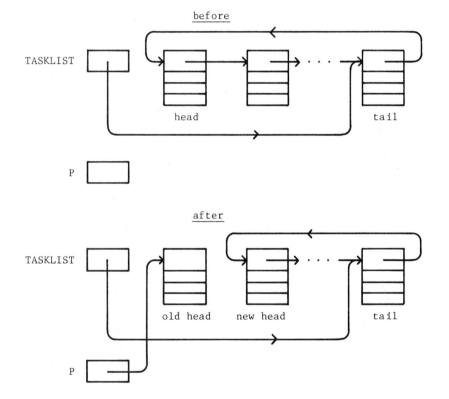

and may be described in Pascal by

```
P := TASKLIST^.NEXT;
TASKLIST^.NEXT := P^.NEXT
```

The two cases may be combined in a single procedure.

```
PROCEDURE UNLINK;

    BEGIN
      IF TASKLIST = NIL THEN P := NIL
        ELSE
          BEGIN
            P := TASKLIST^.NEXT;
            IF TASKLIST = TASKLIST^.NEXT THEN TASKLIST := NIL
                ELSE TASKLIST^.NEXT := P^.NEXT
          END
    END; (* UNLINK *)
```

Displaying the disconnected task requires WRITESTRING. It can no longer remain the monopoly of DISPLAYTASKS and therefore has to be moved from inside DISPLAYTASKS (exercise 19E) to the outer level of the program.

Finally, we ought to release the space occupied by the task we have just removed from the queue so that it is available for reuse but here we meet the problem of Apple Pascal's heap management. Pascal provides for a standard procedure DISPOSE(P) which is the converse of NEW(P). Reference to [Apple, 1980a] shows that DISPOSE is not provided, and that no suitable alternative exists. Versions of UCSD Pascal after IV.0 have a proper DISPOSE procedure and as it is a vital facility for the serious use of the heap, its presence will be assumed throughout the remainder of this book. The sole consequence of its omission from the relatively small programs in this book is that the heap becomes progressively fuller, and the space occupied by unwanted objects is never released for reuse.

The procedure DISPOSE has a parameter which must be a pointer type. The actual parameter must be a pointer variable. The procedure, when called, does two things.

- From the value and type of the parameter it finds the object being pointed at and its size.

- It frees the space occupied by that object on the heap.

EXERCISE 19F: Complete the program, indicating by means of a comment, where the record would be disposed. Save it as USER:REMLIST5.

EXERCISE 19G: The display of tasks is in a strange order. The last is first with the others in sequence. Alter DISPLAYTASKS to display them in sequence. Save this as USER:REMLIST6.

19.3 AN APPLICATION OF LISTS TO GRAPHICS

So far in this course our use of graphics has been solely in the building up of pictures by adding items to the screen, and never by selectively removing an item (such as a windmill or a polygon) from the screen. The reason for this is that we have never kept any record of what was actually on the screen. In the previous section we kept records of tasks to be done for subsequent listing or removal. In this section we do something very similar, but we keep records of pictures rather than records of tasks awaiting completion. We will also explore the more difficult removal of an arbitrary item from a list.

19.3.1 Representation of a Polygon

The program in MACC:POLILIST1.TEXT is based on the solution to exercise 17S. The record structure, defining a polygon, has been extended to enable records to be linked to each other, and to allow identification of a polygon by number. The program allows the user greater flexibility in specifying where and how the polygons (not necessarily convex) should be drawn. (If your Apple has color, you could add that as another field of the record type POLYTYPE.) The salient features of this program are

```
PROGRAM POLILIST1;

USES TURTLEGRAPHICS, TRANSCEND;

CONST PI = 3.141593;

TYPE POLYPTR = ^POLYTYPE;
     POLYTYPE = RECORD
                       NEXT : POLYPTR;
                       IDEN : 1 .. 9999;
                       ORDER : 2 .. 360;
                       EXTANGLE : 0 .. 359;
                       RADIUS : 1 .. 96;
                       COORD : RECORD
                                     X : 0 .. 279;
                                     Y : 0 .. 191
                               END
                END;

VAR REPLY : CHAR;
    POLYNUMBER : 1 .. 9999;
    POLYLIST : POLYPTR;
    POLY : POLYTYPE;
    REALX, REALY : REAL;

PROCEDURE MYMOVE(D : REAL); ...;
PROCEDURE MYMOVETO(X, Y : REAL); ...;

PROCEDURE INITIALIZE;

    BEGIN
        INITTURTLE;
        REALX := TURTLEX;  REALY := TURTLEY;
        POLYNUMBER := 1;
        POLYLIST := NIL
    END; (* INITIALIZE *)

PROCEDURE GETPOLY(VAR POLYGON : POLYTYPE);

    BEGIN
      TEXTMODE;
      WITH POLYGON DO
        BEGIN
            WRITE('ENTER NUMBER OF SIDES [2..360] ');  READLN(ORDER);
            WRITE('ENTER EXTERNAL ANGLE [0..359] ');  READLN(EXTANGLE);
            WRITELN('ENTER RADIUS [1..96] ');  READLN(RADIUS);
            WRITELN('CO-ORDS OF CENTER [0..279 0..191] ');
            WITH COORD DO READLN(X, Y);
            IDEN := POLYNUMBER;  POLYNUMBER := POLYNUMBER + 1
        END;
    END; (* GETPOLY *)
```

```
PROCEDURE DRAWPOLY2(POLY : POLYTYPE);

    VAR SIDENUMBER : 1 .. 60;

    BEGIN
        GRAFMODE;  TURNTO(0);
        WITH POLY DO BEGIN ... END (* WITH *)
    END; (* DRAWPOLY2 *)

PROCEDURE PROMPT;

    BEGIN
        TEXTMODE;  WRITE('A(DD, R(EMOVE, S(TOP: ')
    END; (* PROMPT *)

PROCEDURE GETREPLY(VAR REPLY : CHAR); ...;

PROCEDURE ADDPOLY;

    BEGIN
        GETPOLY(POLY);  DRAWPOLY(POLY)
    END; (* ADDPOLY *)

PROCEDURE REMOVEPOLY;

    BEGIN (* DUMMY *) END; (* REMOVEPOLY *)

BEGIN
    INITIALIZE;
    PROMPT;
    GETREPLY(REPLY);
    WHILE REPLY <> 'S' DO
        BEGIN
            CASE REPLY OF
                'A' : ADDPOLY;
                'R' : REMOVEPOLY
            END;
            PROMPT;
            GETREPLY(REPLY)
        END
END.
```

Since our aim is to erase as well as draw polygons, we have to be
consistent, not only with the location of the polygons but also with their
orientation. Hence DRAWPOLY2 begins with TURNTO(0) as the simplest way to
achieve this.

Adaptation of this program to enable polygons to be erased is left as a
series of exercises. After each exercise, ensure that the program is still
operational. The resulting program will probably stretch to the limit the
version of the compiler which you normally use. It is possible to increase the
capacity of the compiler by allowing it to segment itself. To do this, add, as
the line before the program heading, the compiler option

        (*$S+*)

A complete list of compiler options may be found in [Apple, 1980a].

EXERCISE 19H: Erasure of a polygon will be effected by redrawing it in
                 pencolor BLACK. Adapt the procedure DRAWPOLY2 so that a second
                 parameter specifies the pen color.

EXERCISE 19J: Modify the procedure ADDPOLY so that it links the record of the
                 polygon it draws into the list POLYLIST which is already
                 declared and initialized. (Hint: use the procedure LINK in
                 section 19.2.4.3 with suitable change of identifiers.)

19.3.2 Removing a Polygon

In outline, the removal of a polygon requires the following.

        PROCEDURE REMOVEPOLY;

            BEGIN
                  dialogue to obtain identity of polygon to be removed;
                  find this polygon in POLYLIST;
                  IF polygon exists **THEN**
                        BEGIN
                              detach the record;
                              draw it in black;
                              dispose of the record
                        END
            END;

Before we attempt the removal of a polygon we should recall the removal of
a particular record from the task list (a queue) in section 19.2.6. The record
which it was easiest to remove (the head) was the one following the record we
had an explicit pointer to (the tail). In order to remove an arbitrary record
from POLYLIST (not therefore a queue) we have to find a pointer to the record
before it. This will complicate matters; it also suggests that pointers in
both directions would make things easier. They do, but they take up more space.

The matter of finding the record prior to the one to be removed is perhaps
best done by means of a function which can return a value of a pointer type, as
hinted in section 16.1.1. The function searches the list for a record having
an IDEN field equal to the value of the parameter and returns as the value of
the function either **NIL** if no such record exists, or the pointer to the
record preceding it, if it was found.

EXERCISE 19K: Write such a function which begins

                 FUNCTION POINTERTO(I : INTEGER) : POLYPTR;

                 Note that the type of this function has to be expressed as an
                 identifier.

EXERCISE 19L: The procedure REMOVEPOLY can now be written. Care has to be
                 taken in detaching the record from the list. The two potential
                 pitfalls are

                    - POLYLIST may become empty
                    - POLYLIST itself may be pointing at the record to be
                       detached.

                 Complete the program and save it as USER:POLILIST2. (There
                 remains the problem of black spots when removing a polygon which
                 intersects another. The use of pencolor REVERSE in place of
                 WHITE eliminates the spots on removal at the expense of their
                 appearance during the addition of an intersecting polygon.
                 Short of redrawing the complete picture, this problem is quite
                 severe.)

SOLUTIONS TO THE EXERCISES

19A: It assumes that each written procedure can give rise to only one
         activation at any instant in the execution of a program. Recursive
         procedures may give rise to many activations, the number of which
         may depend on data read by the program, and hence not calculable
         at program writing time. For each activation, a new set of parameters
         and local variables is created.

19B: PROGRAM REMLIST2;

         VAR REPLY : CHAR;

         PROCEDURE INITIALIZE; BEGIN (* DUMMY *) END;

         PROCEDURE PROMPT;

             BEGIN
                 WRITE('A(DD, D(ISPLAY, R(EMOVE, S(TOP: ')
             END; (* PROMPT *)

         PROCEDURE GETREPLY(VAR REPLY : CHAR);

             BEGIN
                 REPEAT READ(REPLY) UNTIL REPLY <> ' ';
                 WRITELN;
                 IF NOT (REPLY IN ['A', 'D', 'R', 'S']) THEN
                     BEGIN
                         WRITELN('SORRY YOU MUST TYPE A, D, R OR S');
                         GETREPLY(REPLY)
                     END
             END; (* GETREPLY *)

         PROCEDURE ADDTASK; BEGIN (* DUMMY *) END;
         PROCEDURE DISPLAYTASKS; BEGIN (* DUMMY *) END;
         PROCEDURE REMOVETASK; BEGIN (* DUMMY *) END;

         BEGIN
             INITIALIZE;
             PROMPT;
             GETREPLY(REPLY);
             WHILE REPLY <> 'S' DO
                 BEGIN
                     CASE REPLY OF
                         'A' : ADDTASK;
                         'D' : DISPLAYTASKS;
                         'R' : REMOVETASK
                     END;
                     PROMPT;
                     GETREPLY(REPLY)
                 END
         END.

```
19C:      PROCEDURE ADDTASK;

              VAR P : ^TASKSPEC;
                  TASKTEXT : STRING70;

              PROCEDURE READSTRING6(VAR ST : STRING70);

                  CONST BS = 8;

                  VAR CHARCOUNT : 0 .. 70;
                      C, DELIMITER : CHAR;

                  BEGIN
                      REPEAT READ(DELIMITER) UNTIL DELIMITER <> ' ';
                      CHARCOUNT := 0;
                      READ(C);
                      WHILE C <> DELIMITER DO
                          BEGIN
                              IF CHARCOUNT < 70 THEN
                                  BEGIN
                                      IF ORD(C) = BS THEN
                                          BEGIN
                                              IF CHARCOUNT > 0 THEN
                                                  BEGIN
                                                      CHARCOUNT := CHARCOUNT - 1;
                                                      WRITE(CHR(BS), ' ', CHR(BS))
                                                  END
                                          END
                                      ELSE
                                          BEGIN
                                              CHARCOUNT := CHARCOUNT + 1;
                                              ST.CH[CHARCOUNT] := C
                                          END
                                  END;
                              READ(C)
                          END;
                      ST.LENGTH := CHARCOUNT
                  END; (* READSTRING6 *)

              BEGIN (* ADDTASK *)
                  NEW(P);
                  WITH P^ DO
                    BEGIN
                      IDEN := TASKNUMBER;  TASKNUMBER := TASKNUMBER + 1;
                      WRITE('ENTER PRIORITY, [0 .. 99] ');
                      READ(PRIORITY);
                      IF PRIORITY < 0 THEN PRIORITY := 0;
                      IF PRIORITY > 99 THEN PRIORITY := 99;
                      WRITELN('ENTER YOUR (DELIMITED) MESSAGE');
                      READSTRING6(TASKTEXT);  WRITELN;
                      MESSAGE := TASKTEXT
                    END;
                  link it into TASKLIST
              END; (* ADDTASK *)
```

```
19D:     PROCEDURE ADDTASK;

             VAR P : ^TASKSPEC;
                 TASKTEXT : STRING70;

             PROCEDURE READSTRING6(VAR ST : STRING70); ...;
             PROCEDURE LINK; ...;

             BEGIN (* ADDTASK *)
                 NEW(P);
                 WITH P^ DO
                   BEGIN ... END;
                 LINK
             END; (* ADDTASK *)


19E:     PROCEDURE DISPLAYTASKS;

             VAR P : ^TASKSPEC;

             PROCEDURE WRITESTRING(S : STRING70);

                 VAR I : 0 .. 70;

                 BEGIN
                     FOR I := 1 TO S.LENGTH DO WRITE(S.CH[I])
                 END; (* WRITESTRING *)

             BEGIN (* DISPLAYTASKS *)
                 IF TASKLIST = NIL THEN WRITELN('NO REMINDERS')
                   ELSE
                     BEGIN
                         WRITELN('LIST OF REMINDERS');   WRITELN;
                         P := TASKLIST;
                         REPEAT
                             WRITE(P^.IDEN : 4);
                             WRITE(' [', P^.PRIORITY : 2, '] ');
                             WRITESTRING(P^.MESSAGE);   WRITELN;
                             P := P^.NEXT
                         UNTIL P = TASKLIST
                     END
             END; (* DISPLAYTASKS *)


19F:     Add the procedure

         PROCEDURE REMOVETASK;

             VAR P : ^TASKSPEC;

             PROCEDURE UNLINK; ...;

             BEGIN (* REMOVETASK *)
                 UNLINK;
                 IF P <> NIL THEN
                     BEGIN
                         WRITESTRING(P^.MESSAGE);   WRITE(' DONE');   WRITELN;
                         (* DISPOSE(P) *)
                     END
             END; (* REMOVETASK *)
```

```
19G:    PROCEDURE DISPLAYTASKS;

            VAR P, P0 : ^TASKSPEC;

            BEGIN
                IF TASKLIST = NIL THEN WRITELN('NO REMINDERS')
                  ELSE
                    BEGIN
                        WRITELN('LIST OF REMINDERS');  WRITELN;
                        P0 := TASKLIST^.NEXT;
                        P := P0;
                        REPEAT
                          WRITE(P^.IDEN : 4);
                          WRITE(' [ ', P^.PRIORITY : 2, '] ');
                          WRITESTRING(P^.MESSAGE);  WRITELN;
                          P := P^.NEXT
                        UNTIL P = P0
                    END
            END; (* DISPLAYTASKS *)


19H:    PROCEDURE DRAWPOLY2(POLY : POLYTYPE; COL : SCREENCOLOR);

            VAR SIDENUMBER : 1 .. 60;

            BEGIN
                GRAFMODE;
                WITH POLY DO
                    BEGIN
                        WITH COORD DO MYMOVETO(X, Y);
                        MYMOVE(RADIUS);
                        TURN(90 + EXTANGLE DIV 2);
                        PENCOLOR(COL);
                        FOR SIDENUMBER := 1 TO ORDER DO
                          BEGIN
                            MYMOVE(2 * RADIUS * SIN(EXTANGLE*PI/360));
                            TURN(EXTANGLE)
                          END;
                        PENCOLOR(NONE);
                        TURN(-(90 + EXTANGLE DIV 2));
                        MYMOVE(-RADIUS);
                        READLN
                    END (* WITH *)
            END; (* DRAWPOLY2 *)


19J:    PROCEDURE ADDPOLY;

            VAR P : POLYPTR;

            PROCEDURE LINK;

                BEGIN
                    IF POLYLIST = NIL THEN POLYLIST := P
                                      ELSE P^.NEXT := POLYLIST^.NEXT;
                    POLYLIST^.NEXT := P;
                    POLYLIST := P
                END; (* LINK *)


            BEGIN (* ADDPOLY *)
                NEW(P);
                GETPOLY(P^);
                LINK;
                DRAWPOLY(P^, WHITE)
            END; (* ADDPOLY *)
```

```
19K:    FUNCTION POINTERTO(I : INTEGER) : POLYPTR;

            (* POINTS TO RECORD BEFORE THE ONE FOUND *)

            VAR P, NEXTP, PO : POLYPTR;
                STATE : (LOOKING, FOUND, NOTTHERE);

            BEGIN
                IF POLYLIST = NIL THEN POINTERTO := NIL
                ELSE
                  BEGIN
                    P := POLYLIST;
                    NEXTP := P^.NEXT;
                    PO := NEXTP;
                    STATE := LOOKING;
                    REPEAT
                      IF NEXTP^.IDEN = I THEN STATE := FOUND
                        ELSE
                          BEGIN
                            P := NEXTP;
                            NEXTP := NEXTP^.NEXT;
                            IF NEXTP = PO THEN STATE := NOTTHERE
                          END
                    UNTIL STATE <> LOOKING;
                    IF STATE = FOUND THEN POINTERTO := P ELSE POINTERTO := NIL
                  END
            END; (* POINTERTO *)


19L:    PROCEDURE REMOVEPOLY;

            VAR I : 1 .. 9999;
                P, Q : POLYPTR;

            FUNCTION POINTERTO(I : INTEGER) : POLYPTR; ...;

            BEGIN (* REMOVEPOLY *)
                IF POLYLIST <> NIL THEN
                  BEGIN
                    WRITE('ENTER NUMBER OF POLYGON TO BE REMOVED: ');
                    READLN(I);

                    P := POINTERTO(I);

                    IF P = NIL THEN WRITELN('NO SUCH POLYGON')
                      ELSE
                        BEGIN
                          (* Q POINTS TO DETACHED RECORD *)
                          Q := P^.NEXT;
                          IF P = Q THEN POLYLIST := NIL
                                ELSE
                                    BEGIN
                                      P^.NEXT := Q^.NEXT;
                                      POLYLIST := P
                                                (* ENSURES POLYLIST STILL
                                                    POINTS TO LIST! *)
                                    END;

                          TURNTO(0);
                          DRAWPOLY(Q^, BLACK);

                          (* DISPOSE(Q) *)
                        END (* ELSE *)
                END (* IF *)
            END; (* REMOVEPOLY *)
```

CHAPTER 20
Pointers and their Application

In the previous chapter the pointer was used as a means of accessing unnamed objects in a program. Unnamed objects give the programmer greater freedom to devise structures which can grow and diminish in response to the data a program is provided with. This freedom was used to create queues and lists but other structures are possible, for example binary trees and directed graphs (figure 20.1).

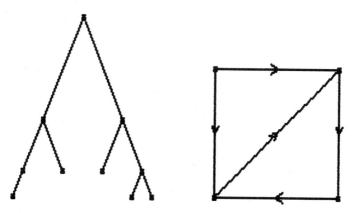

Fig 20.1   Binary tree & directed graph

Structures like these will be studied in greater depth in chapters 21, 23 and 24. In this chapter we first take another look at pointers and then examine one of the least Pascal-like features of Pascal, the variant record.

20.1 POINTERS

In Pascal, a pointer is always associated with the type of object it may
point to. This reflects Pascal's principle of strong typing and enables many
programming errors associated with pointers to be picked up at program
compilation time.

20.1.1 Declaration of Pointer Types and Pointer Variables

A pointer type is represented by a caret (^) followed by an identifier
naming the type of object which may be pointed to. (Some books and computers
represent this character by a vertical arrow (↑).) Thus

        ^INTEGER   ^TASKSPEC

are possible types but

        ^(ACTIVE, RETIRED, COMPLETED)   ^1 .. 31
        ^ARRAY [1 .. 10] OF INTEGER

are not, although the intentions are realizable by naming the types. The
syntax of a pointer type is expressed by the diagram

pointer type:

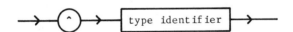

Normally Pascal insists that all references to an identifier occur after
the identifier has been declared. Recall the problem with mutual recursion in
section 5.5. However, in the case of pointers, the definition of the type
identifier may be placed later in the TYPE section in which it is referred.
For example, the type definition

        TYPE TASKSPEC = RECORD
                        NEXT : ^TASKSPEC;
                        IDEN : 1 .. 9999;
                        PRIORITY : 0 .. 99;
                        MESSAGE : ARRAY [1 .. 70] OF CHAR
                    END;

could have been written

        TYPE TASKPTR = ^TASKSPEC;
             TASKSPEC = RECORD
                        NEXT : TASKPTR;
                        IDEN : 1 .. 9999;
                        PRIORITY : 0 .. 99;
                        MESSAGE : ARRAY [1 .. 70] OF CHAR
                    END;

The type pointed to can be any of the types we have encountered so far, even
another pointer. For example,

```
P = ^THING;
PP = ^P;
```

Variables of a pointer type (called <u>pointer variables</u>) are declared in the **VAR** section in the usual way, with the pointer type being either named or explicit; for example

```
TASKLIST : TASKPTR;
```

or

```
TASKLIST : ^TASKSPEC;
```

Functions may be of a pointer type, provided that the type is given as a type identifier. (See exercise 19K.)

EXERCISE 20A: Define pointer types for the three incorrectly specified types above.

EXERCISE 20B: Draw a syntax diagram for type, including all types encountered so far.

20.1.2 Use of Pointers in Expressions

We have to be careful to distinguish between the value of a pointer and the thing it points to. One particular pointer value is represented by the reserved word **NIL**. It points to nothing at all, and any attempt to follow it leads to quite unpredictable data. The value of a pointer variable is represented in an expression by the name (or identifier) of a variable, and whilst it is tempting to use a pointer variable freely in this context, a pointer value may only be

- assigned
- compared for equality or inequality with another pointer value
- passed as a parameter.

For example,

```
P := NIL;
IF PP = NIL THEN ...;
NEW(P);
```

No other operations are possible on pointers except that of following, which we next consider.

Pointers are followed (or <u>de-referenced</u>) by appending the <u>pointer follower symbol</u> (^) to a variable in an expression. (Some books and computers represent this character by a vertical arrow (↑).) Do not confuse the two uses of ^ in connection with pointers. If

P

is a pointer variable whose value points to an object, then

            P^

is the object pointed to. Most frequently, pointers point to records, so P^
generally stands for a record and a particular field of the record is selected
by appending the field selector symbol (.) and the name of the field. Examples
from the previous chapter are

        P^.IDEN   P^.MESSAGE

Where the pointer points to a pointer, for example PP in section 20.1.1, then

        PP   is a pointer to a pointer to a THING
        PP^   is a pointer to a THING
        PP^^   is a THING.

    The syntax is based on that of a variable. Gathering together subscripted
variables and field identifiers as instances of a variable, we have

variable:

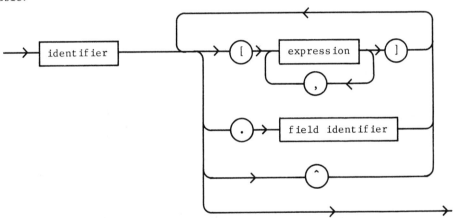

Thus a variable is essentially an identifier followed by an arbitrary sequence
of selectors or pointer follower symbols. The selectors and pointer followers
are applied in order from left to right. Whilst this gives the programmer
great descriptive and constructive freedom, it is essential that each kind of
operator (selector or pointer follower) is only applied to the appropriate kind
of structure. Consider, for example, the type TASKSPEC and associated
variables defined in section 20.1.1, namely

        TYPE TASKSPEC = RECORD
                        NEXT : ^TASKSPEC;
                        IDEN : 1 .. 9999;
                        PRIORITY : 0 .. 99;
                        MESSAGE : ARRAY [1 .. 70] OF CHAR
                    END;

        VAR P : ^TASKSPEC;

and suppose that the ponter P points to the record

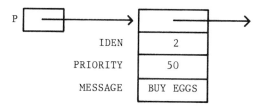

Then the variable

       P^.MESSAGE[1]

is interpreted as follows.

P	pointer to the record of task number 2
P^	the record of task number 2
P^.MESSAGE	the message field of the record of task number 2
P^.MESSAGE[1]	the first character of the message field of the record of task number 2, namely 'B'.

Examples of the incorrect application of selectors and pointer followers are

P[1]	P is not an array; it is a pointer.
P.MESSAGE	P is not a record; it is a pointer.
P^[1]	P^ is not an array; it is a record.
P^.MESSAGE.1	P^.MESSAGE is not a record; it as an array.

EXERCISE 20C: Suppose that, in the context of section 19.2, there is the following additional definition and declaration.

         TYPE GUY = (JACK, MARY, JIM, ANN);

         VAR REMINDER : **ARRAY** [GUY] OF ^TASKSPEC;

Write down variables for

(a) a pointer to Mary's reminder list
(b) the tail record of Jim's reminder list
(c) the message in the tail record of Jack's reminder list
(d) the third letter of the tail record of Ann's reminder list
(e) the priority of the head record of Mary's reminder list.

20.2 APPLICATION TO QUEUES

In the previous chapter, the program which kept a list of reminders did so by means of a queue. Queues are of such general usefulness that it is worth expressing the basic operations on queues in terms of more general procedures. In the discussion that follows, we think of a record type called

THING. Our procedures will only deal with queues of THINGs. They are easily
adapted to handle queues of other types of record.

     The procedures to handle queues have to

          - initialize a queue,
          - add a record to a queue and
          - remove a record from a queue.

The queue in question will be specified as a parameter so that the procedures
can be used to handle any number of queues (of the same type) in a program.

20.2.1 Initialization

     This procedure follows the corresponding procedure INITIALIZE in section
19.2. Note that the parameter has to be a variable parameter.

```
PROCEDURE INITQUEUE(VAR Q : THINGPOINTER);

    BEGIN
        Q := NIL
    END; (* INITQUEUE *)
```

     It is rather extravagant to use a procedure for such a simple task, but
it maintains a sense of completeness in that all operations on queues are then
specified by procedures.

20.2.2 Adding to a Queue

     In section 19.2.4.3, the diagrams describing the linking of a record into
a queue show that the named pointer is always changed to point to the newly
added record. Thus the parameter representing the queue must be a variable
parameter. We further assume that the new record has been created by the
procedure NEW and set up with appropriate values outside this procedure. We
therefore get

```
PROCEDURE ADDTOQUEUE(P : THINGPOINTER; VAR Q : THINGPOINTER);

    (* LINKS RECORD P^ INTO QUEUE Q *)

    BEGIN
        IF Q = NIL THEN Q := P
                   ELSE P^.NEXT := Q^.NEXT;
        Q^.NEXT := P;
        Q := P
    END; (* ADDTOQUEUE *)
```

20.2.3 Removing from a Queue

     Here we follow section 19.2.6. In this case the procedure has to
disconnect the head of the queue and return a variable parameter of type
THINGPOINTER which points to the disconnected record. We assume that

subsequent processing of this record and its disposal will be dealt with outside this procedure. If the queue is empty, we return the value **NIL**, and let the calling section of program decide what to do about it. Again, there is a possibility that the named queue pointer is changed, so it too must be a variable parameter. We get

PROCEDURE REMOVEFROMQUEUE(**VAR** P, Q : THINGPOINTER);

    (* DISCONNECTS HEAD OF QUEUE Q. P THEN POINTS TO THIS RECORD *)

    BEGIN
        IF Q = NIL **THEN** P := NIL
        ELSE
            BEGIN
                P := Q^.NEXT;
                IF Q = Q^.NEXT **THEN** Q := NIL
                            ELSE Q^.NEXT := P^.NEXT
            END
    END; (* REMOVEFROMQUEUE *)

EXERCISE 20D: Express the procedure REMOVEFROMQUEUE as a function.

EXERCISE 20E: In what sense does the program in section 19.2 strictly violate the organization of the queue TASKLIST.

EXERCISE 20F: Rewrite the program in USER:REMLIST6, making use of the three procedures in this section.

20.3 VARIANT PARTS OF RECORDS

So far, a record type has given rise to record variables whose structures are identical. For instance, in the program developed in section 19.3, the type POLYTYPE specified records which described polygons. These records could not describe windmills for example. If, in that program, we had wished to create a picture consisting of windmills and polygons (not a totally unreasonable aspiration), we should have kept two separate lists. This would have led to the duplication of most of the procedures used in that program.

Pascal allows records to have what it calls variant parts. In the variant part of a record, several different structures may be specified. Each actual instance of such record types will be in just one of the variant forms. A field called the tag field indicates which variant form a particular record takes.

If we apply this to the record type POLYTYPE of section 19.3 by extending it to accommodate either polygons or windmills, we have to gather together the common part of the records first and place the variant part last. The new record type, called OBTYPE, might be defined thus.

```
TYPE ANGLE = 0 .. 359;
     OBKIND = (POLYGON, WINDMILL);
     OBPTR = ^OBTYPE;
     OBTYPE = RECORD

                    (* FIRST, THE COMMON PART *)

                    NEXT : OBPTR;
                    IDEN : 1 .. 9999;
                    COORD : RECORD
                                 X : 0 .. 279;
                                 Y : 0 .. 191
                            END;

                    (* THEN THE VARIANT PART *)

                    CASE KIND : OBKIND OF
                              POLYGON : (ORDER : 2 .. 360;
                                         EXTANGLE : 0 .. 359;
                                         RADIUS : 1 .. 96);
                              WINDMILL : (SIZE : INTEGER;
                                          THETA : ANGLE)
          END; (* OBTYPE *)
```

The reserved word **CASE** is used in a related but different sense to that in the case statement. Here it marks the start of the variant part and denotes the tag field, the field which in this example is called KIND, and whose value is either POLYGON or WINDMILL indicating the kind of object the record describes and hence its structure. Following the reserved word **OF** are the variant parts, two in this example. In this context, **CASE** is not terminated by **END.** An instance of a record of type OBTYPE will have one or other of the variants but not both. It is as though record instances are either of type

```
OBTYPE = RECORD
              NEXT : OBPTR;
              IDEN : 1 .. 9999;
              COORD : RECORD
                           X : 0 .. 279;
                           Y : 0 .. 191
                      END;
              KIND : OBKIND;    (* THE VALUE OF THIS FIELD IS
                                      POLYGON *)
              ORDER : 2 .. 360;
              EXTANGLE : 0 .. 359;
              RADIUS : 1 .. 96
         END;
```

or of type

```
OBTYPE = RECORD
              NEXT : OBPTR;
              IDEN : 1 .. 9999;
              COORD : RECORD
                           X : 0 .. 279;
                           Y : 0 .. 191
                      END;
              KIND : OBKIND;    (* THE VALUE OF THIS FIELD IS
                                      WINDMILL *)
              SIZE : INTEGER;
              THETA : ANGLE
         END;
```

One might assume from this that for a particular record instance, given the value of the tag field, a Pascal program should be able to ensure that reference is only made to an appropriate field. In the example above, this would mean that any attempt to refer to the radius of a windmill or the sail angle of a polygon would be trapped. Unfortunately, Apple Pascal, like most Pascal implementations, does not check for this, leaving a chink in the armor of its strong typing. It is the responsibility of the programmer to ensure type correspondence in the case of records having a variant part.

The most secure way to do this is to precede all processing of a record having a variant part by a case statement which reflects the record type definition. For example, the processing of a record OB of type OBTYPE might best be done by

```
WITH OB DO
    CASE KIND OF
        POLYGON  : BEGIN ... END;
        WINDMILL : BEGIN ... END
    END
```

Whilst this does not guarantee avoidance of any incorrect references, it does at least ensure that any such error is in an obviously incorrect part of the program.

Suppose P is a pointer variable of type OBPTR. If a record with a variant part is created by NEW(P) then it will occupy sufficient space to accommodate the largest variant. A record created in this manner would (in standard Pascal) be disposed of by DISPOSE(P). However, to create the minimum-sized record suitable for, say, the description of a windmill, we may write

```
NEW(P, WINDMILL)
```

and to create the minimum sized record suitable for the description of a polygon, we write

```
NEW(P, POLYGON)
```

The tag field (KIND in this example) still has to be assigned with either WINDMILL or POLYGON, but should not otherwise be changed by the program. In standard Pascal, a record created by NEW(P, WINDMILL) would be disposed of in like manner, by writing

```
DISPOSE(P, WINDMILL)
```

The syntax of a variant part is

variant part: [incomplete]

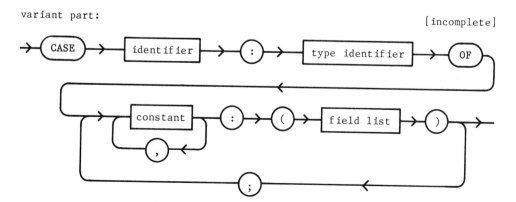

field list:

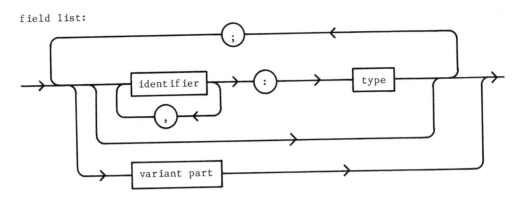

From these definitions it is clear that variant parts may be nested and a record may therefore have several tag fields. In this situation, the alternative form of NEW is

$$NEW(P, t_1, t_2, \ldots, t_n)$$

where t_1, t_2, $\ldots$ t_n are the values of the corresponding tag fields in the order in which they appear in the text. In standard Pascal, such a record would be disposed of by

$$DISPOSE(P, t_1, t_2, \ldots, t_n)$$

The syntax diagram above implies that all variant parts must have a tag field. This restriction is applied to some versions of Pascal, but not to Apple Pascal, but it is to be strongly recommended that variant parts normally be tagged. An untagged record with a variant part suddenly presenting itself for processing is not properly processable, unless information external to the record is available to resolve the kind of variant to hand. Apple Pascal and standard Pascal allow untagged records and the syntax diagram for variant part should be modified to begin

variant part:

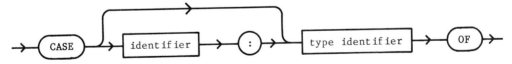

In such cases, a variant is permitted for each value of the named type. The most common type used in this context is the type BOOLEAN, offering two variant parts corresponding to the values false and true. An example of this will be found in the next section.

EXERCISE 20G: In the reminder list program of section 19.2, it is found to be desirable to "date stamp" certain entries by adding, before the entry, an extra record containing the date and time. Redefine the record type TASKSPEC.

20.4 PEEK AND POKE

The chink in the armor of strong typing which records with variant parts expose is logically wide enough to drive a coach and horses through. We shall show in this section how any part of the Apple's memory may be accessed (PEEK) or altered (POKE) from a Pascal program, but will also stress that this is a highly dangerous activity unless the programmer knows exactly what he or she is doing.

The memory of the Apple can be thought of an array of 65536 elements of type CHAR, addresssed by the integers 0, 1, 2, ..., 65535.

The use of a variant parts here enables an item of data, namely a memory address, to be viewed in two different ways. It will first be regarded as an integer (in the range 0 to 65535) which addresses the Apple's memory in the conventional manner, and then as a pointer to a CHAR, which when followed gives the contents of the specified integer address. (This is only possible because a pointer in Apple Pascal happens to be implemented as an integer in the range 0 to 65535.)

The procedure POKE which assigns to memory is perhaps easier to understand. (PEEK, which interrogates memory, is left as an exercise for the reader.) If the heading of the procedure POKE is

        PROCEDURE POKE(A : INTEGER; C : CHAR);

we can then write, for example,

        POKE(1026, 'B')

(This sends a letter 'B' to part of the memory from which the screen is displayed.)

Our first inconclusive attempts to write this procedure will show the way forward. Although A is of type INTEGER, we know it is really an address, so we try

        PROCEDURE POKE(A : INTEGER; C : CHAR);

            BEGIN
                A^ := C
            END; (* POKE *)

But Pascal is not so easily deceived. It insists that since A is of type INTEGER, A^ is not valid. Let us therefore declare a variable, local to POKE, which can be viewed either as an integer or as a pointer.

        VAR MEMREF : RECORD
                        CASE BOOLEAN OF
                            FALSE : (ADDRESS : INTEGER);
                            TRUE : (POINTER : ^CHAR)
                    END;

The variable MEMREF introduced by this declaration can be referred to either as MEMREF.ADDRESS (of type INTEGER) or as MEMREF.POINTER (of type pointer to CHAR). Thus, in the former guise we may write

        MEMREF.ADDRESS := A

This assigns to MEMREF the address of the memory element to be written to. To assign the character C to this address, we refer to MEMREF as a pointer to a CHAR and write

```
MEMREF.POINTER^ := C
```

Gathering all this together, we get

```
PROCEDURE POKE(A : INTEGER; C : CHAR);

    VAR MEMREF : RECORD
                    CASE BOOLEAN OF
                        FALSE : (ADDRESS : INTEGER);
                        TRUE : (POINTER : ^CHAR)
                 END;

    BEGIN
        MEMREF.ADDRESS := A;
        MEMREF.POINTER^ := C
    END; (* POKE *)
```

EXERCISE 20H: PEEK produces a value of type CHAR, and should therefore be a function. Write the function beginning

```
FUNCTION PEEK(A : INTEGER) : CHAR;
```

Test PEEK with the statement

```
FOR I := 1 TO 200 DO C := PEEK(-16336)
```

where C is a CHAR. It should produce a note on the speaker.

The dangerous nature of PEEK and POKE cannot be overstressed. It is even possible to cause corruption of a disk by the injudicious use of POKE, and as exercise 20H shows, some PEEKs even have side effects.

SOLUTIONS TO THE EXERCISES

```
20A:   TYPE STATE    = (ACTIVE, RETIRED, COMPLETED);
            STATEPTR = ^STATE;
            MONTHINT = 1 .. 31;
            MONTHPTR = ^MONTHINT;
            A10      = ARRAY [1 .. 10] OF INTEGER;
            APTR     = ^A10;
```

20B: type:

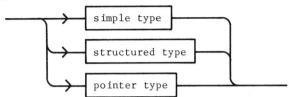

See section 12.4.1 for the diagram for simple type.

structured type:

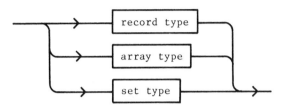

20C: (a)   REMINDER[MARY]
        (b)   REMINDER[JIM]^
        (c)   REMINDER[JACK]^.MESSAGE
        (d)   REMINDER[ANN]^.MESSAGE[3]
        (e)   REMINDER[MARY]^.NEXT^.PRIORITY

20D: Note the change of name from the imperative REMOVEFROMQUEUE to the
        nominative HEADOFQUEUE for a function. Note also that this function
        has a side effect through its variable parameter.

```
FUNCTION HEADOFQUEUE(VAR Q : THINGPOINTER) : THINGPOINTER;

    (* DISCONNECTS RECORD FROM QUEUE Q *)

    VAR P : THINGPOINTER;

    BEGIN
        IF Q = NIL THEN P := NIL
        ELSE
            BEGIN
                P := Q^.NEXT;
                IF Q = Q^.NEXT THEN Q := NIL
                              ELSE Q^.NEXT := P^.NEXT
            END;
        HEADOFQUEUE := P
    END; (* HEADOFQUEUE *)
```

20E: If a queue is defined to be a structure on which only the operations

                initialize queue
                add item to tail of queue
                remove item from head of queue

        are defined, then it is not possible to display any element of the
        queue without first removing it. In order to preserve this element it
        must be added to another queue. In other words, to display the entire
        queue, it must be copied.

```
20F:     PROGRAM REMLIST6A;

         TYPE STRING70 = RECORD ... END;

             TASKPTR = ^TASKSPEC;

             TASKSPEC = RECORD ... END;

         VAR REPLY : CHAR;
             TASKLIST : TASKPTR;
             TASKNUMBER : 1 .. 9999;

         PROCEDURE INITQUEUE(VAR Q : TASKPTR); ...;
         PROCEDURE ADDTOQUEUE(P : TASKPTR; VAR Q : TASKPTR); ...;
         PROCEDURE REMOVEFROMQUEUE(VAR P, Q : TASKPTR); ...;

         PROCEDURE INITIALIZE;

             BEGIN
                 INITQUEUE(TASKLIST);   TASKNUMBER := 1
             END; (* INITIALIZE *)

         PROCEDURE PROMPT; ...;
         PROCEDURE GETREPLY(VAR REPLY : CHAR); ...;

         PROCEDURE ADDTASK;

             VAR P : TASKPTR;
                 TASKTEXT : STRING70;

             PROCEDURE READSTRING6(VAR ST : STRING70); ...;

             BEGIN (* ADDTASK *)
                 NEW(P);
                 WITH P^ DO
                   BEGIN
                     IDEN := TASKNUMBER;   TASKNUMBER := TASKNUMBER + 1;
                     WRITE('ENTER PRIORITY, [0 .. 99] ');
                     READ(PRIORITY);
                     IF PRIORITY < 0 THEN PRIORITY := 0;
                     IF PRIORITY > 99 THEN PRIORITY := 99;
                     WRITELN('ENTER YOUR (DELIMITED) MESSAGE');
                     READSTRING6(TASKTEXT);   WRITELN;
                     MESSAGE := TASKTEXT
                   END;

                 ADDTOQUEUE(P, TASKLIST)

             END; (* ADDTASK *)

         PROCEDURE WRITESTRING(S : STRING70); ...;
         PROCEDURE DISPLAYTASKS; ...;

         PROCEDURE REMOVETASK;

             VAR P : TASKPTR;

             BEGIN
                 REMOVEFROMQUEUE(P, TASKLIST);
                 IF P <> NIL THEN
                   BEGIN
                     WRITESTRING(P^.MESSAGE);   WRITE(' DONE');   WRITELN;
                     (* DISPOSE OF THIS RECORD *)
                   END
             END; (* REMOVETASK *)

         BEGIN ... END.
```

```
20G:     TYPE RECKIND = (DATESTAMP, REMINDER);
            TASKSPEC = RECORD
                           NEXT : ^TASKSPEC;
                           CASE KIND : RECKIND OF
                             DATESTAMP : (DATE : RECORD
                                                    DAY : 1 .. 31;
                                                    MONTH : 1 .. 12;
                                                    YEAR : INTEGER
                                                 END;
                                          TIME : RECORD
                                                    HOURS : 0 .. 23;
                                                    MINS : 0 .. 59;
                                                    SECS : 0 .. 59
                                                 END);
                             REMINDER : (IDEN : 1 .. 9999;
                                         PRIORITY : 0 .. 99;
                                         MESSAGE : ARRAY [1 .. 70] OF CHAR)
                       END;


20H:     FUNCTION PEEK(A : INTEGER) : CHAR;

             VAR MEMREF : RECORD
                             CASE BOOLEAN OF
                               FALSE : (ADDRESS : INTEGER);
                               TRUE : (POINTER : ^CHAR)
                          END;

             BEGIN
                 MEMREF.ADDRESS := A;
                 PEEK := MEMREF.POINTER^
             END; (* PEEK *)
```

CHAPTER 21
Experimenting with Trees

Trees are hierarchical structures. The trees of nature are hierarchical in that if any branch be sawn off, the detached part is similar to (although smaller than) the tree itself. With some species, a carefully detached branch can be re-rooted enabling it to develop into another tree. Trees do not contain loops. The flow of sap from trunk to leaf splits but never rejoins. In other words, from the root to any leaf there is a unique path, corresponding to the flow of sap.

Trees in mathematics and computing share these properties, but they are generally drawn upside down, with the sap flowing down the page. As you might expect, mathematicians have a more formal definition of a tree than the description above. It is an important definition, for it suggests how trees may be processed by program.

A tree is either empty or else it is a node (known as the root, and usually represented in a program by a record) consisting of

- a value field or fields, and
- a finite set of one or more subtrees which are themselves trees.

The definition is clearly recursive, as was the informal description, since a tree is essentially a recursive structure. We shall consider the tree in the context of three applications: first, as a representation of a family structure, then in the context of placing the reminders of chapter 19 in order, and finally as a natural representation of an algebraic expression.

21.1 A FAMILY TREE

When we trace the descendants of a person, we usually draw them as a family tree. Family trees become complicated as a result of marriage and therefore in order to keep things simple, we shall deal here only with people of one sex. The text and program solutions are in terms of the male sex. To

change the programs to deal with the female sex, apply the following Editor
commands

> /RVL/MAN//WOMAN/   and   /RVL/SON//DAUGHTER/

Our objective is to write a procedure DISPLAY which displays the root node of
any family tree and then offers the opportunity for

- a son to be born to that person, or
- the subtree of any son to be dealt with, or
- the termination of the root node.

To keep the program simple we shall restrict the maximum number of sons to 9
and define the user interface as follows.

Key	Action
'B'	arrange for a birth
'1', '2', ..., '9'	display son 1, 2, ..., 9
'F'	finish with this node
any other	ignore.

Again this is recursive: the processing of a node can involve the processing of
a son which is itself a node. This reflects the recursive nature of the tree.

Consider, for example, part of the tree of male descendants of Noah shown
in figure 21.1 (Genesis, chapter 10, verses 1-25; also in [Knuth, 1973]
section 2.3).

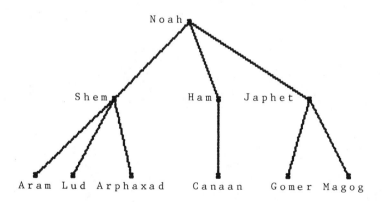

Fig 21.1   Some descendants of Noah

A procedure call equivalent to

> DISPLAY(node of Shem)

should display Shem's record and then invite a response. If, say, key '2' is
pressed, then the record of Lud (the second son) should be displayed, and when
Lud is finished with we should be back with Shem. If on the other hand key 'B'
were pressed, a fourth son (Asshur) could be added to Shem's family. In
outline, the procedure to display the tree corresponding to a given node is

```
PROCEDURE DISPLAY( ... );

   VAR REPLY : CHAR;

   BEGIN
     REPEAT
       DISPLAYNAMES;
       PROMPT;
       READ(REPLY);
       CASE REPLY OF
         '1', '2', '3', '4', '5', '6', '7', '8', '9' :
               DISPLAY(tree of son number REPLY);
         'B' : ARRANGEBIRTH
       END (* CASE *)
     UNTIL REPLY = 'F'
   END; (* DISPLAY *)
```

Before we can refine this we must decide upon the structure of a family
tree or, more precisely, the structure of a node representing a man. A man,
as far as this exercise is concerned, is a name with 0 to 9 sons. We represent
a man by the following definitions.

```
CONST MAXSONS = 9;

TYPE STRING40 = RECORD
                   LENGTH : 0 .. 40;
                   CH : PACKED ARRAY [1 .. 40] OF CHAR
               END;

   MAN = RECORD
            NAME : STRING40;
            NUMSONS : 0 .. MAXSONS;
            SON : ARRAY [1 .. MAXSONS] OF ???
         END;
```

Part of the family tree of Noah can be pictured thus.

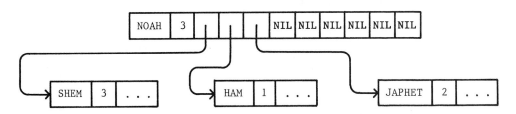

At this stage we must decide how to refer to a tree by means of a
variable. We seem to have two options to consider,

        - a pointer to the root, or
        - the record of the root.

Returning to the definition of a tree, we recall that a tree is either empty
or else a node consisting of value fields and a finite set of subtrees.
Records which can be either empty or non-empty can be handled by means of
variant parts (see section 20.3) but the attendant difficulties of variant
parts means we should consider an alternative if possible. Another reason is
that Pascal does not permit a record to be defined in terms of itself. We
cannot have

```
      SON : ARRAY [1 .. MAXSONS] OF MAN;
```

as a field of the record type MAN. A pointer is therefore used as a reference
to a tree and we observe that the value NIL neatly refers to an empty tree.
We define such a pointer, namely MANPOINTER and the record type MAN as

```
      TYPE STRING40 = ...;

           MANPOINTER = ^MAN;

           MAN = RECORD
                    NAME : STRING40;
                    NUMSONS : 0 .. MAXSONS;
                    SON : ARRAY [1 .. MAXSONS] OF MANPOINTER
                 END;
```

and the family tree itself is represented by a pointer

```
      VAR FAMTREE : MANPOINTER;
```

which points to the root of the tree. We can now improve on the outline
procedure DISPLAY.

```
      PROCEDURE DISPLAY(P : MANPOINTER);

         VAR REPLY : CHAR;

         BEGIN
           REPEAT
             DISPLAYNAMES;
             PROMPT;
             READ(REPLY);
             WITH P^ DO
                CASE REPLY OF
                   '1', '2', '3', '4', '5', '6', '7', '8', '9' :
                        DISPLAY(SON[ORD(REPLY) - 48]);
                   'B' : ARRANGEBIRTH
                END (* CASE AND WITH *)
           UNTIL REPLY = 'F'
         END; (* DISPLAY *)
```

EXERCISE 21A: Complete this program, adapting READSTRING6 (exercise 15D) and
                WRITESTRING (section 13.3.1) for 40 character strings and
                removing the need for delimiters. Add data validation to
                prevent the attempted descent to a non-existent son. You will
                need to make special provision for the naming of the root node.

                What is the state of the family tree immediately before
                termination of the program? How does this contrast with the
                state of named variables at the same time?

     Trees do not have to be represented as records on the heap. It is
possible to use an array, if the maximum number of nodes can be determined at
the time the program is written. If an array is used, then in place of
pointers, values of the index type are used to "point" to the subtrees.

21.2 TREE SORT

The hierarchical nature of a tree lends itself to the arrangement or
sorting of a sequence of objects (usually records) according to the
value of one or more fields, called keys. The method of sorting to be
described is generally referred to as a tree sort. In this discussion we
shall base the ordering on the value of a single key field, and arrange records
in ascending order of the value of their keys.

Returning to the definition of a tree, consider the special kind of tree
that we get if we restrict the set of subtrees to exactly two. Such trees are
known as binary trees. It is useful to label the subtrees as the left
subtree and the right subtree. Suppose that the nodes of a binary tree
are a collection of records each having a single field designated as a key
field. Suppose further that

- all records in the left subtree have keys less than the key of the
  root and

- all records in the right subtree have keys greater than or equal
  to the key of the root

- and that all subtrees of the left and right subtrees have the two
  properties above.

The tree in figure 21.2 satisfies these conditions.

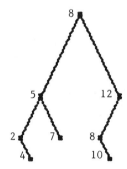

Fig 21.2   Tree sort

If we have access to a procedure which can display the records of the left or
right subtrees in ascending order of their keys, then the following outline
procedure will display the records of the complete tree in ascending order.

```
PROCEDURE DISPLAYTREE(completetree : ...);

    BEGIN
        DISPLAYTREE(left subtree);
        displayroot;
        DISPLAYTREE(right subtree)
    END; (* DISPLAYTREE *)
```

It is, of course, recursive, but as it stands, it suffers from the defect of
having no escape. As it stands it must go on for ever, displaying the left
subtree of the left subtree of the ... We refer back to the definition of a
tree again, and recall that a tree may be empty. Empty trees don't need to be
displayed! This suggests

```
PROCEDURE DISPLAYTREE(completetree : ...);

    BEGIN
       IF completetree <> NIL THEN
          BEGIN
             DISPLAYTREE(left subtree);
             displayroot;
             DISPLAYTREE(right subtree)
          END
    END; (* DISPLAYTREE *)
```

We next have to define the structure of a node in this tree. To simplify the program, we shall ignore all the non-key fields of the record, and assume that the key field is of type INTEGER.

```
TYPE TREEPTR = ^NODE;
     NODE = RECORD
                    LEFT  : TREEPTR;
                    KEY   : INTEGER;
                    RIGHT : TREEPTR
             END;
```

and the procedure becomes

```
PROCEDURE DISPLAYTREE(T : TREEPTR);

    BEGIN
       IF T <> NIL THEN
          BEGIN
             DISPLAYTREE(T^.LEFT);
             WRITE(T^.KEY, '  ');
             DISPLAYTREE(T^.RIGHT)
          END
    END; (* DISPLAYTREE *)
```

It is the simplicity and elegance of this procedure that provides the motivation for this method of sorting.

Next we should consider the main program in outline. We wish to demonstrate that the method works satisfactorily, arranging integers in ascending order as we enter them. For convenience we stop after zero has been entered.

```
PROGRAM TREESORT;

TYPE ...;

VAR N : INTEGER;
    NEWREC, TREE : TREEPTR;

BEGIN
    TREE := NIL;
    READ(N);
    WHILE N <> 0 DO
        BEGIN
            CREATEREC(N, NEWREC);
            GRAFT(NEWREC, TREE);
            WRITELN;  DISPLAYTREE(TREE);  WRITELN;
            READ(N)
        END
END.
```

The procedure call CREATEREC(N, NEWREC) creates a record from the integer N, with **NIL** as the value of both left and right subtree, and leaves NEWREC pointing to it.

EXERCISE 21B: Write the procedure CREATEREC.

The remaining procedure call is GRAFT(NEWREC, TREE) which grafts the record pointed to by NEWREC into the tree pointed to by TREE. Since the value of TREE will change from **NIL** to NEWREC as the first record is grafted to form the root, it must be a variable parameter. The procedure heading may therefore be

> **PROCEDURE** GRAFT(P : TREEPTR; **VAR** T : TREEPTR);

The procedure has to deal with two cases: that of an empty tree and that of a non-empty tree. If the tree T is empty then the value of T is simply P, but if T is not empty, then the record which P points to has to be grafted onto either T^.LEFT or T^.RIGHT, depending on whether P^.KEY is less than or greater than T^.KEY. This is easier to describe in Pascal than in English!

```
     PROCEDURE GRAFT(P : TREEPTR; VAR T : TREEPTR);

        (* GRAFT RECORD POINTED TO BY P INTO TREE POINTED TO BY T *)

        BEGIN
           IF T = NIL THEN T := P
           ELSE
               IF P^.KEY < T^.KEY THEN GRAFT(P, T^.LEFT)
                                  ELSE GRAFT(P, T^.RIGHT)
        END; (* GRAFT *)
```


EXERCISE 21C: Complete the program and save it as USER:TREESORT.

EXERCISE 21D: If the main program of USER:TREESORT were

```
           PROGRAM TREESORT;

           TYPE ...;

           VAR N : INTEGER;
               NEWREC, TREE : TREEPTR;

           BEGIN
               REPEAT
                   TREE := NIL;
                   READ(N);
                   WHILE N <> 0 DO
                       BEGIN
                           CREATEREC(N, NEWREC);
                           GRAFT(NEWREC, TREE);
                           READ(N)
                       END;
                   WRITELN;  DISPLAYTREE(TREE);  WRITELN
               UNTIL FALSE
           END.
```

what problem of storage will eventually arise, and in standard Pascal where is the obvious place to deal with it? (Hint: see exercise 21A.)

21.3   TREES THAT REPRESENT EXPRESSIONS

The hierarchical property of binary trees makes them suitable for the representation, without parentheses, of linearly written expressions. Expressions are normally written in <u>infix</u> notation, with the operator between the operands. This is generally how expressions are written in Pascal but, whilst it is the easiest form for us to understand, it is not the easiest form for automatic conversion to binary trees. We begin by analyzing expressions in a notation in which the operator is placed before the operands and show how expressions in this form may be converted to trees. (This notation should not be completely new to you. It is essentially the notation of functions. If you think of HCF (highest common factor) as an operand, then HCF(56, 21) is in a kind of prefix notation.) Throughout this section you should note that the programs we write will read expressions (in various forms) from the keyboard and display them in some other form on the screen. The programs will in fact be doing one small thing that the Pascal Compiler does.

21.3.1   Prefix Notation

In <u>prefix</u> notation, the operator precedes the operands. If we restrict basic operands to a single character (other than +, -, *, /) we can demonstrate the correspondence between infix and prefix notations by the following examples.

Infix	Prefix
a	a
a+b	+ab
a+b*c	+a*bc
(a+b)*c	*+abc
a*a+b*b	+*aa*bb
(a+b)*(c+d)	*+ab+cd

Observe that parentheses are not required in the prefix notation, and that the need for operator precedence (section 8.2.2) also disappears. An operator applies to the two expressions which follow it. We can express the syntax of an expression in prefix notation as a syntax diagram. This diagram, which describes the data for a program, is in exactly the same style as the diagrams that describe the syntax of Pascal, but it is not part of that set of diagrams and will not be found in appendix 6.

expression (prefix notation):

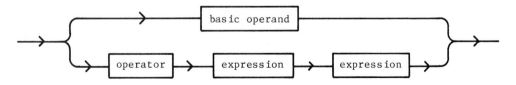

The tree representation of an expression is independent of the notation used. Some examples are given in figure 21.3.

Our program will repeatedly read a prefix expression, convert it to a tree and then display the tree. In outline it is

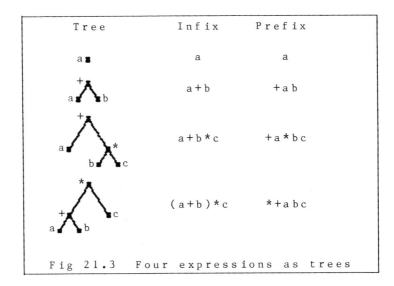

Tree	Infix	Prefix
a	a	a
+	a + b	+ a b
+	a + b * c	+ a * b c
*	(a + b) * c	* + a b c

Fig 21.3   Four expressions as trees

```
PROGRAM PREFIX;

TYPE TREEPTR = ^TREENODE;
     TREENODE = RECORD
                    LEFT : TREEPTR;
                    VAL : CHAR;
                    RIGHT : TREEPTR
                END;

VAR TREE : TREEPTR;

BEGIN
    REPEAT
        TREE := NIL;
        EXPRESSION(TREE);
        WRITELN;  DISPLAYTREE(TREE);  WRITELN
    UNTIL FALSE
END.
```

The procedure EXPRESSION must therefore read characters and build the corresponding tree. The definition of a prefix expression above suggests the form of the procedure. This is a good example of how the structure of the data is reflected in the structure of the procedure that processes it. To keep the program simple, spaces will not be allowed in prefix expressions. The procedure is

```
PROCEDURE EXPRESSION(VAR T : TREEPTR);

    VAR C : CHAR;
        P : TREEPTR;

    BEGIN
        READ(C);  CREATEREC(C, P);
        IF NOT (C IN ['+', '-', '*', '/']) THEN GRAFT(P, T)
        ELSE
          BEGIN
            GRAFT(P, T);
            EXPRESSION(T^.LEFT);
            EXPRESSION(T^.RIGHT)
          END
    END; (* EXPRESSION *)
```

where the procedure CREATEREC is very similar to the procedure of the same name in TREESORT. The procedure GRAFT, on the other hand, does not have to search for the place to graft the record P^. It goes at T, and the procedure is

```
PROCEDURE GRAFT(P : TREEPTR; VAR T : TREEPTR);

    BEGIN
        T := P
    END; (* GRAFT *)
```

Finally, to convince ourselves that the tree is correct, we write a procedure to display the expression in infix notation. It is very similar to the procedure DISPLAYTREE in the treesort program. An expression, in the form of a tree, consists of either

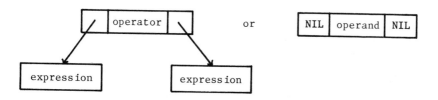

and so the procedure is essentially

```
PROCEDURE DISPLAYTREE(T : TREEPTR);

    BEGIN
        IF T <> NIL THEN
          BEGIN
            DISPLAYTREE(T^.LEFT);
            WRITE(T^.VAL);
            DISPLAYTREE(T^.RIGHT)
          END
    END; (* DISPLAYTREE *)
```

but since the infix notation needs parentheses to express certain operator priorities, we add them (some of which may be unnecessary) so that an expression involving an operator is displayed as

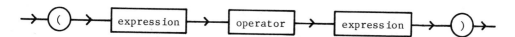

The procedure is

```
PROCEDURE DISPLAYTREE(T : TREEPTR);

  BEGIN
    IF T <> NIL THEN
      BEGIN
        IF T^.LEFT <> NIL THEN WRITE('(');
        DISPLAYTREE(T^.LEFT);
        WRITE(T^.VAL);
        DISPLAYTREE(T^.RIGHT);
        IF T^.RIGHT <> NIL THEN WRITE(')')
      END
  END; (* DISPLAYTREE *)
```

EXERCISE 21E: Assemble the complete program and test it on the expressions at
               the head of this section. Type CTRL-@ to stop the program.
               Save it as USER:PREFIX.

     Prefix notation is sometimes called Polish notation after the Polish
mathematician Lucasiewicz who first explored it.

21.3.2 Postfix Notation

     Make the following changes to the program USER:PREFIX.

     - Change the name of the program to PRETOPOSTFIX.

     - Remove the 2 statements that display parentheses
        from DISPLAYTREE.

     - In the procedure DISPLAYTREE, move the statement

             WRITE(T^.VAL)

        so that it immediately follows

             DISPLAYTREE(T^.RIGHT)

EXERCISE 21F: Type in the following expressions at the program PRETOPOSTFIX
              and observe the responses.

                    A
                    +AB
                    +A-B*CD
                    +*-ABCD
                    *+AB+CD

EXERCISE 21G: Modify the program to display the tree in its original prefix
               notation.

     The forms which the program in exercise 21F displays are in postfix
notation or Reverse Polish Notation (RPN). The general form of an
expression in postfix notation is

expression (postfix notation):

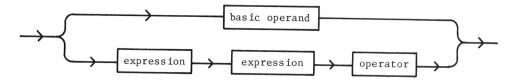

Expressions written in postfix notation are more difficult to analyze in
the manner of the program USER:PREFIX since the definition above leads you down
blind alleys from which it is necessary to <u>backtrack</u>. On the other hand,
expressions in this form are extremely easy to analyze and evaluate using a
stack, and the reader is referred to a standard text on compilers for further
discussion of this technique.

The three different ways of displaying a tree (often called <u>traversing</u>
a tree) given in this section are known by the following terms.

<u>preorder</u>:	root	left subtree	right subtree
<u>inorder</u>:	left subtree	root	right subtree
<u>postorder</u>:	left subtree	right subtree	root

21.3.3 <u>Infix Notation to Tree</u>

In the previous section it should have become apparent that when
structured as a tree, an expression is in a very useful form. It is easy to
display it in any of the three linear notations. It also happens to be in a
form which makes it easy to evaluate and also, rather surprisingly, fairly
easy to differentiate symbolically, that is, to convert the string

        X*X + 3*X

into the string

        1*X + X*1 + 3*1 + 0*X

which, after being tidied up, becomes

        2*X + 3

Symbolic differentiation is left for the reader's consideration, but to
conclude this section, we develop a program which will construct a tree from a
parenthesized infix expression (similar to the <u>simple expression</u> of
Pascal without the leading '+' or '-') and then evaluate the expression from
the tree. All operands will be integer constants. The resulting program will
have an effect not unlike that of a calculator operating in algebraic hierarchy
mode with parentheses.

The tree in this case will have two different kinds of node, one with an
integer value, the other with a character representing an operator (+, -, * or
/). This calls for nodes being represented by records having a variant part;
for example

```
TYPE TREEPTR = ^TREENODE;
     OPTYPE = (OPERAND, OPERATOR);
     TREENODE = RECORD
                     LEFT : TREEPTR;
                     RIGHT : TREEPTR;
                     CASE KIND : OPTYPE OF
                          OPERAND  : (VAL : INTEGER);
                          OPERATOR : (INOP : CHAR)
                END;
```

In outline, the program will be

```
PROGRAM INFIX;

VAR TREE : TREEPTR;

BEGIN
    REPEAT
        TREE := NIL;
        SIMPEXPRESSION(TREE);
        WRITELN(VALOF(TREE));   WRITELN
    UNTIL FALSE
END.
```

where the procedure SIMPEXPRESSION transforms the input to a tree, whilst the function VALOF calculates the value of the simple expression pointed to by its parameter.

In order to see more clearly why the former procedure is worth writing, consider how simple the function appears to be.

```
FUNCTION VALOF(T : TREEPTR) : INTEGER;

BEGIN
  WITH T^ DO
    CASE KIND OF
      OPERAND:
        BEGIN
          VALOF := VAL;
          (* DISPOSE(T, OPERAND) *)
        END;
      OPERATOR:
        BEGIN
          CASE INOP OF
            '+': VALOF := VALOF(LEFT) + VALOF(RIGHT);
            '-': VALOF := VALOF(LEFT) - VALOF(RIGHT);
            '*': VALOF := VALOF(LEFT) * VALOF(RIGHT);
            '/': VALOF := VALOF(LEFT) DIV VALOF(RIGHT)
          END;
          (* DISPOSE(T, OPERATOR) *)
        END
    END (* CASE *)
END; (* VALOF *)
```

EXERCISE 21H: Why, in the function VALOF, do the two DISPOSE statements have
                 two parameters each? Explain the purpose of these statements.
                 What important precept of programming style is broken? Is it
                 justified?

Before we attempt to write the procedure to evaluate an infix expression, we recall the syntax diagrams for the simple expression of Pascal (section 8.2.3). With the restriction that operands be only integer constants, they are simple expression:

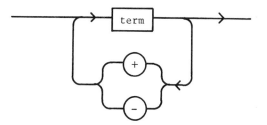

term:

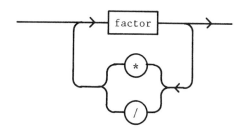

factor:

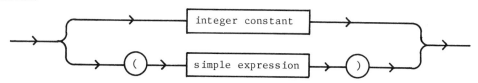

Our first attempt at a procedure to recognize a simple expression will be something like this.

```
PROCEDURE SIMPEXPRESSION;

    BEGIN
        TERM;
        WHILE next character IN ['+', '-'] DO TERM
    END; (* SIMPEXPRESSION *)
```

The general form of the iteration is correct but reference to the next character seems to require a crystal ball to find out what we would next read if we were to read a character. The only satisfactory way around this problem is to ensure that the next character to be processed is already in a variable one step ahead of its use. Thus the procedure for simple expression would be

```
PROCEDURE SIMPEXPRESSION;

    BEGIN
        TERM;
        WHILE CH IN ['+', '-'] DO
            BEGIN
                GETACHAR;
                TERM
            END
    END; (* SIMPEXPRESSION *)
```

where the procedure TERM not only recognizes a term but puts the next
character into the variable CH. Since there is only one input stream and CH
will be used in several procedures, CH has to be declared at the outermost
level, and in the main program a call for GETACHAR must precede the call for
SIMPEXPRESSION.

So much for recognition, but what of the tree that has to be generated?
Suppose the simple expression takes the form

$$t_1 + t_2 - t_3 - t_4$$

where t_1, t_2, t_3, t_4 are terms. The tree has to reflect the left to right
evaluation of the operators.

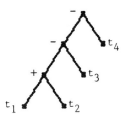

Fig 21.4   The expression $t_1 + t_2 - t_3 - t_4$

The procedure SIMPEXPRESSION must create the appropriate tree and return
the value of a pointer to the tree it has created. Thus we develop the
procedure one stage further.

```
PROCEDURE SIMPEXPRESSION(VAR ET : TREEPTR);

    VAR P, Q, R : TREEPTR;
        ADOP : CHAR;

    BEGIN
      TERM(P);
      WHILE CH IN ['+', '-'] DO
        BEGIN
          ADOP := CH;  GETACHAR;
          TERM(Q);
          NEW(R, OPERATOR);
          WITH R^ DO
            BEGIN
              KIND := OPERATOR;
              LEFT := P;  INOP := ADOP;  RIGHT := Q
            END;
            P := R
        END;
      ET := P
    END; (* SIMPEXPRESSION *)
```

Here the new node representing

        TERM(P)   ADOP   TERM(Q)

is set up with R pointing to it. This then becomes subtree P in readiness for
another ADOP and TERM. On exit the parameter ET points to the last ADOP node.

EXERCISE 21J: The procedure for TERM is almost the same. Write it.

The procedure FACTOR is quite different and reflects the different structure of a factor. Our first attempt might be

```
PROCEDURE FACTOR(VAR FT : TREEPTR);

    VAR V : INTEGER;

    BEGIN (* NOTE THAT THIS PROCEDURE ADMITS A NULL FACTOR *)

        IF CH = '(' THEN SIMPEXPRESSION(FT)
        ELSE
          BEGIN
            GETANINT(V);
            NEW(FT, OPERAND);
            WITH FT^ DO
              BEGIN
                KIND := OPERAND;
                LEFT := NIL;  VAL := V;  RIGHT := NIL
              END
          END
    END; (* FACTOR *)
```

but it does not deal properly with the parentheses. Recognition of the simple expression in parentheses needs the first character to be in CH, and the closing parenthesis needs to be absorbed. The if statement should begin

```
IF CH = '(' THEN
    BEGIN
      GETACHAR;
      SIMPEXPRESSION(FT);            (* CLOSING PARENTHESIS IN CH *)
      GETACHAR
    END
  ELSE ...
```

All that remains are two procedures: GETACHAR gets the next character, and whilst we are at it we might as well ignore leading spaces; GETANINT reads an integer, something we have left to the Pascal READ and READLN statements so far in this book. We cannot do this here because the first character has already been read. It is also necessary for GETANINT to ensure that it leaves the next non-space character following the integer in the variable CH. In the procedure that follows, note how a character representing a decimal digit is converted to an integer value by means of the function ORD.

```
PROCEDURE GETANINT(VAR V : INTEGER);

    BEGIN
      V := 0;
      WHILE CH IN ['0' .. '9'] DO
        BEGIN
          V := V*10 + (ORD(CH) - 48);  (* ORD(0) = 48 *)
          READ(CH)
        END;
      IF CH = ' ' THEN GETACHAR
    END; (* GETANINT *)
```

EXERCISE 21K: Complete the program, test it and save it as USER:INFIX.

EXERCISE 21L: Modify the program in USER:INFIX to produce real valued results.

SOLUTIONS TO THE EXERCISES

21A: PROGRAM FAMILY;

         CONST MAXSONS = 9;

         TYPE ...;

         VAR FAMTREE : MANPOINTER;
             ROOTNAME : STRING40;

         PROCEDURE PAUSE;

             VAR COUNT : INTEGER;

             BEGIN
                 FOR COUNT := 0 TO 4999 DO
             END; (* PAUSE *)

         PROCEDURE READSTRING(VAR ST : STRING40);

             CONST BS = 8;

             VAR CHARCOUNT : 0 .. 40;
                 C : CHAR;

             BEGIN
               CHARCOUNT := 0;
               READ(C);
               WHILE NOT EOLN DO
                 BEGIN
                    ...
                 END;
               ST.LENGTH := CHARCOUNT
             END; (* READSTRING *)

         PROCEDURE WRITESTRING(S : STRING40); ...;

         PROCEDURE NEWMANREC(VAR PERSON : MANPOINTER; NEWNAME : STRING40);

             VAR SONNUMBER : 0 .. MAXSONS;

             BEGIN
               NEW(PERSON);
               WITH PERSON^ DO
                 BEGIN
                   NAME := NEWNAME; NUMSONS := 0;
                   FOR SONNUMBER := 1 TO MAXSONS DO SON[SONNUMBER] := NIL
                 END
             END; (* NEWMANREC *)

         PROCEDURE DISPLAY(P : MANPOINTER);

             VAR REPLY : CHAR;

             PROCEDURE GETREPLY(VAR C : CHAR);

                 BEGIN
                     REPEAT READ(KEYBOARD, C) UNTIL C <> ' ';
                     WITH P^ DO
                       IF NOT (C IN ['B', 'F', '1' .. CHR(48+NUMSONS)]) THEN
                         GETREPLY(C)
                 END; (* GETREPLY *)

```
PROCEDURE DISPLAYNAMES;

    VAR SONNUMBER : 0 .. MAXSONS;

    BEGIN
        WRITE(CHR(12), CHR(25));
        WITH P^ DO
          BEGIN
            WRITESTRING(NAME);  WRITELN;
            WRITELN('HIS SONS ARE : ');
            FOR SONNUMBER := 1 TO NUMSONS DO
              BEGIN
                WRITE(SONNUMBER : 8, '     ');
                WRITESTRING(SON[SONNUMBER]^.NAME);  WRITELN
              END
          END (* WITH *)
    END; (* DISPLAYNAMES *)

PROCEDURE PROMPT;

    VAR SONNUMBER : 0 .. MAXSONS;

    BEGIN
      GOTOXY(0, 16);
      WRITE('F' : 18, ' TO RETURN TO FATHER');
      IF P^. NUMSONS < MAXSONS THEN
        BEGIN
          GOTOXY(0, 18);  WRITE('B' : 18, ' TO ADD A SON')
        END;
      IF P^.NUMSONS >= 1 THEN
        BEGIN
          GOTOXY(0, 20);  WRITE(' ' : 2*(MAXSONS - P^.NUMSONS));
          FOR SONNUMBER := 1 TO P^.NUMSONS DO WRITE(SONNUMBER : 2);
          WRITE(' TO DISPLAY A SON')
        END;
      GOTOXY(0, 14);  WRITE('PRESS ONE KEY AS FOLLOWS : ')
    END; (* PROMPT *)

PROCEDURE ARRANGEBIRTH;

    VAR BABY : MANPOINTER;
        BABYSNAME : STRING40;

    BEGIN
        WITH P^ DO
          IF NUMSONS = MAXSONS THEN
            BEGIN
              GOTOXY(6, 22);
              WRITE('TOO BAD, HIS QUIVER IS FULL');
              PAUSE
            END
          ELSE
            BEGIN
              GOTOXY(0, 22);  WRITE('NAME PLEASE : ');
              READSTRING(BABYSNAME);
              NEWMANREC(BABY, BABYSNAME);
              NUMSONS := NUMSONS + 1;  SON[NUMSONS] := BABY
            END
    END; (* ARRANGEBIRTH *)

BEGIN
  REPEAT
    DISPLAYNAMES;
    PROMPT;
    GETREPLY(REPLY);
    WITH P^ DO ...
  UNTIL REPLY = 'F'
END; (* DISPLAY *)
```

```
BEGIN
    GOTOXY(0, 10);
    WRITE('ENTER NAME OF ROOT PERSON : ');
    READSTRING(ROOTNAME);
    NEWMANREC(FAMTREE, ROOTNAME);
    DISPLAY(FAMTREE)
END.
```

At termination, the records of the tree still occupy space on the heap.
The named pointer that pointed to the root of the tree no longer
exists.

21B: **PROCEDURE** CREATEREC(N : INTEGER; **VAR** P : TREEPTR);

```
    BEGIN
      NEW(P);
      WITH P^ DO
        BEGIN
          LEFT := NIL;   KEY := N;   RIGHT := NIL
        END
    END; (* CREATEREC *)
```

21C: **PROGRAM** TREESORT;

TYPE ...;

VAR N : INTEGER;
    NEWREC, TREE : TREEPTR;

PROCEDURE CREATEREC(N : INTEGER; **VAR** P : TREEPTR); ...;

PROCEDURE GRAFT(P : TREEPTR; **VAR** T : TREEPTR); ...;

PROCEDURE DISPLAYTREE(T : TREEPTR); ...;

BEGIN ... **END.**

21D: For each execution of **REPEAT ... UNTIL**, a new tree is created.

Each execution of

```
    TREE := NIL
```

removes the sole pointer to that tree, which still occupies space on
the heap, and has become inaccessible. As the program continues, more
of the heap is turned into inaccessible trees, and the program must
eventually terminate in an "Execution Error". In standard Pascal,
to avoid this, add to the procedure DISPLAYTREE, at its end, a
statement to dispose of the node just displayed. This disposes of the
entire tree node by node, by a process analogous to branch-by-branch
pruning.

21E: **PROGRAM** PREFIX;

TYPE ...;

VAR TREE : TREEPTR;

PROCEDURE CREATEREC(CH : CHAR; **VAR** P : TREEPTR); ...;
PROCEDURE GRAFT(P : TREEPTR; **VAR** T : TREEPTR); ...;
PROCEDURE EXPRESSION(**VAR** T : TREEPTR); ...;
PROCEDURE DISPLAYTREE(T : TREEPTR); ...;

BEGIN ... **END.**

21F: A
         AB+
         ABCD*-+
         AB-C*D+
         AB+CD+*

21G: Change DISPLAYTREE to

                 PROCEDURE DISPLAYTREE(T : TREEPTR);

                         BEGIN
                             IF T <> NIL THEN
                                 BEGIN
                                     WRITE(T^.VAL);
                                     DISPLAYTREE(T^.LEFT);
                                     DISPLAYTREE(T^.RIGHT)
                                 END
                         END; (* DISPLAYTREE *)

21H: They assume that the records (having variant parts) were created by
         NEW(P, OPERAND) and NEW(P, OPERATOR) respectively. (See section 20.3.)

         They systematically return nodes of the tree to the reusable part of
         the heap, as soon as they are finished with.

         They cause side effects within a function.

         This is certainly the natural place to dispose of these nodes. A
         procedure for dismantling the tree, based on the postorder traverse
         (section 21.3.2) could be written to do this task more explicitly.

21J: PROCEDURE TERM(VAR TT : TREEPTR);

                 VAR P, Q, R : TREEPTR;
                     MOP : CHAR;

                 BEGIN   (* TERM *)
                     FACTOR(P);
                     WHILE CH IN ['*', '/'] DO
                         BEGIN
                             MOP := CH; GETACHAR;
                             FACTOR(Q);
                             NEW(R, OPERATOR);
                             WITH R^ DO
                                 BEGIN
                                     KIND := OPERATOR;
                                     LEFT := P; INOP := MOP; RIGHT := Q
                                 END;
                             P := R
                         END;
                     TT := P
                 END; (* TERM *)

21K: PROGRAM INFIX;

         TYPE ...;

         VAR TREE : TREEPTR;
             CH : CHAR;

         PROCEDURE GETACHAR;

                 BEGIN
                     REPEAT READ(CH) UNTIL CH <> ' '
                 END; (* GETACHAR *)

```
PROCEDURE SIMPEXPRESSION(VAR ET : TREEPTR);

    VAR P, Q, R : TREEPTR;
        ADOP : CHAR;

    PROCEDURE TERM(VAR TT : TREEPTR);

        VAR P, Q, R : TREEPTR;
            MOP : CHAR;

        PROCEDURE FACTOR(VAR FT : TREEPTR);

            VAR V : INTEGER;

            PROCEDURE GETANINT(VAR V : INTEGER); ...;

            BEGIN ... END; (* FACTOR *)

        BEGIN ... END; (* TERM *)

    BEGIN ... END; (* SIMPEXPRESSION *)

FUNCTION VALOF(T : TREEPTR) : INTEGER; ...;

BEGIN (* MAIN PROGRAM *)
    REPEAT
        TREE := NIL;
        GETACHAR;
        SIMPEXPRESSION(TREE);
        WRITELN(VALOF(TREE));   WRITELN
    UNTIL FALSE
END.
```

21L: Change the function header to

```
FUNCTION VALOF(T : TREEPTR) : REAL;
```

and change the last line of the case statement to

```
'/': VALOF := VALOF(LEFT) / VALOF(RIGHT)
```

CHAPTER 22
Experimenting with Files

The program in chapter 19 which kept a reminder list was perhaps of educational value but it was of no practical use whatsoever. The problem lay in the inability of data to survive beyond the duration of the execution of a program. In fact, it is the fresh start with all variables having to be initialized that makes our programs deterministic. Such determinism has helped us to debug programs. However, we have noticed that our programs (both in TEXT and CODE forms) do survive from one day to the next. They are kept in files by the Filer and files survive the programs that use them. If data is to survive from one execution of a program to another then it too must be placed in a file. To make the reminder list program of chapter 19 viable, it will be necessary to place the list of tasks in a file before execution of the program ends, and recover the list from the file just after the next execution begins. As in chapter 19, we will process the data internally as a list (on the heap).

Files have another property that makes them useful in other situations: they can be very much larger than the internal memory of the computer. Depending on the medium on which they reside, they may be of almost unlimited size. The problem of space gives way to the problem of keeping processing time within reasonable limits. On the Apple, the capacity of a floppy disk imposes an upper limit of about 140 000 characters on a file. This is tiny compared with some large commercial files but many times larger than the memory of the computer. (Do not confuse general file limits with the limits of size of files that can be edited with the Editor. In the former case, only a very small part of the file would ever be in memory at one time, but in the latter case, the Editor requires the entire file to be in memory; hence it imposes a much lower limit.)

Files are ordered sequences of homogeneous components. So far the definition seems suspiciously like that of an array. However, there is no limit to the number of components but there is a severe limitation on which component may be accessed next. Generally, only the next component in sequence can be accessed. In standard Pascal, components are not indexed (as in arrays) nor named (as in records). In UCSD Pascal it is possible to access directly any component of a file through the SEEK procedure. For further details of random access, see [Apple, 1980a] or [Clark and Koehler, 1982].

Since access to a standard Pascal file has to be in strict sequence, it is often essential to be able to arrange the components of a file in a particular order before processing that file. Later in this chapter, we give a method of sorting files, and then discuss the general approach to processing data in a file.

22.1 REMEMBERING THE REMINDER LIST

We shall base the developments in this section on the program that was saved at exercise 19G as REMLIST6. Later developments of this program, such as that in exercise 20F, may also be used.

The version of the program using file storage will have a main program section something like

```
PROGRAM REMLIST7;

BEGIN
    INITIALIZE;
    GETLIST;
    DISPLAYTASKS;
    PROMPT;
    GETREPLY(REPLY);
    WHILE REPLY <> 'S' DO
        BEGIN
            CASE REPLY OF
                'A' : ADDTASK;
                'D' : DISPLAYTASKS;
                'R' : REMOVETASK
            END;
            PROMPT;
            GETREPLY(REPLY)
        END;
    PUTLIST
END.
```

Two procedure calls have been added.

- GETLIST   transfers the reminders from a file into the form of a
             linked list
- PUTLIST   is the converse. It transfers the reminders in a linked
             list into the form of a file.

It now makes sense to display the list of reminders automatically, immediately after reading them from the file; hence the procedure statement

    DISPLAYTASKS

is included as the third statement of the main program.

EXERCISE 22A: Why does the procedure statement INITIALIZE have to precede the
               statement GETLIST?

Before we proceed further, it is worth contemplating an important consequence of what we have decided to do. The main program, as we have outlined it, needs a file for GETLIST to get. Such a file will be created by PUTLIST, but on the very first execution of the program there will not be a file! Furthermore, we cannot use the Editor to create such a file. The Editor can only create textfiles and this is not going to be a textfile. In practice, this problem seldom arises since a file maintenance program such as the one we are writing usually forms part of a suite of programs, one of which is a file creation program.

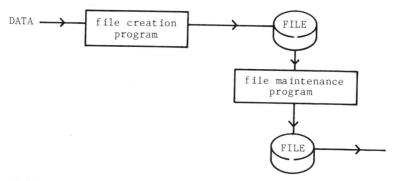

If we were following the usual commercial practice we would first write the file creation program, and use it to create an empty reminder file. Here, we shall adopt a different approach which saves writing an extra program. We start at the end, and implement PUTLIST first!

22.1.1 Writing to a File

To the program in USER:REMLIST6, add only the PUTLIST statement. This implies that we next consider the procedure PUTLIST.

The file to which we will send the reminders will have, as its basic component, a record of type TASKSPEC. The file must have one name (identifier) by which the program refers to it, and another by means of which the Filer refers to it. If you compare the syntax of an identifier (exercise 4G(a)) with that of a file specification (appendix 2, section 2.4) you will see one reason why files have two different names. The name by which the program refers to a file is declared in the VAR section by writing

        REMFILE : **FILE OF** TASKSPEC;

To process any file (either writing to it or reading from it) a strict protocol has to be observed, namely

    -   open the file
    -   process the file
    -   close the file.

You can think of opening a file as making essential checks and preparations prior to processing, and closing a file as tidying up and deeming the file to be finished with. Remember that files survive program execution and are vulnerable compared with the internal variables and structures of a program. This is especially so in multi-user systems, where opening includes checking whether the agent attempting to open the file has the authority to do so and closing may include the application of protection to ensure privacy. On the single-user Apple the principal check on opening a file is that of its existence! To open REMFILE for writing we write

        REWRITE(REMFILE, 'USER:MYLIST.DATA')

This statement associates the identifier REMFILE with the disk file USER:MYLIST.DATA until such time as the file is closed, whereupon the association is broken. If a file with the name USER:MYLIST.DATA exists, then it is deleted and a new file with no components is established, and in the case of UCSD Pascal, the file will be written to the largest unused area on the disk (see appendix 10).

To close REMFILE and ensure that it is kept, we write

    CLOSE(REMFILE, LOCK)

To close REMFILE and have it deleted, we write

    CLOSE(REMFILE)   or   CLOSE(REMFILE, NORMAL)

For our reminder list program, it is essential to keep the new file and therefore, in outline, the procedure PUTLIST will be

    PROCEDURE PUTLIST;

        BEGIN
            REWRITE(REMFILE, 'USER:MYLIST.DATA');
            IF TASKLIST <> **NIL THEN** copy tasklist to REMFILE;
            CLOSE(REMFILE, LOCK)
        END; (* PUTLIST *)

This leaves us with the writing of the reminders in TASKLIST to the file. The order in which the reminders are to be written should be that in which we displayed them. (See the solution to exercise 19G.) If we declare two local pointer variables

    VAR P, P0 : ^TASKSPEC;

the if statement becomes

    IF TASKLIST <> **NIL THEN**
        BEGIN
            P0 := TASKLIST^.NEXT;
            P := P0;
            REPEAT
                send P^ to REMFILE;
                P := P^.NEXT
            UNTIL P = P0
        END;

To complete this procedure we need to consider in more detail how Pascal files are structured. A file is a homogeneous sequence of components which, in this example, are records. The file variable, REMFILE, is effectively a pointer to a <u>buffer</u> which is of the same type as the components of the file. In this example, REMFILE^ may be regarded as a record of type TASKSPEC. Thus,

    REMFILE^.NEXT
    REMFILE^.IDEN
    REMFILE^.MESSAGE

are all valid references to variables. The buffer is not strictly part of the file but belongs to the block in which the file is declared. Two standard procedures transfer components between buffer and file. They are

    PUT(FILENAME)   buffer to file
    GET(FILENAME)   file to buffer.

For our present purposes, we clearly use PUT(REMFILE) to transfer from the buffer REMFILE^ to the file REMFILE. However, the buffer must first be filed from the linked list. The statements that effect the transfer of record P^ to REMFILE are

```
REMFILE^ := P^;
PUT(REMFILE)
```

Before we leave this we should note that the NEXT field is not relevant when the record is transferred to a file. Records are only implicitly sequenced on file. We would do well to set this field to **NIL** on the file, but not in the linked list. We can do this by changing the field in the buffer just before it is written.

```
REMFILE^ := P^;
REMFILE^.NEXT := NIL;
PUT(REMFILE)
```

EXERCISE 22B: Complete the procedure PUTLIST and execute this version of the program leaving some reminders in the list when the program terminates. Leave the program in the workfile. When the program has terminated use the Filer to check that a file USER:MYLIST.DATA exits. Do not attempt to edit this file and do not proceed until you have this file on your disk.

22.1.2 Getting it Back

    This is the purpose of the procedure GETLIST, the call for which should be put into the main program as indicated at the beginning of section 22.1.

    Again we have to follow the protocol: open the file, process the file, close the file. Here we have to open the file REMFILE for reading and a different procedure is used. We write

```
RESET(REMFILE, 'USER:MYLIST.DATA')
```

The association between the two names of the file are exactly as for REWRITE (section 22.1.1). The procedure checks for the existence of the disk file USER:MYLIST.DATA, and then primes the buffer with the first record of the file.

    In outline the procedure GETLIST will be

```
PROCEDURE GETLIST;

    BEGIN
        RESET(REMFILE, 'USER:MYLIST.DATA');
        copy REMFILE to TASKLIST;
        CLOSE(REMFILE)
    END; (* GETLIST *)
```

    Closure of REMFILE after opening by RESET, by CLOSE(REMFILE) does not delete the file, unless we add the rather drastic option PURGE. Were we to write CLOSE(REMFILE, PURGE) no disk file USER:MYLIST.DATA would exist during program execution, leaving the reminder system vulnerable to program or computer failure. Using CLOSE(REMFILE), should the program fail to complete its execution, the disk file still contains the state of the reminder list, as it was at the start of the abortive run. We have therefore made limited provision for recovery or fall-back.

Remembering that RESET has already primed the buffer with the first record we can refine "copy REMFILE to TASKLIST" into

```
WHILE we are not at the end of REMFILE DO
    BEGIN
        make space for a record on the heap (NEW);
        copy the buffer to this space;
        link this record into TASKLIST; (see ADDTASK)
        replenish the buffer (GET);
    END
```

The first matter to be resolved is clearly how to know when we are at the end of a file. More precisely, we need to know when the attempt to get another record has failed because we have previously read the last record of the file. Pascal provides a standard function, EOF, of type BOOLEAN, which determines whether the specified file has reached its end. To determine this condition in the context of the while statement above, we write

```
WHILE NOT EOF(REMFILE) DO
```

We can now refine the procedure into

```
PROCEDURE GETLIST;

    VAR P : ^TASKSPEC;

    BEGIN
        RESET(REMFILE, 'USER:MYLIST.DATA');
        WHILE NOT EOF(REMFILE) DO
          BEGIN
            NEW(P);                (* MAKE SPACE ON THE HEAP ... *)
            P^ := REMFILE^;        (* ... FOR RECORD IN THE BUFFER *)
            IF TASKLIST = NIL THEN P^.NEXT := P
              ELSE
                BEGIN
                  P^.NEXT := TASKLIST^.NEXT;
                  TASKLIST^.NEXT := P
                END;
            TASKLIST := P;
            GET(REMFILE)
          END;
        CLOSE(REMFILE)
    END; (* GETLIST *)
```

EXERCISE 22C: One thing remains. As it stands, the program above numbers newly added tasks from 1, with the result that the IDEN field no longer uniquely defines a record. We should renumber all tasks from the file (starting from 1) and continue with this numbering for all new tasks. Modify GETLIST accordingly. Save this version as USER:REMLIST7.

EXERCISE 22D: Making use of the tree sort of section 21.2, modify the procedure GETLIST so that it sorts the reminders on the value of the field PRIORITY. Comment on the efficiency of your program. Save this as USER:REMLIST8.

In this example the file REMFILE is opened and closed once only. A file may be opened and closed any number of times in a program, provided the sequence open   close   open   close   ...   open   close

is maintained. Always ensure that there are no ways of terminating execution
that leave files unclosed.

22.2 FILES IN MORE DETAIL

We now define the standard procedure statements GET, PUT, REWRITE and
RESET more formally. We use the following diagram to represent a file F
declared by **VAR F : FILE OF R;**

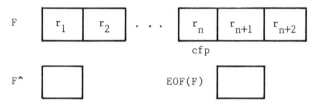

cfp

The components of the file (generally records) are represented by r_1,
r_2, ... each r_i being of type R. cfp stands for the current file
position. The file buffer is represented by F^ and EOF(F) yields a Boolean
value.

Much of this section is specific to UCSD Pascal and its implementations
such as Apple Pascal.

22.2.1 Opening a File for Output – the REWRITE Statement

In UCSD Pascal the REWRITE statement takes the form

        REWRITE(F, FILENAME)

where F is a file variable and FILENAME is either a string constant (as in the
example of section 22.1) or a UCSD Pascal string whose value denotes the
name of the disk file to be opened. (Standard Pascal makes no explicit
provision for naming disk files.) In UCSD Pascal, STRING is a pre-declared
type. UCSD Pascal strings can be read and written by READ and WRITE
statements, and can be processed using quite powerful procedures and functions
specific to UCSD Pascal. For further details see appendix 7.

REWRITE prepares a new file to be written to (see appendix 10). It is
made to be empty. The diagram becomes

F   (empty)

The file buffer is undefined, as is the current file position (cfp).

22.2.2 Writing to a File - the PUT Statement

The statement PUT(F) transfers the contents of the buffer to the end of the file F. The value of EOF(F) must be true before a PUT. As a result of PUT(F), the diagram

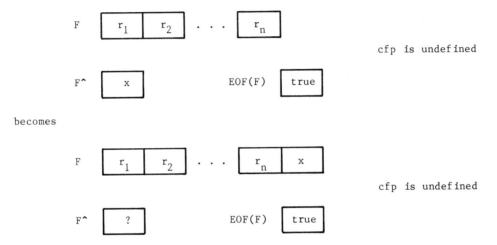

becomes

The record x effectively becomes record r_{n+1}. Note that the file buffer becomes undefined after a PUT.

22.2.3 Opening a File for Input - the RESET Statement

In UCSD Pascal the RESET procedure statement takes the form

RESET(F, FILENAME)

where the parameters have the same meaning as those of REWRITE (see section 22.2.1).

RESET prepares an existing file for reading. In the case of a non-empty file, the diagram becomes

If the file to be read from is empty, the diagram becomes

F   (empty)

                                                        cfp is undefined

F^ [?   ]   EOF(F) [true]

22.2.4 Reading From a File - the GET Statement

There are two cases to consider resulting from the execution of the
statement GET(F): one in which it is possible to advance cfp and the other in
which it is not. In the first case, the diagram becomes

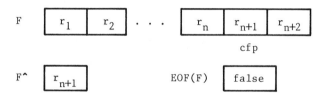

F   [r_1 | r_2 | . . . | r_n | r_{n+1} | r_{n+2}]
                                        cfp

F^   [r_{n+1}]   EOF(F) [false]

In the second case, we are at the end of the file (suppose the last record is
r_n) and the diagram becomes

F   [r_1 | r_2 | . . . | r_{n-2} | r_{n-1} | r_n]
                                                cfp

F^   [?   ]   EOF(F) [true]

22.2.5 Adding to a File

The definitions above allow a file F to be extended. First it must be
opened for reading by RESET. Then the end-of-file must be reached by a series
of GET statements, at which point PUT statements may be executed since EOF(F)
is true. The file may be closed by CLOSE(F); there is no need to apply the
option LOCK to a file which was opened by RESET.

Note that the definitions do not allow the converse. That is, it is never
possible to issue a GET after a PUT unless the file is first closed and then
reopened with a RESET.

22.2.6 Shortening a File (UCSD Pascal Feature)

A file F may be shortened if, after opening for reading (RESET) it is
closed by

```
CLOSE(F, CRUNCH)
```

The last component "got" becomes the last component of the file.

22.3 FILES AS TYPES

In Pascal files are structured types, as are arrays and records. We have used arrays of records, records of arrays and records of records, and in section 22.1, the reminder list program used a file of records. It is natural to ask whether such things as file of array, file of file, array of file or record of file are meaningful and if so, whether they are sensible.

Files of arrays are similar in concept to files of records and are allowed.

Arrays of files, and records of files are not allowed in UCSD Pascal, but are not prohibited in standard Pascal. The lack of arrays of files can be a problem where the number of files needed by a program is bounded, but not known at the time of writing the program.

Files of integers, reals, and Booleans are permitted but are unlikely to be of much use. Files of CHAR are a special case and are discussed in section 22.6.

A file of files is an attractive idea, suggesting the implementation of subfiles, but UCSD Pascal does not implement them.

Files may be passed as parameters, but in UCSD Pascal, only as variable parameters. If a procedure were to have a value parameter of a file type, then by arguments similar to those in section 16.2.3, a local copy of a file would have to be made on entry to a procedure.

22.4 MERGE SORTING

The tree sorting method described in section 21.2 can sort no more data than it can accommodate on the heap. Data in excess of this has to be sorted by other means, and since quantities of data of such magnitudes are likely to reside in files anyway, we need a sorting method that takes its unsorted input from a file, uses files for intermediate storage purposes, and puts the sorted data out to a file. One such method is the merge sort, so named because it continually merges ordered subsequences together into fewer but longer subsequences until only one such subsequence remains. This is then copied to (or renamed as) the file wherein the sorted data is required.

22.4.1 The Method of Merge Sorting

In the following discussion, we again use records consisting of only a single key. It is easily extended, merely by changing a record type, to deal with records containing data fields as well. Records will be sorted into ascending order of their keys.

We shall frequently refer to an ordered subsequence of a file, known as a
run. The set of keys

        14   20   2   6   21   11   8   3

consists of 5 runs, namely

        14   20   of length 2
         2   6   21   of length 3
        11   of length 1
         8   of length 1
         3   of length 1

    If two runs are merged together, we get one run, whose length is the sum
of the lengths of the two merged runs. For example, if we merge

        14   20
         2   6   21

we get one run of length 5, namely

         2   6   14   20   21

Provided that we can keep merging, we can keep reducing the number of runs to
just one. As we shall see, the advantage of merge sorting is that the runs to
be merged only need to be processed sequentially and we need only hold one
component from each run in memory at any time. Higher order merges, in which
3, 4 or more runs may be merged at a time, are simple extensions of the method
which will be described only for the second order merge.

    Before we can merge an unsorted file, it must be split or distributed
onto 2 files. We do this by copying runs alternately to two temporary files,
TEMPA and TEMPB. The set of keys given above would be distributed as follows.

        TEMPA   -   14   20 /   11   /   3
        TEMPB   -   2   6   21 /   8

The symbol / merely shows the end of one run and the start of another. It is
not written to the files.

    Bearing in mind that the next stage (called a pass) in the sorting
process has to be repeated many times in practice, we must ensure that at the
end of each pass we leave runs on a pair of files, to enable the following
pass to continue merging. Pass 1, on our sample data, merges from TEMPA and
TEMPB onto TEMPC and TEMPD.

        TEMPC   -   2   6   14   20   21   /   3
        TEMPD   -   8   11

Note that when only a single run remains on a file (3 in the example above) it
can only be copied. This is equivalent to merging with an empty run. Files
TEMPA and TEMPB are finished with and can be reused as output files. Files
TEMPC and TEMPD will be the input files for the next pass. At the end of that
pass we get

        TEMPA   -   2   6   8   11   14   20   21
        TEMPB   -   3

One more pass onto TEMPC and TEMPD produces

```
TEMPC    -        2   3   6   8   11   14   20   21
TEMPD    -        (empty)
```

The file TEMPC should now be copied to (or renamed as) the required output file.

An important consequence of this method is that files have to be reused for different purposes. At one time they may be used for input and at another for output. For this reason, we have to find a way of keeping either file variables or the disk filenames in variables that can be manipulated in the program. The disk filename can only be held in a variable of the UCSD type STRING, due to the nature of the parameters of RESET and REWRITE. The file variables present more of a problem. An array of files would solve this neatly but we noted that UCSD Pascal does not implement them. We therefore use filenames as the means of identifying files in the program that follows.

22.4.2 A Merge Sorting Program

We shall write a program that accepts appropriate unsorted input from any named file and puts its sorted output onto any named file. In practice, these generally have different names, so that the original, unsorted, data is available for fallback. Filenames are kept in UCSD Pascal strings. In outline the program will be

```
PROGRAM MERGESORT;

TYPE RECTYPE = RECORD
                      KEY : INTEGER
               END;
       FILETYPE = FILE OF RECTYPE;

VAR UNSORTEDFN, SORTEDFN : STRING;        (* UCSD PASCAL STRING *)

BEGIN
     WRITE('ENTER FULL NAME OF FILE TO BE SORTED: ');
     READLN(UNSORTEDFN);
     WRITE('ENTER FULL NAME OF SORTED OUTPUT FILE: ');
     READLN(SORTEDFN);
     LISTFILE(UNSORTEDFN);
     SORT(UNSORTEDFN, SORTEDFN);
     LISTFILE(SORTEDFN)
END.
```

The two calls for the procedure LISTFILE are included here solely for the purpose of checking that the program appears to work correctly.

EXERCISE 22E: Write a program to make a file called USER:MYFILE.DATA whose records each consist of only an integer key. Enter the values on the keyboard. Arrange to stop on reading the value zero.

EXERCISE 22F: Bearing in mind that a file may be empty, write the procedure LISTFILE. Provide a dummy procedure for SORT and test the outline program. Leave it in the workfile.

We now turn our attention to the procedure SORT. Following the discussion in section 22.4.1, we can roughly outline the procedure.

```
PROCEDURE SORT(INNAME, OUTNAME : STRING);

   BEGIN
       DISTRIBUTE(INNAME, ...);
       MERGE;
       COPYFILE(..., OUTNAME)
   END; (* SORT *)
```

Each of the procedures DISTRIBUTE, MERGE, COPYFILE, needs to be given the names of the files it has to operate on. In particular, COPYFILE needs to know where the final sorted data is. Only the procedure MERGE knows this, so it must communicate this back to the procedure SORT via a variable parameter. The actual parameter used below is named FINAL. For the reasons given in appendix 10, we have to specify the sizes of the temporary files. Four blocks should be more than enough for the purpose of these exercises. If we assign the disk filenames USER:TEMPA.DATA, USER:TEMPB.DATA, USER:TEMPC.DATA and USER:TEMPD.DATA to the variables AN, BN, CN and DN, the procedure SORT becomes

```
PROCEDURE SORT(INNAME, OUTNAME : STRING);

   VAR AN, BN, CN, DN, FINAL : STRING;

   BEGIN
       AN := 'USER:TEMPA.DATA[4]';  BN := 'USER:TEMPB.DATA[4]';
       CN := 'USER:TEMPC.DATA[4]';  DN := 'USER:TEMPD.DATA[4]';
       DISTRIBUTE(INNAME, AN, BN);
       MERGE(AN, BN, CN, DN, FINAL);
       COPYFILE(FINAL, OUTNAME)
   END; (* SORT *)
```

We next consider the procedure DISTRIBUTE. It has to handle 3 files, reading from one, and writing runs to two. The essential structure of a file, as far as this (and other) procedures is concerned, is a set of runs (ordered sub-sequence of records). Runs are copied alternately to the output files. The procedure can be written

```
PROCEDURE DISTRIBUTE(PN, QN, RN : STRING);

   VAR P, Q, R : FILETYPE;

   BEGIN
       RESET(P, PN);  REWRITE(Q, QN);  REWRITE(R, RN);
       WHILE NOT EOF(P) DO COPYRUNTOEITHER(P, Q, R);
       CLOSE(P);  CLOSE(Q, LOCK);  CLOSE(R, LOCK)
   END; (* DISTRIBUTE *)
```

Note that, because the files are already open, the parameters P, Q and R passed to COPYRUNTOEITHER are the internal file names. Note also that the use of the while statement admits an empty file as input.

We next consider the procedure COPYRUNTOEITHER. If a run exists at all it must have at least one record, and since we will only call this procedure when we are not at end-of-file, we use a repeat statement to copy individual records until the end of a run is detected. The procedure may therefore be written

```
PROCEDURE COPYRUNTOEITHER(VAR SOURCE, DEST0, DEST1 : FILETYPE);

   BEGIN
       REPEAT COPYRECTOEITHER(SOURCE, DEST0, DEST1) UNTIL ENDOFRUN
   END; (* COPYRUNTOEITHER *)
```

where ENDOFRUN is a Boolean variable which is set to true by COPYRECTOEITHER. It is tempting to declare ENDOFRUN in this procedure, but we shall soon

discover another procedure which requires it, and so we declare it in the
procedure SORT by adding

        ENDOFRUN : BOOLEAN;

to the **VAR** section of SORT.

Next we write the procedure COPYRECTOEITHER. This has two related but
different jobs to do. It has to look out for and signal the end of a run, and
it must also decide which of the destination files to write the record to.
Since the end of a run can only be detected by comparing keys on two
successive records from the source file, a buffer in addition to SOURCE^ will
be required. This will hold the last record copied, whilst SOURCE^ will
generally hold the next record to be copied. The procedure, in outline, is

```
        PROCEDURE COPYRECTOEITHER(VAR SOURCE, DEST0, DEST1 : FILETYPE);

            VAR COPIEDREC : RECTYPE;

            BEGIN
                COPIEDREC := SOURCE^;  GET(SOURCE);
                send copiedrec to either dest0 or dest1;
                set endofrun
            END; (* COPYRECTOEITHER *)
```

The end of a run is detected when either the end of the source file is
reached or when the record just copied has a key lower than the next record.
The file buffer SOURCE^ holds the next record ready as a result of GET(SOURCE),
so ENDOFRUN has the value assigned by

```
        IF EOF(SOURCE) THEN ENDOFRUN := TRUE
                       ELSE ENDOFRUN := COPIEDREC.KEY > SOURCE.KEY
```

EXERCISE 22G: Why should we not write, instead of the statement above,

```
        ENDOFRUN := EOF(SOURCE) OR (COPIEDREC.KEY > SOURCE.KEY)
```

The other question COPYRECTOEITHER has to resolve is which destination
file to write to. This is most clearly arranged by having an integer variable
count 0,1,0,1,... every time a run is ended. If we call this variable
OUTFILENO, then the procedure can be completed.

```
        PROCEDURE COPYRECTOEITHER(VAR SOURCE, DEST0, DEST1 : FILETYPE);

            VAR COPIEDREC : RECTYPE;

            BEGIN
                COPIEDREC := SOURCE^;  GET(SOURCE);
                CASE OUTFILENO OF
                    0: BEGIN DEST0^ := COPIEDREC;  PUT(DEST0) END;
                    1: BEGIN DEST1^ := COPIEDREC;  PUT(DEST1) END
                END;
                IF EOF(SOURCE) THEN ENDOFRUN := TRUE
                               ELSE ENDOFRUN := COPIEDREC.KEY > SOURCE^.KEY
            END; (* COPYRECTOEITHER *)
```

We have to return to the procedure COPYRUNTOEITHER, which is best placed
to do the counting and we add the statement

```
        OUTFILENO := (OUTFILENO + 1) MOD 2
```

after the completion of the copying of each run.

EXERCISE 22H: Write out the final version of COPYRUNTOEITHER. Where should
                 OUTFILENO be declared and where should it be initialized? This
                 completes the procedure DISTRIBUTE. Test it before proceeding.

We now turn our attention to the procedure MERGE. In rough outline it is

```
        PROCEDURE MERGE(PN, QN, RN, SN : STRING;  VAR DESTN : STRING);

            BEGIN
                REPEAT
                    open files;
                    WHILE neither input file is at EOF DO merge runs;
                    copy what is left;
                    close files;
                    interchange input and output filenames;
                UNTIL NUMBEROFRUNS = 1;
                DESTN := PN
            END; (* MERGE *)
```

This needs considerable refinement. First we need local file identifiers
P, Q, R and S for the 4 files. We also need an integer variable in which to
count the number of runs and a temporary string variable TN to enable the
interchange of filenames (see exercise 12A). Remember to initialize OUTFILENO
and NUMBEROFRUNS before each pass begins. Merging of runs is left to another
procedure, but the copying of runs has already been provided in the procedure
COPYRUNTOEITHER. Unfortunately, COPYRUNTOEITHER is within DISTRIBUTE, and its
scope does not include the procedure MERGE. We must move it and
COPYRECTOEITHER to a place, still within SORT, but accessible to both
DISTRIBUTE and MERGE. We must also move the declaration of OUTFILENO to this
level in order that it be available to COPYRUNTOEITHER.

We get the complete procedure MERGE.

```
        PROCEDURE MERGE(PN, QN, RN, SN : STRING;  VAR DESTN : STRING);

            VAR NUMBEROFRUNS : INTEGER;
                P, Q, R, S : FILETYPE;
                TN : STRING;

            BEGIN
                REPEAT
                    RESET(P, PN);  RESET(Q, QN);
                    REWRITE(R, RN); REWRITE(S, SN);

                    OUTFILENO := 0;
                    NUMBEROFRUNS := 0;
                    WHILE NOT (EOF(P) OR EOF(Q)) DO
                        BEGIN
                            MERGERUNTOEITHER(R, S);
                            NUMBEROFRUNS := NUMBEROFRUNS + 1
                        END;
                    WHILE NOT EOF(P) DO
                        BEGIN
                            COPYRUNTOEITHER(P, R, S);
                            NUMBEROFRUNS := NUMBEROFRUNS + 1
                        END;
```

```
WHILE NOT EOF(Q) DO
    BEGIN
        COPYRUNTOEITHER(Q, R, S);
        NUMBEROFRUNS := NUMBEROFRUNS + 1
    END;

CLOSE(P);  CLOSE(Q);  CLOSE(R, LOCK);  CLOSE(S, LOCK);

TN := PN; PN := RN; RN := TN;
TN := QN; QN := SN; SN := TN
    UNTIL NUMBEROFRUNS = 1;
    DESTN := PN
END; (* MERGE *)
```

This leaves only MERGERUNTOEITHER, which merges 2 runs. This works in
two phases: until either run terminates there is genuine choice as to which
record is to be sent next, but as soon as one run ends what is left of the
other is merely copied to the appropriate destination file. We can safely use
COPYRUNTOEITHER for this since any sub-sequence of a run is also a run. This
is expressed in terms of COPYRECTOEITHER and COPYRUNTOEITHER.

```
PROCEDURE MERGERUNTOEITHER(VAR R, S : FILETYPE);

BEGIN
    REPEAT
        IF P^.KEY < Q^.KEY THEN
            BEGIN
                COPYRECTOEITHER(P, R, S);
                IF ENDOFRUN THEN COPYRUNTOEITHER(Q, R, S)
            END
        ELSE
            BEGIN
                COPYRECTOEITHER(Q, R, S);
                IF ENDOFRUN THEN COPYRUNTOEITHER(P, R, S)
            END
    UNTIL ENDOFRUN
END; (* MERGERUNTOEITHER *)
```

EXERCISE 22J: Assemble and test the complete program.

A simpler but less efficient version of the merge sort program appears in
[Welsh and Elder, 1982]. Their program is written in standard Pascal which
has rather less flexible file handling.

22.5 BATCH TRANSACTION PROCESSING

Large sequential files, such as the files of standard Pascal, which we
have discussed in the previous sections of this chapter, can only be
efficiently processed if, on a single pass over the entire file, all
processing to hand is carried out. If some operation on the file is omitted,
the entire file will have to be re-processed.

In the real world of computing, files generally represent the state of
some subset of the world. Earlier in this chapter we created a file that
represented the state of tasks to be done. This was an example of a
master file. In business, master files are often used to represent the
state of customers' accounts, employees' wages, items held in stock, suppliers'
names and addresses, books in the library, registered students, current menus

in a restaurant, theater bookings etc. In all but a tiny minority of
instances, the subset of the real world, represented by a master file, will
change from time to time and, if it is to continue to be of value, it must be
changed or updated. In some cases you can wait until the end of the day,
week, or month, and update all changed master file components in a relatively
leisurely operation called batch transaction processing. In other cases,
the master file must be updated instantaneously, even if this means inhibiting
file activity during the short period of updating. This is called real-time
processing.

     In standard Pascal, updating a record implies writing a new copy of the
entire record to a file, and the only place where a file may be written to is
at the end. It is not possible to write a record in the middle of a file, and
then read records between the one just written and the end. Thus the only way
to update a record of a master file is to copy the entire file. Whilst we are
copying the file, we might as well update all records that need to be updated.
We distinguish between the original and the updated versions of the master
file, calling them old master files and new master file respectively.
The changes which are to be made to the master file can generally be expressed
as records and placed in a file which is called the transaction file. It
is essential that the transaction file be sorted on the same key as the master
file, if we are to update the master file on a single pass. It provides a nice
symmetry if all output from such processing is sent to an output or report
file.

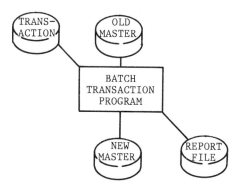

     We shall assume, in the worked example that follows, that the records of
the old master are sorted on a key field and that the keys are unique. The
batch transaction program will preserve this property on the new master file.
The transaction file will also be sorted on the same key but its keys are not
necessarily unique. A set of transactions with the same key will be applied
to the master file in the order in which they are read from the file.

     In practice, transactions can be of diverse forms, implemented by records
with variant parts. They can cause fields in the master file's records to be
updated; they can also cause records to be created or deleted from the master
file. In the example that follows, transactions will be only of one kind,
updating only the PRIORITY field of the records of the file USER:MYLIST.DATA,
but with care the method can be adapted to cater for more general transactions.
Before we write the updating program we need to write a small program to create
the file of transactions.

22.5.1 A Program to Create a Transaction File

     To create this file, we need a simple program that accepts pairs of
integers representing a task IDEN number, and new PRIORITY from the keyboard.
For each pair, it creates a record and writes it to a file, USER:TRANS.DATA.

In outline, the program will be

```
PROGRAM MAKETRANS;

TYPE PRIOSPEC = RECORD
                        IDEN : 1 .. 9999;
                        PRIORITY : 0 .. 99
                END;

VAR TRANSFILE : FILE OF PRIOSPEC;
    INIDEN, INPRIO : INTEGER;

BEGIN
    REWRITE(TRANSFILE, 'USER:TRANS.DATA');
    PROMPT;
    READ(INIDEN, INPRIO);
    WHILE INIDEN <> 0 DO
      BEGIN
        IF ... THEN
          BEGIN
              create transaction record and write it
          END
        ELSE
          IF ... THEN WRITELN('ERROR IN INPUT');
        PROMPT;
        READ(INIDEN, INPRIO)
      END;
    CLOSE(TRANSFILE, LOCK)
END.
```

EXERCISE 22K: Complete this program ensuring that the input is validated
                before a record is written to file.

22.5.2   **The File Updating Program**

     We will take the file of reminders, created by the program in section
22.1, and a file of transactions which specify changed priorities, and write an
updating program in the style of the batch transaction processing program.
All files will be assumed to be sorted on the key field IDEN. Output to the
report file will be directed to the screen, so that the reader can obtain
instant feedback from the program.

In outline, the program will be

```
PROGRAM UPDATE;

TYPE STRING70 = RECORD
                    LENGTH : 0 .. 70;
                    CH : ARRAY [1 .. 70] OF CHAR
                END;

     TASKSPEC = RECORD
                    NEXT : ^TASKSPEC;
                    IDEN : 1 .. 9999;
                    PRIORITY : 0 .. 99;
                    MESSAGE : STRING70
                END;

     PRIOSPEC = RECORD
                    IDEN : 1 .. 9999;
                    PRIORITY : 0 .. 99
                END;

VAR TRANS : FILE OF PRIOSPEC;
    OMF, NMF : FILE OF TASKSPEC;

BEGIN
     RESET(TRANS, 'USER:TRANS.DATA');
     RESET(OMF, 'USER:OLDLIST.DATA');
     REWRITE(NMF, 'USER:NEWLIST.DATA');

     WHILE NOT EOF(OMF) DO
         BEGIN
             process transaction records with keys less than master;

             IF TRANS^.IDEN <> OMF^.IDEN THEN
                 process master record with no transactions
             ELSE
                 process transaction records with keys equal to master;

             do any other processing on each record destined for the new
             master file;

             write OMF record to new master;

             GET(OMF)
         END;

     mop up end of transaction file;

     CLOSE(TRANS);        CLOSE(OMF);        CLOSE(NMF, LOCK)
END.
```

There are three essentially different kinds of processing implied by this
outline.

- TRANSONLY: transaction record with no corresponding master. In
               this example an error is reported.

- MASTERONLY: master record with no transaction. In this example
               it reports that this master record is not updated.

- UPDATEOLD: transaction record with key equal to master. In this
               example it updates OMF record and reports.

We can now elaborate on the informal parts of the outline program.

"process transaction records with keys less than master"

becomes

```
REPEAT
    IF NOT EOF(TRANS) THEN
        IF TRANS^.IDEN < OMF^.IDEN THEN TRANSONLY;
    IF EOF(TRANS) THEN NOMORE := TRUE
                  ELSE NOMORE := TRANS^.IDEN >= OMF^.IDEN
UNTIL NOMORE
```

"process master record with no transactions"

becomes

```
MASTERONLY
```

"process transaction records with keys equal to master"

becomes

```
REPEAT
    IF NOT EOF(TRANS) THEN
        IF TRANS^.IDEN = OMF^.IDEN THEN UPDATEOLD;
    IF EOF(TRANS) THEN NOMORE := TRUE
                  ELSE NOMORE := TRANS^.IDEN > OMF^.IDEN;
UNTIL NOMORE
```

"write OMF record to new master"

becomes

```
NMF^ := OMF^;   PUT(NMF)
```

"mop up end of transaction file"

becomes

```
WHILE NOT EOF(TRANS) DO TRANSONLY
```

All that remains is to write the three basic processing procedures which characterize the particular problem we are solving.

```
PROCEDURE TRANSONLY;

    BEGIN
        WRITELN('TRANSACTION FOR KEY ', TRANS^.IDEN, ' BUT NO MASTER');
        GET(TRANS)
    END; (* TRANSONLY *)

PROCEDURE UPDATEOLD;

    BEGIN
        OMF^.PRIORITY := TRANS^.PRIORITY;
        WRITELN('RECORD IDEN ', OMF^.IDEN,
                ' GETS PRIORITY ', TRANS^.PRIORITY);
        GET(TRANS)
    END; (* UPDATEOLD *)

PROCEDURE MASTERONLY;

    BEGIN
        WRITELN('MASTER RECORD WITH KEY ', OMF^.IDEN, ' NOT UPDATED')
    END; (* MASTERONLY *)
```

EXERCISE 22L: Assemble the complete program. Copy USER:MYLIST.DATA to
                USER:OLDLIST.DATA, and test the program on suitable transaction
                files.

      In practical applications, certain transactions may have the effect of
creating or deleting records from the master file. New master records can be
created and written to the new master file in TRANSONLY, whilst the deletion
of a record in the master file is discovered in UPDATEOLD and implemented
by suppressing the writing of the OMF record to the new master file.

22.6   TEXTFILES

      None of the files we have processed by program so far can be handled by
the Editor. The Editor can only process textfiles. Textfiles are of type

          FILE OF CHAR

and occur sufficiently commonly to be a pre-defined type, namely

          TEXT

In fact, in UCSD Pascal the three following types are all equivalent

          FILE OF CHAR
          PACKED FILE OF CHAR
          TEXT

      Textfiles have an internal structure consisting of a sequence of lines
separated by end-of-line markers. (Readers should note the similarity between
a textfile and the supply of characters from the terminal. See sections 10.3
to 10.5.) Textfiles may be read in a very similar fashion to other kinds of
file. Try the following program which will copy the named file to the screen.
In it, replace USER:??????.TEXT by the name of one of the shorter textfiles on
your USER: disk.

```
          PROGRAM DISPLAYFI1;

          VAR INFILE : TEXT;
              C : CHAR;

          BEGIN
              RESET(INFILE, 'USER:??????.TEXT');
              WHILE NOT EOF(INFILE) DO
                  BEGIN
                      C := INFILE^;
                      WRITE(C);
                      GET(INFILE)
                  END;
              CLOSE(INFILE)
          END.
```

      The most obvious deficiency of this program is its failure to recognize
the end of a line and do the appropriate thing with it. The function EOLN
can be used to ascertain the end-of-line status of a textfile, but you should

note a subtle difference between its application to a textfile and UCSD
Pascal's terminal input. The function reference EOLN(INFILE) yields the
value true when the current file position is the end-of-line marker. The
buffer (INFILE^) will then contain a space. The only way to place an end-of-
line marker into a file OUTFILE is to use WRITELN(OUTFILE) and to inject an
end-of-line into the screen use WRITELN. Thus to correct the program above we
can write

```
PROGRAM DISPLAYFI2;

VAR INFILE : TEXT;
    C : CHAR;

BEGIN
    RESET(INFILE, 'USER:??????.TEXT');
    WHILE NOT EOF(INFILE) DO
        BEGIN
            C := INFILE^;
            IF EOLN(INFILE) THEN WRITELN ELSE WRITE(C);
            GET(INFILE)
        END;
    CLOSE(INFILE)
END.
```

Make this modification, try it, and convince yourself that it is correct.

So far, so good. But are we really to believe that the most elementary
operation of reading a character from a textfile needs two statements, namely

```
C := INFILE^;
GET(INFILE)
```

Remember that RESET primes the buffer, hence the first characters of the file
would be missed were we to reverse the order of the statements. Pascal
provides a shorter equivalence of the statements above. Instead we may write

```
READ(INFILE, C)
```

Replace the while statement in the program above by

```
WHILE NOT EOF(INFILE) DO
    BEGIN
        READ(INFILE, C);
        IF EOLN(INFILE) THEN WRITELN ELSE WRITE(C)
    END
```

and see what happens! The last character of each line has been lost, since
EOLN becomes true when the last character on a line has been read. The problem
here has arisen partly because we have failed to analyze properly the structure
of a textfile. A textfile is a sequence of lines separated by end-of-line
markers. The while statement in the program should be thought of as

```
WHILE NOT EOF(INFILE) DO copy a line
```

where copy a line is

```
BEGIN
    WHILE NOT EOLN(INFILE) DO
        BEGIN
            READ(INFILE, C);
            WRITE(C)
        END;
    WRITELN;
    READ(INFILE, C)
END
```

EXERCISE 22M: Make this modification and save the program as USER:DISPLAYFI3.

Having come to terms with the underlying structure of a textfile, it is, of course, possible to read the lines of the file with READLN and to display them with WRITELN. In UCSD Pascal, this is made easier by the existence of the type STRING, variables of which type can hold complete lines. We then get the comparatively simple program

```
PROGRAM DISPLAYFI4;

VAR INFILE : TEXT;
    LINE : STRING;

BEGIN
    RESET(INFILE, 'USER:???????.TEXT');
    WHILE NOT EOF(INFILE) DO
        BEGIN
            READLN(INFILE, LINE);
            WRITELN(LINE)
        END;
    CLOSE(INFILE)
END.
```

Both UCSD Pascal and standard Pascal have two predeclared files, whose file identifiers are

        INPUT   OUTPUT

They are automatically opened at the start of every program, and closed at the end. The file INPUT is the terminal, considered as a keyboard and echoing screen. All READ and READLN statements which do not specify a file name as the first parameter, are assumed to be from the file INPUT. The file OUTPUT is the screen. All WRITE and WRITELN statements which do not specify a file name as the first parameter, are assumed to be destined for the file OUTPUT. UCSD Pascal has a third predeclared file called KEYBOARD, which is a non-echoing version of INPUT. (See section 10.3.8.)

We can summarize the reading of text as follows.

-   READ(C) from the terminal in UCSD Pascal is equivalent to

        GET(INPUT);
        C := INPUT^

-   READ(F, C) from a file F in both USCD and standard Pascal is equivalent to

        C := F^;
        GET(F)

This difference would make it awkward to write a program in UCSD Pascal which could take its input from either the terminal or from a file, and so UCSD Pascal offers an alternative to the type TEXT, known as

    INTERACTIVE

The statement READ(F, C) from a file of type INTERACTIVE is equivalent to

    GET(F);
    C := F^

making it compatible with input from the terminal. The files named INPUT and KEYBOARD are of type INTERACTIVE, and the file named OUTPUT is of type TEXT.

SOLUTIONS TO THE EXERCISES

22A: INITIALIZE sets TASKLIST to the value **NIL**, and GETLIST adds
        items to that list.

22B: **PROCEDURE** PUTLIST;

            VAR P, PO : ^TASKSPEC;

            BEGIN
                REWRITE(REMFILE, 'USER:MYLIST.DATA');
                IF TASKLIST <> **NIL THEN**
                  BEGIN
                    PO := TASKLIST^.NEXT;
                    P := PO;
                    REPEAT
                      REMFILE^ := P^;
                      REMFILE^.NEXT := NIL; (* THIS FIELD NOT NEEDED ON FILE *)
                      PUT(REMFILE);
                      P := P^.NEXT
                    UNTIL P = PO
                  END;
                CLOSE(REMFILE, LOCK)
            END; (* PUTLIST *)

22C: In GETLIST, immediately after P^ := REMFILE; add the statements

            P^.IDEN := TASKNUMBER;   TASKNUMBER := TASKNUMBER + 1;

22D: **PROCEDURE** GETLIST;

            TYPE TREEPTR = ^NODE;
                  NODE = **RECORD**
                            LEFT, RIGHT : TREEPTR;
                            BODY : TASKSPEC
                         END;

            VAR P : ^TASKSPEC;
                  TREE, T : TREEPTR;

```
        PROCEDURE GRAFT(P : TREEPTR; VAR T : TREEPTR);

            (* GRAFT RECORD POINTED TO BY P INTO TREE POINTED TO BY T *)

            BEGIN
                IF T = NIL THEN T := P
                ELSE
                    IF P^.BODY.PRIORITY < T^.BODY.PRIORITY THEN
                        GRAFT(P, T^.LEFT)
                    ELSE GRAFT(P, T^.RIGHT)
            END; (* GRAFT *)

        PROCEDURE COPYTREE(T : TREEPTR);

            BEGIN
                IF T <> NIL THEN
                  BEGIN
                    COPYTREE(T^.LEFT);
                    NEW(P);
                    P^ := T^.BODY;
                    P^.IDEN := TASKNUMBER;  TASKNUMBER := TASKNUMBER + 1;
                    IF TASKLIST = NIL THEN P^.NEXT := P
                        ELSE
                            BEGIN
                              P^.NEXT := TASKLIST^.NEXT;
                              TASKLIST^.NEXT := P
                            END;
                    TASKLIST := P;
                    COPYTREE(T^.RIGHT)
                  END
            END; (* COPYTREE *)

        BEGIN (* GETLIST *)
            RESET(REMFILE, 'USER:MYLIST.DATA');  TREE := NIL;
            WHILE NOT EOF(REMFILE) DO
              BEGIN
                NEW(T);
                T^.BODY := REMFILE^;  T^.LEFT := NIL;  T^.RIGHT := NIL;
                GRAFT(T, TREE);
                GET(REMFILE)
              END;
            CLOSE(REMFILE);
            COPYTREE(TREE)
        END; (* GETLIST *)


22E:    PROGRAM MAKEFILE;

        TYPE RECTYPE = RECORD
                         KEY : INTEGER
                       END;
            FILETYPE = FILE OF RECTYPE;

        VAR FILENAME : STRING;
```

```
PROCEDURE MAKE(FNAME : STRING);

    VAR F : FILETYPE;
        REC : RECTYPE;

    BEGIN
        REWRITE(F, FNAME);
        REPEAT
            READ(REC.KEY);
            IF REC.KEY <> 0 THEN
              BEGIN
                F^ := REC;
                PUT(F)
              END
        UNTIL REC.KEY = 0;
        CLOSE(F, LOCK)
    END; (* MAKE *)

BEGIN
    WRITE('ENTER FULL NAME OF FILE TO BE MADE: ');
    READ(FILENAME);
    MAKE(FILENAME)
END.
```

22F:
```
PROCEDURE LISTFILE(FNAME : STRING);

    VAR F : FILETYPE;

    BEGIN
        RESET(F, FNAME);
        WHILE NOT EOF(F) DO
          BEGIN
            WRITELN(F^.KEY);
            GET(F)
          END;
        CLOSE(F)
    END; (* LISTFILE *)
```

22G: All operands of expressions are evaluated in Pascal, whether or not they contribute to the resultant value. Even if EOF(SOURCE) is true, the value of (COPIEDREC.KEY > SOURCE.KEY) is calculated. From section 22.2.4 we see that when EOF(SOURCE) is true, SOURCE^ is undefined. Therefore, the assignment statement will involve a reference to an undefined variable at the end of the file.

22H:
```
PROCEDURE COPYRUNTOEITHER(VAR SOURCE, DEST0, DEST1 : FILETYPE);

    BEGIN
      REPEAT COPYRECTOEITHER(SOURCE, DEST0, DEST1) UNTIL ENDOFRUN;
      OUTFILENO := (OUTFILENO + 1) MOD 2
    END; (* COPYRUNTOEITHER *)
```

OUTFILENO should be declared (for the time being) and initialized in the procedure DISTRIBUTE.

At this stage the program structure should be as follows.

PROGRAM MERGESORT;

TYPE ...;

VAR UNSORTEDFN, SORTEDFN : STRING;

PROCEDURE LISTFILE(FNAME : STRING); ...;

```
PROCEDURE SORT(INNAME, OUTNAME : STRING);

    VAR AN, BN, CN, DN, FINAL : STRING;
        ENDOFRUN : BOOLEAN;

    PROCEDURE DISTRIBUTE(PN, QN, RN : STRING);

        VAR P, Q, R : FILETYPE;
            OUTFILENO : 0 .. 1;

        PROCEDURE COPYRUNTOEITHER(VAR SOURCE, DESTO, DEST1 : FILETYPE);

            PROCEDURE COPYRECTOEITHER(VAR SOURCE, DESTO, DEST1
                                                        : FILETYPE);

                VAR COPIEDREC : RECTYPE;

                BEGIN ... END; (* COPYRECTOEITHER *)

            BEGIN ... END; (* COPYRUNTOEITHER *)

        BEGIN (* DISTRIBUTE *)
            RESET(P, PN);  REWRITE(Q, QN);  REWRITE(R, RN);
            OUTFILENO := 0;
            WHILE NOT EOF(P) DO COPYRUNTOEITHER(P, Q, R);
            CLOSE(P);  CLOSE(Q, LOCK);  CLOSE(R, LOCK)
        END; (* DISTRIBUTE *)

    PROCEDURE MERGE(PN, QN, RN, SN : STRING;  VAR DESTN : STRING);

        BEGIN  END; (* MERGE *)

    PROCEDURE COPYFILE(PN, FNAME : STRING);

        VAR F, P : FILETYPE;

        BEGIN  END; (* COPYFILE *)

    BEGIN ... END; (* SORT *)

BEGIN ... END.


22J:    PROGRAM MERGESORT;

    TYPE ...;

    VAR UNSORTEDFN, SORTEDFN : STRING;

    PROCEDURE LISTFILE(FNAME : STRING); ...;

    PROCEDURE SORT(INNAME, OUTNAME : STRING);

        VAR AN, BN, CN, DN, FINAL : STRING;
            ENDOFRUN : BOOLEAN;
            OUTFILENO : 0 .. 1;

        PROCEDURE COPYRECTOEITHER(VAR SOURCE, DESTO, DEST1 : FILETYPE);

            VAR COPIEDREC : RECTYPE;

            BEGIN ... END; (* COPYRECTOEITHER *)

        PROCEDURE COPYRUNTOEITHER(VAR SOURCE, DESTO, DEST1 : FILETYPE);

            BEGIN ... END; (* COPYRUNTOEITHER *)
```

```
      PROCEDURE MERGE(PN, QN, RN, SN : STRING;  VAR DESTN : STRING);

            VAR NUMBEROFRUNS : INTEGER;
                P, Q, R, S : FILETYPE;
                TN : STRING;

            PROCEDURE MERGERUNTOEITHER(VAR R, S : FILETYPE);

                BEGIN ... END; (* MERGERUNTOEITHER *)

            BEGIN ... END; (* MERGE *)

      PROCEDURE DISTRIBUTE(PN, QN, RN : STRING);

            VAR P, Q, R : FILETYPE;

            BEGIN
                OUTFILENO := 0;
                ...
            END; (* DISTRIBUTE *)

      PROCEDURE COPYFILE(PN, FNAME : STRING);

            VAR F, P : FILETYPE;

            BEGIN
                RESET(P, PN);  REWRITE(F, FNAME);
                WHILE NOT EOF(P) DO
                    BEGIN
                        F^ := P^;
                        PUT(F);  GET(P)
                    END;
                CLOSE(P);  CLOSE(F, LOCK)
            END; (* COPYFILE *)

      BEGIN ... END; (* SORT *)

   BEGIN ... END.


22K:  PROGRAM MAKETRANS;

   TYPE PRIOSPEC = RECORD
                       IDEN : 1 .. 9999;
                       PRIORITY : 0 .. 99
                   END;

   VAR P : ^PRIOSPEC;
       TRANSFILE : FILE OF PRIOSPEC;
       INIDEN, INPRIO : INTEGER;
```

```
        BEGIN
            REWRITE(TRANSFILE, 'USER:TRANS.DATA');
            WRITE('ENTER IDEN [1 .. 9999]  PRIORITY [0 .. 99], ',
                                            'IDEN = 0 TO STOP: ');
            READ(INIDEN, INPRIO);
            WHILE INIDEN <> 0 DO
              BEGIN
                IF (INIDEN >= 1) AND (INIDEN <= 9999)
                                AND (INPRIO IN [0 .. 99]) THEN
                    BEGIN
                      NEW(P);
                      P^.IDEN := INIDEN;
                      P^.PRIORITY := INPRIO;
                      TRANSFILE^ := P^;
                      PUT(TRANSFILE)
                    END
                ELSE IF INIDEN <> 0 THEN WRITELN('ERROR IN INPUT');
                WRITE('ENTER IDEN [1 .. 9999]  PRIORITY [0 .. 99], ',
                                            'IDEN = 0 TO STOP: ');
                READ(INIDEN, INPRIO)
              END;
            CLOSE(TRANSFILE, LOCK)
        END.


22L:    PROGRAM UPDATE;

        TYPE STRING70 = RECORD
                          LENGTH : 0 .. 70;
                          CH : ARRAY [1 .. 70] OF CHAR
                        END;

             TASKSPEC = RECORD
                          NEXT : ^TASKSPEC;
                          IDEN : 1 .. 9999;
                          PRIORITY : 0 .. 99;
                          MESSAGE : STRING70
                        END;

             PRIOSPEC = RECORD
                          IDEN : 1 .. 9999;
                          PRIORITY : 0 .. 99
                        END;

        VAR TRANS : FILE OF PRIOSPEC;
            OMF, NMF : FILE OF TASKSPEC;
            NOMORE : BOOLEAN;

        PROCEDURE TRANSONLY;

          BEGIN
              WRITELN('TRANSACTION FOR KEY ', TRANS^.IDEN, ' BUT NO MASTER');
              GET(TRANS)
          END; (* TRANSONLY *)

        PROCEDURE UPDATEOLD;

          BEGIN
            OMF^.PRIORITY := TRANS^.PRIORITY;
            WRITELN('RECORD IDEN ', OMF^.IDEN,
                    ' GETS PRIORITY ', TRANS^.PRIORITY);
            GET(TRANS)
          END; (* UPDATEOLD *)
```

```
PROCEDURE MASTERONLY;

    BEGIN
        WRITELN('MASTER RECORD WITH KEY ', OMF^.IDEN, ' NOT UPDATED')
    END; (* MASTERONLY *)

BEGIN
    RESET(TRANS, 'USER:TRANS.DATA');
    RESET(OMF, 'USER:OLDLIST.DATA');
    REWRITE(NMF, 'USER:NEWLIST.DATA');

    WHILE NOT EOF(OMF) DO
        BEGIN
            REPEAT  (* TRANSACTION RECORDS WITH KEYS LESS THAN MASTER *)
                IF NOT EOF(TRANS) THEN
                    IF TRANS^.IDEN < OMF^.IDEN THEN TRANSONLY;
                IF EOF(TRANS) THEN NOMORE := TRUE
                              ELSE NOMORE := TRANS^.IDEN >= OMF^.IDEN
            UNTIL NOMORE;

            IF TRANS^.IDEN <> OMF^.IDEN THEN
                MASTERONLY  (* MASTER RECORD WITH NO TRANSACTIONS *)
            ELSE
                REPEAT (* TRANSACTION RECORDS WITH KEYS EQUAL TO MASTER *)
                    IF NOT EOF(TRANS) THEN
                        IF TRANS^.IDEN = OMF^.IDEN THEN UPDATEOLD;
                    IF EOF(TRANS) THEN NOMORE := TRUE
                                  ELSE NOMORE := TRANS^.IDEN > OMF^.IDEN;
                UNTIL NOMORE;

            (* ANY OTHER PROCESSING ON EACH RECORD DESTINED FOR THE
               NEW MASTER FILE MAY BE INCLUDED HERE *)

            NMF^ := OMF^;   PUT(NMF);

            GET(OMF)
        END; (* WHILE *)

    (* OLD MASTER FINISHED, MOP UP END OF TRANSACTION FILE *)

    WHILE NOT EOF(TRANS) DO TRANSONLY;

    CLOSE(TRANS);
    CLOSE(OMF);
    CLOSE(NMF, LOCK)
END.


22M:    PROGRAM DISPLAYFI3;

VAR INFILE : TEXT;
    C : CHAR;

BEGIN
    RESET(INFILE, 'USER:??????.TEXT');
    WHILE NOT EOF(INFILE) DO
        BEGIN
            WHILE NOT EOLN(INFILE) DO
                BEGIN
                    READ(INFILE, C);
                    WRITE(C)
                END;
            WRITELN;
            READ(INFILE, C)
        END;
    CLOSE(INFILE)
END.
```

CHAPTER 23
Graphs and the Shortest Path Problem

In an earlier chapter we hinted at the possibility of structures other than lists and trees. One such structure is a graph (or network). A graph is a set of nodes (points) and arcs (paths, edges). An arc connects a pair of nodes (usually but not necessarily distinct) and may have a weight such as length or cost. Weights will always be assumed to be non-negative in this and the following chapter. A sequence of contiguous arcs is known as a path. The length of a path is the sum of the weights of its component arcs. An example of a graph is shown in figure 23.1. Its nodes are named A, B, C and D. CA and AB are examples of arcs, and {CA, AB} is a path of length 6.

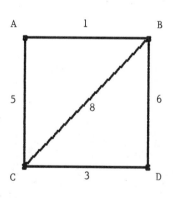

Fig 23.1   A graph

Graphs can be qualified by the following adjectives.

directed:	all arcs have direction shown by arrows on the arc (directed graphs are also known as digraphs)
non-directed:	no arc has direction
connected:	between any pair of nodes there is a path
non-connected:	there exist at least two nodes with no path between them

| simple graph: | between any ordered pair of nodes there is at most one arc |
| multi-graph: | between any ordered pair of nodes there may be more than one arc. |

EXERCISE 23A: For each of the graphs in figure 23.2, say whether it is

directed   or   non-directed
connected   or   non-connected
a simple graph   or   a multi-graph

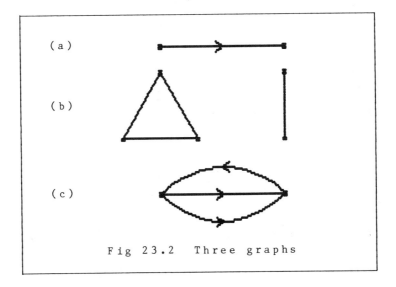

(a)

(b)

(c)

Fig 23.2   Three graphs

The shortest path between any two nodes of a graph may be defined for either directed or non-directed graphs. We shall consider only non-directed graphs although all the methods of this chapter apply equally to directed graphs. The road maps we shall use as examples are non-directed graphs, since travel in either direction along an arc is allowed.

A cycle in a directed graph is a non-empty path whose start and finish nodes coincide (see figure 23.3(a)). If a directed graph is free from cycles (see figure 23.3(b)) then the longest path (or critical path) may be found by a simple adaptation of the shortest path algorithm.

The longest path problem is at the heart of Critical Path Analysis (or Programme Evaluation Review Techniques - PERT), used for analyzing and optimizing complex procedures such as plant maintenance and production engineering schedules.

The shortest path algorithm is therefore of practical significance and the program to implement it embodies most of the features of Pascal and the principles of programming that we have studied. But first we do well to study the representation of a graph, and consider two methods of finding the shortest path other than the one to be implemented in chapter 24.

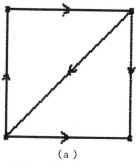 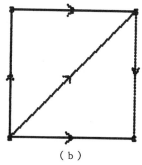

(a)   (b)

Fig 23.3   Graphs (a) with cycle,
                  (b) without cycles

23.1 REPRESENTATION OF A GRAPH

A good program is one which operates correctly with the least restrictive
conditions. We shall therefore aim to write a program that copes with non-
connected graphs (exercise 23A(b)) as well as multi-graphs (exercise 23A(c)).
To guide our thoughts, consider the following simple, connected, non-directed
graph.

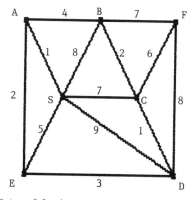

Fig 23.4   Another graph

One possible representation of a graph is an array. The graph of
figure 23.4 could be represented by

A	B,4	E,2	S,1	–	–
B	A,4	C,2	F,7	S,8	–
C	B,2	D,1	F,6	S,7	–
D	C,1	E,3	F,8	S,9	–
E	A,2	D,3	S,5	–	–
F	B,7	C,6	D,8	–	–
S	A,1	B,8	C,7	D,9	E,5

Each row of the array represents the node named on the left. The entry pairs in each row represent the nodes to which the node on the left is connected, and the lengths of the arcs. Such an array must have as many rows as there are nodes in the graph, and room for as many entry pairs as the maximum number of arcs leaving a node. The graph above, which has been drawn non-directed, is represented as a directed graph, with each arc specified in both directions. A directed graph could therefore be represented in this form. A multi-graph may also be represented in this manner.

An alternative representation using a square array removes the need to name the nodes explicitly. The graph above could be represented by

	A	B	C	D	E	F	S
A	–	4	–	–	2	–	1
B	4	–	2	–	–	7	8
C	–	2	–	1	–	6	7
D	–	–	1	–	3	8	9
E	2	–	–	3	–	–	5
F	–	7	6	8	–	–	–
S	1	8	7	9	5	–	–

but multiple arcs between pairs of nodes cannot be represented in this form. The array is symmetric for a non-directed graph, and therefore only the lower (or upper) triangle need be kept. Pascal does not have triangular array structures. An n x n triangular array may be represented by a one-dimensional array of length n(n+1)/2, and a function, tri(i,j) which converts a pair of two-dimensional array subscripts to a one-dimensional subscript.

EXERCISE 23B: Write such a function for a lower triangular array.

The use of an array to represent a graph seems to destroy the rather free character of a graph. Arcs are essentially links between nodes, and the most natural linking object in Pascal is the pointer. A tree is clearly a special case of a graph, and we used pointers to represent the branches of a tree. Thus a more natural representation of a graph is by a set of nodes with arcs represented by pointers. As with the first representation by an array, we are forced to describe in advance the maximum number of arcs that may leave a node. We will use a constant (in the **CONST** section) to represent this number in order to make it easy to adjust if necessary. It is also necessary to know, for each node, how many arcs leave it. Using an analogous term from chemistry, we call this the <u>valency</u> of the node. We can now sketch out the structure of a node (not to scale).

```
              name      ┌──────────────────┐
                        │                  │
           valency      ├──────────────────┤
                        │                  │
   arc : pointer/length ├─────────┬────────┤
                        │         │        │
   arc : pointer/length ├─────────┼────────┤
                        │         │        │
                 .      │    .    │   .    │
                 .      │    .    │   .    │
                 .      │    .    │   .    │
   arc : pointer/length ├─────────┼────────┤
                        │         │        │
                        └─────────┴────────┘
```

Nodes are clearly going to be represented by records and the only place to put them, where the pointers can point to other records, is on the heap. When we come to develop algorithms for determining the shortest path we will find

that it is necessary to extend a node to make provision for other fields used
during the computation.

EXERCISE 23C: For the graph in figure 23.4, what are the valencies of the
                nodes A, B, S? What is the maximum valency in this graph?

EXERCISE 23D: Sketch the record representing the node named A in the graph in
                figure 23.4.

EXERCISE 23E: By inspection, what is the shortest path from the node named S
                to the node named F in the graph in figure 23.4?

23.2   SHORTEST PATH ALGORITHMS

We now look at four approaches to solving the shortest path problem in
preparation for the implementation of a solution in chapter 24. In each case
we refer to two special nodes as the start node and the finish node.
The four methods are described in terms of finding the shortest route through
a network of roads (arcs) joining towns (nodes).

23.2.1   The Lee Algorithm

This is the easiest method to explain and its correctness is almost self-
evident. At the center of each town there is a blackboard which can be used
to record, amongst other things, the distance by the shortest route from the
start to that town. Initially, all the blackboards are clear. First mark the
blackboard at the start town as distance 0 from the start. At the start town,
assemble a sufficiently large cohort of people so that in the subsequent
divisions no subgroup becomes empty. Divide the people into subgroups and
send a subgroup along each road leading from the start. Each group must march
at the same constant rate. Whenever a group reaches another town it does one
of two things. If the town has not already been reached by some group, mark
the town as now having been visited, record on the blackboard the distance
travelled, and split the group into subgroups which again proceed along each
road as before. If the town has been previously visited, the group disbands.
The first group to reach the finish town has found the shortest path, and all
other groups may be told to stop. If, on the other hand, all groups are
allowed to continue until all towns have been visited, all will eventually
disband and the process will terminate with the shortest paths to all connected
towns having been found. If the graph is not connected, then only those nodes
reachable from the start node will have been visited.

This method is awkward to turn into a standard Pascal program for it is
described in terms of the simultaneous activities of varying numbers of
autonomous groups of people. We can regard time as the basic event marker and
then compute what happens during each interval of time, creating and disposing
of the representations of the marching groups. Thus, in addition to the graph,
we need to create structures representing the groups of marchers. The nodes of
the graph need additional fields to denote recorded distance, and whether or
not a node has been visited. We will not pursue this method further, save to
recommend the following exercise.

EXERCISE 23F: The following table summarizes the progress of the Lee algorithm
               over the graph in figure 23.4. It starts from node S, and
               finishes at node F. Complete the table and hence find the
               minimum distance from S to F and determine at what distance
               marched the last group disbands.

Distance	Subgroup number

Distance	1	2	3	4	5	6	7	8	9	10	11	12	13	14	15	16	17	18	19	20	21	22
0	sA	sB	sC	sD	sE																	
1	*	–	–	–	–	aB	aE	aS														
2		–	–	–	–	–	–	#														
3		–	–	–	–	*			eA	eD	eS											
4		–	–	–	–				–	–	–											
5		–	–	–	#	*			#	–	–				bA	bC	bF					
6																						
7																						
8																						
9																						
10																						
11																						
12																						
13																						
14																						
15																						

Notation:

aB	group sets off from A towards B
–	group continues
*	group reaches destination first, records distance from start and divides
#	group reaches destination too late and disbands
=	more than one group reaches destination simultaneously, any one of them divides, the rest disband.

23.2.2 Finding the Shortest Path

     The method described in the previous section marks nodes with their
minimum distance from the start node, and that is all. It is interesting to
note that from only this information, we can deduce the shortest path, not
from start to finish but from finish to start.

     Starting at the finish town look for a neighboring town such that its
blackboard distance, plus the distance between the towns, equals the finish
town's blackboard distance. That town must be on the shortest path. Move to
it and repeat the process until the start is reached. This suggests that,
instead of recording distances from the start, we should record distances to
the finish and enable the route to be displayed from start to finish. The
interesting feature of this method is that only one town is specified and the
minimum distance to every connected town is found. It is known as a single-
source method. If the start and finish nodes are not connected, the
blackboard at the start will have no number on it. We shall return later to
the properties of the solutions which are common to the four methods of
solution.

     Alternatively, the Lee algorithm can be modified so that whenever a group
arrives at a town for the first time, it adds to the blackboard the name of
the town from which it came, or a pointer to that town. This makes it possible
to retrace the path from any town to the start by merely following pointers.

EXERCISE 23G: Without the use of reverse pointers, trace the path from node F
to node S, in the graph of figure 23.4, explaining each step.

23.2.3 Iterative Method

If the Lee algorithm is elegant but awkward to program, the iterative
method is somewhat inelegant but simple to program.

At the center of each town, there is a signpost pointing to each adjacent
town, with the corresponding distance indelibly inscribed upon it. Alongside
each signpost is a blackboard, chalk and eraser. Initially, all blackboards
are empty, except the one at the start town. It has a zero on it. Each
blackboard will be used to record the length of the shortest path so far
discovered from the start to that town. In contrast to the Lee algorithm, this
method needs only a single person to operate it.

The basic procedure is one of spreading information from a town to each
of its neighbors. Imagine visiting a particular town and (provided there is
a number on its blackboard) setting up a temporary base there. If the
blackboard has no distance on it, pass straight on to the next town. (We
assume that the towns are arranged in some sequence (what sequence does not
matter) so that "next town" has some meaning.) Using the current distance on
the blackboard at base and the information on the signpost, attempt to improve
upon the distances on each surrounding town's blackboard. Each time a distance
on a blackboard is changed, add one to a variable called CHANGES. Call this
procedure IMPROVE. The algorithm can be stated in outline as follows.

```
REPEAT
    CHANGES := 0;
    FOR each town DO
        IF blackboard has a distance on it THEN
            FOR each neighbor DO IMPROVE
UNTIL CHANGES = 0
```

The algorithm terminates when you have completed a sequence of visits to
each town and have been unable to make any improvement to the distances on any
neighboring blackboard. (For the algorithm to terminate, "improvement" means
finding a strictly smaller distance.)

The route may be obtained by either of the methods of section 23.2.2. If
pointers are to be recorded then they must be updated every time the procedure
IMPROVE makes an improvement.

EXERCISE 23H: Using the iterative method, complete the following table showing
its progress.

Pass no	Base node	Best distance so far from S to						
		S	A	B	C	D	E	F
		0	−	−	−	−	−	−
1	S	0	1	8	7	9	5	−
2	A	0	1	5	7	9	3	−
	B	0	1	5	7	9	3	12
	C							

Compare the results with those from exercise 23F. How many passes are necessary? Altogether, how many times is the procedure IMPROVE called?

The principal disadvantage of this method is its complete lack of insight into whereabouts in the graph the action should be concentrated. For example, if, on a cycle of the **REPEAT ... UNTIL**, only one change is made, the next cycle will still set up base at every town in the entire graph and attempt to improve all their neighbors.

23.2.4 Iterative Method with Markers

This method is related to the iterative method insofar as it uses the same procedure to improve the distances on neighboring towns' blackboards. It differs only in its approach to where it sets up base, being more selective. In fact it only sets up base at towns which have previously had their blackboard distances changed. More precisely, when a blackboard distance is changed, a marker is placed on the town denoting that further attention is required; and when every neighbor of a base town has been improved, the marker is removed from the base town. The algorithm terminates when there are no markers left on any towns.

The algorithm of section 23.2.3 can be modified thus.

```
REPEAT
    NUMBEROFMARKERS := 0;
    FOR each town DO
        BEGIN
            IF marked THEN
                BEGIN
                    FOR each neighbor DO IMPROVE;
                    remove marker from this town
                END
        END
UNTIL NUMBEROFMARKERS = 0
```

where IMPROVE, amongst other things, sets markers and counts them.

EXERCISE 23J: Complete the following table which describes the iterative method with markers.

Pass no	Base node	Best distance so far from S to						
		S	A	B	C	D	E	F
		0M	–	–	–	–	–	–
1	S	0	1M	8M	7M	9M	5M	–
2	A	0	1	5M	7M	9M	3M	–
	B	0	1	5	7M	9M	3M	12M
	C							

How many times is the procedure IMPROVE called?

The **REPEAT ... UNTIL** is still extravagant, requiring repeated scanning of the markers at all towns in the network, until on the final scan it discovers that no markers remain.

23.2.5 Depth-first Recursive Method

The recursive approach to the problem focuses attention on a single node instead of the whole set of nodes. Recall that this was the tactic adopted in processing trees. In outline the procedure to find minimum distances from a given node to all other nodes on the network is

```
PROCEDURE FINDMINDISTS(NODE : ...);

    BEGIN
        FOR each neighbor DO IMPROVE;
        remove marker from this node;
        FOR each neighbor DO
            IF marked THEN
                FINDMINDISTS(NEIGHBOR)
    END; (* FINDMINDISTS *)
```

This algorithm, along with the others in this chapter, is expressed in a form which is independent of the representation of the graph. It can be applied to a representation based either on arrays or on pointers. Usually the choice of representation affects an algorithm to a greater extent than this. The array and pointer representations are in fact closer than they appear to be at first sight.

EXERCISE 23K: Using the depth-first recursive method, complete the following table showing its progress.

Base node at level							Best distance so far from S to					
0	1	2	3	4	5	6	S	A	B	C	D	E	F
S							0	1M	8M	7M	9M	5M	–
	A						0	1	5M	7M	9M	3M	–
		B					0	1	5	7M	9M	3M	12M
			C										

The method is described as <u>depth-first</u> because of the way the procedure FINDMINDISTS calls itself. The recursive part is essentially the second for statement, which causes the if statement to be executed a number of times equal to the valency of node. From the viewpoint of the finish node, the call to FINDMINDISTS of the first node's neighbors must terminate before it moves on to its second node's neighbors. The algorithm therefore initially explores the first neighbor of the first neighbor ... of the first neighbor, until the whole of the accessible part of the network has been explored. Only then do second neighbors get considered.

In contrast, the Lee algorithm (section 23.2.1) employs a <u>breadth-first</u> search. All neighbors of the finish node are approached at the same rate and the point of activity spreads out on a broad front. The method known as "Dijkstra's algorithm", is likewise breadth-first, but uses a technique

called <u>next event simulation</u> to disguise the simultaneous independent
activities referred to in section 23.2.1. [Dijkstra, 1976]

23.3 SPANNING TREES

If, in any of the methods described in this chapter, reverse pointers are
established, and if we draw the graph of figure 23.4 with only these
"recommended" arcs, we get figure 23.5. This is in fact a tree with its root
at node F. Furthermore, every node of the original graph is in the tree. The
tree is said to <u>span</u> the graph.

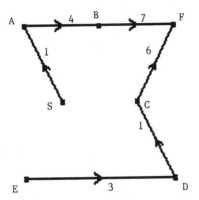

Fig 23.5   A spanning tree

EXERCISE 23L: Find the shortest path tree, rooted at S, which spans the graph.
               This tree is not unique. Find another tree that spans the same
               graph. What is the significance of the non-uniqueness of the
               spanning tree in this case?

SOLUTIONS TO THE EXERCISES

23A: (a) directed   connected   simple graph
         (b) non-directed   non-connected   simple graph
         (c) directed   connected   multi-graph

23B: **FUNCTION TRI(ROW, COL : INTEGER);**

         (* CONVERTS LOWER TRIANGULAR ARRAY TO LINEAR SUBSCRIPTS.
            IT DOES NOT CHECK THAT ROW >= COL *)

         BEGIN
             TRI := ROW*(ROW - 1) **DIV** 2 + COL
         END; (* TRI *)

23C: Valency of node A is 3
                                  B is 4
                                  S is 5 (maximum)

23D:

	name	A	
	valency	3	
arc : pointer/length	->B	4
arc : pointer/length	->E	2
arc : pointer/length	->S	1
	.	.
	.	.
	.	.
arc : pointer/length	**NIL**	-

23E: S -> A -> B -> F

23F:

Distance	Subgroup number																					
	1	2	3	4	5	6	7	8	9	10	11	12	13	14	15	16	17	18	19	20	21	22
0	sA	sB	sC	sD	sE																	
1	*	-	-	-	-	aB	aE	aS														
2		-	-	-	-	-	#															
3		-	-	-	-	-	*		eA	eD	eS											
4		-	-	-	-				-	-	-											
5		-	-	-	#	*			#	-	-	bA	bC	bF								
6		-	-	-			*		-	-	-	-	-	dC	dE	dF	dS					
7		-	=	-					-	-	=	-	-	=	-	-			cB	cD	cF	cS
8	#	-							#	-		-	-	-	-				#	-		
9			#							#		-		#	-	-		#			-	-
10												-		-	-						-	-
11												-		-	-						-	-
12												*		-	-						-	-
13														-	-				#	-		
14														#	-						#	
15															#							

The last group disbands at distance 15.

23G: dist(F) = 12. Test each of the following.

                dist(F) - length(FB) = dist(B)   true
                dist(F) - length(FC) = dist(C)   false
                dist(F) - length(FD) = dist(D)   false

Therefore B is on path. dist(B) = 5. Test each of the following.

                dist(B) - length(BA) = dist(A)   true
                dist(B) - length(BC) = dist(C)   false
                dist(B) - length(BF) = dist(F)   false
                dist(B) - length(BS) = dist(S)   false

Therefore A is on path. dist(A) = 1. Test each of the following.

```
dist(A) - length(AB) = dist(B)          false
dist(A) - length(AE) = dist(E)          false
dist(A) - length(AS) = dist(S)          true
```

S is the start node. Therefore path is S -> A -> B -> F.

23H:

Pass no	Base node	Best distance so far from S to						
		S	A	B	C	D	E	F
		0	-	-	-	-	-	-
1	S	0	1	8	7	9	5	-
2	A	0	1	5	7	9	3	-
	B	0	1	5	7	9	3	12
	C	0	1	5	7	8	3	12
	D	0	1	5	7	8	3	12
	E	0	1	5	7	6	3	12
	F	0	1	5	7	6	3	12
	S	0	1	5	7	6	3	12
3	A	0	1	5	7	6	3	12
	B	0	1	5	7	6	3	12
	C	0	1	5	7	6	3	12
	D	0	1	5	7	6	3	12
	E	0	1	5	7	6	3	12
	F	0	1	5	7	6	3	12
	S	0	1	5	7	6	3	12

No change in pass 3, therefore algorithm terminates.

Let V_X be the valency of node X. The number of times the procedure IMPROVE is called is

$$V_S + 2*(V_A + V_B + V_C + V_D + V_E + V_F + V_S)$$
$$= \quad 5 + 2*(3 + 4 + 4 + 4 + 3 + 3 + 5)$$
$$= \quad 57$$

23J:

Pass no	Base node	Best distance so far from S to						
		S	A	B	C	D	E	F
		0M	-	-	-	-	-	-
1	S	0	1M	8M	7M	9M	5M	-
2	A	0	1	5M	7M	9M	3M	-
	B	0	1	5	7M	9M	3M	12M
	C	0	1	5	7	8M	3M	12M
	D	0	1	5	7	8	3M	12M
	E	0	1	5	7	6M	3	12M
	F	0	1	5	7	6M	3	12
3	D	0	1	5	7	6	3	12

The number of times the procedure IMPROVE is called is

$$V_S + V_A + V_B + V_C + 2*V_D + V_E + V_F$$

$$= \quad 5 + 3 + 4 + 4 + 8 + 3 + 3$$

$$= \quad 30$$

23K:

	Base node at level							Best distance so far from S to						
0	1	2	3	4	5	6		S	A	B	C	D	E	F
S								0	1M	8M	7M	9M	5M	-
	A							0	1	5M	7M	9M	3M	-
		B						0	1	5	7M	9M	3M	12M
			C					0	1	5	7	8M	3M	12M
				D				0	1	5	7	8	3M	12M
					E			0	1	5	7	6M	3	12M
						D		0	1	5	7	6	3	12
					F			0	1	5	7	6	3	12

23L: Two possible trees are shown in figures 23.6 and 23.7.

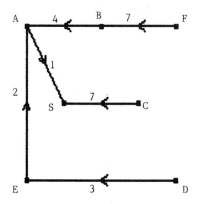

Fig 23.6   Spanning tree (i)

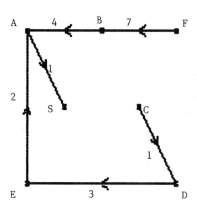

Fig 23.7   Spanning tree (ii)

There are alternative paths of length 7 from node S to node C.   There
is a third tree in the case above.   Can you find it?

CHAPTER 24
A Shortest Path Algorithm Realized

As a practical example of the solution to the shortest path problem, we will develop a program which finds the shortest route through a road map.

In the program we are about to construct, we shall attempt to keep the user interface as simple as possible, to enable us to concentrate on the algorithm and the data structures. More attractive user interfaces are left to the reader's imagination and initiative. We shall deliberately leave the choice of shortest path algorithm as late as possible in the construction of the program so as to make it easy to replace one method by another.

24.1 A SIMPLE USER INTERFACE

The program will first read the graph from a file, and then invite the user to type in the names of two towns which it calls the start and the finish. It then computes the route and displays it. If the start and the finish towns are the same, the program terminates. In outline it looks like

```
PROGRAM MINPATH;

(* THE PROGRAM FINDS AND DISPLAYS THE SHORTEST PATH BETWEEN TWO
   NAMED NODES IN A DIRECTED GRAPH. *)

VAR START, FINISH : STRING20;

BEGIN
    READGRAPH;

    REPEAT
       REPEAT
          WRITE('ENTER START NODE''S NAME: ');
          READSTRING(START)
       UNTIL start is the name of a node;
```

```
        REPEAT
            WRITE('ENTER FINISH NODE''S NAME: ');
            READSTRING(FINISH);
        UNTIL finish is the name of a node;

        DISPLAYPATH(START, FINISH)
    UNTIL START = FINISH
END.
```

This outline raises a few questions. First the type STRING20 is a simple adaptation of the STRING80 type of chapter 13. Then there is the question of how we find out whether the name we have read is the name of a town or not. Underlying the latter issue is the question of how to represent the graph. Until this is resolved we cannot begin to attempt to write the procedure READGRAPH.

24.2 REPRESENTATION OF A GRAPH

Let us begin where we left off in chapter 23 with the following sketch of the structure of a node.

To this we must add a number of fields, regardless of which algorithm we use. They correspond to the blackboard used in chapter 23.

- distance   minimum distance found so far, as on the blackboard
- known   a Boolean to enable us to distinguish between an empty blackboard and a zero distance
- markerset   a Boolean
- path   a pointer to the next node on the shortest path.

We need one more field to enable the nodes of the graph to be processed sequentially, for example, when checking that a town name typed by the user in the dialogue is in fact the name of some town in the graph. For this, and other purposes, we also organize the nodes as a linked linear list in the manner of section 19.2. We therefore need to add a field called

    NEXT

We will declare a pointer variable MAP, which will be the named reference to the linear list of nodes, and will use this variable to refer to the network as a whole.

In programs which operate on a single data structure, such as the one we are now considering and the timetable analyzing program of section 14.6, it is questionable whether the data structure should be passed as a parameter to the procedures that process it, or whether it should be referred to as a non-local variable by these procedures. In the timetable analyzing program we adopted the latter approach, and as a consequence, that program and its procedures could only handle a single timetable. In the shortest path program, we will make our procedures refer to the road network by means of a parameter, noting that this makes the program easily adaptable to the handling of more than one graph.

EXERCISE 24A: Incorporate into the outline program a type declaration for a record of a node of a graph, and a variable declaration for a pointer named MAP that points to the graph.

Returning to the outline program above, the procedure call to READGRAPH should be given a variable parameter through which it can return a value to the variable MAP.

We saw in the previous chapter and the exercise above that the nodes of the graph itself contain fields that are used for the solution of the shortest path problem. These fields must be reset to their initial values before the solution is attempted (RESETGRAPH(MAP)). We can also be more explicit about the graph which the procedure DISPLAYPATH is to operate on. The outline program can now be written as follows.

```
PROGRAM MINPATH;

    (* THE PROGRAM FINDS AND DISPLAYS THE SHORTEST PATH BETWEEN TWO
       NAMED NODES IN A DIRECTED GRAPH. *)

CONST MAXVAL = 12;

TYPE STRING20 = ...;
     NODEPOINTER = ^NODE;
     NODE = ...;

VAR  MAP : NODEPOINTER;
     START, FINISH : STRING20;

BEGIN
     READGRAPH(MAP);

     IF MAP <> NIL THEN
        BEGIN
           REPEAT
              RESETGRAPH(MAP);   WRITELN;

              REPEAT
                 WRITE('ENTER START NODE''S NAME: ');
                 READSTRING(START)
              UNTIL start is the name of a node;

              REPEAT
                 WRITE('ENTER FINISH NODE''S NAME: ');
                 READSTRING(FINISH);
              UNTIL finish is the name of a node;

              DISPLAYPATH(START, FINISH, MAP)
           UNTIL START = FINISH
        END (* IF *)
END.
```

DISPLAYPATH is the major part of the outline to be developed, but before we look further into that we should resolve the conditions in the clauses

UNTIL START is the name of a node

UNTIL FINISH is the name of a node

These conditions have to determine whether the names read into the variables START and FINISH are names of nodes in the network. We had to perform a similar search in the program USER:POLILIST2 (section 19.3.2) where we used a function whose value was a pointer to the record sought (or rather the record prior to it in that case) or NIL if no such record were found. We therefore assume that a function named PTR exists, so that we can write the until clauses as

UNTIL PTR(START,MAP) <> NIL

UNTIL PTR(FINISH,MAP) <> NIL

Make these refinements to the outline program and leave it in the workfile. It should be possible now to compile the outline with only errors related to the still unwritten procedures and functions.

24.3 READING THE GRAPH

Two road maps of North America are provided on the MACC: disk in the files USA18.TEXT and USA94.TEXT. They contain 18 and 94 towns respectively. The 18-town map should be used during program development, whilst the 94-town map is more impressive as a demonstration. It is recommended that you use the Filer to transfer the map you are working with to the file USER:USA.TEXT and make the program refer only to that file.

The maps have been provided as TEXT files to enable them to be inspected by the Editor. The maps begin with a list of towns and then the routes from each town in the same sequence. The shorter map begins:

```
ALBUQUERQUE
ATLANTA
BOSTON
CHICAGO
CLEVELAND
DALLAS
DENVER
DETROIT
LOS ANGELES
MIAMI
MINNEAPOLIS
NEW ORLEANS
NEW YORK
ST.LOUIS
SALT LAKE CITY
SAN FRANCISCO
SEATTLE
WASHINGTON D.C.
*

ALBUQUERQUE
     DALLAS   670
     DENVER   449
     SALT LAKE CITY   617
     LOS ANGELES   820
     *
```

```
ATLANTA
     CLEVELAND  735
     WASHINGTON D.C.  640
     MIAMI  691
     NEW ORLEANS  488
     ST.LOUIS  589
     *

BOSTON
     CLEVELAND  654
     NEW YORK  219
     *

CHICAGO
     CLEVELAND  364
     MINNEAPOLIS  430
     ST.LOUIS  314
     DETROIT  291
     *

CLEVELAND
     DETROIT  178
     ST.LOUIS  585
     WASHINGTON D.C.  386
     NEW YORK  476
     *
etc.
```

Note that routes are only included once. For example, the Boston to Cleveland route is under the routes from Boston but not from Cleveland. The reverse route will be assumed during the creation of the graph. We use a single asterisk (*) to denote the end of a section, and indentation merely to assist the human reader.

EXERCISE 24B: Assuming that procedures READSTRING, WRITESTRING, ADDTOLIST and function PTR exist, write the first part of a procedure which begins

PROCEDURE READGRAPH(**VAR** G : NODEPOINTER);

and reads the list of town names up to the first asterisk (*). Having opened the file USER:USA.TEXT, it reads a town name, displays it, checks it has not been used before, sets up a new record for the town with the valency field initially zero, and adds the record to a list G. When a town name consisting of an asterisk (*) has been read, the first part of the procedure terminates.

We next consider the procedure READSTRING. We want it to be able to read strings both from file and from the keyboard. However, as we discovered in section 22.6, files of type text are treated differently from the keyboard, as far as end of line is concerned in UCSD Pascal. (In standard Pascal, they are the same - both like files.) We use UCSD Pascal's alternative textfile type, INTERACTIVE, files of which type behave like input from the keyboard; that is EOLN becomes true when the end-of-line marker has been read (as a space). We will give READSTRING an extra parameter to say where to read from. It begins

PROCEDURE READSTRING(**VAR** SOURCE : INTERACTIVE; **VAR** ST : STRING20);

EXERCISE 24C: Modify the procedure READSTRING6 (exercise 15D) so that

- delimiters are not used

- a string is terminated by end-of-line or two consecutive spaces

- the maximum string length is 20 characters.

Adapt WRITESTRING (section 13.3.1) to the needs of this program. Supply dummy procedures for RESETGRAPH, DISPLAYPATH and ADDTOLIST, and add a dummy function for PTR which always returns the value **NIL**. Check out the program so far. It should display a list of 18 towns in the USA followed by an asterisk, and then stop.

EXERCISE 24D: Complete the function PTR which begins

FUNCTION PTR(GIVENNAME : STRING20; G : NODEPOINTER)
                                                  : NODEPOINTER;

and the procedure ADDTOLIST which begins

PROCEDURE ADDTOLIST(P : NODEPOINTER; **VAR** Q : NODEPOINTER);

(See section 19.3.2 where a similar function, POINTERTO, was given, but beware of important differences. See section 20.2.2 for a procedure very similar to ADDTOLIST.)

Test these additions to the program. Its visible effect should be the same as before, except that this time a list of nodes will have been created.

EXERCISE 24E: Complete the procedure READGRAPH, noting that the arc information is given in the same town sequence as the names in the first part of the file. Include plenty of checks to ensure that information does not get misplaced. Ensure that the valency of no node exceeds the constant MAXVAL. Remember that routes appear only one way in the file but have to be represented both ways in the graph. Test the procedure READGRAPH before proceeding.

EXERCISE 24F: To be sure that the graph has been read correctly, write a procedure DISPLAYGRAPH that can be called after READGRAPH. It should display the nodes in a similar format to that on file, but include routes both ways. The display should begin

```
ALBUQUERQUE
    DALLAS   670
    DENVER   449
    SALT LAKE CITY   617
    LOS ANGELES   820
    *

ATLANTA
    CLEVELAND   735
    WASHINGTON D.C.   640
    MIAMI   691
    NEW ORLEANS   488
    ST.LOUIS   589
    *
```

```
BOSTON
        CLEVELAND  654
        NEW YORK  219
        *

CHICAGO
        CLEVELAND  364
        MINNEAPOLIS  430
        ST.LOUIS  314
        DETROIT  291
        *

CLEVELAND
        ATLANTA  735
        BOSTON  654
        CHICAGO  364
        DETROIT  178
        ST.LOUIS  585
        WASHINGTON D.C.  386
        NEW YORK  476
        *
etc.
```

24.4 RESETTING THE GRAPH

Before any attempt is made to find the shortest path, the following fields
of each node should be set to the values stated.

```
        KNOWN            FALSE
        MARKERSET        FALSE
        PATH             NIL
```

EXERCISE 24G: Write the procedure RESETGRAPH.

24.5 FINDING AND DISPLAYING THE SHORTEST PATH

We next focus on the procedure DISPLAYPATH, which has to find the shortest
route between two named nodes and display it. The four methods of finding
shortest paths which were discussed in chapter 23 had the following in common.

-   They were single-source methods.
-   They set, (or could easily set) in the field PATH, pointers which
    define the spanning tree.

Our first attempt at the procedure is

```
PROCEDURE DISPLAYPATH(START, FINISH : STRING20; G : NODEPOINTER);

    (* DISPLAYS MINIMUM DISTANCE AND ROUTE FROM START TO FINISH. *)

    VAR P : NODEPOINTER;

    BEGIN
        SPAN(PTR(FINISH, G));

        P := PTR(START, G);

        IF NOT P^.KNOWN THEN
            WRITELN('START AND FINISH NODES ARE NOT CONNECTED')
        ELSE display distance and nodes on path
    END; (* DISPLAYPATH *)
```

Notice how the value of P^.KNOWN (where P points to the start), after the graph has been spanned from the finish, tells us whether the start and finish are connected.

The procedure SPAN prepares the ground for finding the shortest path,

```
PROCEDURE SPAN(S : NODEPOINTER);

    (* FINDS MINIMUM DISTANCES FROM NODE S TO ALL REACHABLE NODES.
       ROUTES ARE IMPLIED BY THE SPANNING TREE. *)

    BEGIN
        S^.DISTANCE := 0;
        S^.KNOWN := TRUE;
        FINDMINDISTS(S)
    END; (* SPAN *)
```

and leaves the procedure FINDMINDISTS to represent the chosen method.

We will implement the depth-first recursive method (see section 23.2.5), leaving another method as the final exercise of the chapter.

EXERCISE 24H: Convert the outline in section 23.2.5 into the complete
                procedure. Assume you have a procedure IMPROVE.

EXERCISE 24J: The procedure IMPROVE has to do the following: for a given base
                town, if the distance field at a particular neighbor is not
                known, or if the route to a particular neighbor via the base
                town is shorter than the present one, replace the distance field
                of the neighbor by the shorter distance; set the marker at the
                neighbor to true; set KNOWN to true and PATH to point back to
                the current town.

                Write the procedure.

EXERCISE 24K: Complete the procedure DISPLAYPATH so that its output looks
                something like

                        SHORTEST ROUTE BETWEEN
                        ATLANTA AND BOSTON IS 1078 MILES

                        AND IS VIA:
                                    ATLANTA
                                    WASHINGTON D.C.
                                    NEW YORK
                                    BOSTON

EXERCISE 24L: Assemble and execute the complete program. Check that it works
                on USER:USA94.TEXT which is not a connected graph.

EXERCISE 24M: Replace the procedure FINDMINDISTS by one which uses the
                iterative method with markers (section 23.2.4).

SOLUTIONS TO THE EXERCISES

24A: **PROGRAM** MINPATH;

        (* THE PROGRAM FINDS AND DISPLAYS THE SHORTEST PATH BETWEEN TWO
           NAMED NODES IN A GRAPH. *)

        CONST MAXVAL = 12;

        TYPE STRING20 = **RECORD**
                            LENGTH : 0 .. 20;
                            CH : **PACKED ARRAY** [1 .. 20] **OF** CHAR
                        END;

            NODEPOINTER = ^NODE;

            NODE =
              RECORD
                NEXT : NODEPOINTER;   (* POINTER TO NEXT NODE IN THE LIST *)
                NAME : STRING20;   (* TWENTY-CHAR NAME OF NODE *)
                VALENCY : 0 .. MAXVAL; (* NUMBER OF ARCS OUT OF THIS NODE *)
                ARC : **ARRAY** [1 .. MAXVAL] **OF**
                        RECORD   (* EACH ARC IS DEFINED BY *)
                            LENGTH : INTEGER;   (* ITS LENGTH ... *)
                            OTHERNODE : NODEPOINTER (* AND THE OTHER NODE *)
                        END;
                DISTANCE : INTEGER;
                KNOWN : BOOLEAN;
                MARKERSET : BOOLEAN;
                PATH : NODEPOINTER
              END;

        VAR MAP : NODEPOINTER;
             START, FINISH : STRING20;

```
        BEGIN
            READGRAPH;

            REPEAT
                REPEAT
                    WRITE('ENTER START NODE''S NAME: ');
                    READSTRING(START)
                UNTIL start is the name of a node;

                REPEAT
                    WRITE('ENTER FINISH NODE''S NAME: ');
                    READSTRING(FINISH);
                UNTIL finish is the name of a node;

                DISPLAYPATH(START, FINISH)
            UNTIL START = FINISH
        END.
```

24B: **PROCEDURE** READGRAPH(**VAR** G : NODEPOINTER);

```
        (* READS A GRAPH FROM THE FILE GRAFILE *)

        VAR NODENAME : STRING20;
            P, Q : NODEPOINTER;
            GRAFILE : INTERACTIVE;

        BEGIN
          G := NIL;
          RESET(GRAFILE, 'USER:USA.TEXT');
          READSTRING(GRAFILE, NODENAME);  WRITESTRING(NODENAME);  WRITELN;
          WHILE NODENAME.CH[1] <> '*' DO
            BEGIN
              Q := PTR(NODENAME, G);
              IF Q <> NIL THEN
                  WRITELN('NAME HAS ALREADY BEEN USED')
                ELSE
                  BEGIN
                      NEW(P);
                      WITH P^ DO
                        BEGIN
                          NAME := NODENAME;
                          VALENCY := 0
                        END; (* WITH *)

                      ADDTOLIST(P, G)

                  END; (* ELSE *)
              READSTRING(GRAFILE, NODENAME); WRITESTRING(NODENAME); WRITELN
            END; (* WHILE *)

          (* NOTE THAT THIS IS INCOMPLETE - SEE EXERCISE 24E *)

        END; (* READGRAPH *)
```

24C: **PROCEDURE** READSTRING(**VAR** SOURCE : INTERACTIVE; **VAR** ST : STRING20);

```
        (* TWO CONSECUTIVE SPACES OR RETURN TERMINATE STRING *)

        CONST BS = 8;

        VAR CHARCOUNT : 0 .. 20;
            DOUBLESPACE : BOOLEAN;
            C : CHAR;
```

```
BEGIN
    CHARCOUNT := 0;  DOUBLESPACE := FALSE;
    REPEAT READ(SOURCE, C) UNTIL C <> ' ';
    WHILE NOT (EOLN(SOURCE) OR DOUBLESPACE) DO
        BEGIN
            IF CHARCOUNT < 20 THEN
                BEGIN
                    IF ORD(C) = BS THEN
                        BEGIN
                            IF CHARCOUNT > 0 THEN
                                BEGIN
                                    CHARCOUNT := CHARCOUNT - 1;
                                    WRITE(CHR(BS), ' ', CHR(BS))
                                END
                        END
                    ELSE
                        BEGIN
                            CHARCOUNT := CHARCOUNT + 1;
                            ST.CH[CHARCOUNT] := C
                        END
                END; (* IF *)
            READ(SOURCE, C);
            IF CHARCOUNT >= 1 THEN
                DOUBLESPACE := (C = ' ') AND (ST.CH[CHARCOUNT] = ' ')
        END; (* WHILE *)

    IF DOUBLESPACE THEN ST.LENGTH := CHARCOUNT - 1
                    ELSE ST.LENGTH := CHARCOUNT;

    FOR CHARCOUNT := ST.LENGTH + 1 TO 20 DO ST.CH[CHARCOUNT] := ' '
END; (* READSTRING *)
```

24D:
```
    FUNCTION PTR(GIVENNAME : STRING20; G : NODEPOINTER) : NODEPOINTER;

        (* SEARCHES FOR GIVENNAME; RETURNS EITHER THE VALUE OF THE POINTER
           TO IT IN GRAPH G OR NIL IF GIVENNAME WAS NOT FOUND *)

        VAR P : NODEPOINTER;
            STATE : (LOOKING, FOUND, NOTTHERE);

        BEGIN
            IF G = NIL THEN PTR := NIL
            ELSE
                BEGIN
                    P := G;  STATE := LOOKING;
                    REPEAT
                        IF P^.NAME = GIVENNAME THEN STATE := FOUND
                            ELSE
                                BEGIN
                                    P := P^.NEXT;
                                    IF P = G THEN STATE := NOTTHERE
                                END
                    UNTIL STATE <> LOOKING;
                    IF STATE = FOUND THEN PTR := P ELSE PTR := NIL
                END
        END; (* PTR *)

    PROCEDURE ADDTOLIST(P : NODEPOINTER; VAR Q : NODEPOINTER);

        (* ADDS RECORD P^ TO TO LIST Q *)

        BEGIN
            IF Q = NIL THEN Q := P ELSE P^.NEXT := Q^.NEXT;
            Q^.NEXT := P;  Q := P
        END; (* ADDTOLIST *)
```

24E: Add the following declarations.

```
        STATE : (MOREARCS, LASTARC);
        DIST : INTEGER;
```

Add to the end of readgraph, in exercise 24B,

```
IF G <> NIL THEN
    BEGIN
       P := G^.NEXT;
       REPEAT
          WITH P^ DO
             BEGIN
                WRITE('.');      (* SHOWS SOMETHING IS HAPPENING *)
                STATE := MOREARCS;
                READSTRING(GRAFILE, NODENAME);
                IF NODENAME <> P^.NAME THEN
                                        WRITELN('ARC DATA OUT OF SEQUENCE')
                  ELSE
                    REPEAT
                       READSTRING(GRAFILE, NODENAME);
                       IF NODENAME.CH[1] = '*' THEN STATE := LASTARC
                         ELSE
                           BEGIN
                              Q := PTR(NODENAME, G);
                              IF Q = NIL THEN
                                 BEGIN
                                    WRITESTRING(NODENAME);
                                    WRITELN('NAME NOT IN GRAPH')
                                 END
                               ELSE
                                 BEGIN
                                    READ(GRAFILE, DIST);
                                    FILLINDIST(G, P, Q, DIST);
                                    FILLINDIST(G, Q, P, DIST)
                                 END
                           END
                    UNTIL STATE = LASTARC;
                P := P^.NEXT
             END (* WITH *)
       UNTIL P = G^.NEXT
    END; (* IF *)
    CLOSE(GRAFILE)
END; (* READGRAPH *)
```

and add the procedure

`PROCEDURE FILLINDIST(G, P, Q : NODEPOINTERS; DIST : INTEGER);`

`(* IN GRAPH G, NODE P IS GIVEN AN ARC OF LENGTH DIST TO NODE Q *)`

```
    BEGIN

       WITH P^ DO
          IF VALENCY < MAXVAL THEN
             BEGIN
                VALENCY := VALENCY + 1;
                ARC[VALENCY].LENGTH := DIST;
                ARC[VALENCY].OTHERNODE := Q
             END
           ELSE
             WRITELN('ATTEMPT TO DEFINE MORE THAN ', MAXVAL, ' ARCS')
    END; (* FILLINDIST *)
```

```
24F:    PROCEDURE DISPLAYGRAPH(G : NODEPOINTER);

            (* SIMPLE LISTING OF EACH NODE *)

            VAR P : NODEPOINTER;
                I : 0 .. MAXVAL;

            BEGIN
                IF G <> NIL THEN
                  BEGIN
                    P := G^.NEXT;  WRITELN;
                    REPEAT
                      WITH P^ DO
                        BEGIN
                          WRITELN;  WRITESTRING(NAME);  WRITELN(':');
                          FOR I := 1 TO VALENCY DO
                            BEGIN
                              WRITE(' ' : 10);
                              WRITESTRING(ARC[I].OTHERNODE^.NAME);
                              WRITELN(ARC[I].LENGTH : 6)
                            END;
                          P := P^.NEXT
                        END (* WITH *)
                    UNTIL P = G^.NEXT
                  END (* IF *)
            END; (* DISPLAYGRAPH *)


24G:    PROCEDURE RESETGRAPH(G : NODEPOINTER);

            (* ENSURES WORKSPACE WITHIN THE GRAPH IS INITIALIZED. *)

            VAR P : NODEPOINTER;

            BEGIN
                IF G <> NIL THEN
                  BEGIN
                    P := G^.NEXT;
                    REPEAT
                      WITH P^ DO
                        BEGIN
                          MARKERSET := FALSE;
                          PATH := NIL;
                          KNOWN := FALSE;
                          P := P^.NEXT
                        END
                    UNTIL P = G^.NEXT
                  END
            END; (* RESETGRAPH *)


24H:    PROCEDURE FINDMINDISTS(P : NODEPOINTER);

            (* DEPTH FIRST RECURSIVE ALGORITHM.

            PROCEDURE ESSENTIALLY COMPUTES THE MINIMUM DISTANCES TO THE FINISH
            OF EACH NODE CONNECTED TO P^.  WHERE A SMALLER DISTANCE IS FOUND
            FOR A NODE, THAT NODE IS MARKED (MARKERSET).  WHEN THESE
            COMPUTATIONS ARE COMPLETED THE SECOND PART OF THE PROCEDURE SCANS
            FOR SURROUNDING NODES WHICH NEED ATTENTION AND CALLS ITSELF
            RECURSIVELY TO DO SO.  *)

            VAR I, V : 0 .. MAXVAL;
```

```
      BEGIN
          V := P^.VALENCY;

          (* ATTEMPT TO IMPROVE SURROUNDING NODES. *)
          FOR I := 1 TO V DO IMPROVE;

          (* NOW MARK THIS NODE AS DONE *)
          P^.MARKERSET := FALSE;

          (* FINALLY MOVE TO THOSE SURROUNDING NODES WHICH ARE MARKED,
                                              AND SPREAD THE NEWS *)
          FOR I := 1 TO V DO
              BEGIN
                 IF P^.ARC[I].OTHERNODE^.MARKERSET
                                THEN FINDMINDISTS(P^.ARC[I].OTHERNODE)
              END

      END; (* FINDMINDISTS *)


24J:   PROCEDURE IMPROVE;

       BEGIN
          WITH P^.ARC[I].OTHERNODE^ DO
            BEGIN
              IF (NOT KNOWN) OR
                 (P^.DISTANCE + P^.ARC[I].LENGTH < DISTANCE) THEN
                 BEGIN
                    DISTANCE := P^.DISTANCE + P^.ARC[I].LENGTH;
                    KNOWN := TRUE;
                    PATH := P;              (* THIS MARKS THE PATH *)
                    MARKERSET := TRUE
                 END
            END (* WITH *)
       END; (* IMPROVE *)


24K:   PROCEDURE DISPLAYPATH(START, FINISH : STRING20; G : NODEPOINTER);

       (* DISPLAYS MINIMUM DISTANCE AND THE ROUTE FROM START TO FINISH. *)

       VAR P : NODEPOINTER;

       PROCEDURE SPAN(S : NODEPOINTER); ...;

       BEGIN
          SPAN(PTR(FINISH, G));

          P := PTR(START, G);

          IF NOT P^.KNOWN THEN
              WRITELN('START AND FINISH NODES ARE NOT CONNECTED')
            ELSE
              BEGIN
                WRITELN;  WRITELN('SHORTEST ROUTE BETWEEN ');
                WRITESTRING(START); WRITE(' AND '); WRITESTRING(FINISH);
                WRITELN(' IS ', P^.DISTANCE, ' MILES');
                WRITELN;  WRITELN('AND IS VIA:');
                WHILE P^.NAME <> FINISH DO
                    BEGIN
                       WRITE(' ' : 10); WRITESTRING(P^.NAME); WRITELN;
                       P := P^.PATH
                    END;
                WRITE(' ' : 10); WRITESTRING(FINISH); WRITELN
              END (* ELSE *)
       END; (* DISPLAYPATH *)
```

```
24L:     PROGRAM MINPATH;

         CONST MAXVAL = 12;

         TYPE STRING20 ...;
              NODEPOINTER = ^NODE;
              NODE ...;

         VAR  MAP : NODEPOINTER;  START, FINISH : STRING20;

         PROCEDURE READSTRING(VAR SOURCE : INTERACTIVE; VAR ST : STRING20); ...;
         PROCEDURE WRITESTRING(S : STRING20); ...;
         FUNCTION PTR(GIVENNAME : STRING20; G : NODEPOINTER) : NODEPOINTER; ...;

         PROCEDURE READGRAPH(VAR G : NODEPOINTER); ...;

             VAR NODENAME : STRING20;
                 P, Q : NODEPOINTER;
                 STATE : (MOREARCS, LASTARC);
                 DIST : INTEGER;
                 GRAFILE : INTERACTIVE;

             PROCEDURE ADDTOLIST(P : NODEPOINTER; VAR Q : NODEPOINTER); ...;
             PROCEDURE FILLINDIST(G, P, Q : NODEPOINTERS; DIST : INTEGER); ...;

             BEGIN ... END; (* READGRAPH *)

         PROCEDURE DISPLAYGRAPH(G : NODEPOINTER); ...;
         PROCEDURE RESETGRAPH(G : NODEPOINTER); ...;

         PROCEDURE FINDMINDISTS(P : NODEPOINTER);

             VAR I, V : 0 .. MAXVAL;

             PROCEDURE IMPROVE; ...;

             BEGIN ... END; (* FINDMINDISTS *)

         PROCEDURE DISPLAYPATH(START, FINISH : STRING20; G : NODEPOINTER);

             VAR P : NODEPOINTER;

             PROCEDURE SPAN(S : NODEPOINTER); ...;

             BEGIN ... END; (* DISPLAYPATH *)

         BEGIN ... END.
```

24M: Two procedures have to be modified.

```
PROCEDURE FINDMINDISTS(P, G : NODEPOINTER);

    (* ITERATIVE METHOD WITH MARKERS *)

    VAR I, V : 0 .. MAXVAL;
        NUMOFMARKERS : INTEGER;

    PROCEDURE IMPROVE; ...;

    BEGIN (* FINDMINDISTS *)
        IF G <> NIL THEN
            REPEAT
                NUMOFMARKERS := 0;
                P := G^.NEXT;
                REPEAT
                    WITH P^ DO
                      BEGIN
                        V := VALENCY;
                        IF MARKERSET THEN
                            FOR I := 1 TO V DO IMPROVE;
                        MARKERSET := FALSE;
                        P := P^.NEXT
                      END
                UNTIL P = G^.NEXT
            UNTIL NUMOFMARKERS = 0
    END; (* FINDMINDISTS *)

PROCEDURE SPAN(S : NODEPOINTER);

    BEGIN
        S^.DISTANCE := 0;
        S^.KNOWN := TRUE;
        S^.MARKERSET := TRUE;
        FINDMINDISTS(S, G)
    END; (* SPAN *)
```

APPENDIX 1
Turtlegraphics

The turtlegraphics package introduced in chapter 1 is a system of relative polar coordinates, designed to make the drawing of plane figures simple. It is provided as a unit, and is made available to a program by including

        USES TURTLEGRAPHICS;

immediately following the **PROGRAM** ...; line in the source program.

This form of graphics first appeared around 1969 in a language called LOGO, designed by Seymour Papert of Massachusetts Institute of Technology. It was originally used with an electro-mechanical "turtle" (an American generic word which includes the land tortoise) which held a pen that could be raised and lowered and driven around the floor under the control of a computer. In the Apple implementation the turtle has to be imagined, and the floor becomes the screen. The turtle is to be thought of as a movable dispenser of dots of various colors, having coordinate position (x, y) and a direction (or heading) in which it is facing. The Apple turtlegraphics package is broadly compatible with that described in [Bowles, 1977]. For the definitive and highly readable treatment of the geometry of the turtle, [Abelson and diSessa, 1980] is recommended.

The Apple screen can display one of two internally held images. One is the text area used by the p-System and the WRITE, WRITELN, READ and READLN statements. To display this area the Apple must be in textmode (the default). The other area is that to which all the turtlegraphics statements send their output. To display this area, the Apple must be in grafmode.

In grafmode the screen is regarded as an array of 280 (horizontal) by 192 (vertical) dots or pixels. The coordinate axes are conventionally arranged with the origin (0, 0) at the bottom left-hand corner of the screen. Horizontal and vertical movements of equal given sizes are displayed as equal length lines on a properly adjusted screen. Angles are always specified in degrees.

The effect of the **USES** TURTLEGRAPHICS declaration is to make available the following type, procedures and functions.

```
TYPE SCREENCOLOR = (NONE, WHITE, BLACK, REVERSE, RADAR, BLACK1,
                    GREEN, VIOLET, WHITE1, BLACK2, ORANGE, BLUE,
                    WHITE2);

PROCEDURE INITTURTLE;
PROCEDURE MOVE(RELDIST : INTEGER);
PROCEDURE TURN(RELANGLE : INTEGER);
PROCEDURE MOVETO(X, Y : INTEGER);
PROCEDURE TURNTO(ANGLE : INTEGER);
PROCEDURE PENCOLOR(COLOR : SCREENCOLOR);
PROCEDURE TEXTMODE;
PROCEDURE GRAFMODE;
PROCEDURE VIEWPORT(LEFT, RIGHT, BOTTOM, TOP : INTEGER);
PROCEDURE FILLSCREEN(COLOR : SCREENCOLOR);
PROCEDURE WCHAR(C : CHAR);
PROCEDURE WSTRING(S : STRING);

FUNCTION TURTLEX : INTEGER;
FUNCTION TURTLEY : INTEGER;
FUNCTION TURTLEANG : INTEGER;
FUNCTION SCREENBIT(X, Y : INTEGER) : BOOLEAN;
```

There are two further procedures DRAWBLOCK and CHARTYPE which are described in the Apple Pascal Language Reference Manual. They are not referred to in this book.

The type SCREENCOLOR defines a set of values which describe all possible pen colors. On an Apple with a monochrome screen, only the first 4 values are required. NONE causes no change to the screen as the pen moves; WHITE and BLACK force the pixels passed by the pen to become the specified color; and REVERSE changes black pixels to white and vice-versa.

INITTURTLE is the procedure which initializes the turtle. It should be called before your program uses any other turtlegraphics feature. It clears the screen, puts the Apple in grafmode and initializes the variables used inside the package. It also moves the turtle to the center of the screen (139, 95), sets the heading to 0 degrees (pointing east) and selects the pen color NONE. You should also call it from your program if, for instance, you wish to draw a second screenful.

MOVE provides relative translation in the direction in which the turtle is pointing, and TURN effects relative rotation. MOVETO and TURNTO set the turtle to an absolute position and heading.

PENCOLOR selects a new pen color from those of the range defined by the type SCREENCOLOR.

TEXTMODE and GRAFMODE force the Apple into the stated mode.

VIEWPORT causes subsequent traces on the screen to be clipped, that is, only points (x, y) within the rectangle defined by $x \geq$ LEFT, $x \leq$ RIGHT, $y \geq$ BOTTOM and $y \leq$ TOP are plotted.

FILLSCREEN, as the name suggests, saturates the screen (or that part defined by the latest VIEWPORT) with the specified color.

WCHAR places the specified character in the 7 pixel (wide) by 8 pixel (high) rectangle whose bottom left-hand corner is at the current position of the turtle. The turtle is moved 7 to the right as a result of a WCHAR. WSTRING effectively calls WCHAR once for each character of the specified string.

TURTLEX and TURTLEY are integer functions which return the current position of the turtle in integer coordinates. TURTLEANG returns the direction in which it is currently pointing, in degrees. SCREENBIT is a Boolean function which returns the state of the specified pixel as true if it is not BLACK, and false if it is BLACK.

APPENDIX 2
Apple Pascal Operating System Summary

This appendix provides a concise description of the Apple Pascal Operating System. It is described in greater detail in the Apple Pascal Operating System Reference Manual [Apple, 1980b].

1 AT THE OUTERMOST LEVEL OF COMMAND

The Apple Pascal Operating System is hierarchically organized in a number of levels. The system generally displays a list or "menu" of those options available at each level. Known as a prompt, it is generally displayed on the top line of the screen although only part of it may be seen at a time on a 40-character screen Apple. (Press CTRL-A to see the other part.) Sometimes there are more commands than will fit on even the 80-character screen. In this case, typing '?' causes another 80 characters worth of prompt line to be displayed (although only part of it may be seen ...). Options are usually selected by typing a single character on the keyboard. For example, the prompt for the outermost level of command is

COMMAND: E(DIT, R(UN, F(ILE, C(OMP, L(INK, X(ECUTE, A(SSEM, D(EBUG,? [...]

To select the Filer, for example, type F. The Filer then displays its outer level prompt line, indicating the options it provides. To return to a level from which you have descended, there are various methods, usually indicated in the prompt line itself. For example, to leave the Filer whilst at its outer level, you type Q for Quit. At other levels you may be asked for the name of a file; responding with just RETURN, generally takes you back to the level above. In a very few commonly occurring situations short cuts are provided whereby you may be taken up and then down to some other option. For example, there is a short cut of this kind out of the Compiler: when you type E you Exit the Compiler and enter the Editor which displays the location of the error.

In order to expedite the development of programs, the edit-compile-debug-edit cycle may be based on a single set of files called the workfile. The Editor and Compiler are designed to look out for and use the workfile if it exists, and the Filer is used to control its creation, annihilation and all

intermediate states of existence. The most common use of the workfile is
described in section 3.6.4 of chapter 3. For a more detailed description, see
[Apple, 1980b].

   The options available at the outermost level of command are as follows.

– E for Edit	The Editor is brought into memory from disk. If it exists, the text workfile is read into the Editor buffer, otherwise the Editor asks for a filename (no need to type .TEXT), suggests RETURN to create a new file, or ESC RETURN to get back to the outermost level of command. See section 3 for details.
– F for Filer	The Filer is brought into memory from disk. See section 2 for details.
– C for Compile	The system Compiler is initiated. If it exists, the text workfile is compiled and a code workfile is opened. If there is no workfile you are asked to name a textfile and a codefile (no need to type .TEXT or .CODE). If a syntax error is detected, the Compiler stops and and give you the choice of returning to the Editor, abandoning the compilation or continuing. No codefile is created if an error is detected. See [Apple, 1980a] for full details of the Compiler.
– L for Link	The Linker is not required for the exercises associated with this book.
– R for Run	If it exists, the code workfile is executed. If no such codefile exists, the Compiler is called as in C above. After an error free compilation, the program is executed.
– X for eXecute	You are asked for the name of a codefile which is executed; if the file does not exist "NO FILE" is displayed. (Note that the .CODE suffix on such a file is implicit in this context and need not be typed.)
– A for Assemble	The Assembler is not required for the exercises associated with this book.
– U for User restart	The previously executed program is restarted.
– I for Initialize	Type I for a fresh start.
– D for Debug	Not implemented. Do not use.

2 THE FILER

2.1 Files

   A file is a collection of values which is usually stored on disk.
All files have names, known as filenames of up to 15 characters length.
When responding to the Filer's prompts, a file specification is given

which, in addition to the filename, has to say where the file is. How to write
file specifications is covered in section 2.4. Under Apple Pascal a disk is
divided into 280 blocks of 512 bytes. The first 6 (blocks numbered 0 to 5) are
reserved, and include the file directory which contains the filename and
block number of each of up to 77 files on the disk; blocks 6 to 279 are for
files. The maximum length of a file, determined only by the capacity of the
disk, is 274 blocks. Files are kept on disk in contiguous blocks. As the disk
is used, the file area becomes fragmented and unused areas appear on the disk
between files. When the largest unused area is not large enough for a file
being written to the disk and yet the total number of unused blocks is
sufficient, the disk must be reorganized using the Filer's Krunch command
(section 2.5.16).

Files are of various types. The type of a file is determined by its
creator. It suggests, and in most cases constrains its use. File types may
also be signified by the last part of the filename (or suffix). Reserved
suffixes for filenames are

.TEXT   Human and Compiler readable textfile created by the Editor
         or by a program writing a file of type TEXT, **FILE OF** CHAR,
         PACKED FILE OF CHAR or INTERACTIVE.

.CODE   Machine executable codefile created by the Compiler.

.BAD   An unmovable file covering a physically damaged area of a
         disk created by the Filer's eXamine command.

.DATA   File, not of type TEXT, etc., created by a program.

The file type cannot be changed by changing the suffix in the filename
(section 2.5.9).

2.2 Volumes

A volume is an input or output device, such as the screen, the
keyboard, a disk or a printer. A block-structured device is one that can
have a directory and is usually a disk of some sort. A non-block-structured
device does not have internal structure, it simply produces or consumes a
stream of data, such as the keyboard and the screen. The table below lists the
reserved volume names and volume numbers on a basic two-drive Apple Pascal
system.

Volume number	Volume name	Description
1	CONSOLE:	screen and keyboard with echo
2	SYSTERM:	keyboard without echo
3		unused
4	APPLE1:	the system disk (drive 1)
5	USER:	the user's disk (drive 2)
6 - 12		reserved for specific uses

2.3 Volume Specification

To refer to a volume in the Filer, a volume specification is used,
various forms of which allow both flexibility and brevity. The syntax may be
described by the diagram,

volume specification:

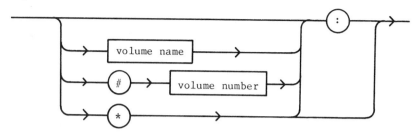

A volume name must be from 1 to 7 characters long and may not contain an equals
sign (=), a dollar sign ($), a question mark (?), a colon (:) or a comma (,).
An asterisk (*) alone is an alternative volume specification for the system
disk (the disk that was in drive 1 when the system was loaded, sometimes called
the root volume). The system recognizes a default volume. This is
the volume which is referred to when a file is specified (section 2.4) without
a volume specification or by a colon (:) alone. The default volume can be
changed by means of the Filer's Prefix command (section 2.5.13). The volume
specification #<volume number> is equivalent to the name of the volume in that
device at that time. See also section 3.6.1 in chapter 3.

2.4 File Specification

A file specification may be described by the following syntax diagrams.

file specification:

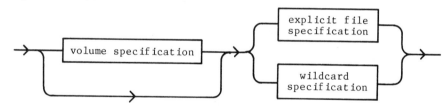

explicit file specification:

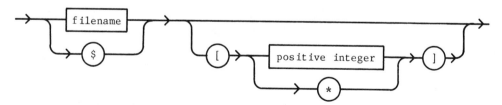

wildcard specification:

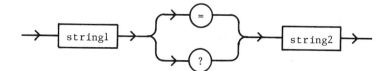

The filename may be from 1 to 15 characters, including the suffix (section
2.1). Spaces and non-visible characters are removed from the filename.
Allowable characters for a filename are the alphanumerics and the characters
'-', '/', '\', '_' and '.'. The special filename '$' is only used in the
Filer's Transfer command (section 2.5.11). The positive integer and the
asterisk in square brackets are known as file <u>size specifications</u> which
may be used in connection with the Filer's Transfer command (section 2.5.11),
the Make command (section 2.5.17) and Pascal's REWRITE statement (chapter
22 and appendix 10). In other Filer commands where it is not relevant, the
size specification is ignored.

The wildcard option is a shorthand notation for specifying multiple files
in the same volume. A set of files whose names match the given subset-
specifying strings is selected and delivered to the Filer in sequence. If
equals (=) is used, all the selected files are delivered without user
intervention, but if the question mark (?) is used, the user has the final say
as to which of the selected files is delivered. Either or both of the strings
may be omitted. Files are selected in two stages. In stage 1, if the string1
is present, then any filename beginning with string1 is passed on to stage 2,
but if string1 is omitted, each filename is passed on to stage 2. In stage 2,
if the string2 is omitted, the filename is selected but if string2 is present,
selection depends on matching the end of the filename with string2.

For example, given a volume FELLS: containing the files

            LINGMELL.CODE
            ALLEN.CODE
            ROSSETT.TEXT
            ILLGILL.CODE
            LINGMOOR.TEXT

the file specification FELLS:LING=TEXT selects only LINGMOOR.TEXT; the
specification FELLS:=.CODE selects LINGMELL.CODE, ALLEN.CODE and ILLGILL.CODE;
the file specification FELLS:L? allows the user to select either or both of
LINGMELL.CODE and LINGMOOR.TEXT for consideration. The specification FELLS:=
selects all five files and FELLS:A?.TEXT selects none. If string1 and string2
overlap, as in FELLS:ALLEN.C=N.CODE, then a match would not be found in the set
of filenames above. However, the filename ALLEN.CAN.CODE would produce a
match, as indeed would ALLEN.CN.CODE. Only the following Filer commands allow
the use of wildcards:

            List directory
            Extended directory listing
            Change
            Remove
            Transfer

2.5 <u>The Filer Commands</u>

Type F at the outer level of command to enter the Filer and one of the
following prompts is displayed. (Press CTRL-A if necessary to see the other
half.)

FILER: G(ET, S(AVE, W(HAT, N(EW, L(DIR, R(EM, C(HNG, T(RANS, D(ATE, Q(UIT

FILER: G, S, N, L, R, C, T, D, Q [...]

Typing '?' in response to either version makes more Filer commands available.

FILER: B(AD-BLKS, E(XT-DIR, K(RNCH, M(AKE, P(REFIX, V(OLS, X(AMINE, Z(ERO

FILER: W, B, E, K, M, P, V, X, Z [...]

The individual Filer commands are invoked by typing the letter to the left of the parenthesis (or the letter itself). For example, S would invoke the Save command.

In the Filer, answering a Yes/No question with any character other than Y constitutes the answer 'No'. Simply typing RETURN when a file specification is expected returns you direct to the outer level of the Filer.

In response to a request for a file specification, you may enter as many specifications as desired, separating them with commas, and terminating the list with RETURN. Commands operating on single files read specifications from the list and operate on them until none is left. Commands operating on pairs of files (such as Change, Transfer and the directory Listing commands) read specifications in pairs and operate on them until only one or none remains. If one specification remains, the Filer prompts for the final member of the pair. If an error is detected in the list, the remainder of the list is flushed.

2.5.1 G for Get

The designated file is named as the workfile. In spite of the message indicating that a file has been loaded, this is not the case. However, the next time the Editor or Compiler is used, they will use this filename as the name of the workfile. The suffix part of the file specification (.TEXT or .CODE) is not necessary. Typical responses to the prompt "GET ? " are

        MACC:TWOBUGS

        STARTIME   In the context of chapter 1, this assumes the
                                    default volume is MACC:

2.5.2 S for Save

Saves the workfile. If the workfile has been named, you can choose to have it saved under this name or under a filename specified by you. If the workfile is not named, or if you choose to name it, then the suffix must not be given since the Filer automatically appends the suffixes .TEXT and .CODE to files of the appropriate type.

If the workfile is saved on the system disk, it is not copied, but merely renamed.

2.5.3 N for New

Clears the workfile. Any SYSTEM.WRK files are removed, and no workfile name remains. If a physical workfile exists, the user is prompted "THROW AWAY CURRENT WORKFILE ? ". The response Y clears the workfile, whilst N returns the user to the outer level of the Filer.

2.5.4 Q for Quit

Returns the user to the outermost level of command.

2.5.5 W for What

Displays the name and state (whether saved or not) of the workfile.

2.5.6 V for Volumes

Displays volumes currently on-line, with their associated volume numbers. The ROOT volume is the volume from which the system was loaded. The PREFIX is the current name of the default disk (section 2.4). Block-structured devices are indicated by # on this display.

2.5.7 L for List directory

Lists the disk directory, denoted by the first specification, to the destination denoted by the second specification. The second specification is normally omitted, indicating that the directory is to be copied onto the screen (the default being CONSOLE:). To list only a subset of a directory, the wildcard '=' may be used in the first specification. (Use of the wildcard '?' will be found to be rather tedious.) The directory may be sent to a volume or file other than CONSOLE:. For each file on the volume being listed the filename, the length of the file and the date of latest modification are listed.

The number of files, number of blocks used and largest unused blocks of the volume are given at the end of the listing, but some of this information is unreliable when a subset of the directory is called for.

The first specification consists of a mandatory volume specification, and optional subset-specifying strings. The second specification consists of a volume specification and, if the volume is a block-structured device such as a disk, a filename. Typical responses to the prompt "DIR LISTING OF ?" are

MACC:	Entire directory of MACC: to screen.
USER:=.TEXT	Textfiles in directory of USER: to screen.
#4,USER:SYSDIR.TEXT	Entire directory of disk in drive 1 to the file USER:SYSDIR.TEXT.

2.5.8 E for Extended directory listing

Lists the directory in more detail than the L command. Unused areas of the disk are included. In addition to the information given by the L command, the starting block number and the file type are given. Otherwise it is as for the L command.

2.5.9   C for Change

Changes a file's filename or a disk's volume name. This command requires two specifications. The first specifies either the file or the volume whose name is to be changed; the second specifies either the new filename or the new volume name to which it is to be changed. In the case of a filename change, any volume specification in the second specification is ignored, since the old file and the new file must be on the same volume. The Change command does not affect the file type.

If a wildcard is used in the first file specification, then a wildcard (either kind) must be used in the second file specification. The subset-specifying strings in the first file specification are replaced by the analogous strings given in the second file specification. The Filer will not change the filename if the change would have the effect of making the filename too long (>15 characters). Remember that any of the subset-specifying strings or the replacement strings may be empty.

The following examples are each to be interpreted in the context of the volume FELLS: in section 2.4. In response to the Change command's prompt "CHANGE ? ",

FELLS:,HILLS: Changes the volume name to HILLS:

FELLS:=SETT.TEXT,=THWAITE.FELL
                       Changes the name of the file ROSSETT.TEXT to ROSTHWAITE.FELL but the file remains a textfile. To specify this file for the Editor or the Compiler it is necessary to append a full stop to the filename. For example, in response to the prompt "COMPILE WHAT TEXT ? " type "FELLS:ROSTHWAITE.FELL.".

FELLS:LING?,CART?   Allows the user to choose which of the files LINGMELL.CODE and LINGMOOR.TEXT should have their names changed to CARTMELL.CODE and CARTMOOR.TEXT

FELLS:=.TEXT,=   Changes the name of ROSSETT.TEXT to ROSSETT and LINGMOOR.TEXT to LINGMOOR (files remaining textfiles).

2.5.10   R for Remove

Removes files from the specified or implied volume's directory. Because of the drastic effect of this command, the user is finally prompted with "UPDATE DIRECTORY ? ", allowing any specified removals to be cancelled by the response N. The response Y causes all specified files to be removed.

The file specification '=' alone requests the removal of every file from the specified or implied volume's directory.

Do not use Remove to remove SYSTEM.WRK.TEXT and/or SYSTEM.WRK.CODE from the system disk. Use the command New (section 2.5.3).

The following examples are each to be interpreted in the context of the volume FELLS: in section 2.4. Typical responses to the Remove command's prompt "REMOVE ? " are,

FELLS:ALLEN   No file is removed.

FELLS:ALLEN.CODE   The file ALLEN.CODE will be removed if the user confirms this by typing Y at the final prompt.

FELLS:LING=   Both of the files LINGMELL.CODE and
                               LINGMOOR.TEXT will be removed if the user
                               confirms this by typing Y at the final prompt.

FELLS:?   The user is asked about the removal of each of
                               the five files separately. Finally, the user
                               accepts or rejects the selected removals as a
                               whole, by typing Y or N at the final prompt.

FELLS:=   All five files will be removed if the user
                               confirms this by typing Y at the final prompt.

2.5.11   T for Transfer

Copies the specified file to the given destination. Two file
specifications are required, one for the source file, and one for the
destination file, separated with either a comma or RETURN. Wildcards are
permitted, and size specification information is recognized for the destination
file. The Transfer command does not change the file type of the files it
copies.

To transfer a file between two disks, neither of which is the system
disk, type F to enter the Filer before removing the system disk. On a one-
drive Apple, files may be transferred between different disks provided volume
names, and not volume numbers, are used to identify the disks. Follow the
instructions on the screen telling you to load first one disk and then the
other.

When transferring a file with no change of filename, you may write the
character $ in the destination file specification to stand for the filename of
the source file.

If the second file specification has the filename completely omitted,
there is a danger that the destination disk will be wiped out!

Files may be transferred to volumes that are not block-structured, such
as CONSOLE: by giving the appropriate volume specification (section 2.2) as the
destination file specification. It is generally a good idea to make certain
that the destination volume is on-line before giving this command. You may
also transfer from non-block-structured devices, providing they are input
devices.

If the source file specification contains a wildcard, and the destination
is a block-structured device, then the destination file specification must
either contain a wildcard or be the special filename '$'. The subset-
specifying strings in the source file specification are replaced by the
analogous strings given in the destination file specification. Remember that
any of the subset-specifying strings may be empty. In the source file
specification, '=' alone specifies every file on the volume but in the
destination filename specification, '=' alone has the effect of replacing the
subset-specifying strings in the source specification with nothing. If '?' is
used in place of '=', the user is asked for verification before each transfer
takes place.

A file can be transferred within a volume by specifying the same volume
specification for both source and destination file specifications. This is
useful when a file is to be relocated on the disk. Appending a size
specification (section 2.4) causes the Filer to copy the file into the first
unused area of at least that size. The size specification denoted by '*'
stands for the second largest unused area. If no size specification is given,
the file is written into the largest unused area.

If the same filename is given for both source and destination file
specifications on a same-volume transfer, then the Filer copies the file to the
unused area determined according to the paragraph above, and then removes the
original file.

To do an entire volume-to-volume transfer both source and destination file specifications should be volume specifications only. Transferring a block-structured volume to another block-structured volume causes the destination volume to be wiped out so that it becomes an exact copy of the source volume, including the volume name. Immediately after such a transfer, remove one of the disks and give the Filer a Volumes command (section 2.5.6) to convince it that it does not have two volumes with the same name.

If a disk contains a marked bad block (section 2.5.15) it cannot be copied by a volume-to-volume transfer. However all the files may be copied to another disk by means of a wildcard source file specification.

The following examples are each to be interpreted in the context of the volume APPLE1: on drive 1 and FELLS: on drive 2. Typical responses to the prompt "TRANSFER ? " are,

FELLS:ALLEN.CODE,FELLS:ALLEN.CRAGS
> A copy of the file ALLEN.CODE is made on the same disk (FELLS:). The file is still a codefile, and the original file also remains, still named ALLEN.CODE

FELLS:ALLEN.CODE,APPLE1:$
> A copy of the file ALLEN.CODE is made on the APPLE1: disk with the same filename.

FELLS:R=,CONSOLE:
> The file ROSSETT.TEXT is sent to the screen at high speed. Press CTRL-S to freeze the display.

FELLS:LING?,APPLE1:LANG?
> The files LINGMELL.CODE and LINGMOOR.TEXT are copied, at the user's discretion, to the disk APPLE1: where they are given the names LANGMELL.CODE and LANGMOOR.TEXT respectively.

FELLS:=,PIKES:$
> A disk whose volume name is PIKES: must first be loaded in drive 1. All the files on FELLS: are copied to PIKES: where they retain their original filenames. An alternative destination file specification is PIKES:=

FELLS:ILLGILL.CODE,FELLS:$[8]
> The file ILLGILL.CODE is relocated on the FELLS: disk in the first unused area of at least 8 blocks.

FELLS:,BLANK:
> A disk whose volume name is BLANK: must first be loaded in drive 1. In reply to the prompt "TRANSFER 280 BLOCKS ? (Y/N) ", type Y, and in reply to "DESTROY BLANK: ? ", type Y. A volume-to-volume copy ensues as a result of which the disk which was called BLANK: becomes a block-for-block copy of the disk called FELLS: This cannot be used if the source disk has any bad blocks. Use FELLS:=,BLANK:= and then Change the volume name from BLANK: to FELLS:

2.5.12   <u>D for system Date</u>

Displays current system date, and enables it to be changed. The response the prompt "NEW DATE ? " may be in one of four formats. Note the day-month-year order.

    (a)   DD-MMM-YY RETURN

                        where DD is a 1- or 2-digit day number,
MMM is the first 3 letters of the month name
and YY is the last 2 digits of the year.
The components must be separated by '-'.
(The year 2000 is going to cause problems!)
All 3 components of the system date are set.

    (b)   DD-MMM RETURN   As above, but the year is unchanged.

    (c)   DD RETURN   As above but year and month remain unchanged.

    (d)   RETURN   The entire date is unchanged.

For examples of the use of the Date command, see section 1.3 in chapter 1. The system date is associated with all files written to or saved on disk, and is the date displayed along with the filename when a directory is listed.

2.5.13   P for Prefix

Changes the name of the default volume (section 2.3). This command requires only a single volume specification. The volume need not be on-line, but if the volume specification is given as a volume number, which at that time is on-line, the prefix is set to the corresponding volume name.

Typical responses to the prompt "PREFIX TITLES BY ? ", are

    USER: The default volume becomes USER:

    #5:   If drive 2 has no disk, the default volume becomes #5: otherwise it becomes the volume name of the disk therein.

    *   The default volume becomes the root volume.

2.5.14   B for Bad block scan

Scans the disk and checks for bad blocks. This command requires a volume specification which must relate to an on-line volume. To check the whole disk answer Y to the prompt "SCAN FOR 280 BLOCKS ? (Y/N) ". Bad blocks can sometimes be fixed (section 2.5.15).

2.5.15   X for eXamine

Attempts to recover suspected bad blocks which have been detected by a bad block scan. In response to the prompt "EXAMINE BLOCKS ON ? ", enter a volume specification which must relate to an on-line volume. In response to "BLOCK RANGE" enter the first and last block numbers of the bad area as reported by the bad block scan. If any files are endangered, the following conversation occurs.

Apple: FILE(S) ENDANGERED:
           filename <first block number> <last block number>
           FIX THEM ?

User: Y

The Filer examines the blocks and displays either

Apple: BLOCK <block-number> MAY BE OK
           in which case the bad block may have been fixed, or

Apple: MARK BAD BLOCKS ?   (FILES WILL BE REMOVED !) (Y/N)

Responding with Y to this prompt, causes the block(s) to be marked
BAD. Blocks which are marked BAD are not shifted during a Krunch, and
are thus rendered relatively harmless. (See 2.5.11 regarding restrictions on
Transferring from a disk with marked bad blocks.) Responding with N to the
"FIX THEM ? " prompt returns the user to the outer level of the Filer.

A block which is claimed to be "fixed" may still contain garbage. "MAY
BE OK" merely means that the block has been read, written back to the disk,
read again, and the two reads found to be the same. Only if the two reads are
different, is the block considered to be bad enabling it to be marked as such.

2.5.16 K for Krunch

Reorganizes the files on the specified volume, which must be on-line, so
that all unused blocks are combined into one. There is a degree of choice as
to where the unused area is to be. If you want the files to be at the front
(blocks numbered 6, 7 etc.) then answer Y to the prompt "FROM END OF DISK,
BLOCK 280 ? (Y/N) ". Otherwise, it attempts to leave the block number given in
response to the next prompt within the unused area.

As each file is moved, its filename is displayed on the screen. If the
file SYSTEM.PASCAL is moved, the system must be reinitialized (section 1).

Do not touch the disk-drive door, the power switch or RESET until the
operation is complete; otherwise serious damage may be done to the disk.

It is recommended that a bad block scan be done before Krunching in
order to avoid writing files over bad areas of the disk. If bad blocks are
detected by the scan, they must be either fixed or marked before the Krunch
(section 2.5.15).

2.5.17 M for Make

Creates a directory entry on the specified volume with the specified
filename. The file type of the newly-created file is dependent upon
recognition of a reserved suffix (section 2.1). An unrecognized suffix
results in a file of type equivalent to one with suffix .DATA being created.
The Make command is most frequently used to attempt to recover a file believed
to be occupying an unused area of a disk. The filename must be given in full,
and wildcards are not allowed. The size specification option (section 2.4)
is generally used, since, if it is omitted, the Filer creates the specified
file in the whole of the largest unused area of the disk. If the size
specification is a positive integer, the first unused area of at least that
size accommodates the file. Special cases of the size specification are

           [0] - equivalent to omitting the size specification. The file is
                   created in the largest unused area.

           [*] - the file is created in the second largest area, or half the
                   largest area, whichever is larger.

2.5.18 Z for Zero

Puts a new empty directory on the specified volume. If a directory already exists on this volume, you are warned that it and all its files will be lost.

In response to the two less obvious prompts, you are recommended to reply

```
        DUPLICATE DIR ?          N
        ARE THERE 280 BLKS ...   Y
```

3 THE EDITOR

3.1 Commands and Modes

At the outer level of the Editor the prompt line offers several options, which are called either <u>commands</u> or <u>modes</u>. If the selection of an option executes a task and returns control directly to the outer level of the Editor, it is called a command, but if the selection results in the issue of a further prompt, giving the user another menu, it is called a mode.

3.2 Repeat-factors

Some of the Editor's commands and modes allow repeat-factors. A repeat-factor is applied to a command or mode by typing an unsigned integer immediately before it. The command or mode is then repeated the number of times indicated by the repeat-factor. For example, typing 2 CTRL-L causes the cursor to move down two lines. Commands and modes which allow a repeat-factor assume it to be 1 if no integer precedes it. A '/' typed before the command or mode implies repetition until the end (or beginning) of the file being edited is reached. Repeat-factors are not generally echoed on the screen.

3.3 The Cursor

The cursor, although shown as a reversed character, is actually in the gap to the left of the reversed character. For example if the letter G of PROGRAM is reversed, then the cursor is between the letter O and the letter G. This is most obvious in the Insert mode which inserts new characters in front of the reversed character.

3.4 Direction

Certain commands and modes are affected by direction. If the direction is <u>forward</u> (the default) they operate from beginning to end through the file. The opposite direction is <u>backward</u>.

Direction is changed by typing '<' or '>' or ',' or '.' or '+' or '-' and is shown as the first character of most of the Editor's prompt lines. Forward is shown as '>' and backward as '<'.

3.5 Cursor-moving Commands and Modes

Whilst at the outer level of the Editor, the following keys control the movement of the cursor.

CTRL-L	Moves down one line
CTRL-O	Moves up one line
\<left-arrow\>	Moves left one character
\<right-arrow\>	Moves right one character
\<spacebar\>	Moves one character according to direction
CTRL-I	Tabs according to direction to the next position which is a multiple of 8 spaces from the left side of the screen
RETURN	Moves according to direction to the beginning of the next line above or below
=	Moves to the beginning of the last text Inserted, Found or Replaced
J	Jump mode (see below)
P	Page (see below) according to direction.

Repeat-factors can be used with any of the above except that they are not relevant in the case of '=' and 'J'.

The Editor maintains the screen column position of the cursor when using CTRL-O and CTRL-L although when this puts the cursor outside the text, it is considered to be immediately after the last character or immediately before the first character of the line.

Jump mode is reached by typing J while at the Editor's outer level. Typing B (or E) moves the cursor to the beginning (or the end) of the file. Typing M, followed by the name of a marker, moves the cursor to that marker (section 3.8.1.1).

The Page command is invoked by typing P while at the Editor's outer level. Depending on the current direction, Page moves the cursor one screenful (24 lines) up or down. The cursor is reset to the start of a line. A repeat-factor may be used to move several screenfuls.

3.6 Text-changing Commands and Modes

3.6.1 I for Insert

Insert mode is reached by typing I while at the Editor's outer level. To accept inserted text, press CTRL-C; to reject it, press the ESC key. Whilst in Insert mode, use ← to erase the character to the left of the cursor. (You cannot reverse the cursor back beyond the start of the insertion.) Use CTRL-X to erase the current line. Typing RETURN moves the cursor to the start of the line below, at the indentation specified by the options selected in the Environment option of the Set mode. See section 3.8.1.2. The cursor may be forced to the left-hand edge of the screen by typing CTRL-Q.

If Auto-indent is True, RETURN causes the cursor to move to the next line immediately "under" the leftmost character of the line above. If Auto-indent is False, RETURN moves the cursor to the first position in the line below. If Filling (see below) is True, the first position is the Left margin, unless the line above is blank, in which case the first position is that of Paragraph margin. See section 3.8.1.2.

If Filling is True, the Editor forces all insertions to be between the Right and Left margins by automatically inserting a RETURN between words whenever the Right margin would have been exceeded, and by indenting to the Left margin whenever a new line is started. The Editor considers anything between two spaces, hyphens or normal punctuation marks to be a word. See section 3.8.1.2.

If both Auto-indent and Filling are True, Auto-indent controls the Left margin while Filling controls the Right margin. The level of indentation may be changed by using the spacebar and ← keys immediately and only immediately after a RETURN.

Filling also causes the Editor to adjust the margins on the portion of the paragraph following the insertion. Any line beginning with the Command character (section 3.7.3) is not touched during this adjustment and that line is considered to terminate the paragraph.

The direction does not affect the Insert mode although still indicated by the direction of the arrow on the prompt line.

If an insertion is made and accepted, that insertion is available for use in the Copy mode (section 3.6.4). However, if the ESC key is used to terminate the insertion, the copy buffer is empty.

3.6.2   D for Delete

Delete mode is reached by typing D while at the Editor's outer level. On entering the Delete mode, the Editor remembers where the cursor is. That position is called the anchor. As the cursor is moved from the anchor in any direction by use of →, ←, CTRL-L, CTRL-O, CTRL-I, RETURN or the spacebar, text in its path disappears from view. Opposite cursor movements may be used to restore to view text which had disappeared. To accept the deletion from the file of what has disappeared from view, press CTRL-C; to reject the deletion, press the ESC key.

Deleted characters, whether accepted or not, are copied into the buffer. Unless the Editor has stated otherwise, you may then use the Copy mode to copy the deleted characters at any place to which the cursor is next moved. This gives the Editor what is sometimes called a "cut and paste" facility.

A repeat-factor may also be used to delete several lines at once by preceding a RETURN or any other of the moving commands with a repeat-factor while in the Delete mode.

3.6.3   Z for Zap

The Zap command is invoked by typing Z while at the Editor's outer level. Zap is useful for deleting large quantities of text several pages long. Zap deletes all text between the start of what was previously Found, Replaced or Inserted and the current position of the cursor. It is intended to be used immediately after one of the Find, Replace or Insert modes. If more than 80 characters are about to be Zapped the Editor will ask for verification.

If a preceding Find or Replace is made with a repeat-factor then only the last Find or Replacement will be Zapped. All others will be left as found or replaced.

Unless the Editor has stated otherwise, the text deleted by a Zap command may be used in the Copy mode.

3.6.4 C for Copy

The Copy mode is reached by typing C while at the Editor's outer level.
As the next prompt line indicates, it may be used to copy text from another
file (type F) or from its own Copy buffer (type B).

If copying from another file, another prompt will appear.

>COPY: FROM WHAT FILE[MARKER,MARKER]?

Any textfile on any volume may now be specified, but .TEXT is assumed and need
not be typed. In order to copy only part of a file, one or two markers must
already have been set to mark the start and/or end of the text to be copied
(section 3.8.1.1). To copy from the start of a file to a marker, type
"[,marker]" after the filename; to copy from a marker to the end of a file,
type "[marker,]". Use of the Copy mode does not change the contents of the
file being copied from.

To copy the text in the Copy buffer into the file at the current position
of the cursor, type B. After the Copy the contents of the Copy buffer remain
unchanged.

The Copy buffer is affected by Delete, Insert and Zap as indicated
in the descriptions of those commands and modes.

The Copy buffer is of limited size. As the length of text being edited
increases, the Copy buffer decreases. Whenever a Deletion or Zap is longer
than the available buffer, a warning is given to the effect that the buffer
will not be filled with the about-to-be-deleted text on this occasion. If
the deletion is part of a "cut and paste" operation, then smaller chunks
will have to be used.

3.6.5 X for eXchange

Exchange mode is reached by typing X while at the Editor's outer level.
In eXchange mode, one character in the file is replaced by each character of
text typed. Exchanges may only be made on the current line to the right of the
initial position of the cursor. The line may not be lengthened in this mode.

The only cursor-moving keys which may be used during eXchange mode are
< which is used to correct typing errors, and the spacebar which is used
conventionally. CTRL-C quits eXchange mode with the line changed to what you
see on the screen. ESC quits eXchange mode with no changes made to the line.

The use of eXchange mode does not affect the Copy buffer.

3.6.6 Find and Replace

Strictly speaking, Find is a moving mode (section 3.5) but is included
here because of its close affinity to the Replace mode. Searching for given
strings is the essence of both modes.

In either mode a repeat-factor may precede the F or the R. The repeat-
factor is echoed in square brackets on the prompt line.

Both modes operate on delimited strings. The Editor has two string
variables. One called <TARG> in the prompt line is the target string and is
referred to by both modes while the other, called <SUB> by the prompt line,
is the substitute and is used only by Replace. The following rules apply to
the way these strings are used.

- Both delimiters of the string must be the same. Any character
  which is not a letter or a number is considered to be a delimiter.

- Both modes operate from the position of the cursor to scan the
  text in the current direction as indicated by the arrow on the
  prompt line. The target pattern can only be found if it appears
  in that section of the text. See section 3.4 regarding how to
  change the direction.

- The search occurs in one of two ways called Literal searching
  and Token searching (section 3.8.1.2.5). If Literal searching
  is selected, the Editor looks for any occurrence of the target
  string. If Token searching is selected, "isolated" occurrences
  of the target string are sought. A string is "isolated" if it is
  surrounded by any pair of characters which are not letters or
  digits, such as words in sentences and identifiers in a Pascal
  program. To select Token searching as the default, set the value
  of TOKEN to TRUE in the Environment, and to select Literal
  searching as the default set TOKEN to FALSE (section 3.8.1.2.5).
  To override the default, type T or L after the F for Find or R for
  Replace. In Token searching, spaces in the <TARG> string are not
  significant in the matching process. Thus a Token search for
  "OVER DRIVE" will find both "OVER DRIVE" and "OVERDRIVE" in the
  file.

- In both Find and Replace, typing S in place of a delimited string
  denotes the Same string as was used previously. For example,
  typing "RS/<any-string>/" causes the Replace mode to use the
  previous <TARG> string, while typing "R/<any-string>/S" causes _he
  previous <SUB> string to be used.

The Set Environment mode (section 3.8.1.2) displays the current <TARG> and
<SUB> strings.

3.6.6.1 F for Find

Find mode is reached by typing F while at the Editor's outer level. The
Find mode finds the n-th occurrence of the target string starting with
the current postition and moving in the direction shown by the arrow at the
beginning of the prompt line. The number n is the repeat-factor and is shown
on the prompt line in the brackets [ ].

3.6.6.2 R for Replace

Replace mode is reached by typing R while at the Editor's outer level.
Repeat-factors and the Literal/Token search options are as for Find mode.

The Verify option, permits the user to examine the <TARG> string (up to
the limit set by the repeat-factor) and decide whether it is to be replaced.
To select this option, type V after the R, or after the overriding T or L.
A prompt line appears whenever the <TARG> pattern in the file has been found
and verification has been requested. Type an R to effect replacement; type a
space to skip this occurrence and search for the next, provided the repeat-
factor has not been reached; and type ESC to return you direct to the outer
level of the Editor. The repeat-factor counts the number of times an
occurrence is found, not the number of times you actually type R. Use '/' as
a repeat-factor in order to examine every occurrence of the target string.

3.7 Formatting Commands and Modes

3.7.1 A for Adjust

Adjust mode is reached by typing A while at the Editor's outer level.
Adjust moves entire lines to the left or right, allowing the indentation of
a line to be altered. The <left-arrow> and <right-arrow> cursor-moving

commands move the line in which the cursor is, to the left and right
respectively, by one character position at a time. When the adjustment is
satisfactory, press CTRL-C. The ESC key will not terminate Adjust.

A sequence of consecutive lines may be adjusted by the same displacement.
First Adjust the top (bottom) line using <left-arrow> and <right-arrow>; then
use CTRL-L (CTRL-O) commands repeatedly to apply the same adjustment to the
lines below (above) automatically. Terminate with CTRL-C. You may alter the
displacement by inserting further <left-arrow> and <right-arrow> commands which
are also applied to succeeding lines. Once you have embarked upon a sequence
of Adjustments, use only CTRL-L or only CTRL-O. Mixing them may have
unexpected effects.

Repeat-factors, including '/', may be used before any of the four cursor-
moving commands while in Adjust mode.

Text may be centered or justified in Adjust mode. Type L (R) to left-
justify (right-justify) the current line to the margin set in the Environment
(section 3.8.1.2.3). Type C to center the current line between the set
margins. Typing CTRL-O (CTRL-L) will cause the line above (below) to be
adjusted in the same manner as the previously adjusted line.

3.7.2 M for Margin

The Margin command is invoked by typing M at the Editor's outer level.
Margin rearranges paragraphs of text according to the three margins,
Right margin, Left margin and Paragraph margin, set in the Environment
(section 3.8.1.2.3). Lines are left-justified, leaving a ragged right margin.
Margin may only be used when Filling is TRUE and Auto-indent is FALSE
(section 3.8.1.2).

A paragraph is a set of adjacent lines bounded by any two of the
following: a blank line, the beginning of a file, the end of a file or a line
which starts with the Command character (section 3.7.3). Blanks (spaces) and
hyphens are regarded as word separators and all other characters are taken to
be parts of words. It does not hyphenate words.

To Margin a paragraph move the cursor to anywhere within the paragraph and
type M. When Margining a long paragraph a second or more may elapse before the
screen is re-displayed.

3.7.3 Command character

Lines of text can be protected from being Margined by the use of what is
called the "Command character". A line whose first non-blank character is the
Command character is protected from being Margined. Furthermore, such a line
bounds a paragraph and limits the effect of the Margin command.

3.8 Miscellaneous Commands and Modes

3.8.1 S for Set

Set mode is entered by typing S at the Editor's outer level. There are
two options.

3.8.1.1 M for Marker

When editing, it is sometimes convenient to be able to jump directly to
certain places in a long file by using markers. Once set, it is possible to
jump to a marker using the Marker option in the Jump mode. When in Set mode,
a marker may be set at the current position of the cursor, by typing M,

followed any name up to 8 characters, followed by RETURN. (If a marker with
that name already exists, it will be reset to the new position of the cursor.)

Only a limited number (10) of markers are allowed in a file at any one
time. If on typing SM, the prompt "MARKER OVFLW" appears, you will be asked
which marker to remove in order to make room for the new one. A list of all
current marker names is included in the Environment display.

If a copy or deletion is made between the beginning of the file and the
position of the marker, a jump to that marker may not subsequently return to
the desired place as the absolute position has changed.

3.8.1.2 E for Environment

Certain characteristics of the Editor's operation on a particular file
may be set by the user. Collectively these are known as the Environment.
The Environment is kept with a textfile when it it written to disk.
The user may set these characteristics to suit the file being edited. By
typing the appropriate letters, any options may be changed.

3.8.1.2.1 A for Auto-indent

Auto-indent affects only the Insert mode and the Margin command in the
Editor. Auto-indent is set to TRUE by typing AT and to FALSE by typing AF
(section 3.6.1). Auto-indent should be TRUE when editing Pascal programs.

3.8.1.2.2 F for Filling

Filling affects only the Insert mode and the Margin command in the Editor.
Filling is set to TRUE by typing FT and to FALSE by typing FF (section 3.6.1).
Filling should be FALSE when editing Pascal programs.

3.8.1.2.3 L, R and P for Left, Right and Paragraph Margin

Following the L, R or P type the column number (a positive integer
counting from 0) to correspond to that margin. Terminate the column number
with a space or RETURN. The positive integer typed replaces the old value for
that margin. Positive integers with four or fewer digits are valid margin
values.

When Filling is true the margins set in the Environment are the margins
which affect the Insert mode and the Margin command. They also affect the
centering and justifying options in the Adjust mode.

3.8.1.2.4 C for Command character

The Command character affects the Margin command and the Filling option
in the Insert mode as described in section 3.7.3. To change the Command
character type C followed by the new Command character.

3.8.1.2.5 T for Token definition

This option affects Find and Replace. Token is set to TRUE by typing
TT and to FALSE by typing TF. If Token is true, Token is the default and if
Token is false, Literal is the default. (See section 3.6.6.)

3.8.2 V for Verify

The Verify command (not to be confused with the Verify option in the
Replace mode) is executed by typing V at the Editor's outer level. The screen
is redisplayed with the cursor at the center of the screen (unless the cursor
is in the first screenful of the file, in which case the first screenful is
displayed). Use this command whenever you are unsure about what is actually in
the file or simply to centralize the cursor on the screen.

3.8.3 Q for Quit

Quit mode is reached by typing Q at the Editor's outer level. One of five options must be selected by typing U, E, R, W or S.

3.8.3.1 U for Update the Workfile

The file being edited is written to the system disk, as the workfile and named SYSTEM.WRK.TEXT. It may be used subsequently by the Compile or Run options or for the Save option in the Filer.

3.8.3.2 E for Exit

This causes the system to leave the Editor without saving the file being edited. Any changes made during the current session are about to be lost and you are therefore reminded of this before confirming that you wish to leave in this manner.

3.8.3.3 R for Return

This option returns to the Editor without updating. The cursor is returned to the place it occupied when Q was typed. This is useful after unintentionally typing Q.

3.8.3.4 W for Write

The modified file may now be written with any filename. This option can be aborted by pressing RETURN instead of a filename and returning to the Editor. After writing, you have the option of returning either to the Editor (R), or to the outermost level of command (E).

3.8.3.5 S for Same Name

The modified file can be written to a file with the same name as that with which it was obtained for the Editor. The prompt, asking whether the old file be purged before saving, should normally be answered by N. Should any mishap occur during the save, you still have the old file to revert to. But if free disk space is scarce, you may not be able to afford to have two copies existing (albeit for a fleeting moment) on the disk. In these circumstances, type Y and keep your fingers crossed.

It is whilst quitting the Editor that sooner or later you will see the message "OUTPUT FILE FULL". The most likely reason for this warning is that the disk being written to has insufficient room for the file in its largest unused area. Press the spacebar in accordance with the message on the screen. You may have to find another volume on which there is room to write this file. If you were trying to Update the workfile, then try to Write to a disk on #5; if you were trying to Write to #5, try Saving there instead, using the Y option; failing that try Updating the workfile, and failing that, try another disk in #5. In any event, it is likely that one of your disks is getting too full for comfort. Can any files be removed? Does it need to be Krunched? Or is it time to start on another disk?

4 CONTROL KEYS ON THE APPLE

The CTRL key provides another set of characters, known as control characters, when it is depressed prior to, and held down during, the depression of another key. Some control characters are interpreted specially in Apple Pascal.

CTRL-A   On a 40-character screen, this shows the other half of the screen. Can be used at any time the Apple is waiting for you to type something.

CTRL-C   Used in the Editor to denote the acceptance of a string of text or the end of a sequence of cursor moving commands. See the description of the Insert, Delete, Adjust commands in the Editor.

CTRL-F   Flush output. That is stop sending output to the screen, but allow the program to continue to run. Another CTRL-F resumes output on the screen.

CTRL-I   In the Editor, this tabs across the screen to the next tab position. Tabs are set every 8 characters at columns 8, 16, 24, ...

CTRL-K   Delivers the left square bracket character, [. Can be used at any time.

CTRL-L   In the Editor, this moves the cursor down one line.

CTRL-O   In the Editor, this moves the cursor up one line.

CTRL-Q   While inserting text in the Editor, this moves the cursor to the left margin provided this is not to the left of the start of the insertion.

CTRL-S   Halts the current program. No prompt is given. The program may be resumed by typing a second CTRL-S. This command is useful to pause, for example, during rapidly scrolling output, and may be given at most times. This is your "Panic Button".

CTRL-X   Whilst Inserting text in the Editor, CTRL-X erases the current line and moves the cursor back to the end of the previous line.

CTRL-Z   Puts the 40-character screen into auto-follow mode so that it follows the horizontal movement of the cursor. Can be used at any time the Apple is waiting for you to type something. Type CTRL-A to cancel.

CTRL-@   Both CTRL and SHIFT keys must be held down whilst the key labelled '@' and '2' is pressed. This interrupts the current program and prompts for a space to be typed, whereupon the system returns to the outermost level of command. The program will only be interrupted by CTRL-@ when it executes an input or output statement. To stop a program in an endless loop which does no input or output you have to resort to RESET (or CTRL-RESET).

APPENDIX 3
Reserved Words and Composite Symbols

Reserved words may not be used as identifiers. Therefore, some familiarity with the following lists will be useful, whether or not the features to which they relate are used in programs. The reserved words of standard Pascal are

AND	ARRAY	BEGIN	CASE	CONST	DIV	DO
DOWNTO	ELSE	END	FILE	FOR	FORWARD	FUNCTION
GOTO	IF	IN	LABEL	MOD	NIL	NOT
OF	OR	PACKED	PROCEDURE	PROGRAM	RECORD	REPEAT
SET	THEN	TO	TYPE	UNTIL	VAR	WHILE
WITH						

In Apple Pascal there are a few additional Reserved Words.

EXTERNAL	IMPLEMENTATION	INTERFACE	SEGMENT	UNIT	USES

Spaces may not be placed between the characters constituting the following composite symbols which, like reserved words, are regarded as indivisible tokens.

<>   <=   >=   (*   *)   :=   ..

APPENDIX 4
Disk Recovery Strategies

1   DISK HANDLING PRACTICE

Prevention is better than the cure. By taking good care of your disks, you will reduce considerably the likelihood of the kind of disk problems this appendix addresses. Disks should at all times be kept flat, clean, dry, away from direct sunlight and at a moderate temperature. Never touch either surface of the disk. Do not write on a label on a disk except with a soft fibre tipped pen. Keep them away from strong magnetic fields and x-ray sources such as those used by airport security services. Always keep the disk either in an Apple drive or in its envelope.

2   BACKING UP A DISK

If you value the files on a disk, you should take time to make and keep an up-to-date copy, called a backup disk. Use the Filer's Transfer command in its volume-to-volume mode of operation to create a bit-for-bit copy of the disk. Be very careful which drive has the original and which drive has the backup disk, for since both disks will have the same volume name, you will have to specify the volumes to be transferred by their device numbers (#4 and #5). At the end of such a copying process the system believes it has two disks with the same volume name, and a warning is issued. Remove the new backup copy, do a Volume listing and the situation will become clear again. Physically label the backup disk with the same volume name as the original, and mark it as a "backup" copy. To be quite sure that you have got a good backup copy, do a bad block scan of the new backup disk. Ideally the backup disk should be stored apart from the original, but this makes it inconvenient to use, and reduces your chances of keeping the backup disk current. Work out some acceptable compromise.

3 WHAT TO DO WHEN A FILE CANNOT BE READ

When the Apple experiences difficulty reading a file, it tries several times. Total failure results in a message of the form "I/O ERROR". There is a possibility that the disk has not centered properly in the drive unit. Unload the disk, reload it carefully, and try the transfer again. If that fails, read on.

(a) Make a written record of the fact that some difficulty has been experienced with this disk. If and when the problem recurs with this disk you will wish to take stronger measures. If the trouble is with one of the APPLE system disks go to (b), otherwise go to (c).

(b) Try making another copy from a master disk onto the suspect disk, and re-check it with a bad block scan. If that fails discard the disk, and make a new working copy onto a formatted disk. If that fails, suspect the disk drive.

(c) Try a bad block scan on as many different drives as you can reasonably access, and if you get 0 BAD BLOCKS on one of them, copy the disk (using a volume-to-volume transfer) from that drive to a formatted disk as in section 2 above. If the suspect disk has hitherto given no trouble, attempt to reformat it, and allow it to be reused. If the disk will not format, or if it has previously given trouble, discard it and regard yourself fortunate. If bad blocks were persistent in blocks 0 to 5 or if the bad block scan module reckoned there were other than 280 blocks on the disk, go to (g); if there were persistent bad blocks in the range 6 to 279 go to (d).

(d) You must now attempt to restore the disk to a readable condition. Use the eXamine command of the Filer as directed in appendix 2, section 2.5.15. Write down the names of the files endangered. There are 2 possible outcomes: if all bad blocks "MAY BE OK" go to (e); otherwise go to (f).

(e) The files which are declared "MAY BE OK" have to be replaced, checked, corrected or removed. Follow the sequence of advice below.

- Make a temporary backup copy of the suspect disk now. Any tidying of the suspect disk should be done on this copy.

- For each endangered file, if you have a current copy on a backup disk, copy that file to the temporary backup file.

- Each endangered TEXT file should be checked, either visually with the Editor, or by compilation if appropriate. Common sense is the most valuable guide here.

- Each endangered CODE file should be removed and recreated by compilation.

- Each endangered DATA file should be removed and recreated by running the program that created it.

- If you have applied any corrections to the disk in this sequence, copy the temporary backup disk to the original suspect disk. You now have 2 copies of the restored disk, a working copy and a backup copy.

(f) The file(s) lost by the marking process at (d) will have to be recovered (unless you are prepared to lose them). TEXT files should be recovered from a backup disk, but recent updates may have to be applied again. Files of other types should be recreated as described in (e) above. The disk which now has marked bad blocks should be labelled accordingly, for it is now less convenient to back it up! (See appendix 2, section 2.5.11.) In spite of this, back it up now before the process of restoration is regarded as complete. If resources permit, you are strongly advised to discard such disks as soon as they can be replaced.

(g) You have a corrupt directory and you are in serious trouble. If a recent backup disk exists, destroy the bad disk (with scissors as if it were a credit card), make a new working copy from the backup and bring all the files up to date as best you can. If no backup exists, a tedious and hazardous process which carries no guarantee of success may be followed.

- Attempt an Extended directory listing (appendix 2, section 2.5.8) and write down all normal-looking entries corresponding to TEXT files.

- Attempt to Zero the directory (appendix 2, section 2.5.18) on the bad disk. If this fails, you are finished; there is no way back using the facilities of Apple Pascal.

- Assuming you now have a readable but zeroed directory, copy the bad disk (volume-to-volume) onto a fresh disk, and destroy the bad disk. With the copy, attempt to reconstruct the directory you wrote down by Making (appendix 2, section 2.5.17) a file of the correct length for every TEXT file and for every gap between the TEXT files. You must work forwards through the disk from block 6 to block 279. Call the files FILE1.TEXT, FILE2.TEXT, ... and the gaps GAP1.TEXT, GAP2.TEXT, ... Use the Editor to identify the files you are expecting to find, and Change their names back to their original filenames. Then do the same to the files called GAP1, GAP2, ... and see whether there be anything of value lurking therein.

Programs which attempt the recovery of disks with lost directories may be available from your local software supplier.

After the trauma experienced in the wake of this kind of disaster, you are unlikely ever again to neglect the backing up of disks.

APPENDIX 5
Debugging

In an ideal world, debugging should not be necessary. If programs are always constructed in the manner of chapters 3 and 4, and if procedures are thoroughly tested before being incorporated into major programs, the likelihood of obscure errors is greatly diminished. A combination of structured program design, and defensive coding of procedures and functions will facilitate the business of program development.

This appendix describes two complementary sets of aids to program development: first (in sections 1 to 5) those provided by the system itself and then (in section 6) some you should consider adding yourself, preferably at the time the program is being written.

1 THE COMPILER

During compilation, the Compiler indicates its progress by messages to the screen. For example, the unsuccessful compilation of TWOBUGS on the system disk appears on the screen as follows:

```
APPLE PASCAL COMPILER [...]
<   0>....
TURTLEGR [ 2307 WORDS]
<   4>..............................
FOURSQUA [ 1156 WORDS]
<  34>....
       PENCOLOR(BLACK);
       FOR SIDENUMBER : <<<<
LINE 38, ERROR 51: <SP>(CONTINUE), <ESC>(TERMINATE), E(DIT
```

The angle brackets and dots show the number of lines compiled (including blank lines and invisible lines of text referred to in the TURTLEGRAPHICS unit). When the start of a used unit, procedure or function body is reached, its name (truncated to the first eight characters if necessary) is shown followed by the number of words of spare memory available to the Compiler.

If the Compiler encounters a syntax error, or is unable to continue because of an input or output error, it issues an error message. The previous line and the current line up to the point of the error are displayed, with the arrow (<<<<) pointing to where the error was detected. Syntax and input/output errors are identified by line number and error number, and the Compiler offers the option of continuing compilation (spacebar), terminating (ESC key) or entering the Editor (E). You are recommended to enter the Editor which will then display that part of the program text containing the context of the error and a description of the error on the top line of the screen. The cursor will be positioned at the point in the source text where the error was found.

2   EXECUTION ERRORS

If an error occurs during the execution of a program (that is, after the compiled and linked program has been loaded and started to run) and it is detected by the system, an error message will be given and the program stopped. The error message will be in one of the forms

```
VALUE RANGE ERROR           EXEC ERR #  1
S# 1, P# 3, I# 42           S# 1, P# 3, I# 42
TYPE <SPACE> TO CONTINUE    TYPE <SPACE> TO CONTINUE
```

The first line indicates what went wrong. Examples of some of the common execution error messages, and their meanings, are

Error number	Message	Description
1	VALUE RANGE ERROR	A subrange variable, an enumerated type variable or array index contained an illegal value.
4	*STACK OVERFLOW*	The system exhausted its stack space, perhaps because of infinite recursion in the user program.
6	DIVIDE BY ZERO	Self-explanatory.
8	PROGRAM INTERRUPTED BY USER	CTRL-@ was typed on the keyboard. (See section 4 below.)
10	I/O ERROR (followed by more precise details)	Normally self-explanatory.
12	FLOATING POINT ERROR	
13	STRING OVERFLOW	The result of a string operation was too large for the receiving string to contain.

The second line indicates whereabouts in the program the error was detected. This is in 3 parts.

(a) Segment number. In all programs given in or suggested in this book, the segment number is 1.

(b) Procedure number. To work out which procedure is referred to,
remember that the Compiler numbers the procedures in the order
in which it encounters **PROGRAM**, **PROCEDURE** or **FUNCTION** in
the source (regardless of nesting). Remember that the main
program is user procedure number 1 even though its body is
textually last. Include any external procedures in the count,
and where a procedure is declared to be **FORWARD**, count it at
its first appearance only. In the following simple example

```
        PROGRAM EXAMPLE;

            PROCEDURE PROCA;

                PROCEDURE PROCC;
                    BEGIN
                        ...
                    END; (* PROCC *)

                BEGIN
                    ...
                END; (* PROCA *)

            FUNCTION FUNCB;

                BEGIN
                    ...
                END; (* FUNCB *)

        BEGIN
            ...
            ...
        END.
```

The main program is "procedure" #1, PROCA is #2, PROCC is #3,
and FUNCB is #4.

(c) Instruction offset. The interpretive program counter (offset)
is more difficult to understand. It is the number of the p-code
instruction in which the interpreter found the error. As the
roughest of guesses, allow one p-code instruction per
identifier, reserved word or other character of Pascal, ignoring
blank lines, declarations and comments.

You should be able to pin-point most execution errors using the guide
lines above. Should this not be sufficiently precise, then you need a
compilation listing.

3 COMPILATION LISTING

To obtain a compilation listing you will need to make a minor change to
the program text and recompile. (You can make other changes if you wish.)
Add, as the very first line of the program (before the **PROGRAM** ...; line)
the compiler option

        (*$LCOMPLIST.TEXT*)

which instructs the Compiler to write the compilation listing to the system
disk and call it COMPLIST.TEXT. Leave no spaces at all inside the comment
brackets. The file COMPLIST.TEXT will be much larger that the program
textfile, perhaps three times larger, so make sure there will be room for it.

(The listing can be sent to the USER: disk instead.) The compilation is
noticeably slower. Rerun the program allowing the program to run into the
error again. Make a note of the cause of the error, the Segment number,
Procedure number and Instruction offset. Save the program textfile on USER:.
Then use the Editor to examine the file called COMPLIST.TEXT. It contains 5
columns mainly of numbers, and your program text including the text of any unit
which it used. The meaning of these columns, reading from left to right, is

     (a)   line number in the program text file.

     (b)   segment number.

     (c)   procedure number, followed by a colon.

     (d)   D means a declaration, and a number means the depth of nesting
          of compound statements and iterative statements.

     (e)   offset of the first p-code instruction generated by the first
          statement to commence on that line.

Thus, to identify the line of program text in which the error occurred, first
locate the procedure; look in the 5th column for the instruction offset
displayed in the error message (or the nearest number below) and that is the
line in question. Do not forget to Remove the file COMPLIST.TEXT when the
error has been identified.

4 PROGRAMS THAT LOOP INDEFINITELY

    If the computer becomes unexpectedly uncommunicative and shows no outward
signs of activity (for example, no apparent disk activity) it is probably
executing an endless loop of instructions, such as **WHILE** TRUE **DO.** To
interrupt such a loop, try typing CTRL-@, and information as described in
sections 2 and 3 above should help you to discover, if not the precise loop it
is in, at least one of the lines of text through which the loop passes.
Otherwise press RESET to reboot the system.

5 AN EXAMPLE OF EXECUTION ERROR DEBUGGING

    The following program is a variant on the solution to exercise 3N.
Type it in, or modify your solution to the exercise.

       (*$LCOMPLIST.TEXT*)

       PROGRAM REGULARPOLYGONS;

       USES TURTLEGRAPHICS;

       VAR ORDER : INTEGER;

```
PROCEDURE DRAWPOLYGON(N, S : INTEGER);

(* THIS PROCEDURE FAILS TO MAINTAIN THE ANGULAR AND COORDINATE
   INVARIANCE OF THE TURTLE, BECAUSE N * (360 DIV N) IS NOT ALWAYS
   EQUAL TO 360 *)

    VAR SIDENUMBER, EXTANGLE : INTEGER;

    BEGIN
        PENCOLOR(WHITE);
        EXTANGLE := 360 DIV N;
        FOR SIDENUMBER := 1 TO N DO
            BEGIN
               MOVE(S);
               TURN(EXTANGLE)
            END;
        PENCOLOR(NONE)
   END; (* DRAWPOLYGON *)

BEGIN
    INITTURTLE;
    FOR ORDER := 4 DOWNTO 0 DO
        BEGIN
          MOVETO(115, 20);     (* THESE TWO STATEMENTS ARE HERE *)
          TURNTO(0);           (* BECAUSE OF THE DEFICIENCY NOTED
                                  ABOVE *)
          DRAWPOLYGON(ORDER, 50)
        END;
    READLN
END.
```

Run the program and see if you can locate the error without reference to the compilation listing. If you cannot find it, read on. The error message says

```
DIVIDE BY ZERO
S# 1, P# 2, I# 8
TYPE <SPACE> TO CONTINUE
```

By counting,

```
procedure 1 is the main program, REGULARPOLYGONS
procedure 2 is DRAWPOLYGON
```

Can you find the error? If not, read on. The error was found at Instruction offset 8. Count through the text as indicated in section 2(c) above. It is apparently somewhere near the beginning of the procedure. Look around for a statement that changes the value of a variable such that a DIVIDE BY ZERO error could occur. Press the spacebar and then return to the Editor where the correction may be made. If you still can't find it, look at the values the parameter N can be given. If you still can't find it, obtain a listing as described in section 3 above.

6 AN ALTERNATIVE APPROACH TO DEBUGGING

Sometimes a program will give incorrect results yet terminate normally. To find out where things go wrong, it is often useful to display intermediate results, and check them. If they are right, the trouble is probably after that point in the program; if they are wrong, then before. Further intermediate values may be needed to pin down the problem more precisely. Such values will probably have to be labelled if they are to be readily interpreted, as in

        WRITELN('*** X, Y AND Z ', X : 6, Y : 6, Z : 6)

    If many such debugging aids are written into a program you may find it convenient, when getting rid of them, to use the Editor to search for the ***.

    If you wish to leave debugging aids such as these in the program but be able to use them or not at will, you can make them conditional.

```
        VAR ... DEBUG : BOOLEAN;
                C : CHAR;
        BEGIN
            WRITE('DEBUGGING? Y OR N');
            READ(C);
            DEBUG := (C = 'Y');
            ...
            IF DEBUG THEN WRITELN('*** X, Y AND Z ', X : 6, Y : 6, Z : 6);
            ...
        END.
```

    Note that all this takes time and space. Avoid adding such debugging statements to the inner loops of programs which are repeated many times.

    Sometimes the techniques described in this appendix show where the error is first detected, but give no clue as to how the program execution arrived at that point. In this case, some form of procedure trace is useful. Try adding a WRITE statement at the start of important procedures so that the program produces a list of procedures that have been entered.

APPENDIX 6
Apple Pascal Syntax Diagrams

The syntax diagrams shown here describe the subset of Apple Pascal which this book covers. The only aspects of the syntax not dealt with are those relating to units. The syntax is introduced in a "constructive" sequence: that is, objects are generally defined before they are used to define more complex objects. It is the recursive nature of the syntax that provides the exceptions to this rule.

identifier:

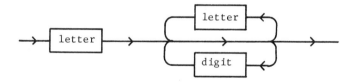

unsigned integer:

unsigned number:

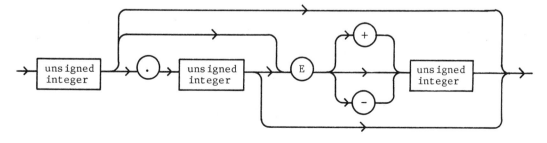

unsigned constant:

constant:

simple type:

field list:

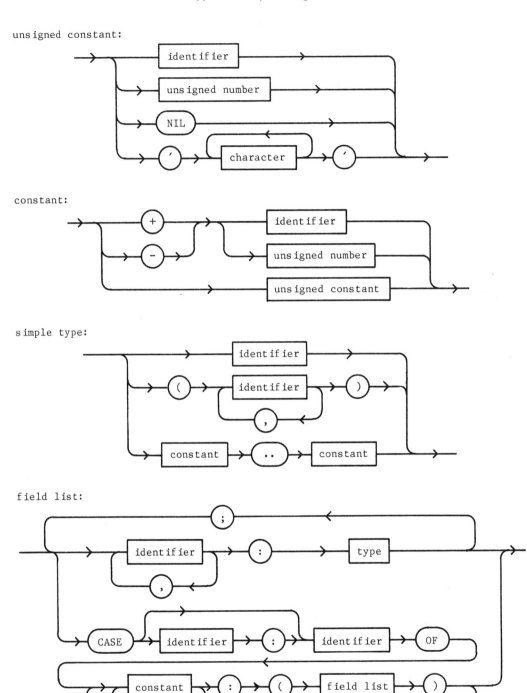

type:

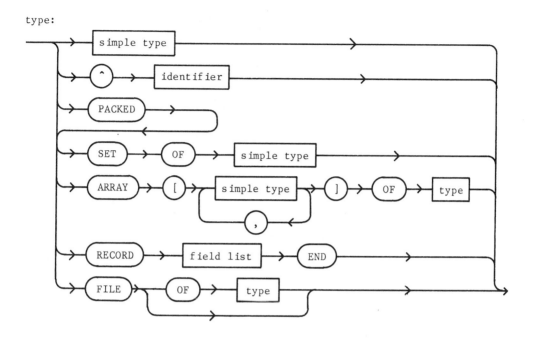

expression:

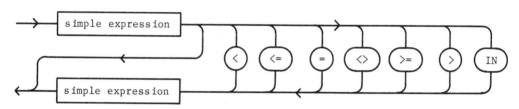

simple expression:

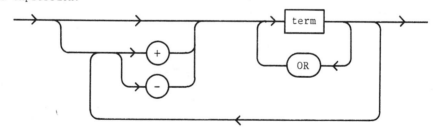

term:

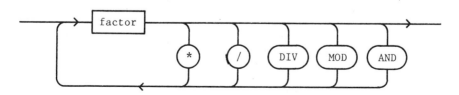

factor:

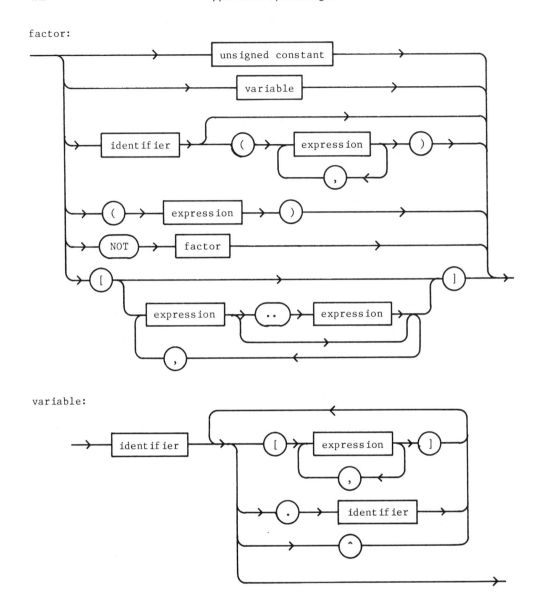

variable:

statement:

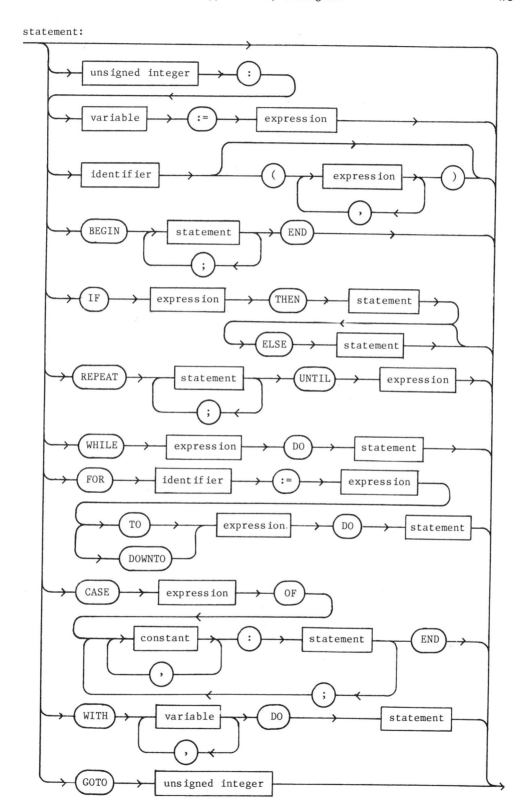

parameter list:

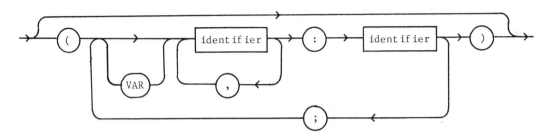

function declaration:

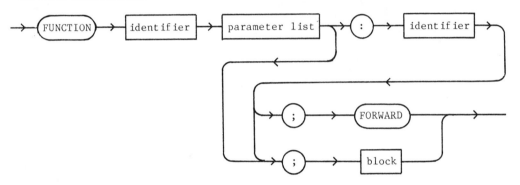

procedure declaration:

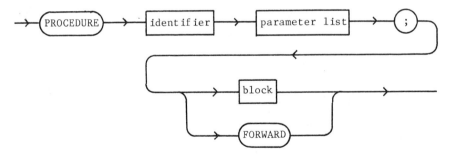

block:

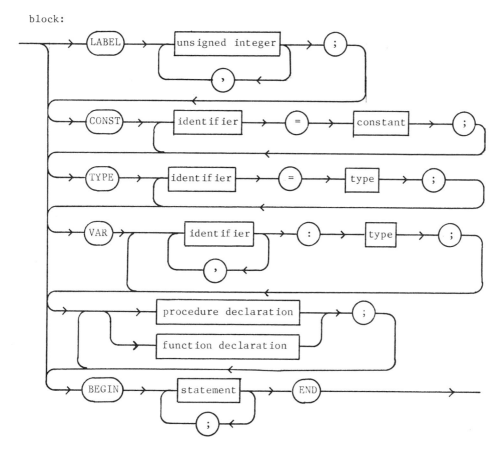

program:

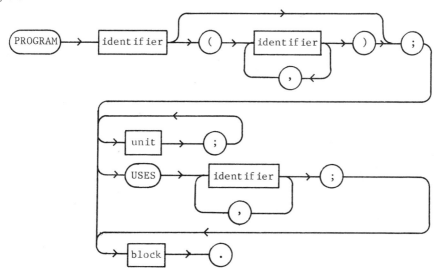

APPENDIX 7
UCSD Pascal Strings

1 THE TYPE STRING

UCSD Pascal has introduced a pre-declared type which makes string handling very much simpler and more powerful than in standard Pascal. This appendix therefore does not apply to non-UCSD Pascal implementations.

In the main body of the text we had to develop some procedures (at some length) in standard Pascal to perform some of the functions which are directly available in UCSD Pascal. The predeclared type denoting UCSD Pascal strings is named

          STRING

Constants of type STRING are written exactly as in sections 9.1 and 10.1.2, the same form as the string constant in standard Pascal.

STRINGs are normally of any length from 0 to 80 characters, but the maximum length may be changed to any value in the range 1 .. 255 by appending an integer constant to the type identifier. Thus the declarations

          VAR S : STRING;
              SHORT : STRING[8];
              LONG : STRING[132];

introduce 3 <u>string variables</u> S, SHORT and LONG whose maximum lengths are 80, 8 and 132 characters respectively. We may therefore write

          S := 'FOR WHAT I HAVE ';
          SHORT := 'I NEED ';
          LONG := 'NOT TO REPEAT,'

but not

          SHORT := 'FOR WHAT I HAVE '

which would produce an execution error - string overflow.

Do not confuse the type STRING with either the record type STRING80 introduced in section 13.3 or with the type **ARRAY** [1 .. 80] **OF** CHAR. The three types are different. Remember Pascal's strong typing policy and do not mix them.

2   PROCEDURES AND FUNCTIONS FOR STRING HANDLING

In the following description of functions and procedures provided in UCSD Pascal for string handling, it is assumed that S1, S2, ... are declared as string variables (that is, STRING[80]) and I1, I2, ... are integer variables.

2.1   READLN

STRINGs may be read from any text or interactive file by the READLN statement, having one, and only one, parameter of type STRING.

        READLN(S1)

This reads characters from the keyboard. The string is terminated by RETURN. String overflow is not detected if more than 80 characters are typed before RETURN.

Do not use the READ statement to read a STRING.

2.2.   WRITE and WRITELN

STRINGs may be written to any text file (including the screen) in the manner of section 10.1.2, but string variables may be included as parameters. For example, in the context of section 1,

        WRITE(S);   WRITELN(SHORT, LONG);

        S1 := 'AND WHAT I WANT ';
        WRITELN(S1, 'IT BOOTS NOT TO COMPLAIN.')

displays

        FOR WHAT I HAVE I NEED NOT TO REPEAT,
        AND WHAT I WANT IT BOOTS NOT TO COMPLAIN.

                                            [Richard II, iii, 4

You may also use a field width indicator in the way described in section 10.1.2.

2.3 CONCAT

This is one of four functions, two of which return results which are of type STRING. (The programmer may also write functions of type STRING.) The function CONCAT, used to join or concatenate strings,

```
CONCAT(S1, S2, ..., SN)
```

may take any number of parameters (rather like READ, READLN, WRITE and WRITELN) all of type STRING. For example

```
S1 := 'WILL THESE TURTLES ';
S2 := 'BE GONE?';
S3 := CONCAT(S1, S2);
WRITELN(S3)
```

displays

```
WILL THESES TURTLES BE GONE?
```
                                                      [Love's Labour's Lost, iv, 3

Also,

```
WRITELN(CONCAT('YEA FROM THE TABLE ', 'OF MY MEMORY'));
S1 := 'I''LL WIPE AWAY ';
S2 := 'ALL TRIVIAL ';
S3 := 'FOND RECORDS,';
WRITELN(CONCAT(CONCAT(S1, S2), S3))
```

displays

```
YEA FROM THE TABLE OF MY MEMORY
I'LL WIPE AWAY ALL TRIVIAL FOND RECORDS.
```
                                                      [Hamlet, i, 5

2.4 LENGTH

The function LENGTH returns an integer value equal to the current length of its single parameter of type STRING, not the maximum length. For example, if

```
S1 := 'O! THOU HAST DAMNABLE ITERATION, ';
S2 := CONCAT(S1, 'AND ART INDEED ABLE TO CORRUPT A SAINT.')
```

then

```
I1 := LENGTH(S1);
I2 := LENGTH(S2)
```

gives I1 the value 33, and I2 the value 72. (Incidentally, LENGTH('I''LL') has the value 4.)

2.5 COPY

The function COPY is used to make a copy of all or part of another string. Its general form is

        COPY(S, START, SIZE)

where

        S   is a STRING
        START   is the starting position of the substring to be copied
        SIZE   is the length of the substring to be copied.

For example, if in the context of section 2.4, we write

        S1 := COPY(S2, 1, LENGTH(S2))

to copy an entire string, (losing the original S1,) the statement

        WRITELN(COPY(S1, 1, LENGTH(S1)))

displays

    O! THOU HAST DAMNABLE ITERATION, AND ART INDEED ABLE TO CORRUPT A SAINT.
                                                        [1 Henry IV, i, 2

As examples of the copying of only part of a string,

        WRITE(' ' : 31);
        S3 := 'HERE; THAT WE BUT TEACH';
        S4 := COPY(S3, 7, 17);
        WRITELN(S4);

        WRITELN('BLOODY INSTRUCTIONS, WHICH, BEING TAUGHT, RETURN');

        S5 := 'TO PLAGUE THE INVENTOR; THIS EVEN-HANDED JUSTICE';
        S6 := COPY(S5, 1, LENGTH(S5)-25);
        WRITELN(S6)

displays

                                THAT WE BUT TEACH
        BLOODY INSTRUCTIONS, WHICH, BEING TAUGHT, RETURN
        TO PLAGUE THE INVENTOR;
                                                        [Macbeth, i, 7

In the last example, S3 and S5 remain unaltered by the COPY function. If the SIZE is too long, that is

        START + SIZE - 1 > LENGTH(S),

or if START < 1, then COPY returns an empty string.

2.6 <u>POS</u>

This is the pattern matching function. It's general form is

```
POS(PATTERN, S)
```

where PATTERN is of type STRING. If PATTERN occurs in S the value of POS is the character position (starting at 1) of the first character of PATTERN in S. If PATTERN does not occur in S, it returns the value 0. For example,

```
S1 := 'THE THE STRINGS, MY LORD, ARE FALSE.';
S2 := 'TRUE';
S3 := 'Y LO';
S4 := 'LORD.';
I1 := POS(S2,S1);
I2 := POS(S3,S1);
I3 := POS(S4,S1)
```

puts the values 0, 19, 0 into I1, I2, I3 respectively.

2.7 <u>DELETE</u>

This is a procedure. It deletes part or all of a string. Its general form is

```
DELETE(S, START, SIZE)
```

It deletes SIZE characters from the string S beginning at character number START. If SIZE is too long, that is, if

```
START + SIZE - 1 > LENGTH(S)
```

or if START < 1 then the procedure does nothing. For example, in the context of section 2.6,

```
DELETE(S1, 1, 4);
WRITELN(S1)
```

displays

```
THE STRINGS, MY LORD, ARE FALSE.
```

[Julius Caesar, iv, 3

and

```
S1 := 'IS''T REAL ESTATE THAT I SEE?';
DELETE(S1, 11, 7);
WRITELN(S1)
```

displays

    IS'T REAL THAT I SEE?
                                    [All's Well that Ends Well, v, 3

The functions DELETE, POS and LENGTH can be usefully combined as in the following example,

    S3 := 'HOW PROVE YOU THAT, IN THE GREAT HEAP OF YOUR ACKNOWLEDGE?';
    S4 := 'AC';
    DELETE(S3, POS(S4, S3), LENGTH(S4));
    WRITELN(S3)

which displays

    HOW PROVE YOU THAT, IN THE GREAT HEAP OF YOUR KNOWLEDGE?
                                    [As you Like it, i, 2

2.8 INSERT

    This is a procedure. It inserts one string into another at a given position. Take care that the resultant string does not overflow. Its general form is

    INSERT(S1, S2, START)

where S1 is the string to be inserted into S2 at the character position denoted by START. For example

    S1 := 'EVERY ';
    S2 := 'SO SCOPE BY THE IMMODERATE USE TURNS TO RESTRAINT.';
    INSERT(S1, S2, 4);
    WRITELN(S2)

displays

    SO EVERY SCOPE BY THE IMMODERATE USE TURNS TO RESTRAINT.
                                    [Measure for Measure, 1, 2

If START < 1 then INSERT does nothing.

    There is no explicit replace procedure, but it is easy to construct one from the functions and procedures given in this section.

    PROCEDURE REPLACE(TARGET, SUBSTITUTE : STRING; VAR S : STRING);

    (* REPLACES "TARGET" IN "S" BY "SUBSTITUTE" *)

    VAR P : INTEGER;

    BEGIN
        P := POS(TARGET, S);
        DELETE(S, P, LENGTH(TARGET));
        INSERT(SUBSTITUTE, S, P)
    END; (* REPLACE *)

For example,

```
          S1 := 'FOLLOW YOUR FUNCTION; GO, AND BATTEN ON HOT BITS.';
          S2 := 'HOT';
          S3 := 'COLD';
          REPLACE(S2, S3, S1);
          WRITELN(S1)
```

displays

          FOLLOW YOUR FUNCTION; GO, AND BATTEN ON COLD BITS.

                                                    [Coriolanus, iv, 5

but

          REPLACE('YOU''RE', 'MY', S1)

results in no change to S1.

2.9 Comparison

     STRINGs may be compared by any of the 6 relational operators. Ordering is
lexicographical. Shorter strings precede longer strings of which they are
leading substrings.

2.10 Access to Individual Characters

     The characters of a STRING may be accessed by subscripts. They are
objects of type CHAR. This should not be allowed to mislead you into thinking
that the type STRING is the same as **ARRAY** [1 .. 80] **OF** CHAR after all. It
is not! If $1 \leq I \leq$ LENGTH(S1), the reference

          S1[I]

has a similar value, but is of a different type to

          COPY(S1, I, 1)

The type of S1[I] is CHAR, whereas the type of COPY(S1, I, 1) is STRING. If I
is outside the range, a value range error will be detected in the former
reference.
     The variable S1[0] is where the length of the string is kept, as an 8-bit
unsigned integer in the range 0 .. 255. It is in fact of type CHAR. To change
the length of a string (up to the maximum prescribed or defaulted to by the
declaration) you must use one of the compiler options, and write

```
          (*$R-*)        (* SWITCH OFF RANGE-CHECKING *)
          S1[0] := CHR(NEWLENGTH);
          (*$R+*)        (* SWITCH ON RANGE-CHECKING *)
```

where NEWLENGTH is an integer expression in the range 0 to the maximum
declared.

There is one situation in which access by subscript is unavoidable. If C
is a variable of type CHAR and it is necessary to turn it into a STRING S,
there is no way that the procedures and functions of sections 2.1 to 2.8 will
do this. None of them has a parameter of type CHAR. The remedy is

```
S := '*';     (* A STRING OF LENGTH 1 *)
S[1] := C     (* CHARACTER 1 OF S BECOMES THE CHARACTER C *)
```

APPENDIX 8
Labels and the Goto Statement

Generally, the control of sequence in programs is best expressed by if, case, for, repeat and while statements, and the sensible use of procedures. Occasionally we have been mildly embarrassed by deficiencies of these statements and have resorted to state variables to resolve our difficulties. The goto statement may also be used to overcome these difficulties but its unbridled use will create much greater chaos. The problem was first encountered in section 11.5 where we had a loop from which we wished to break out. Breaking out of a loop at the beginning or the end is achieved with the while and repeat statements respectively, but it was the breaking from within a loop that presented difficulty. One of the criticisms of Pascal is that it has no special command for breaking out of a compound statement, other than the goto statement.

To illustrate the use of the goto statement, consider the program MILL11 in section 11.5. We could rewrite the main program as follows.

```
BEGIN
    CUSTOMER := ACTIVE;
    FOR MILLSIZE := 1 TO 4 DO
      BEGIN
        WRITE('DO YOU WANT THE NEXT MILL OF SIZE ', MILLSIZE,
            ' (Y/N)?');
        GETREPLY;
        IF REPLY <> 'Y' THEN
            BEGIN
                CUSTOMER := RETIRED;  GOTO 1
            END;
        INITTURTLE;  DRAWMILL(MILLSIZE, 139, 95, 45);
        READLN;  TEXTMODE
      END;
  1: WRITELN;
    IF CUSTOMER <> RETIRED THEN
    WRITELN('CONGRATULATIONS ON COMPLETING THE COURSE.')
    ELSE
    WRITELN(
    'YOU DID NOT COMPLETE THE COURSE.  WE UNDERSTAND YOUR PROBLEM.')
END.
```

In this example, "1" is used to label the statement following the for statement. Like all other naming mechanisms in Pascal, it has to be declared, not in the VAR section, but in a special label section, which precedes the **CONST** sections in a block. The main program above would therefore have to be incorporated into a program as follows.

```
PROGRAM MILLG;

USES TURTLEGRAPHICS;

LABEL 1;

TYPE ...;

VAR ...;

BEGIN
    ... GOTO 1; ...
  1: ...
    ...
END.
```

In the main program above, we have used the goto statement solely to break out of a loop. The label "1" was placed on the statement immediately following the end of the loop. This is the cleanest use of the goto statment and least likely to cause programming difficulties. It is however tempting to write the main program as

```
BEGIN
  CUSTOMER := ACTIVE;
  FOR MILLSIZE := 1 TO 4 DO
    BEGIN
    WRITE('DO YOU WANT THE NEXT MILL OF SIZE ', MILLSIZE,
          ' (Y/N)?');
    GETREPLY;
    IF REPLY <> 'Y' THEN
        BEGIN
            CUSTOMER := RETIRED;  GOTO 1
        END;
    INITTURTLE;  DRAWMILL(MILLSIZE, 139, 95, 45);
    READLN;  TEXTMODE
    END;
  WRITELN('CONGRATULATIONS ON COMPLETING THE COURSE.');
  GOTO 2;
 1: WRITELN(
    'YOU DID NOT COMPLETE THE COURSE.  WE UNDERSTAND YOUR PROBLEM.');
 2: END.
```

This is equivalent to the earlier version (and incidentally shows that a label may be placed before **END**) and has removed an if statement. It has, however, introduced a degree of confusion at the end. The two WRITELN statements are no longer in the immediate context of the condition governing which one is to be selected. That condition is back inside the for statement.

The scope of a label is the procedure within which it is defined and in UCSD Pascal this excludes any nested procedure, making it impossible to jump into a procedure. In UCSD Pascal, every declared label must appear as a label in the program.

To conclude, avoid goto statements if at all possible. If you believe you have to use one, use it only to break out of a compound statement to a label which immediately follows the **END** of the compound statement. Such break statements are included in some structured programming languages. UCSD Pascal has a rather drastic form of break, called an exit statement (see [Clark and Koehler, 1982]) which enables exits from procedures or the program itself but not from a compound statement as in the examples above.

APPENDIX 9
Packed Data

Standard Pascal advises implementors to arrange the storage of structured data (arrays, records and sets) with a view to efficiency of access. However, the programmer may, with no effect on the meaning of a program, request that data be stored with a view to economy of storage space, usually at the expense of access. To do this, the reserved word **PACKED** is prefixed to **ARRAY**, **RECORD** or **SET**. Standard Pascal does not require that the implementation convert between packed and unpacked formats automatically, but provides two procedures, pack and unpack, which are the programmer's responsibility to use.

UCSD Pascal converts data automatically and therefore does not implement pack and unpack. For further discussion, see [Jensen and Wirth, 1978] and [Clark and Koehler, 1982].

APPENDIX 10
REWRITE and the Problem of Opening Multiple Files

The mergesort program of section 22.4 highlights a problem consequent upon UCSD Pacal's organization of files. As can be seen from an Extended directory listing, files are kept in contiguous blocks. If a volume becomes filled to the extent that there are, say, 100 unused blocks and the largest unused area is of only 12 blocks, then there is nowhere to place a 16 block file on that volume. On closing a file, reserved but unused blocks are released.

When REWRITE opens a file for writing, it does not know how long it will be and therefore, in the absence of any other information, it opens the file in the largest unused area on the specified volume, and reserves the whole of that area for the file just opened. If the volume has just been Krunched (see appendix 2, section 2.5.16) then there will be no further unused areas on that volume to accommodate any more files to be opened for writing to. If, on the other hand, the disk is in a fragmented state (for example, prior to Krunching) then there will be unused areas, though not greater than the one reserved. On closing a file, reserved but unused blocks are released.

Thus for applications in which multiple files are to be written, care must be exercised, either to ensure that the volume is suitably fragmented before the program begins, or to provide information to the REWRITE procedure indicating the maximum size of the file to be written. The latter information may be supplied by means of a size specification appended to the filename, as described for the Filer's Make command (see appendix 2, section 2.5.17).

As it stands, the mergesort program of section 22.4 will be able to operate, provided that there are four unused areas of 4 or more blocks. There must also be a fifth unused area large enough for the sorted file, but that could be on a different volume.

Bibliography

ABELSON, H & diSESSA, A A (1980)
       "Turtle Geometry". Cambridge, Mass. MIT Press.

ANGELL, I O (1981)
       "A Practical Introduction to Computer Graphics". London and
       Basingstoke. Macmillan.

APPLE (1980a)   "The Apple Pascal Language Reference Manual". Cupertino,
       Ca. Apple Computer, Inc.

APPLE (1980b)   "The Apple Pascal Operating System Reference Manual".
       Cupertino, Ca. Apple Computer, Inc.

BOWLES, K L (1977)
       "Microcomputer Problem Solving Using Pascal". New York, N.Y.
       Springer-Verlag.

CLARK, R & KOEHLER, S (1982)
       "The UCSD Pascal Handbook". Englewood Cliffs, N.J.
       Prentice-Hall, Inc.

DIJKSTRA, E W (1976)
       "A Discipline of Programming". Englewood Cliffs, N.J.
       Prentice-Hall, Inc.

ISO (1981)   "Second Draft Proposal of the ISO Standard (January 1981)".
       Pascal News, No. 20.

JENSEN, K & WIRTH, N (1978)
       "Pascal User Manual and Report" (2nd ed.). New York, N.Y.
       Springer-Verlag.

KNUTH, D E (1973)
       "Fundamental Algorithms", The Art of Programming, Volume 1
       (2nd ed.). Reading, Mass. Addison-Wesley, Inc.

KNUTH, D E (1969)
       "Semi-numerical Algorithms", The Art of Programming, Volume 2.
       Reading, Mass. Addison-Wesley, Inc.

MOYER, G (1982) "The Gregorian Calendar", Scientific American, May 1982,
       pp 104-111.

SOFTECH (1981) "UCSD Pascal Users Manual, Version IV.0". San Diego, Ca.
                SofTech Microsystems, Inc.

WELSH, J & ELDER, J (1982)
                "Introduction to Pascal" (2nd ed.). Englewood Cliffs, N.J.
                Prentice-Hall, Inc.

WIRTH, N (1976) "Algorithms + Data Structures = Programs". Englewood Cliffs,
                Prentice-Hall, Inc.

Index

(Principal references are in boldface.)

PRENTICE-HALL ADDRESSES

You can order the MACC: disk from any of these
addresses. The disk contains 13 sample programs and
10 explanatory programs. The explanatory programs
take the reader line by line through some of the sample
programs. They illustrate each line, and show its effect
in graphic terms.

Prentice-Hall Inc.
Attn: Ryan Colby
College Operations
Englewood Cliffs
New Jersey 07632
U.S.A.

Prentice-Hall International Inc.
301 Sylvan Avenue
Englewood Cliffs
New Jersey 07632
U.S.A.

Prentice-Hall of Australia Pty Ltd.
7 Grosvenor Place
Brookvale, N.S.W. 2100
Australia

United Book Distributors Pty Ltd.
PO Box 17294
Hillbrow
Transvaal, South Africa

Prentice-Hall of Japan, Inc.
Akasaka Mansion Room 405
12-23 Akasaka 2-chome
Minato-ku, Tokyo 107, Japan

Prentice-Hall of Canada
1870 Birchmont Road
Scarborough
Ontario, Canada

Prentice-Hall International Inc.
Dept 255
66 Wood Lane End
Hemel Hempstead, Herts.
HP2 4RG, England

Whitehall Books Limited
53 Jackson Street
PO Box 38694
Petone, New Zealand

Prentice-Hall of India Private Ltd.
M-97 Connaught Circus
New Delhi 1, India

Prentice-Hall of Southeast Asia Pte Ltd.
4-B, 77 Ayer Rajah Industrial Estate
Ayer Rajah Road
Singapore 5

TO THE PURCHASER

This disk is named MACC:. You are authorized to make one copy
of it for your own use.

Keep this original disk in a safe place. Please note that it cannot be
written to. It is write-protected, to avoid accidental over-writing.

CONTENTS OF MACC: DISK

FIVESTAR.TEXT	REAL2.TEXT	XPLAIN3.1.CODE
TWOBUGS.TEXT	REAL3.TEXT	XPLAIN5.1.CODE
STARTIME.TEXT	POLILIST1.TEXT	XPLAIN5.2.CODE
STARTURN.CODE	USA18.TEXT	XPLAIN5.3.CODE
DIAGONAL1.TEXT	USA94.TEXT	XPLAIN5.4.CODE
VALUEPARAM.TEXT	XPLAIN1.1.CODE	XPLAIN7.1.CODE
SCOPEDEMO.TEXT	XPLAIN1 2.CODE	XPLAIN7.2.CODE
REAL1.TEXT		XPLAIN15.1.COD